Documents
in English History

Early Times to the Present

Brian L. Blakeley

Jacquelin Collins

Department of History
Texas Tech University

John Wiley & Sons, Inc.
New York · London · Sydney · Toronto

Cover Photograph: Courtesy of the National Maritime Museum, London

Library of Congress Cataloging in Publication Data
Blakeley, Brian L comp.
Documents in English History.

1. Great Britain—History—Sources. I. Collins, Jacquelin, 1933–   joint comp. II. Title.

DA26.B55   942   74-18264
ISBN 0-471-07945-6
ISBN 0-471-07946-4 (pbk.)

Printed in the United States of America

10 9 8 7 6 5 4 3 2 1

Preface

The beginning student frequently assumes that history consists of the compilation of facts, the mere learning of which imparts knowledge and wisdom. With experience, however, he comes to the realization that the study of history is essentially a continuing process by which an individual historian asks questions of the evidence he has at hand or can discover. Written history consists of the answers that various historians have arrived at and recorded. It varies according to the questions posed and the beliefs and prejudices of the historians asking the questions and searching for evidence. It is not surprising, therefore, that each generation must write its history anew—not only contemporary history but also that of all previous times. Definitive history is possible only for those historians who have given up the arduous task of seeking new answers to questions both old and new.

There is, nevertheless, a constant factor in history, a factor essential if historians are to be prevented from wandering off into the wilderness of their own imaginations. This factor is the evidence used by historians in answering the questions they have raised. A historian's evidence also provides a means by which other historians can judge the validity of his answers. This evidence is often called "documents." Originally, when the discipline of history was less sophisticated, a document was a written record, and historians believed that only written records could reveal the secrets of man's past action. In the absence of written documents it was assumed that history could not be written. Without written documents there was only the "prehistory" of a mysterious age populated by shadows and visited by lesser beings such as archeologists and anthropologists. However, historians have come to understand that evidence is simply where you find it, and it is worth whatever you can make out of it. Written records obviously remain valuable, but a discerning historian may have his questions answered by a careful examination of other evidence as well—the workmanship of primitive craftsmen, the remains of a Roman city, or the layout of a medieval manor as revealed by a World War II aerial photograph. In using evidence of this kind, the historian may have to ask more subtle questions and accept more tentative answers, but the historical process is essentially the same. Thus evidence of any kind, once recognized and appropriated by a historian, becomes a historical document to be used again and again by himself and others in the same field.

No historian, not even the beginning undergraduate, can remain a passive spectator. Each must ask his own questions and then seek answers to them. At first he will be led to the written accounts of other historians. This approach, however, results in confusion: historical accounts often conflict with one another. Which historian is correct? At this point one should not become discouraged. Instead, one should recognize, in this confusion, frustration and, yes, even anger, the maturing of a historian. As one perseveres, he will be led back at first to the same documents or evidence used by previous historians and then, hopefully, even to new evidence. Along the way one asks his own questions and arrives at his own answers with the same caution and confidence as other historians.

Every historian, from the beginner to the most prominent, needs the assistance of others working in the same field; the task of historical research, with the whole world as evidence, is too immense for a single person. This collection of documents, of appropriated bits of evidence, will help the beginning student of English history in two ways.

1. It will make him aware of the different kinds of evidence available to him. Some evidence cannot be presented here: for instance, a packet of soil analyzed by an agronomist to determine the location of the pilings of a neolithic building, a long list of place-names used by a linguist in tracing the probable routes of the Anglo-Saxon invasions, or a motion picture from the 1920s used by a social historian. Nevertheless nonwritten documents like the Bayeux Tapestry, aerial photographs of medieval fields, and the prints of the famous eighteenth-century artist, William Hogarth, can be included and reveal the variety of historical documents. Most of this book consists of written documents, and this is justifiable, since the majority of historians still rely almost entirely on evidence in this form. Even here, however, we have indicated the numerous types of written documents. Chronicles, governmental records, speeches, diaries, poetry, and nursery rhymes are only examples of this variety.

2. These documents include many that are generally agreed to be among the most important to an understanding of English history. They

provide evidence that has been used and must continue to be used to answer the hardest and most persistent questions.

We have placed the documents in chronological order and have made no attempt to group them topically. Each document is a self-contained unit, sufficiently complete with its introduction to be understood and appreciated by itself. However, in writing the introductions we have been conscious of the place of each document in English history. The introductions provide a thread of continuity from one document to another, should the student choose to read several documents in succession.

Many people have given us help and encouragement in the preparation of this book. Patrick C. Lipscomb III, Brian C. Levack, and Stanford E. Lehmberg read the manuscript and offered suggestions for its improvement. C. Warren Hollister gave needed encouragement. Larry J. Holley, Robert Cain, and Charles Middleton provided invaluable assistance in obtaining documents. Joan Weldon typed the manuscript. Finally, Robert Paradine, now an editor of Pennsylvania State University Press, and Wayne Anderson, history and political science editor at Wiley, made preparation of this book for publication more fun than it might have been. We give thanks to all of these people, to our colleagues at Texas Tech University, and to our long-suffering wives and families.

Finally, let us welcome each new student to the study of English history. Our prejudices, which led us to study this subject and now leads us to invite others to do the same, are apparent but unabashed. For the students who are about to discover England and its history this book was written; to them it is dedicated.

Brian L. Blakeley
Jacquelin Collins

Texas Tech University
St. Adrian's Day, 1974

Contents

1

Prehistoric Britain in Pictures

Prehistory, often defined as the account of events or conditions prior to written or recorded history, is necessarily dependent on the work of the archeologist. A careful search for and interpretation of the surviving artifacts of early man can reveal much about the nature of prehistoric societies. Archeologists have found in Britain simple stone tools dating from the Old Stone Age, some as old as half a million years. It is not, however, until the New Stone Age or about 3000 B.C. that men developed the social organization necessary to construct the monuments for which the early Britons are justly famous.

The best known of Britain's ancient monuments is, of course, Stonehenge, located on the Salisbury Plain in southern England. Stonehenge (Plate A) was built in several stages, being begun about 2100 B.C. and, after several remodelings, achieving its final form about 1450 B.C. Although today it is generally believed that the completed Stonehenge was used to compute the time of the year, uncertainty remains regarding its original purposes and the means by which it was constructed. Stonehenge and similar remains, nevertheless, stand as a reminder that these primitive peoples possessed definite religious beliefs, considerable wealth, and sophisticated political and social structures.

Near Stonehenge are several other impressive remains, many of them associated with the so-called Beaker People, who arrived in Britain about 1900 B.C. and were the heralds of the Bronze Age. They received their name from their practice of burying drinking cups with the dead. Their numerous, large burial mounds resemble cemeteries in many areas (Plate B). Silbury Hill (Plate C), 125 feet high and covering 5 acres, is the largest artificial mound in Europe. It apparently had a religious purpose, but what specifically it was for remains a mystery. Avebury (Plate D) is typical of the numerous stone circles found in southern England from the same period.

The Celts, who began arriving in England about 1000 B.C., were more warlike than the earlier inhabitants, possessing by 500 B.C. the iron weapons

PLATE A
Stonehenge (Cambridge University Collection, copyright reserved).

PLATE B
Prehistoric cemetery (Department of Antiquities, Ashmolean Museum).

PLATE C
Silbury Hill (Crown copyright, reproduced with the permission of the
Controller of Her Majesty's Stationery Office).

PLATE D
Avebury (Crown copyright, reproduced with the permission of the Controller of Her Majesty's Stationery Office).

PLATE E
Maiden Castle (Crown copyright, reproduced with the permission of the
Controller of Her Majesty's Stationery Office).

that enabled them to conquer most of southern England. Their warlike
nature and their stronger tribal government are reflected in their numerous
hill forts, the most famous being Maiden Castle in Dorset (Plate E), enclosing

PLATE F
White Horse (Aerofilms Ltd.)

almost 45 acres of land. The Celts were also artists. Plate F, "White Horse," one of their greatest triumphs, is a figure of a horse 120 yards long cut into the side of a chalk hill.

Britain's prehistoric monuments are among her greatest national treasures. Today most of them are in the custody of, or are protected by, the Department of the Environment.

2

Tacitus *Agricola* (A. D. 98). Roman Britain, A. D. 78-84

Rome's subjugation of Britain, initiated by Julius Caesar in 55 B.C. and completed following the Claudian invasion of A.D. 43, frees the historian from the restrictions imposed by the absence of written evidence. It must be remembered, nevertheless, that to the Romans, Britain was always an expendable frontier province, an outpost of Roman civilization, and that, consequently, few Roman writers treated it in much detail.

Much of our detailed knowledge of Roman Britain comes from P. Cornelius Tacitus's *Agricola,* a brief biography of Gnaeus Iulius Agricola, the most significant governor of Roman Britain (A.D. 78–84). Tacitus not only dealt with Agricola's conquests and his policy of Romanization, but he also included a valuable description of the geography and the people of Britain, part of which is reproduced below.

As with any document, the *Agricola* should not be accepted uncritically. Tacitus was often careless of detail, and his statements must when possible be tested against other evidence, often that produced by the archeologist. More important, Tacitus was Agricola's son-in-law, and thus perhaps not the

SOURCE.   Tacitus, *On Britain and Germany: A Translation of the "Agricola" and the "Germania,"* translated H. Mattingly (Penguin Classics, 1948), pp. 61–63, 70–72. Copyright © the Estate of H. Mattingly, 1948.

best person to provide an objective treatment of Agricola's achievements. Finally, Tacitus wrote the *Agricola* (A.D. 98) during a period of great political turmoil and corruption in Rome. Some specialists argue, therefore, that his favorable descriptions of frontier peoples, in both the *Agricola* and his more famous *Germania,* written at the same time, may have been in part an appeal to the Romans to reassert their primitive virtues against the corruption of their current "civilization." Whatever its limitations, Tacitus's account will obviously remain an essential document for the study of Roman Britain.

In view of the loss of portions of Tacitus's major works, the *Histories* and the *Annals,* it is fortunate, indeed, that four manuscript copies of the *Agricola* have survived, the oldest being from the tenth century. Although the *Agricola* was used by some medieval writers working in the libraries at Fulda and Monte Cassino, Tacitus's writings were not highly regarded until modern times.

Who the first inhabitants of Britain were, whether natives or immigrants, remains obscure; one must remember we are dealing with barbarians. But physical characteristics vary, and that very variation is suggestive. The reddish hair and large limbs of the Caledonians proclaim a German origin, the swarthy faces of the Silures, the tendency of their hair to curl and the fact that Spain lies opposite, all lead one to believe that Spaniards crossed in ancient times and occupied the land. The peoples nearest to the Gauls are correspondingly like them. Perhaps the original strain persists, perhaps it is climatic conditions that determine physical type in lands that converge from opposite directions on a single point. On a general estimate, however, we may believe that it was Gauls who took possession of the neighboring island. In both countries you will find the same ritual, the same religious beliefs. There is no great difference in language, and there is the same hardihood in challenging danger, the same subsequent cowardice in shirking it. But the Britons show more spirit; they have not yet been softened by protracted peace. The Gauls, too, we have been told, had their hour of military glory; but then came decadence with peace, and valour went the way of lost liberty. The same fate has befallen such of the Britons as have long been conquered; the rest are still what the Gauls used to be.

Their strength is in their infantry. Some tribes also fight from chariots. The nobleman drives, his dependants fight in his defence. Once they owed obedience to kings; now they are distracted between the jarring factions of rival chiefs. Indeed, nothing has helped us more in war with their strongest nations than their inability to cooperate. It is but seldom that two or three states unite to repel a common danger; fighting in detail they are conquered wholesale. The climate is objectionable, with its frequent rains and mists, but there is no extreme cold. Their day is longer than is normal in the Roman world. The night is bright and, in the extreme North, short, with only a brief interval between evening and morning twilight. If no clouds block the view, the sun's glow, it is said, can be seen all night long. It does not set and rise, but simply passes along the horizon. The reason must be that the ends of the earth, being flat, cast low shadows and cannot raise the darkness to any height; night therefore fails to reach the sky and its stars. The soil can bear all produce, except the olive, the vine, and other natives of warmer climes, and it is fertile. Crops are slow to ripen, but quick to grow—both facts due to one and the same cause, the extreme moistness of land and sky. Britain yields gold, silver and other metals, to make it worth conquering. . . .

The Britons themselves submit to the levy, the tribute and the other charges of Empire with cheerful readiness, provided that there is no abuse. *That* they bitterly resent; for they are broken in to obedience, not to slavery. . . .

Agricola, however, understood the feelings of a province and had learned from the experience of others that arms can effect little if injustice follows in their train. He resolved to root out the causes of war. . . . He preferred to appoint to official positons and duties men whom he could trust not to transgress, rather than punish the transgressor. He eased the levy of corn and tribute by distributing the burden fairly, and cancelled those charges, contrived by profiteers, which were more bitterly resented than the tax itself. The provincials had actually been compelled to wait at the doors of closed granaries, buy back their own corn and pay farcical prices. Delivery was ordered to destinations off the map or at a great distance, and states that had permanent quarters of troops close by them had to send to remote and inaccessible spots, until a service that should have been easy for all ended by benefiting a few scoundrels only.

By checking these abuses in his very first year of office, Agricola gave men reason to love and honour peace. Hitherto, through the negligence or arbitrariness of former governors, it had been as much feared as war. . . .

The following winter was spent on schemes of the most salutary kind. To induce a people, hitherto scattered, uncivilized and therefore prone to fight, to grow pleasurably inured to peace and ease, Agricola gave private encouragement and official assistance to the building of temples, public squares and private mansions. He praised the keen and scolded the slack, and competition to gain honour from him was as effective as compulsion. Furthermore, he trained the sons of the chiefs in the liberal arts and expressed a preference for British natural ability over the trained skill of the

Gauls. The result was that in place of distaste for the Latin language came a passion to command it. In the same way, our national dress came into favour and the toga was everywhere to be seen. And so the Britons were gradually led on to the amenities that make vice agreeable—arcades, baths and sumptuous banquets. They spoke of such novelties as "civilization," when really they were only a feature of enslavement.

3

Sutton Hoo Ship-Burial

The Sutton Hoo ship-burial is a vivid example of archeology's role in the study of history. Since its excavation in 1939 from a barrow located 6 miles from the North Sea on Mrs. E. M. Pretty's Suffolk estate, Sutton Hoo, the

PLATE A
The excavation (by permission of the Trustees of the British Museum).

ship-burial has been recognized as an archeological discovery of unprecedented importance.

The Sutton Hoo ship, an open rowing boat, measured 80 feet in length and 14 feet in the beam (Plate A). The discovery of its remains, together with a large number of seventh-century artifacts, caused considerable excitement among historians. Despite differences of opinion among specialists in Anglo-Saxon history, some tentative conclusions regarding the importance of the Sutton Hoo ship-burial have emerged. The ship-burial and its artifacts confirm what written evidence, such as *Beowulf,* has said about some of the institutions and practices of the period. The ceremonial whetstone (Plate B) is an emblem that supports the existence of the concept of royal sovereignty during this early period. The dishes, coins, and weaponry reveal extensive contact between the Anglo-Saxons and the rest of Europe, particularly

PLATE B
The ceremonial whetstone (by permission of the Trustees of the British Museum).

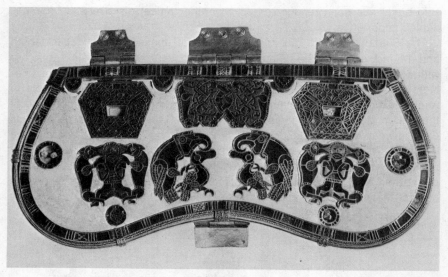

PLATE C
Purse lid with gold frame (by permission of the Trustees of the British Museum).

Sweden. The elaborate gold-framed purse lid (Plate C) and the gold belt buckle (Plate D) have led to a new appreciation of the artistic creativity and craftsmanship of the early Anglo-Saxons. Finally, the bronze fish and es-

PLATE D
The gold belt buckle (by permission of the Trustees of the British Museum).

PLATE E
Bronze fish and escutcheon (by permission of the Trustees of the British Museum).

cutcheon (Plate E) seem to confirm the influence of Christianity in East Anglia during the mid-seventh century.

Sutton Hoo raises further historical questions, however. The date of the ship-burial is usually put at about 655, but some scholars argue for a date as early as 625. The exact purpose of the ship-burial is also a matter of dispute, particularly because of the absence of any evidence of human remains. Why was there no body? Perhaps, if the date of 655 is accepted, it is because the pagan king Aethelhere was killed in battle and his body could not be recovered. Or perhaps if Aethelhere did receive a Christian burial, his entombed ship was simply a pagan centotaph erected in adherence to older traditions. Or was the ship-burial connected with the kings of East Anglia at all? The only thing that seems certain is that Sutton Hoo will remain a topic of controversy.

Following storage in the Aldwich Underground Station during World War II, the Sutton Hoo artifacts received a permanent home in the British Museum. The most accessible collection of photographs of the ship-burial is

R. L. S. Bruce-Mitford, *The Sutton Hoo Ship-Burial: A Handbook* (2nd ed.; London: British Museum, 1972).

4

Bede, *Ecclesiastical History* (731). Synod of Whitby, 664

The Venerable Bede (673–735) was in his time the greatest intellect in Western Europe. He entered a monastery when he was yet a child and remained at Jarrow in Northumbria until his death, loved for his virtue and devotion and respected for his wisdom and learning. His *History,* which he completed in 731, is his most famous work and the first history of England.

The intellectual flowering of Northumbria in the seventh and eighth centuries, of which Bede is the chief product, was due largely to the mingling of the Celtic tradition, which had grown up and flourished in the isolation of Ireland while barbarian tribes were disrupting Western Europe, and the Mediterranean tradition, which in 597 came with Augustine, the first Christian missionary sent by Rome to England. Bede's account of the introduction of Latin and Celtic Christianity into England and of the contest between the two traditions coming to a settlement at the Synod of Whitby in 664 is reproduced below.

In Bede's *History,* the Church occupies a central position, and its bringing of Christianity and civilization to the barbarian Anglo-Saxons is the theme. Not surprisingly the role of God as prime mover in history is acknowledged and miracles are treated as facts of life. What is surprising and noteworthy is Bede's treatment of England as a unit, populated by one people despite

SOURCE. *Bede's Ecclesiastical History of the English People,* eds. Bertram Colgrave and R. A. B. Mynors, pp. 69, 73, 75, 77, 221, 223, 225, 227, 231, 255, 295, 297, 299, 301, 305, 307. © 1969 Oxford University Press. By permission of The Clarendon Press, Oxford.

its political division into the Heptarchy of seven kingdoms. Where he got this notion, how extensive it was, and the impact of his stating it are interesting questions. Also significant is Bede's role in initiating and making popular the new system of dating, *anno domini,* "In the year of our Lord," which is, of course, the way we number the years today.

Copies of Bede's original Latin manuscript soon found their way to all parts of Europe, attesting both to Bede's personal reputation and to the broad influence of Northumbrian learning. Its first partial translation into English was in the reign of Alfred (871–899); its first printing was in 1475.

In the year of our Lord 582, Maurice, the fifty-fourth from Augustus, became emperor; he ruled for twenty-one years. In the tenth year of his reign, Gregory, a man eminent in learning and in affairs, was elected pontiff of the apostolic see of Rome. . . . In the fourteenth year of this emperor and about 150 years after the coming of the Angles to Britain, Gregory, prompted by divine inspiration, sent a servant of God named Augustine and several more God-fearing monks with him to preach the word of God to the English race. In obedience to the pope's commands, they undertook this task and had already gone a little way on their journey when they were paralysed with terror. They began to contemplate returning home rather than going to a barbarous, fierce, and unbelieving nation whose language they did not even understand. They all agreed that this was the safer course; so forthwith they sent home Augustine whom Gregory had intended to have consecrated as their bishop if they were received by the English. Augustine was to beg St. Gregory humbly for permission to give up so dangerous, wearisome, and uncertain a journey. Gregory, however, sent them an encouraging letter in which he persuaded them to persevere with the task of preaching the Word and trust in the help of God. . . .

So Augustine, strengthened by the encouragement of St. Gregory, in company with the servants of Christ, returned to the work of preaching the word, and came to Britain. At that time Æthelberht, king of Kent, was a very powerful monarch. The lands over which he exercised his suzerainty stretched as far as the great river Humber, which divides the northern from the southern Angles. Over against the eastern districts of Kent there is a large island called Thanet. . . . Here Augustine, the servant of the Lord, landed with his companions, who are said to have been nearly forty in number. They had acquired interpreters from the Frankish race according to the command of Pope St. Gregory. Augustine sent to

Æthelberht to say that he had come from Rome bearing the best of news, namely the sure and certain promise of eternal joys in heaven and an endless kingdom with the living and true God to those who received it. On hearing this the king ordered them to remain on the island where they had landed and be provided with all things necessary until he had decided what to do about them. . . .

Some days afterwards the king came to the island and, sitting in the open air, commanded Augustine and his comrades to come thither to talk with him. He took care that they should not meet in any building, for he held the traditional superstition that, if they practised any magic art, they might deceive him and get the better of him as soon as he entered. But they came endowed with divine not devilish power and bearing as their standard a silver cross and the image of our Lord and Saviour painted on a panel. They chanted litanies and uttered prayers to the Lord for their own eternal salvation and the salvation of those for whom and to whom they had come. At the king's command they sat down and preached the word of life to himself and all his *gesiths* there present. Then he said to them: "The words and the promises you bring are fair enough, but because they are new to us and doubtful, I cannot consent to accept them and forsake those beliefs which I and the whole English race have held so long. But as you have come on a long pilgrimage and are anxious, I perceive, to share with us things which you believe to be true and good, we do not wish to do you harm; on the contrary, we will receive you hospitably and provide what is necessary for your support; nor do we forbid you to win all you can to your faith and religion by your preaching." So he gave them a dwelling in the city of Canterbury, which was the chief city of all his dominions. . . .

At last the king, as well as others, believed and was baptized, being attracted by the pure life of the saints and by their most precious promises, whose truth they confirmed by performing many miracles. Every day more and more began to flock to hear the Word, to forsake their heathen worship, and, through faith, to join the unity of Christ's holy Church. . . .

In the year of our Lord 565, when Justin the second took over the control of the Roman Empire after Justinian, there came from Ireland to Britain a priest and abbot named Columba, a true monk in life no less than habit; he came to Britain to preach the word of God to the kingdoms of the northern Picts. . . .

Columba turned them to the faith of Christ by his words and example and so received the island of Iona from them in order to establish a monastery there. . . .

This island always has an abbot for its ruler who is a priest, to whose authority the whole kingdom, including even bishops, have to be subject. This unusual arrangement follows the example of their first teacher, who was not a bishop but a priest and monk. Some written records of his life and teachings are said to have been preserved by his disciples. Whatever he was himself, we know this for certain about him, that he left successors distinguished for their great abstinence, their love of God, and their observance of the Rule. It is true that they used tables of doubtful accuracy in fixing the date of the chief festival, since they were so far away at the ends of the earth that there was none to bring them the decrees of the synods concerning the observance of Easter; but they diligently practised such works of religion and chastity as they were able to learn from the words of the prophets, the evangelists, and the apostles. . . .

Such was the island, such the community, from which Aidan was sent to give the English people instruction in Christ. . . . Aidan taught the clergy many lessons about the conduct of their lives but above all he left them a most salutary example of abstinence and self-control; and the best recommendation of his teaching to all was that he taught them no other way of life than that which he himself practised among his fellows. . . .

With such a man as bishop to instruct them, King Oswald, together with the people over which he ruled, learned to hope for those heavenly realms which were unknown to their forefathers; and also Oswald gained from the one God who made heaven and earth greater earthly realms than any of his ancestors had possessed. In fact he held under his sway all the peoples and kingdoms of Britain, divided among the speakers of four different languages, British, Pictish, Irish, and English. . . .

After Oswald had been translated to the heavenly kingdom, his brother Oswiu succeeded to his earthly kingdom in his place, as a young man of about thirty, and ruled for twenty-eight troubled years. . . .

In those days there arose a great and active controversy about the keeping of Easter. Those who had come from Kent or Gaul declared that the Irish observance of Easter Sunday was contrary to the custom of the universal church. . . .

It is said that in these days it sometimes happened that Easter was celebrated twice in the same year, so that the king had finished the fast and was keeping Easter Sunday, while the queen and her people were still in Lent and observing Palm Sunday. . . .

When this question of Easter and of the tonsure and other ecclesiastical matters was raised, it was decided to hold a council to settle the dispute at a monastery called *Streanæshealh* (Whitby). . . .

King Oswiu began by declaring that it was fitting that those who served one God should observe one rule of life and not differ in the celebration of the heavenly sacraments, seeing that they all hoped for one kingdom in heaven; they ought therefore to inquire as to which was the truer tradition and then all follow it together. He then ordered his bishop Colman to say first what were the customs which he followed and whence they originated. Colman thereupon said, "The method of keeping Easter which I observe, I received from my superiors who sent me here as bishop; it was in this way that all our fathers, men beloved of God, are known to have celebrated it. Nor should this method seem contemptible and blame-worthy seeing that the blessed evangelist John, the disciple whom the Lord specially loved, is said to have celebrated it thus, together with all the churches over which he presided." . . . Then Wilfrid, receiving instruc-tions from the king to speak, began thus: "The Easter we keep is the same as we have seen universally celebrated in Rome, where the apostles St. Peter and St. Paul lived, taught, suffered, and were buried. We also found it in use everywhere in Italy and Gaul when we travelled through those countries for the purpose of study and prayer. We learned that it was observed at one and the same time in Africa, Asia, Egypt, Greece, and throughout the whole world, wherever the Church of Christ is scattered, amid various nations and languages. The only exceptions are these men and their accomplices in obstinacy, I mean the Picts and the Britons, who in these, the two remotest islands of the Ocean, and only in some parts of them, foolishly attempt to fight against the whole world."

"So far as your father Columba and his followers are concerned, whose holiness you claim to imitate and whose rule and precepts (confirmed by heavenly signs) you claim to follow, I might perhaps point out that at the judgment, many will say to the Lord that they prophesied in His name and cast out devils and did many wonderful works, but the Lord will answer that He never knew them. Far be it from me to say this about your fathers, for it is much fairer to believe good rather than evil about unknown people. So I will not deny that those who in their rude simplicity loved God with pious intent, were indeed servants of God and beloved by Him. Nor do I think that this observance of Easter did much harm to them while no one had come to show them a more perfect rule to follow. In fact I am sure that if anyone knowing the catholic rule had come to them they would have followed it, as they are known to have followed all the laws of God as soon as they had learned of them. But, once having heard the decrees of the apostolic see or rather of the universal Church, if you refuse to follow them, confirmed as they are by the holy Scriptures, then without doubt you are committing sin. For though your fathers were holy men, do you think that a handful of people in one corner of the remotest of islands is to be preferred to the universal Church of Christ which is spread throughout the world? And even if that Columba of yours —yes, and ours too, if he belonged to Christ—was a holy man of mighty works, is he to be preferred to the most blessed chief of the apostles, to whom the Lord said, 'Thou art Peter and upon this rock I will build my Church and the gates of hell shall not prevail against it, and I will give unto thee the keys of the kingdom of heaven'?"

When Wilfrid had ended, the king said, "It is true, Colman, that the Lord said these words to Peter?" Colman answered, "It is true, O King." Then the king went on, "Have you anything to show that an equal authority was given to your Columba?" Colman answered, "Nothing." Again the king said, "Do you both agree, without any dispute, that these words were addressed primarily to Peter and that the Lord gave him the keys of the kingdom of heaven?" They both answered, "Yes." Thereupon the king concluded, "Then, I tell you, since he is the doorkeeper I will not contradict him; but I intend to obey his commands in everything to the best of my knowledge and ability, otherwise when I come to the gates of the kingdom of heaven, there may be no one to open them because the one who on your own showing holds the keys has turned his back on me."

5

The Anglo-Saxon Chronicle

The Anglo-Saxon Chronicle is in fact seven related chronicles, which record in an annalistic fashion the events in England's history from the invasion of Julius Caesar, "Sixty years before Christ was born," to the death of Stephen in 1154. The *Chronicle* was initially compiled during the reign of Alfred (871–899), a result of his determination to revive interest in learning. The earliest entries, often little more than identifying labels to help the memory distinguish one year from another, were similar to the brief remarks added by churches and monasteries to the column of years on an Easter table. Where written records such as Bede's *History* were available, entries were longer, and during a writer's own lifetime there was the possibility of considerable

SOURCE. *The Anglo-Saxon Chronicle: A Revised Translation*, ed. Dorothy Whitelock with David C. Douglas and Susie I. Tucker, New Brunswick, N. J.: Rutgers University Press, 1961, pp. 6–7, 9, 14, 22, 26, 28, 35–36, 42, 46–47, 49–50, 52, 58. Reprinted by permission of Eyre & Spottiswoode (Publishers) Ltd.

first-hand information. Thus Alfred's reign and the troubles produced by the invading Danes were emphasized. Copies of the initial compilation, added to with varying degrees of skill and imagination, became the several versions, especially of the later period.

Not only does the *Chronicle* give the historian a wealth of information, but the long period of its compositon by a number of scribes in different locations makes it an equally valuable source of information for the student of the Old English or Anglo-Saxon language. Its very existence, a vernacular chronicle spanning several centuries, is as unique in the field of letters as the Domesday survey is in the field of royal administration, a fact that needs to be pondered and explained.

1   Octavian reigned 66 years and in the 52nd year of his reign Christ was born.

2   The three astrologers came from the East in order to worship Christ, and the children in Bethlehem were slain because of the persecution of Christ by Herod.

6   Five thousand and two hundred years had passed from the beginning of the world to this year.

47   In this year Claudius came to Britain, the second of the kings of the Romans to do so, and obtained the greater part under his control, and likewise subjected the island of Orkney to the rule of the Romans.

410   In this year Rome was destroyed by the Goths, eleven hundred and ten years after it was built. Then after that the kings of the Romans no longer reigned in Britain. Altogether they had reigned there 470 years since Gaius Julius first came to the land.

596   In this year Pope Gregory sent Augustine to Britain with a good number of monks, who preached God's word to the English people.

671   In this year there was the great mortality of birds.

715   In this year Ine and Ceolred fought at "Woden's barrow."

733   In this year Æthelbald occupied Somerton, and there was an eclipse of the sun.

734   In this year the moon looked as if it were suffused with blood, and Tatwine and Bede died.

789   In this year King Brihtric married Offa's daughter Eadburh. And in his days there came for the first time three ships of Northmen

and then the reeve rode to them and wished to force them to the king's residence, for he did not know what they were; and they slew him. Those were the first ships of Danish men which came to the land of the English.

793   In this year dire portents appeared over Northumbria and sorely frightened the people. They consisted of immense whirlwinds and flashes of lightning, and fiery dragons were seen flying in the air. A great famine immediately followed those signs, and a little after that in the same year, on 8 June, the ravages of heathen men miserably destroyed God's church on Lindisfarne, with plunder and slaughter. And Sicga died on 22 February.

851   In this year Ealdorman Ceorl with the contingent of the men of Devon fought against the heathen army at *Wicganbeorg,* and the English made a great slaughter there and had the victory. And for the first time, heathen men stayed through the winter on Thanet. And the same year 350 ships came into the mouth of the Thames and stormed Canterbury and London and put to flight Brihtwulf, king of the Mercians, with his army, and went south across the Thames into Surrey. And King Æthelwulf and his son Æthebald fought against them at *Aclea* with the army of the West Saxons, and there inflicted the greatest slaughter [on a heathen army] that we ever heard of until this present day, and had the victory there.

871   In this year the army came into Wessex to Reading, and three days later two Danish earls rode farther inland. Then Ealdorman Æthelwulf encountered them at Englefield, and fought against them there and had the victory, and one of them, whose name was Sidroc, was killed there. Then four days later King Ethelred and his brother Alfred led a great army to Reading and fought against the army; and a great slaughter was made on both sides and Ealdorman Æthelwulf was killed, and the Danes had possession of the battle-field. . . . And afterwards, after Easter, King Ethelred died, and he had reigned five years, and his body is buried at Wimborne minster.

Then his brother Alfred, the son of Æthelwulf, succeeded to the kingdom of the West Saxons. And a month later King Alfred fought with a small force against the whole army at Wilton and put it to flight far on into the day; and the Danes had possession of the battle-field. And during that year nine general engagements were fought against the Danish army in the kingdom south of the Thames, besides the expeditions which the king's brother Alfred and [single] ealdormen and king's thegns often rode on, which were not counted. And that year nine (Danish) earls were killed and one king. And the West Saxons made peace with the army that year.

878   In this year in midwinter after twelfth night the enemy army came stealthily to Chippenham, and occupied the land of the West Saxons and settled there, and drove a great part of the people across the sea, and conquered most of the others; and the people submitted to them, except King Alfred. He journeyed in difficulties through the woods and fen-fastnesses with a small force.

And afterwards at Easter, King Alfred with a small force made a stronghold at Athelney, and he and the section of the people of Somerset which was nearest to it proceeded to fight from that stronghold against the enemy. Then in the seventh week after Easter he rode to "Egbert's stone" east of Selwood, and there came to meet all the people of Somerset and of Wiltshire and of that part of Hampshire which was on this side of the sea, and they rejoiced to see him. And then after one night he went from that encampment to Iley, and after another night to Edington, and there fought against the whole army and put it to flight, and pursued it as far as the fortress, and stayed there a fortnight. And then the enemy gave him preliminary hostages and great oaths that they would leave his kingdom, and promised also that their king should receive baptism, and they kept their promise. Three weeks later King Guthrum with 30 of the men who were the most important in the army came [to him] at Aller, which is near Athelney, and the king stood sponsor to him at his baptism there; and the unbinding of the chrism took place at Wedmore. And he was twelve days with the king, and he honoured him and his companions greatly with gifts.

886   In this year the Danish army which had gone east went west again, and then up the Seine, and made their winter quarters there at the town of Paris.

That same year King Alfred occupied London; and all the English people that were not under subjection to the Danes submitted to him. And he then entrusted the borough to the control of Ealdorman Ethelred.

900   In this year Alfred the son of Æthelwulf died, six days before All Saints' day. He was king over the whole English people except for that part which was under Danish rule, and he had held the kingdom for one and a half years less than thirty; and then his son Edward succeeded to the kingdom.

6

Anglo-Saxon Dooms of Wihtred (695) and Alfred (871-899)

The Anglo-Saxon's readiness to resort to violence was limited only by his knowledge that a victim's family would return in kind any injury or insult received. This tension produced a vast body of unwritten law and custom that governed the conduct of the folkmoot or court, where responsibility or guilt and an appropriate monetary compensation was determined. A killing required the payment of a wergeld, a lesser physical injury a bot, and other injuries, such as breaking the peace of a man's household, brought other fines. These procedures were both very formal and ancient. Stresses appeared in the system, however, as kings became more powerful, as the solidarity of the family declined, and as outside influences, such as Christianity and commerce, produced conditions for which the customary laws made no provision.

Dooms were written laws issued by a king and his council of wise men, the witenagemot, mainly for the purpose of adapting existing customs to new conditions. The first dooms, those of Ethelbert of Kent (560–616), date from shortly after Augustine's arrival in England in 597. The Church no doubt contributed the idea that laws should be written. The dooms reproduced below were issued by Wihtred of Kent in 695 and by Alfred of Wessex (871–899). The former illustrate the continuing attempt to accommodate the law to the Christian Church, as well as the perennial need to keep the peace. The dooms of Alfred indicate not only his wide-ranging interests but also the profound difficulties he faced during his reign.

SOURCE. *English Historical Documents, Vol. 1, c. 500–1042,* ed. Dorothy Whitelock. 1955, Oxford University Press, Inc., pp. 362–364, 373, 377–380. Reprinted by permission of Oxford University Press, Inc., and Eyre & Spottiswoode (Publishers) Ltd.

The dooms were written in Anglo-Saxon and have survived in various manuscripts, none of which dates back to its original promulgation.

THESE ARE THE DECREES OF WIHTRED, KING OF THE PEOPLE OF KENT.

Prologue

When the most gracious king of the people of Kent, Wihtred, was reigning, in the fifth year of his reign . . . there was collected a deliberate assembly of leading men. . . . There, with the consent of all, the leading men devised these decrees and added them to the lawful usages of the people of Kent, as it says and declares hereafter.

1. The Church [is to be] free from taxation.

2. The [breach of] the Church's protection is to be 50 shillings like the king's.

9. If a servant, against his lord's command, do servile work between sunset on Saturday evening and sunset on Sunday evening, he is to pay 80 *sceattas* to his lord.

10. If a servant rides on his own business on that day, he is to pay six [shillings] to his lord, or be flogged.

16. The word of the bishop and the king without an oath is to be incontrovertible.

17. The head of a monastery is to clear himself with a priest's exculpation.

18. A priest is to purge himself with his own asseveration in his holy vestments before the altar, saying thus: "I speak the truth in Christ, I do not lie." Similarly a deacon is to purge himself.

19. A cleric is to purge himself with three of the same order, and he alone is to have his hand on the altar; the others are to stand by and discharge the oath.

20. A stranger is to purge himself with his own oath on the altar; similarly a king's thegn;

21. A *ceorl* with three of the same class on the altar; and the oath of all these is to be incontrovertible.

25. If anyone kill a man who is in the act of thieving, he is to lie without wergild.

26. If anyone captures a freeman with the stolen goods on him, the king

26.1. He who discovers and captures him, is to have the right to half is to choose one of three things; he is either to be killed or sold across the sea or redeemed with his wergild.

of [the payment for] him; if he is killed, 70 shillings is to be paid to them.

27. If a slave steals and is redeemed, [this is to be at] 70 shillings, which-ever the king wishes. If he is killed, half is to be paid for him to the possessor.

28. If a man from a distance or a foreigner goes off the track, and he neither shouts nor blows a horn, he is to be assumed to be a thief, to be either killed or redeemed.

THE DOOMS OF ALFRED

Int. 43. Judge thou very fairly. Do not judge one judgment for the rich and another for the poor; nor one for the one more dear and another for the one more hateful.

Int. 49.6. A man can think on this one sentence alone, that he judges each one rightly; he has need of no other law-books. Let him bethink that he judge to no man what he would not that he judged to him, if he were giving the judgment on him.

Int. 49.9. Then I, King Alfred, collected these together and ordered to be written many of them which our forefathers observed, those which I liked; and many of those which I did not like, I rejected with the advice of my councillors, and ordered them to be differently observed. For I dared not presume to set in writing at all many of my own, because it was unknown to me what would please those who should come after us. But those which I found anywhere, which seemed to me most just, either of the time of my kinsman, King Ine, or Offa, king of the Mercians, or of Ethelbert, who first among the English received baptism, I collected herein, and omitted the others.

Int. 49.10. Then I, Alfred, king of the West Saxons, showed these to all my councillors, and they then said that they were all pleased to observe them.

26 (29). If anyone with a band of men kills an innocent man of a two-hundred wergild, he who admits the slaying is to pay the wergild and the fine, and each man who was in that expedition is to pay 30 shillings as compensation for being in that band.

27 (30). If it is a man of a six-hundred wergild, each man [is to pay] 60 shillings as compensation for being in that band, and the slayer the wer-gild and full fine.

28 (31). If he is a man of twelve-hundred wergild, each of them [is to pay] 120 shillings, and the slayer the wergild and the fine.

34. Moreover, it is prescribed for traders: they are to bring before the king's reeve in a public meeting the men whom they take up into the

country with them, and it is to be established how many of them there are to be; and they are to take with them men whom they can afterwards bring to justice at a public meeting. . . .

35. If anyone binds an innocent *ceorl,* he is to pay him six shillings compensation.

35.1. If anyone scourges him, he is to pay him 20 shillings compensation.

35.2. If he places him in the stocks, he is to pay him 30 shillings compensation.

35.3. If in insult he disfigures him by cutting his hair, he is to pay him 10 shillings compensation.

35.4. If, without binding him, he cuts his hair like a priest's, he is to pay him 30 shillings compensation.

35.5. If he cuts off his beard, he is to pay 20 shillings compensation.

35.6. If he binds him and then cuts his hair like a priest's, he is to pay 60 shillings compensation.

36. Moreover, it is established: if anyone has a spear over his shoulder, and a man is transfixed on it, the wergild is to be paid without the fine.

36.1. If he is transfixed before his eyes, he is to pay the wergild; if anyone accuses him of intention in this act, he is to clear himself in proportion to the fine, and by that [oath] do away with the fine,

36.2. if the point is higher than the butt of the shaft. If they are both level, the point and the butt end, that is to be [considered] without risk.

38. If anyone fights in a meeting in the presence of the king's ealdorman, he is to pay wergild and fine, as is fitting, and before that, 120 shillings to the ealdorman as a fine.

38.1. If he disturbs a public meeting by drawing a weapon, [he is to pay] 120 shillings to the ealdorman as a fine.

38.2. If any of this takes place before the deputy of the king's ealdorman, or before the king's priest, [there shall be] a fine of 30 shillings.

39. If anyone fights in the house of a *ceorl,* he is to pay six shillings compensation to the *ceorl.*

39.1. If he draws a weapon and does not fight, it is to be half as much.

42. Moreover we command: that the man who knows his opponent to be dwelling at home is not to fight before he asks justice for himself.

42.1. If he has sufficient power to surround his opponent and besiege him there in his house, he is to keep him seven days inside and not fight against him, if he will remain inside; and then after seven days, if he will surrender and give up his weapons, he is to keep him unharmed for 30 days, and send notice about him to his kinsmen and his friends.

42.2. If he, however, reaches a church, it is then to be [dealt with] according to the privilege of the church, as we have said above.

42.3. If he [the attacker] has not sufficient power to besiege him in his house, he is to ride to the ealdorman and ask him for support; if he will not give him support, he is to ride to the king, before having recourse to fighting.

42.5. Moreover we declare that a man may fight on behalf of his lord, if the lord is being attacked, without incurring a vendetta. Similarly the lord may fight on behalf of his man.

42.6. In the same way, a man may fight on behalf of his born kinsman, if he is being wrongfully attacked, except against his lord; that we do not allow.

42.7. And a man may fight without incurring a vendetta if he finds another man with his wedded wife, within closed doors or under the same blanket, or with his legitimate daughter or his legitimate sister, or with his mother who was given as a lawful wife to his father.

7

"The Battle of Maldon," 991

This Anglo-Saxon poem, a 325-line fragment missing the beginning and end, describes a battle fought at Maldon in Essex in 991. The *Anglo-Saxon Chronicle* relates the incident simply: "And Ealdorman Brihtnoth came against him there with his army and fought against him; and they killed the ealdorman there and had control of the field." Thus, Maldon was one of many skirmishes in the renewed onslaught of the Danes against the faltering resistance of King Ethelred the Redeless (978–1016).

The poem, however, gives a far more vivid impression of the battle—of the personal defiance of Byrhtnoth in the face of the Danes' invitation to submit and of the resolution of the slain Byrhtnoth's followers to avenge his death or to die on the field by him. The poem, demonstrating the existence of

SOURCE. Margaret Ashdown, *English and Norse Documents, Relating to the Reign of Ethelred the Unready,* Cambridge University Press, 1930, pp. 23, 25, 29, 31, 33, 35, 37. Reprinted by permission of Cambridge University Press.

poetic artistry of the highest quality, gives a unique touch of individual sentiment and action and forces the historian to see real people and real emo-
tions behind the chronicler's brief catalogue of events.

How different our understanding of the tenth century would be without
this invaluable evidence. Although the only poem of its kind in existence, it
was part of an oral heroic tradition that included *Beowulf.* It differs from
that epic not only in its brevity but in its lateness of composition and in its
dealing with a recent historical event rather than a story remembered dimly
from the past. Like *Beowulf,* however, "Maldon" owed its survival to its
being written down, the result perhaps of a monastery's regard for a dead
benefactor or a widow's commissioning of a memorial for her dead husband.
The poem apparently went unnoticed during the Middle Ages, its first mention coming in the 1696 cataloguing of the manuscripts of the Cottonian
Library, works rescued when the monasteries were dissolved and later left
to the nation by its owner John Cotton. Thomas Hearne, seemingly for no
particular reason, included the poem among the appendices of the *Chronicle
of John of Glastonbury,* which he edited and printed in 1726. Thus, although
the original manuscript burned in 1731, the poem survived, illustrating the
role of good fortune in the historian's quest for knowledge of the past.

Then he bade each warrior leave his horse, drive it afar and go forth
on foot, and trust to his hands and to his good intent.

Then Offa's kinsman first perceived that the earl would suffer no faint-
ness of heart; he let his loved hawk fly from his hand to the wood and
advanced to the fight. By this it might be seen that the lad would not
waver in the strife now that he had taken up his arms.

With him Eadric would help his lord, his chief in the fray. He advanced
to war with spear in hand; as long as he might grasp his shield and broad
sword, he kept his purpose firm. He made good his vow, now that the
time had come for him to fight before his lord.

Then Byrhtnoth began to array his men; he rode and gave counsel and
taught his warriors how they should stand and keep their ground, bade
them hold their shields aright, firm with their hands and fear not at all.
When he had meetly arrayed his host, he alighted among the people where
it pleased him best, where he knew his body-guard to be most loyal.

Then the messenger of the Vikings stood on the bank, he called sternly,
uttered words, boastfully speaking the seafarers' message to the earl, as he
stood on the shore. "Bold seamen have sent me to you, and bade me say,
that it is for you to send treasure quickly in return for peace, and it will

be better for you all that you buy off an attack with tribute, rather than that men so fierce as we should give you battle. . . .

Byrhtnoth lifted up his voice, grasped his shield and shook his supple spear, gave forth words, angry and resolute, and made him answer: "Hear you, searover, what this folk says? For tribute they will give you spears, poisoned point and ancient sword, such war gear as will profit you little in the battle. Messenger of the seamen, take back a message, say to your people a far less pleasing tale, how that there stands here with his troop an earl of unstained renown, who is ready to guard this realm, the home of Ethelred my lord, people and land; it is the heathen that shall fall in the battle." . . .

Then Byrhtnoth drew his blade, broad and of burnished edge, and smote upon his mail. All too quickly one of the seamen checked his hand, crippling the arm of the earl. Then his golden-hilted sword fell to the earth; he could not use his hard blade nor wield a weapon. Yet still the white-haired warrior spoke as before, emboldened his men and bade the heroes press on. He could no longer now stand firm on his feet. The earl looked up to heaven and cried aloud: "I thank thee, Ruler of Nations, for all the joys that I have met with in this world. Now I have most need, gracious Creator, that thou grant my spirit grace, that my soul may fare to thee, into thy keeping, Lord of Angels, and pass in peace. It is my prayer to thee that fiends of hell may not entreat it shamefully."

Then the heathen wretches cut him down, and both the warriors who stood near by, Ælfnoth and Wulfmær, lay overthrown; they yielded their lives at their lord's side. . . .

All the retainers saw how their lord lay dead. Then the proud thanes pressed on, hastened eagerly, those undaunted men. All desired one of two things, to lose their lives or to avenge the one they loved.

With these words Ælfric's son urged them to go forth, a warrior young in years, he lifted up his voice and spoke with courage. Ælfwine said: "Remember the words that we uttered many a time over the mead, when on the bench, heroes in hall, we made our boast about hard strife. Now it may be proved which of us is bold! I will make known my lineage to all, how I was born in Mercia of a great race. Ealhelm was my grandfather called, a wise ealdorman, happy in this world's goods. Thanes shall have no cause to reproach me among my people that I was ready to forsake this action, and seek my home, now that my lord lies low, cut down in battle. This is no common grief to me, he was both my kinsman and my lord."

Then he advanced (his mind was set on revenge), till he pierced with his lance a seaman from among the host, so that the man lay on the earth, borne down with his weapon.

Then Offa began to exhort his comrades, his friends and companions, that they should press on. . . .

Leofsunu lifted up his voice and raised his shield, his buckler to defend him, and gave him answer: "This I avow, that I will not flee a footspace hence, but will press on and avenge my liege-lord in the fight. . . .

Dunhere spoke and shook his lance; a simple churl, he cried above them all, and bade each warrior avenge Byrhtnoth: "He that thinks to avenge his lord, his chief in the press, may not waver nor reck for his life." Then they went forth, and took no thought for life. . . .

They prayed God that they might take vengeance for their lord, and work slaughter among their foes. . . .

Then Offa smote a seaman in the fight, so that he fell to the earth. Gadd's kinsman too was brought to the ground, Offa himself was quickly cut to pieces in the fray. Yet he had compassed what he had promised his chief, as he bandied vows with his generous lord in days gone by, that they should both ride home to the town unhurt or fall among the host, perish of wound on the field. He lay, as befits a thane, at his lord's side.

Then came a crashing of shields; seamen pressed on, enraged by war; the spear oft pierced the life-house of the doomed. Wistan went forth, Thurstan's son and fought against the men. Wighelm's child was the death of the three in the press, before he himself lay among the slain.

That was a fierce encounter; warriors stood firm in the strife. Men were falling, worn out with their wounds; the slain fell to the earth.

Oswold and Eadwold all the while, that pair of brothers, urged on the men, prayed their dear kinsmen to stand firm in the hour of need, and use their weapons in no weak fashion.

Byrhtwold spoke and grasped his shield (he was an old companion); he shook his ash-wood spear and exhorted the men right boldly: "Thoughts must be the braver, heart more valiant courage the greater as our strength grows less. Here lies our lord, all cut down, the hero in the dust. Long may he mourn who thinks now to turn from the battle-play. I am old in years; I will not leave the field, but think to lie by my lord's side, by the man I held so dear."

8

William of Poitiers, *The Deeds of William* (1071). Background to the Norman Conquest, 1064-1066

William of Poitiers's *Gesta Willelmi ducis Normannorum et regis Anglorum,* written about 1071, is one of several "chronicles" surviving from the Norman period. Unlike a pure chronicle, which simply attempts to remind the reader of past events, William's work begins the transition toward a more topically organized "history," which assists the reader to understand, as well as to recall, the past. William stands somewhere between the writers of the *Anglo-Saxon Chronicle* and later historians such as William of Newburgh.

William of Poitiers served for a time as chaplain to Duke William of Normandy. He was a product of Norman feudalism, a warrior-priest like Bishop Odo of Bayeux, who commissioned the Bayeux Tapestry. Although not present at the Battle of Hastings, William knew many of the men who were. His account in Latin of the background to the invasion and of the battle itself is, together with the Bayeux Tapestry, the source of our most detailed knowledge of this central event in English history.

As a Norman and an admirer of Duke William, later William I (1066–1087), William of Poitiers did not write an unbiased account. In the selection that follows his primary concern is to justify William's invasion of England. He stresses Harold's debt to William and insists on the voluntary nature of Harold's oath taken in 1064 and on his treachery in later breaking it, an event

---

SOURCE. *English Historical Documents, Vol. II, 1042–1189,* eds. David C. Douglas and George W. Greenaway. 1953, Oxford University Press, Inc., pp. 217–219. Reprinted by permission of Oxford University Press, Inc., and Eyre & Spottiswoode (Publishers) Ltd.

that supposedly brought William widespread sympathy and support. This account differs sharply from that of the *Anglo-Saxon Chronicle,* a version more favorable to Harold. The latter omits any mention of an oath and stresses Edward the Confessor's choice of Harold, not William, as his successor. Thus, as in so many cases, the historian must attempt to analyze his data critically and to arrive at an independent judgment not necessarily wholly in agreement with any one of his sources of evidence.

About the same time, Edward, king of the English, who loved William as a brother or a son, established him as his heir with a stronger pledge than ever before. The king, who in his holy life showed his desire for a celestial kingdom, felt the hour of his death approaching, and wished to anticipate its inevitable consequences. He therefore dispatched Harold to William in order that he might confirm his promise by an oath. This Harold was of all the king's subjects the richest and the most exhalted in honour and power, and his brother and his cousins had previously been offered as hostages in respect of the same succession. The king, indeed, here acted with great prudence in choosing Harold for this task, in the hope that the riches and the authority of this magnate might check disturbance throughout England if the people with their accustomed perfidy should be disposed to overturn what had been determined. Whilst travelling upon this errand Harold only escaped the perils of the sea by making a forced landing on the coast of Ponthieu where he fell into the hands of Count Guy, who threw him and his companions into prison. He might well have thought this a greater misfortune even than shipwreck, since among many peoples of the Gauls there was an abominable custom utterly contrary to Christian charity, whereby, when the powerful and rich were captured, they were thrown ignominiously into prison, and there maltreated and tortured even to the point of death, and afterwards sold as slaves to some magnate. When Duke William heard what had happened he sent messengers at speed, and by prayers and threats he brought about Harold's honourable release. . . . For the duke rejoiced to have so illustrious a guest in a man who had been sent him by the nearest and dearest of his friends: one, moreover, who was in England second only to the king, and who might prove a faithful mediator between him and the English. When they had come together in conference at Bonneville, Harold in that place swore fealty to the duke employing the sacred ritual recognized among Christian men. And as is testified by the most truthful and most honourable men who were there present, he took an oath of his own free will in the following terms: firstly that he would be the representative of Duke William at the court of his lord, King Edward, as long as the king lived; secondly that he would employ all his influence and wealth to ensure that after the death of King Edward the kingdom of England should be confirmed in the possession of the duke; thirdly that he would place a garrison of the duke's knights in the castle of Dover and maintain these at his own care and cost; fourthly that in other parts of England at the pleasure of the duke he would maintain garrisons in other castles and make complete provision for their sustenance. The duke on his part who before the oath was taken had received ceremonial homage from him, confirmed to him at his request all his lands and dignities. For Edward in his illness could not be expected to live much longer. . . . After this there came the unwelcome report that the land of England had lost its king, and that Harold had been crowned in his stead. This insensate Englishman did not wait for the public choice, but breaking his oath, and with the support of a few ill-disposed partisans, he seized the throne of the best of kings on the very day of his funeral, and when all the people were bewailing their loss. He was ordained king by the unhallowed consecration of Stigand, who had justly been deprived of his priesthood by the zeal and anathema of the apostolic see. Duke William therefore having taken counsel with his men resolved to avenge the insult by force of arms, and to regain his inheritance by war. . . . It would be tedious to tell in detail how by his prudent act ships were made, arms and troops, provisions and other equipment assembled for war, and how the enthusiasm of the whole of Normandy was directed towards this enterprise. Nor did he neglect to take measures for the administration and the security of the duchy during his absence. Further, many warriors came to his support from outside the duchy, some being attracted by his well-known generosity, and all by confidence in the justice of his cause. . . .

At that time there sat in the seat of St. Peter at Rome Pope Alexander, who was worthy of the respect and obedience of the whole Church. . . . Wherever he could throughout all the world he corrected evil without compromise. The duke therefore sought the favour of this apostle for the project he had in hand, and gladly received from him the gift of a banner as a pledge of the support of St. Peter whereby he might the more confidently and safely attack his enemy. . . .

9

The Bayeux Tapestry.
The Battle of Hastings, 1066

The Bayeux Tapestry, which is actually an embroidery, is a most unusual piece of historical evidence. It is unique not only because of its survival but because of its portrayal of a historical event of obvious importance—the Norman conquest of England. The tapestry is approximately 230 feet long and 20 inches wide. Its 73 panels, beginning with the mission of Harold to Normany in 1064 and ending with his death at Hastings, tell in comic-strip fashion a portion of the story of the conquest.

The tapestry was commissioned by Odo, Bishop of Bayeux, William the Conqueror's half-brother, probably sometime between 1066 and 1082. Most likely it was intended for his new cathedral at Bayeux, which was dedicated in 1077. But there is dispute on all of these points. Odo fought with William at Hastings, and the tapestry, although probably produced by Anglo-Saxon craftsmen, is a Norman version of these critical events. In fact, the account given by the Bayeux Tapestry is similar to that of William of Poitiers, although the two do differ on points of detail. The tapestry also emphasizes the oath of 1064 as the justification for William's invasion. The panel dealing with the oath (Plate A) appears near the middle of the tapestry and should be viewed as the central, climactic event. The portrayal of the coming of Halley's Comet (Plate B) is the tapestry's attempt to shown divine displeasure with Harold's usurpation of the throne. The events shown in the rest of the tapestry, Plates C and D, dealing with the invasion of England, and Plates E and F, depicting the battle itself, proceed as if the success of the Normans was inevitable. The tapestry is also of particular value in studying the clothing, weaponry, and architecture of the eleventh century.

SOURCE. *The Bayeux Tapestry: A Comprehensive Survey,* gen. ed. Sir Frank Stenton, London: Phaidon Press, 1957, plates 29, 35, 43, 52, 67, 72. Reproduced with the permission of Phaidon Press.

PLATE A
Harold's oath (Phaidon Press, reproduced with permission of Phaidon Press).

PLATE B
King Harold and the comet (Phaidon Press, reproduced with permission of Phaidon Press).

PLATE C
The invasion fleet (Phaidon Press, reproduced with permission of
Phaidon Press).

The tapestry itself has an interesting history. It is first referred to in an
inventory of 1476, which revealed its occasional display in the nave of the
cathedral. It was not mentioned again until the eighteenth century, when its
historical importance was widely recognized. During the French Revolution

PLATE D
Norman destruction in England (Phaidon Press, reproduced with permission of Phaidon Press).

PLATE E
The battle of Hastings (Phaidon Press, reproduced with permission of Phaidon Press).

it was on two occasions almost destroyed. In 1792 soldiers attempted un-successfully to use it to cover a wagon, and two years later it almost adorned a float honoring the revolution. In 1803 Napoleon exhibited the tapestry at

PLATE F
The death of Harold (Phaidon Press, reproduced by permission of Phaidon Press).

the *Musée Napoléon* in Paris, perhaps hoping to draw attention to his own projected invasion of England. He later returned it to Bayeux, where it is now displayed in the former bishop's palace. It was first photographed in 1871.

10

Domesday Book (1086). Survey of Herefordshire

William the Conqueror (1066–1087), in the meeting of his great council at Christmas in 1085, ordered a survey of the kingdom of England. A rumored Norse invasion and a need for money probably prompted his action. Certainly his motive was to learn the extent of his conquest and particularly to ascertain what taxes and assessments had gone to Edward the Confessor and should now come to him. The *Anglo-Saxon Chronicle* attests to the thoroughness of William's survey: "there was not a single hide or rood of land, nor even was there an ox or a cow or a pig left that was not set down in his writings."

Royal officials went through the shires, hundreds, and villages impaneling sworn inquests, requiring residents to reveal information on ownership, tenure, and taxation. The raw information, digested and reorganized according to feudal tenures within shires, was recopied into two bound volumes, which became known as *Domesday Book*. The title has always been something of a curiosity: does it refer to doomsday, the day of Last Judgment, or to Anglo-Saxon dooms or laws, or to what?

The book is filled with specific detail regarding not only tenures and taxation but further incidental information, which has proved a gold mine, albeit

SOURCE. *Sources of English Constitutional History,* edited and translated by Carl Stephenson and Frederick George Marcham, pp. 41–44. Copyright 1937 by Harper & Row, Publishers, Inc. Reprinted by permission of the publishers.

a difficult one, to the social and economic historian of Norman and Anglo-Saxon England. Also interesting is the obvious question: What does it say of a king who could order such a project, and of the royal administration that could execute it so quickly and so well? *Domesday Book* is a unique document; no other country in Western Europe in the Middle Ages produced its like.

Domesday Book, originally kept in the Treasury at Winchester, is now in the Public Record Office in London. It was printed by the Record Commission in 1783.

In the city of Hereford, in the time of King Edward, there were 103 men dwelling together inside and outside the wall, and they had the customs hereinunder noted. If any of them wished to leave the city, he could, with the consent of the reeve, sell his house to another man who was willing to perform the service owed from it, and the reeve got the third penny from this sale. But if any one, because of his poverty, could not perform the service, he gave up his house without payment to the reeve, who saw to it that the house did not remain vacant and that the king did not lose the service. Every entire messuage inside the wall rendered 7½*d.,* and [also] 4*d.* for the hire of horses; and [the holder] reaped for three

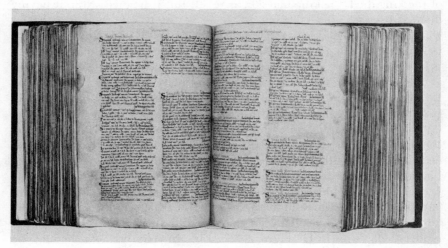

PLATE A
Domesday Book (permission of the Public Record Office, London).

days at Marden and spent one day gathering hay wherever the sheriff wished. Whoever had a horse went thrice a year with the sheriff to the pleas and the hundred [court] at Wormelow. When the king engaged in a hunting expedition, one man customarily went from each house to serve as a beater in the wood. Other men, who did not have entire messuages, found guards for the [royal] hall when the king was in the city. On the death of a burgess who served with a horse, the king had his horse and arms. From him who had no horse, when he died, the king had either 10s. or his land, together with the houses [on it]. If any one, overtaken by death, had not divided what he possessed, the king had all his chattels. These customs were had alike by those living in the city and by those dwelling outside the wall, except that an entire messuage outside the wall rendered only 3½d. The other customs were common [to both groups].

Any man's wife who brewed inside or outside the city gave 10d. according to custom. There were six smiths in the city, each of whom gave 1d. for his forge. Each of them made 120 shoes from the king's iron, and to each of them 3d. was customarily paid on that account, and these smiths were quit of all other custom. Seven moneyers were there; one of them was the bishop's moneyer. When the coinage was changed, each of them gave 18s. to obtain the dies, and from the day on which they returned each of them gave the king 20s. for one month; and in the same way the bishop had 20s. from his moneyer. When the king came to the city, the moneyers made for him as many pennies as he wished—that is to say, of the king's silver. And these seven had their *sac* and *soc*. When any moneyer of the king died, the king had 20s. as relief. But if he died without having divided his cash, the king had all of it. If the sheriff went into Wales with an army, these men [of Hereford] went with him. But if any one was summoned to go and did not do so, he paid 40s. fine to the king.

In this city Earl Harold had 27 burgesses enjoying the same customs as the other burgesses. From this city the reeve rendered £12 to King Edward and £6 to Earl Harold, and he had in his farm all the aforesaid customs. The king, however, had in his demesne three forfeitures: namely, breach of his peace, house-breaking, and assault by ambush. Whoever committed one of these [offenses] paid the king 100s. fine, whosesoever man he was. Now the king has the city of Hereford in demesne, and the English burgesses who dwell there have their previous customs. The French burgesses, however, are quit, through [payment of] 12d., of all forfeitures except the three aforesaid. This city renders to the king £60 by tale in assayed money. Between the city and the eighteen manors that render their farms in Hereford £335. 18s. are accounted for, besides the pleas of the hundred and county [courts]. . . .

Here are set down those holding hands in Herefordshire. . . .

The land of the king. . . . The king holds Leominster. Queen Edith held it. . . . In this manor . . . there were 80 hides, and in demesne 30 ploughs. In it were 8 reeves, 8 beadles, 8 ridingmen, 238 villeins, 75 bordars, and 82 serfs and bondwomen. These together had 230 ploughs. The villeins ploughed 140 acres of the lord's land and sowed it with their own seed grain, and by custom they paid £11. 52d. The ridingmen paid 14s. 4d. and 3 sesters of honey; and there were eight mills [with an income] of 73s. and 30 sticks of eels. The wood rendered 24s. besides pannage. Now in this manor the king has in demesne 60 hides and 29 ploughs; and 6 priests, 6 ridingmen, 7 reeves, 7 beadles, 224 villeins, 81 bordars, and 25 serfs and bondwomen. Among them all they have 201 ploughs. They plough and sow with their own grain 125 acres, and by custom they pay £7. 14s. 8½d.; also 17s. [worth] of fish, 8s. of salt, and 65s. of honey. In it are eight mills [with an income] of 108s. and 100 sticks of eels less 10. A wood 6 leagues long and 3 leagues wide renders 22s. Of these shillings 5 are paid for buying wood at Droitwich, and thence are obtained 30 mitts of salt. Each villein possessing ten pigs gives one pig for pannage. From woodland brought under cultivation come 17s. 4d. An eyrie of hawks is there. . . . Altogether this revenue, except the eels, is computed at £23. 2s. This manor is at farm for £60 in addition to the maintenance of the nuns. The county says that, if it were freed [of that obligation], this manor would be worth six score, that is to say, £120.

Establishment of the King's Household (c. 1135)

This document is what it appears to be: a list of the pay and allowances due various members of the king's household. Someone from the court of Henry I (1100–1135) prepared it for Stephen (1135–1154) shortly after he came to the throne. Its importance lies in the light it sheds on the king's management of his personal household and, more important, of his kingdom.

Norman kings had, like all feudal lords, a court that their tenants-in-chief were obliged to attend. This great council, meeting several times a year, at Christmas, Easter, and Whitsuntide, discussed major problems and projects such as the Domesday survey. More obscure is the king's personal or household staff and its relationship to the small council, in theory the same as the great council but in practice containing only those men needed to run the government. Between the small council and the household there was considerable overlap of personnel and functions; it was only natural for the king to rely on men who were at hand and whose talents he knew. Thus the small council was formed in large part out of the household, and the household was the training ground for royal administrators. In time some officials left the household completely; for example, the chancellor began as the king's priest and confessor, later became his personal secretary, and eventually ended by heading the secretarial staff of the royal government. This development produced conflicts between household officers who had already become public officials (e.g., the chancellor and the treasurer) and servants, specifically from the chamber and wardrobe, whose relationship with the king remained more personal. It was a problem to men in the Middle Ages, as

SOURCE. *The Course of the Exchequer by Richard, Son of Nigel,* translated and edited by Charles Johnson, London: Thomas Nelson and Sons, Ltd., 1950, pp. 129–130, 132–133. By permission of The Clarendon Press, Oxford.

well as to historians now, to distinguish government officials from personal servants of the king.

Although the original manuscript has been lost, the document survived by being appended to two thirteenth-century copies of *The Dialogue of the Exechequer.*

THIS IS THE ESTABLISHMENT OF THE KING'S HOUSEHOLD PAY AND ALLOWANCES

Chancery and Chapel

Chancellor.   5*s.* a day, and one superior and two salt simnels, one sextary of dessert wine, and one of *vin ordinaire,* one large wax candle and forty candle-ends.

Master of the Writing-Chamber.   Originally 10*d.* a day, and one salt simnel, and half a sextary of *vin ordinaire,* and one large candle and twenty-four candle-ends. But King Henry so increased Robert de Sigillo, that on the day of the King's death he had 2*s.*, and one sextary of *vin ordinaire,* and one salt simnel, and one small wax candle and twenty-four candle-ends.

Chaplain—in charge of the chapel and relics.   Diet for two men. And four serjeants of the chapel, each double rations. And two sumpter-horses of the chapel, each 1*d.* a day, and a penny a month for shoeing them. For the chapel service, two wax candles on Wednesday and two on Saturday, and every night one wax candle before the relics, and thirty candle-ends, and one gallon of dessert wine for mass, and one gallon of *vin ordinaire* on Holy Thursday to wash the altar. On Easter day at communion, one sextary of dessert wine and one of *vin ordinaire.*

Steward's Department

Sewers.   Sewers as the Chancellor, if they eat out. If indoors, 3*s.* 6*d.*, two salt simnels, one sextary of *vin ordinaire* and candles at discretion.

Clerk of the Spence of bread and wine.   2*s.* a day, and a salt simnel, and one sextary of *vin ordinaire,* and one small wax candle and twenty-four candle-ends.

PANTRY

Dispensers of bread.   The master-dispenser of bread, a permanent officer, if he eats out-of-doors, 2*s.* 10*d.* a day, and one salt simnel, one sextary of *vin ordinaire,* one small wax candle and twenty-four candle-ends. But if indoors, 2*s.* a day, half a sextary of *vin ordinaire* and candles at discretion.

Dispensers serving in turn. If out-of-doors, 19*d.* a day, one salt simnel, one sextary of *vin ordinaire,* one large candle and twenty candle-ends. If indoors, 10*d.,* half a sextary of *vin ordinaire* and candles at discretion.

Buttery

Master-Butler. As a sewer; the same livery and in like manner.

Master-Dispenser of the Buttery. As the Master-Dispenser of bread and wine. *Dispensers of the Buttery* serving in turn. As the dispensers of the Spence serving in turn; but they have more candles, because they have a small wax candle and twenty-four candle-ends. *Usher of the Buttery:* The customary diet, and three halfpence for his man. The *Cellarmen* shall eat in the house, and have three halfpence each for their men.

Chamber

The *Master-Chamberlain's* livery is the same as that of a sewer. The *Treasurer* as the Master-Chamberlain, if he is at Court and serves in the Treasury. William Mauduit 14*d.* a day; and shall eat permanently in the house, and have one large candle and fourteen ends, and two sumpter-horses with their liveries.

The *Bearer of the King's Bed* shall eat in the house, and have three halfpence a day for his man, and one sumpter-horse with its livery. A *Chamberlain* serving in his turn, 2*s.* a day, one salt simnel, and sextary of *vin ordinaire,* one small wax candle and twenty-four candle-ends. The *Chamberlain of the Chandlery:* 8*d.* a day, and half a sextary of *vin ordinaire.* The *King's Tailor* shall eat in his own house, and have three halfpence a day for his man. A *Chamberlain* without livery [i.e. not on duty] shall eat in the house, if he wishes. The *Ewer* has double diet; and when the King goes on a journey, 1*d.* for drying the King's clothes; and when the King bathes, 4*d.* except on the three great feasts of the year. The wages of the *Laundress* are in doubt.

12

The Assize of Clarendon (1166). Royal Justice in the Twelfth Century

The term "assize" means not only a sitting or session of a court or council, but also the enactment of that sitting. The Assize of Clarendon, produced by Henry II (1154–1189) and his great council in 1166, ordered the members of the king's council acting as itinerant justices to convert the old Anglo-Saxon county courts into royal courts, thereby enforcing the king's will throughout the whole countryside. To strengthen the faltering Anglo-Saxon system of accusation by personal appeal, the assize expanded the use of the sworn inquest, now literally an accusation or grand jury. An indictment resulting from the action of a sworn inquest would represent an accusation by the entire community. Men thus accused would still "make their law," that is be tried by the traditional ordeal of hot water or hot iron.

This assize, extended and regularized by the Assize of Northampton (1176), was no doubt a product of the moment, a vigorous king's answer to immediate problems. The aptness of Henry's response is demonstrated by its success. The success of Henry's experiment insured its survival as a fundamental part of the English legal system. The grand jury's accusations soon gained greater credence than the ordeal's acquittals. The rapidly expanding royal courts quickly eroded the traditional jurisdictions not only of Anglo-Saxon courts but of the feudal courts as well. Henry's bold innovations can be considered, on the one hand, as efficiency in government and as providing law and order; they were, on the other, an enhancement of royal power at the expense of ancient rights and privileges.

SOURCE. *Sources of English Constitutional History,* edited and translated by Carl Stephenson and Frederick George Marcham, pp. 76–79. Copyright 1937 by Harper & Row, Publishers, Inc. Reprinted by permission of the publishers.

HERE BEGINS THE ASSIZE OF CLARENDON MADE BY KING HENRY, NAMELY THE SECOND, WITH THE ASSENT OF THE ARCHBISHOPS, BISHOPS, ABBOTS, EARLS, AND BARONS OF ALL ENGLAND

1. In the first place the aforesaid King Henry, by the counsel of all his barons, has ordained that, for the preservation of peace and the enforcement of justice, inquiry shall be made in every county and in every hundred through twelve of the more lawful men of the hundred and through four of the more lawful men of each vill, [put] on oath to tell the truth, whether in their hundred or in their vill there is any man accused or publicly known as a robber or murderer or thief, or any one who has been a receiver of robbers or murderers or thieves, since the lord king has been king. And let the justices make this investigation in their presence and the sheriffs in their presence.

2. And whoever is found by the oath of the aforesaid men to have been accused or publicly known as a robber or murderer or thief, or as a receiver of them since the lord king has been king, shall be seized; and he shall go to the ordeal of water and swear that, to the value of 5s., so far as he knows, he has not been a robber or murderer or thief, or a receiver of them, since the lord king has been king.

9. And let there be no one . . . who forbids the sheriffs to enter upon his jurisdiction or his land for view of frankpledge; and let all men be placed under sureties, and let them be sent before the sheriffs under frankpledge.

10. And within cities or boroughs no one shall have men, or shall receive [men] without his house or his land or his soke for whom he will not be sponsor, [guaranteeing] that he will bring them before the justice, should they be summoned, or that they are under frankpledge.

11. And let there be no persons . . . who forbid the sheriffs to enter upon their land or their soke for the purpose of seizing those who have been accused or publicly known as robbers or murderers or thieves, or receivers of them, or outlaws, or those accused under forest [law]; on the contrary, [the king] commands them to give assistance in seizing those [suspects].

12. And if any one is seized who possesses [the proceeds] of robbery or theft, should he be a notorious person and have a bad reputation, and should he not have a warrantor, let him not have his law. And if he is not notorious, let him, on account of his [suspicious] possessions, go to the [ordeal of] water.

13. And if any one, in the presence of lawful men or of a hundred [court], has confessed robbery or murder or theft, or the reception of those [who have committed such crimes], and should he then wish to deny it, let him not have his law.

14. The lord king also wills that those who make their law and are cleared by the law, if they are of very bad reputation, being publicly and shamefully denounced by the testimony of many lawful men, shall abjure the lands of the king, so that they shall cross the sea within eight days unless they are detained by the wind; then, with the first [favourable] wind that they have, they shall cross the sea and thenceforth not return to England, except at the mercy of the lord king; [so that] they shall there be outlaws and shall be seized as outlaws if they return.

19. And the lord king wills that, as soon as the sheriffs have received the summons of the itinerant justices to come before the latter together with [the courts of] their counties, they shall bring together [the courts of] their counties and make inquiry concerning all who recently, after this assize, have come into their counties; and they shall put those [new-comers] under pledge to appear before the justices, or they shall guard those [newcomers] until the justices come to them, and then they shall bring [the newcomers] before the justices.

13

William of Newburgh, *History of England* (c. 1198). The Becket Controversy, 1170

The struggle between Henry II (1154–1189) and Archbishop Thomas Becket, ending with Becket's murder in Canterbury Cathedral in 1170, captured and still holds the imagination of the general public. Their rivalry was largely the result of the conflict between the church and the state, in England going back to the Norman Conquest. Two major issues contributed to the conflict. First,

SOURCE. *The History of William of Newburgh*, translated by Joseph Stevenson, in *The Church Historians of England*, vol. IV, part II (London: Seeleys, 1856), pp. 478–481.

was the Investiture Controversy over who should appoint the bishops and invest them with the symbols of office. In England, this issue had been compromised in 1107, the Church to invest those who, in fact, were selected by the king. Second was the question concerning the extent of the jurisdiction of church courts. In 1164, Henry II asserted in the Constitutions of Clarendon the power of royal courts over churchmen accused of secular crimes, the so-called criminous clerks. Becket championed, and by his death won, the right of the Church to try its own. Fundamental to these specific disputes was the question of ultimate authority in medieval society. Viewed in this light, the Becket controversy represented one in a series of challenges to the growth of a royal authority which might easily have become arbitrary and tyrannical.

William of Newburgh (c. 1135–1198) was born in Yorkshire and was educated at the Augustinian priory at Newburgh, where he returned in 1182 after deserting his wealthy wife. There he wrote his justly famous *Historia Rerum Anglicarum,* a study of England from the Conquest to 1197. The most remarkable thing about William is not his accuracy or his style but his attempt to subject earlier writers and contemporary historical evidence to critical analysis. He also attempted to present his material topically rather than simply listing it chronologically. Finally, he tried to be impartial in his treatment of controversial events. In the following selection he has recognized the underlying causes as well as the personality conflicts leading to the break between Henry II and Becket.

The Latin text of William's work was, like the most important medieval chronicles, published in the Rolls Series.

William of Newburgh
History of England (c. 1198)

In the year one thousand one hundred and seventy from the delivery of the Virgin, which was the seventeenth of the reign of Henry the second, the king caused his son Henry, yet a youth, to be solemnly anointed and crowned king at London, by the hands of Roger, archbishop of York. For the king not being yet appeased, the venerable Thomas, archbishop of Canterbury, was still an exile in France, though the Roman pontiff and the king of France had interested themselves extremely to bring about a reconciliation. The moment Thomas heard of this transaction, jealous for his church, he quickly informed the pope of it (by whose favour and countenance he was supported), alleging that this had taken place to the prejudice of himself and his see: and he obtained letters of severe rebuke, for the purpose of correcting equally the archbishop of York, who had performed the office in another's province, and the bishops, who, by their presence, had sanctioned it. The king, however, continued but a short time in England after the coronation of his son, and went beyond sea; and when urged by the frequent admonitions of the pope, and the earnest entreaties of the illustrious king of France, that he would, at least, condescend to be reconciled to the dignified exile, after a seven years' banishment, he at length yielded; and a solemn reconciliation took place between them, which was the more desired and the more grateful in proportion to the time of its protraction. While the king, therefore, continued abroad, the archbishop, by royal grant and permission, returned to his diocese; having in his possession, unknown to the king, letters obtained from the pope against the archbishop of York, and the other prelates who had assisted at that most unfortunate coronation; which was the means of breaking the recently concluded peace, and had become the incentive to greater rage. . . .

The bishops, on account of the offence before mentioned (which I could wish to have remained unnoticed at the time), being suspended, at the instance of the venerable Thomas, from all episcopal functions, by the authority of the apostolic see, the king was exasperated by the complaints of some of them, and grew angry and indignant beyond measure, and losing the mastery of himself, in the heat of his exuberant passion, from the abundance of his perturbed spirit, poured forth the language of in-discretion. On which, four of the bystanders, men of noble race and re-nowned in arms, wrought themselves up to the commission of iniquity through zeal for their earthly master; and leaving the royal presence, and crossing the sea, with as much haste as if posting to a solemn banquet, and urged on by the fury they had imbibed, they arrived at Canterbury on the fifth day after Christmas, where they found the venerable arch-bishop occupied in the celebration of that holy festival with religious joy. Proceeding to him just as he had dined, and was sitting with certain honourable personages, omitting even to salute him, and holding forth the terror of the king's name, they commanded (rather than asked, or admonished him) forthwith to remit the suspension of the prelates who had obeyed the king's pleasure, to whose contempt and disgrace this act redounded. On his replying that the sentence of a higher power was not to be abrogated by an inferior one, and that it was not his concern to pardon persons suspended not by himself, but by the Roman pontiff, they had recourse to violent threats. Undismayed at these words, though uttered by men raging and extremely exasperated, he spoke with singular freedom and confidence. In consequence, becoming more enraged than before, they hastily retired, and bringing their arms, (for they had entered without them,) they prepared themselves, with loud clamour and indignation, for the commission of a most atrocious crime. The venerable prelate was per-suaded by his friends to avoid the madness of these furious savages, by retiring into the holy church. When, from his determination to brave every danger, he did not acquiesce, on the forcible and tumultuous approach of his enemies, he was at length dragged by the friendly violence of his associates to the protection of the holy church. The monks were solemnly chanting vespers to Almighty God, as he entered the sacred temple of Christ, shortly to become an evening sacrifice. The servants of Satan pursued having neither respect as Christians to his holy order, nor to the sacred place, or season; but attacking the dignified prelate as he stood in prayer before the holy altar, even during the festival of Christmas, these truly nefarious Christians most inhumanly murdered him. Having done the deed, and retiring as if triumphant, they departed with unhallowed joy. Recollecting, however, that perhaps the transaction might displease the person in whose behalf they had been so zealous, they retired to the northern parts of England, waiting until they could fully discover the disposition of their monarch towards them.

The frequent miracles which ensued manifested how precious, in the sight of God, was the death of the blessed prelate, and how great the atrocity of the crime committed against him, in the circumstances of time, place, and person. Indeed, the report of such a dreadful outrage, quickly pervading every district of the western world, sullied the illustrious king of England, and so obscured his fair fame among christian potentates, that, as it could scarcely be credited to have been perpetrated without his consent and mandate, he was assailed by the execrations of almost all, and deemed fit to be the object of general detestation. . . .

Whilst almost all persons then attributed the death of this holy man to the king, and more especially the French nobles, who had been jealous of his good fortune, were instigating the apostolical see against him, as the true and undoubted author of this great enormity, the king sent representatives to Rome, to mitigate, by submissive entreaty, the displeasure which was raging against him. When they arrived at Rome, (as all men joined in execrating the king of England,) it was with difficulty that they were admitted. Constantly affirming, however, that this dreadful outrage was not committed either by the command or concurrence of their master, they, at length, obtained, that legates *a latere* from the pope, vested with full power, should be sent into France, who, on carefully investigating, and ascertaining the truth of the matter, should admit the king either to the purgation of his fame, or punish him, if found guilty, by ecclesiastical censure, which was done accordingly. . . . Indeed, he did not deny that those murderers had, perhaps, taken occasion and daring to their excessive fury from some words of his too incautiously uttered; when, hearing of the suspension of the prelates, he became infuriated, and spake unadvisedly. "And, on this account," said he, "I do not refuse the discipline of the Church: I will submit devotedly to whatever you decree, and I will fulfil your injunction." Saying this, and casting off his clothes, after the custom of public penitents, he submitted himself naked to ecclesiastical discipline. The cardinals, overjoyed at the humility of so great a prince, and weeping with joy, while numbers joined their tears, and gave praise to God, dissolved the assembly,—the king's conscience being quieted, and his character in some measure restored. Richard, prior of Dover, then succeeded the blessed Thomas in the see of Canterbury.

14

Richard FitzNigel, *The Dialogue of the Exchequer* (c. 1179)

As treasurer of England, Richard FitzNigel was well qualified to play the part of the "Master" in his dialogue describing the form and function of the exchequer. The exchequer, which met at Easter and at Michaelmas to receive and to audit accounts due the king, had two parts. The lower exchequer received and assayed the monies and issued receipts in the form of wooden tallies (see Plate A), sticks notched to indicate pounds, shillings, and pence and then split to give the sheriff and the treasury identifiable, duplicate copies. These quaint tallies, still accumulating in the nineteenth century and stored in the basement of the House of Commons, were lost when that building burned in 1834. The upper exchequer, the exchequer of account, consisted of a table covered with a checkered cloth, around which sat members of the king's small council, special exchequer officials, and the sheriff whose account was being audited. The abacus-like tablecloth facilitated computations in Roman numerals and allowed even an illiterate sheriff readily to see the status of his account. The results of the audit became an entry in the Pipe Roll such as the following: "Miles of Gloucester accounts for 80 pounds

---

SOURCE. *The Course of the Exchequer by Richard, Son of Nigel,* translated and edited by Charles Johnson, London: Thomas Nelson and Sons, Ltd., 1950, pp. 3, 6–8, 24–25. By permission of The Clarendon Press, Oxford.

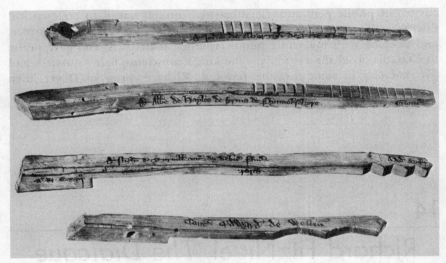

PLATE A
Exchequer tallies (by permission of the Public Record Office, London).

and 14 pence. . . . He has paid this in the Treasury. And he is quit." The exchequer's development can be seen from the surviving annual Pipe Rolls —one in 1130 under Henry I and then nothing until the nearly continuous series that began in 1155 under Henry II.

Besides the intriguing technical details of the exchequer's operations, the most interesting feature of its development is the role it played in the creation of a central royal bureaucracy. The upper exchequer, which began as a special function of the small council, soon split off to become a specialized department. This recurring process of development was confirmed by the central common law courts. The early history of the exchequer, as described by Richard FitzNigel, forms an important chapter in the creation of the best organized and most efficient government in Western Europe.

Three basic manuscript copies of the *Dialogue,* once belonging to various officials of the exchequer, are now deposited in the Public Record Office and the British Museum.

The Exchequer has its own rules. They are not arbitrary, but rest on the decisions of great men; and if they are observed scrupulously, individuals will get their rights, and Your Majesty will receive in full the revenue due to the Treasury, which your generous hand, obeying your noble mind, may spend to the best advantage. . . .

Scholar: What is the Exchequer?

Master: The exchequer [*chess-board*] is an oblong board measuring about ten feet by five, used as a table by those who sit at it, and with a rim round it about four finger-breadths in height, to prevent anything set on it from falling off. Over the [*upper*] exchequer is spread a cloth, bought in Eastern term, of a special pattern, black, ruled with lines a foot, or a full span, apart. In the spaces between them are placed the counters, in their ranks, as will be explained in another place. But though such a board is called "exchequer," the name is transferred to the Court in session at it; so that if a litigant wins his case, or a decision on any point is taken by common consent, it is said to have happened "at the Exchequer" of such a year. But where we now say "at the Exchequer," they used to say "at the Tallies."

Scholar: Why is the Court so called?

Master: I can think, for the moment, of no better reason than that it resembles a chess-board.

Scholar: Was its shape the only reason why our wise forefathers gave it that name? For they might equally well have called it a draught-board.

Master: I was justified in calling you "precise." There is another less obvious reason. For as on the chess-board the men are arranged in ranks, and move or stand by definite rules and restrictions, some pieces in the foremost rank and others in the foremost position; here, too, some [*the barons*] preside, others assist *ex officio,* and nobody is free to overstep the appointed laws, as will appear later. Again, just as on a chess-board, battle is joined between the kings; here too the struggle takes place, and battle is joined, mainly between two persons, to wit, the Treasurer and the Sheriff who sits at his account, while the rest sit by as judges to see and decide.

Scholar: Does the Treasurer really take the account when there are many present who appear by reason of their power to be more important?

Master: It is obvious that the Treasurer takes the account from the Sheriff, because it is from him that an account is required when the King so pleases. Nor would that be demanded of him unless he had received it. . . .

Scholar: Is the Exchequer where this conflict takes place the only Exchequer?

Master: No. For there is a Lower Exchequer, also called the Receipt, where the money received is counted and entered on rolls and tallies, in order that the account may be made up from them in the Upper Exchequer. But both spring from the same root, because whatever is found in the Upper Exchequer to be due, is paid in the Lower, and what is paid in the Lower is credited in the Upper. . . .

Master: [In the Upper Exchequer] sits the man who, by the King's command, makes out the account, using coins for counters. It is a confusing and laborious process, and without it the business of the Exchequer would be interminable, or nearly so. But it is not the specific duty of any officer sitting at the Exchequer unless the King or the Justiciar has committed the task to him. I call it laborious, because every other official duty is carried out by using the tongue or the hand or both. But in this:

> Tongue, eyes, hand and restless brain
> Work with all their might and main

But the system of this is according to the usual course of the Exchequer, not by the rules of Arabian arithmetic. You remember my saying, I imagine, that a cloth is laid on the Exchequer table ruled with lines, and that the coins used as counters are placed in the spaces between them. The Accountant sits in the middle of his side of the table, so that everybody can see him, and so that his hand can move freely at his work. In the lowest space, on the right, he places the heap of the pence, eleven or fewer. In the second the shillings, up to nineteen. In the third he puts the pounds; and this column should be directly in front of him, because it is the centre column in the Sheriff's usual accounts. In the fourth is the heap of the scores of pounds. In the fifth, hundreds, in the sixth, thousands, in the seventh, but rarely, tens of thousands. I say "rarely"; that is, when an account of the whole receipt of the realm is taken by the King, or by the magnates of the realm at his command from the Treasurer and Chamberlains. The Accountant may substitute a silver halfpenny for ten shillings, and a gold one for ten pounds for convenience in counting. But he must take care that his hand does not outrun his tongue or *vice versa*; but as he reckons, he must put out the counters and state the number simultaneously, lest there should be a mistake in the number. So, when the sum demanded of the Sheriff has been set out in heaps of counters, the payments made into the Treasury or otherwise are similarly set out in heaps underneath. If the demand made on him is for a farm or other debt payable "by tale," the lower line is simply subtracted from the upper, and the Sheriff will be liable for the remainder.

15

Rannulf Glanvill, *Treatise on the Laws and Customs of the Realm of England* (c. 1189)

Whether Rannulf Glanvill, Henry II's justiciar from 1180 to 1189, was the author of this *Treatise* is uncertain. Written late in his tenure as justiciar, it has been attributed to him for so long that it is commonly referred to simply as "Glanvill."

"Glanvill" is the first textbook on English common law. Where earlier there had been separate laws of Wessex, Mercia, and the Danelaw and a host of local peculiarities, by Glanvill's time a royal law common to all of England was rapidly taking shape. Unlike on the continent, where the emphasis was on the study of Roman and canon law, in England the major concern was the expansion of royal justice at the expense of old local and feudal courts, witnessed by Henry II's Assizes of Clarendon and Northampton.

It was the purpose of the author of "Glanvill" to do for the judicial part of Henry II's administration what Richard FitzNigel had done for the fiscal, to describe its workings in a straightforward and intelligible manner. He stressed the importance of royal writs, in bringing cases before the courts and in enforcing their decisions, and the jury, the sworn inquest, in presenting the facts and deciding the case. The passage below, which deals with one of the possessory assizes, illustrates this.

Also interesting and significant is Glanvill's assertion that the laws of England were unwritten. However, by describing the earliest processes and func-

SOURCE. *The Treatise on the Laws and Customs of the Realm of England, commonly called Glanvill,* ed. G. D. G. Hall, London: Nelson, in Association with the Selden Society, 1965, pp. 1–3, 148–153. © 1965, Oxford University Press. By permission of The Clarendon Press, Oxford.

tions of the common law, he contributed both to its development and to its survival as a discrete system from that day to this. Anyone seeking to understand the original workings of the common law has of necessity begun with "Glanvill." More than 30 manuscript copies of the *Treatise* exist. The first printed edition appeared in 1554.

Here begins the treatise on the laws and customs of the realm of England, composed in the time of King Henry the Second when justice was under the direction of the illustrious Rannulf Glanvill, the most learned of that time in the law and ancient customs of the realm.

Prologue

Not only must royal power be furnished with arms against rebels and nations which rise up against the king and the realm, but it is also fitting that it should be adorned with laws for the governance of subject and peaceful peoples; so that in time of both peace and war our glorious king may so successfully perform his office that, crushing the pride of the unbridled and ungovernable with the right hand of strength and tempering justice for the humble and meek with the rod of equity, he may both be always victorious in wars with his enemies and also show himself continually impartial in dealing with his subjects.

No one doubts how finely, how vigorously, how skillfully our most excellent king has practised armed warfare against the malice of his enemies in time of hostilities, for now his praise has gone out to all the earth and his mighty works to all the borders of the world. Nor is there any dispute how justly and how mercifully, how prudently he, who is the author and lover of peace, has behaved towards his subjects in time of peace, for his Highness's court is so impartial that no judge there is so shameless or audacious as to presume to turn aside at all from the path of justice or to digress in any respect from the way of truth. For there, indeed, a poor man is not oppressed by the power of his adversary, nor does favour or partiality drive any man away from the threshold of judgment. For truly he does not scorn to be guided by the laws and customs of the realm which had their origin in reason and have long prevailed; and, what is more, he is even guided by those of his subjects most learned in the laws and customs of the realm whom he knows to excell all others in sobriety, wisdom and eloquence, and whom he has found to be most prompt and clear-sighted in deciding cases on the basis of justice and in settling disputes, acting now with severity and now with leniency as seems expedient to them.

Although the laws of England are not written, it does not seem absurd to call them laws—those, that is, which are known to have been promulgated about problems settled in council on the advice of the magnates and with the supporting authority of the prince—for this also is a law, that "what pleases the prince has the force of law." For if, merely for lack of writing, they were not deemed to be laws, then surely writing would seem to supply to written laws a force of greater authority than either the justice of him who decrees them or the reason of him who establishes them.

It is, however, utterly impossible for the laws and legal rules of the realm to be wholly reduced to writing in our time, both because of the ignorance of scribes and because of the confused multiplicity of those same laws and rules. But there are some general rules frequently observed in court which it does not seem to me presumptuous to commit to writing, but rather very useful for most people and highly necessary to aid the memory. I have decided to put into writing at least a small part of these general rules, adopting intentionally a commonplace style and words used in court in order to provide knowledge of them for those who are not versed in this kind of inelegant language.

[Book XIII]

THE VARIOUS KINDS OF RECOGNITION

So far the questions which most often arise in pleas about right have been dealt with. There remain for discussion those which are concerned with seisin only. By virtue of a constitution of the realm called an assize these questions are for the most part settled by recognition, and therefore the various kinds of recognition must now be considered.

One kind of recognition is called mort d'ancestor. Another concerns the last presentation of parsons to churches; another, whether a tenement is ecclesiastic or lay fee.

There is also the recognition called novel disseisin.

When anyone dies seised of a free tenement, if he was seised in his demesne as of fee, then his heir can lawfully claim the seisin which his ancestor had, and if he is of full age he shall have the following writ:

THE WRIT OF MORT D'ANCESTOR

The king to the sheriff, greeting. If G. son of O. gives you security for prosecuting his claim, then summon by good summoners twelve free and lawful men from the neighbourhood of such-and-such a vill to be before me or my justices on a certain day, ready to declare on oath whether O. the father of the aforesaid G. was seised in his demesne as of his fee of one virgate of land in that vill on the day he died, whether he died after my first coronation, and whether the said G. is his next heir. And meanwhile let them view the land; and you are to see that their names are endorsed on this writ. And summon by good summoners R., who holds that land, to be there then to hear the recognition. And have there the summoners and this writ. Witness, etc.

THE PROCEDURE LEADING TO THIS ASSIZE

When the sheriff has received the writ of mort d'ancestor and security for prosecuting the claim has been given in the county court, then the procedure leading to the assize is as follows. First, in accordance with the terms of the writ, twelve free and lawful men from the neighbourhood are to be elected in the presence of both demandant and tenant, or even in the absence of the tenant provided he has been summoned at least once to attend the election. He must be summoned once to come and hear who are elected to make the recognition, and he can if he wishes reject some of them for reasonable cause so that they are excluded from the recognition. If, however, he has not come when the first summons is properly attested in court, then he shall be waited for no longer, and in his absence the twelve jurors shall be elected and sent by the sheriff to view the land or other tenement of which seisin is claimed. Here again the tenant shall have one summons only. The sheriff shall see that the name of the elected twelve are endorsed on the writ.

Then the sheriff shall arrange for the tenant to be summoned to be before the king or his justices on the day stated in the writ of the king or his justices, to hear the recognition. If the demandant is of full age, the tenant can essoin himself on the first and second return days but not on the third day, for then the recognition shall be taken whether the tenant comes or not, because no more than two essoins are allowed in any recognition which concerns only seisin. Indeed, in the recognition of novel disseisin no essoin is allowed. On the third return day, then, as stated above, the assize shall be taken whether the tenant has come or not. And if the jurors declare in favour of the demandant, seisin shall be adjudged to him and the sheriff ordered by the following writ to have put in seisin:

THE WRIT FOR DELIVERING SEISIN AFTER THE RECOGNITION

The king to the sheriff, greeting. Know that N. has proved in my court, by a recognition concerning the death of a certain ancestor of his,

his right against R. to the seisin of so much land in such-and-such a vill. And therefore I command you to have him put in seisin without delay. Witness, etc.

16

Charter for Bristol (1189)

The charter, first used in Anglo-Saxon times, was a legal instrument for granting a privilege or recognizing a right. It is the most important type of document for the study of Anglo-Norman feudalism. Royal charters, usually issued by the chancery, were of two basic kinds: the *diploma,* a long document normally in Latin describing in a formal, stylized manner a grant of great importance, and the *writ* or *writ-charter,* a simpler, more efficient document usually in the vernacular and dealing with a more routine matter. Private charters assumed a variety of forms. Both royal and private charters, however, normally began with an introduction or greeting, proceeded to the terms of the grant itself, and concluded by stating the agreement of all parties. Finally, there was usually a list of witnesses, not necessarily present, and a seal or seals to authenticate the grant.

The charter below, issued in 1189 by John, then count of Mortain but later king (1199–1216), is a confirmation of the privileges Henry II granted to the city of Bristol in 1155. It is typical of the charters granted to the rising towns of the twelfth century, a recognition by the monarchy of the importance of their goodwill and wealth as a counterweight to an unruly baronage. The rights and privileges guaranteed to the burgesses of Bristol were those deemed essential for them to carry out their mercantile functions—a separate system of justice, the right to regulate their own economic affairs, and freedom from many of the traditional feudal obligations. Because towns had common needs, their charters tended to be similar. In England, the privileges

SOURCE. *Bristol Charters, 1155–1373,* ed. N. Dermott Harding, Bristol Record Society, 1930, pp. 9, 11, 13.

of Newcastle-upon-Tyne, dating from the reign of Henry I, became a model for other towns, although local conditions inevitably led to many modifications.

A large number of royal and private charters from the twelfth century have been preserved. In 1199 the chancery, in order to have a complete record of grants made, initiated the Charter Rolls, on which all royal charters were copied. In 1201 the *writ-charters*, now called letters patent, were inscribed on the Patent Rolls. These rolls, plus others, such as the Close Rolls (1204), are not only of great value to the historian but are yet another indication of the sophistication of royal government in medieval England.

John, Count of Moreton, to all men and to his friends, French and English, Welsh and Irish, present and to come, greeting. Know ye that I have granted and by this present charter have confirmed to my burgesses of Bristol dwelling within the walls and without the walls unto the metes of the town, to wit, between Sandbrook and Bewell and Brightnee-bridge and the spring in the way near Aldebury of Knowle, all their liberties and free customs, as well, freely and entirely, or more so, as ever they had them in my time or in the time of any of my predecessors. Now the liberties which have been granted to them are these, to wit:— That no burgess of Bristol shall plead without the walls of the town concerning any plea except pleas of exterior tenements which do not pertain to the Hundred of the town. And that they shall be quit of murder within the metes of the town. And that no burgess shall wage battle except he have been appealed concerning the death of a foreign man who has been killed in the town and who was not of the town. And that no one shall take a hospice within the walls by assize or by livery of the marshals against the will of the burgesses. And that they shall be quit of Toll and Lastage and Passage and Pontage and of all other customs throughout all my land and power. . . . And that the Hundred shall be held only once in the week. . . .

And that they shall have justly their lands and tenures and their pledges and debts throughout all my land whosoever shall owe to them. And that concerning lands and tenures which are within the town, right shall be done to them according to the custom of the town. And that concerning debts which have been contracted in Bristol and concerning pledges made in the same place pleas shall be held in the town, according to the custom of the town. And that if anyone anywhere in my land shall take Toll of the men of Bristol if he have not restored it after he shall have been required to restore [it], the Prepositor of Bristol shall take thereupon a distress at Bristol and shall destrain to restore [it]. And that no strange merchant shall buy within the town of any strange man hides or corn or wool except of the burgesses. And that no stranger shall have a tavern except in a ship, nor shall he sell cloths for cutting except in the fair. And that no stranger shall tarry in the town with his wares in order to sell his wares except for forty days. And that no burgess anywhere in my land or power shall be attached or destrained for any debt except he be debtor or pledge. And that they shall be able to marry themselves and their sons and daughters and widows without license of their lords. And that none of their lords on account of foreign lands shall have custody or gift of their sons or daughters or widows, but only custody of their tenements which are of their fee until they shall be of age. . . . And that they shall be able to grind their corn wheresoever they will. And that they shall have all their reasonable gilds as well as, or better than, they had them in the time of Robert and William his son, Earls of Gloucester. . . . I have granted also that everyone of them shall be able to make improvement as much as he be able in making edifices everywhere upon the bank and elsewhere without damage to the borough and town. And that they shall have and possess all lands and void places which are contained within the aforesaid metes to be built on at their will. Wherefore, I will and firmly command that my aforesaid burgesses of Bristol and their heirs shall have and shall hold all their aforesaid liberties and free customs as is above written of me and my heirs as well and entirely, or more so, as ever they had them at what time they have been effectual, well and in peace and honourably without all impediment or molestation which any one shall do to them thereupon. Witnesses: Stephen Ridel, my Chancellor, William de Wenneval, Roger de Planes, Roger de Newburgh, Maurice de Berkeley, Robert his brother, Hamo de Valonis, Simon de Marisco, Gilbert Rass', William de la Faleise, Master Benedict, Master Peter and many others. At Bristol.

17

Magna Carta (1215)

Magna Carta is universally recognized as England's most important constitutional document. Disaffected barons and churchmen, fearing the growth of royal authority and exasperated with King John personally, reacted in the only way they knew. By force of arms, they extracted in June 1215 John's promise to acknowledge the freedom of the Church, to respect the traditional laws and customs of England and the feudal system, and to recognize a makeshift grievance committee established to insure that his promise was kept. Charters of liberties had been issued by earlier kings for political purposes, the most important being that of Henry I in 1100, but Magna Carta was the first actually imposed by force.

Pope Innocent III's nullification of Magna Carta revived the civil war, which continued until John's death in October 1216. The barons accepted John's nine-year-old son Henry as king, but took advantage of his youth to have a shortened version of Magna Carta confirmed in 1216, 1217, and 1225 (in the text below the words deleted are indicated by italics). This version was subsequently confirmed more than 50 times, the last being in 1416. The most noteworthy confirmation was in 1297 when Edward I had it copied onto the Statute Rolls. Though almost forgotten during the fifteenth and sixteenth centuries, Magna Carta was revived in the seventeenth by lawyers like Sir Edward Coke to counter the Stuart kings' theory of divine right and to support the general idea that the government as well as the governed must obey the law. It was now regarded as a charter guaranteeing liberty in general, an implication that can be found in the original but which was hardly intended by either the barons in 1215 or the kings who later confirmed it.

Another feature of Magna Carta is the belief in the necessity of machinery

SOURCE. *Sources of English Constitutional History,* edited and translated by Carl Stephenson and Frederick George Marcham, pp. 115–121, 123, 125–126. Copyright 1937 by Harper & Row, Publishers, Inc. Reprinted by permission of the publishers.

by which its terms could be enforced. The barons could think of nothing better than a collective *diffidatio*, a formalization of a vassal's right to resort to arms if his lord violated the feudal contract. But as the centuries passed the barons' counterparts gradually evolved more effective machinery—control of taxation in parliament and ultimately responsible government.

Both the significance of Magna Carta and the historian's difficulty in understanding it are results of its position as a fundamental part of a living, developing constitution. Its role and its meaning (see especially clauses 12, 14, and 39) have changed as times and occasions demanded. Its specific provisions have to a great extent been repealed and forgotten, but the conviction, inherent in it from the beginning, that it was the charter of the people's liberties has grown along with the constitution's understanding of those liberties.

The 1215 version of Magna Carta, although it disappeared when the shortened version replaced it, was found again in the seventeenth century and in 1759 was published by William Blackstone. What is believed to be the original manuscript to which John affixed his seal is in the British Museum.

1. We have in the first place granted to God and by this our present charter have confirmed, for us and our heirs forever, that the English Church shall be free and shall have its rights entire and its liberties inviolate. . . . We have also granted to all freemen of our kingdom, for us and our heirs forever, all the liberties hereinunder written, to be had and held by them and their heirs of us and our heirs.

2. If any one of our earls or barons or other men holding of us in chief dies, and if when he dies his heir is of full age and owes relief, [that heir] shall have his inheritance for the ancient relief: namely, the heir or heirs of an earl £100 for the whole barony of an earl. . . . And let whoever owes less give less, according to the ancient custom of fiefs.

3. If, however, the heir of any such person is under age and is in wardship, he shall, when he comes of age, have his inheritance without relief and without fine.

4. The guardian of the land of such an heir who is under age shall not take from the land of the heir more than reasonable issues and reasonable customs and reasonable services, and this without destruction and waste of men or things. . . .

6. Heirs shall be married without disparagement; *yet so that, before the marriage is contracted, it shall be announced to the blood-relatives of the said heir.*

7. A widow shall have her marriage portion and inheritance immediately after the death of her husband and without difficulty. . . .

8. No widow shall be forced to marry so long as she wishes to live without a husband. . . .

9. Neither we nor our bailiffs will seize any land or revenue for any debt, so long as the chattels of the debtor are sufficient to repay the debt; nor shall the sureties of that debtor be distrained so long as the chief debtor is himself able to pay the debt. . . .

10. *If any one has taken anything, whether much or little, by way of loan from Jews, and if he dies before that debt is paid, the debt shall not carry usury so long as the heir is under age.* . . .

12. *Scutage or aid shall be levied in our kingdom only by the common counsel of our kingdom, except for ransoming our body, for knighting our eldest son, and for once marrying our eldest daughter; and for these [purposes] only a reasonable aid shall be taken.* . . .

13. And the city of London shall have all its ancient liberties and free customs, *both by land and by water.* Besides we will and grant that all the other cities, boroughs, towns, and ports shall have all their liberties and free customs.

14. *And in order to have the common counsel of the kingdom for assessing aid other than in the three cases aforesaid, or for assessing scutage, we will cause the archbishops, bishops, abbots, earls, and greater barons to be summoned by our letters individually; and besides we will cause to be summoned in general, through our sheriffs and bailiffs, all those who hold of us in chief—for a certain day, namely, at the end of forty days at least, and to a certain place. And in all such letters of summons we will state the cause of the summons; and when the summons has thus been made, the business assigned for the day shall proceed according to the counsel of those who are present, although all those summoned may not come.*

17. Common pleas shall not follow our court, but shall be held in some definite place.

18. Assizes of novel disseisin, of mort d'ancestor, *and of darrein presentment* shall be held only in their counties [of origin] and in this way: we, or our chief justice if we are out of the kingdom, will send two justices through each county *four times a year; and they, together with four knights of each county elected by the county [court], shall hold the aforesaid assizes in the county, on the day and at the place [set for the meeting] of the county [court].*

28. No constable or other bailiff of ours shall take grain or other chattels of any one without immediate payment therefor in money. . . .

32. We will hold the lands of those convicted of felony only for a year

and a day, and the lands shall then be given to the lords of the fiefs [concerned].

35. There shall be one measure of wine throughout our entire kingdom, and one measure of ale; also one measure of grain, namely, the quarter of London. . . . With weights, moreover, it shall be as with measures.

36. Nothing henceforth shall be taken or given for the writ of inquisition concerning life and limbs, but it shall be issued gratis and shall not be denied.

39. No freeman shall be captured or imprisoned or disseised or outlawed or exiled or in any way destroyed, nor will we go against him or send against him, except by the lawful judgment of his peers or by the law of the land.

40. To no one will we sell, to no one will we deny or delay right or justice.

41. All merchants may safely and securely go away from England, come to England, stay in and go through England, by land or by water, for buying and selling under right and ancient customs and without any evil exactions, except in time of war if they are from the land at war with us.

52. *If any one, without the lawful judgment of his peers, has been disseised or deprived by us of his lands, castles, liberties, or rights, we will at once restore them to him. And if a dispute arises in this connection, then let the matter be decided by the judgment of the twenty-five barons, concerning whom provision is made below.*

54. No one shall be seized or imprisoned on the appeal of a woman for the death of any one but her husband.

60. Now all these aforesaid customs and liberties, which we have granted, in so far as concerns us, to be observed in our kingdom toward our men, all men of our kingdom, both clergy and laity, shall, in so far as concerns them, observe toward their men.

61. *Since moreover for [the love of] God, for the improvement of our kingdom, and for the better allayment of the conflict that has arisen between us and our barons, we have granted all these [liberties] aforesaid, wishing them to enjoy those [liberties] by full and firm establishment forever, we have made and granted them the following security: namely, that the barons shall elect twenty-five barons of the kingdom, whomsoever they please, who to the best of their ability should observe, hold, and cause to be observed the peace and liberties that we have granted to them and have confirmed by this our present charter; so that, specifically, if we or our justiciar or our bailiffs or any of our ministers are in any respect delinquent toward any one or trangress any article of the peace or the*

security, and if the delinquency is shown to four barons of the aforesaid twenty-five barons, those four barons shall come to us, or to our justiciar if we are out of the kingdom, to explain to us the wrong asking that without delay we cause this wrong to be redressed. And if within a period of forty days, counted from the time that notification is made to us, or to our justiciar if we are out of the kingdom, we do not redress the wrong, or, if we are out of the kingdom, our justiciar does not redress it, the four barons aforesaid shall refer that case to the rest of the twenty-five barons, and those twenty-five barons, together with the community of the entire country, shall distress and injure us in all ways possible— namely, by capturing our castles, lands, and possessions and in all ways that they can—until they secure redress according to their own decision, saving our person and [the person] of our queen and [the persons] of our children. And when redress has been made, they shall be obedient to us as they were before. . . .

18

Royal Seals of the Thirteenth and Fourteenth Centuries

Seals were used by both private and official persons in the Middle Ages to authenticate documents, much as personal signatures are today. The practice was begun in Carolingian France. Edward the Confessor (1042–1066) was probably the first English king to use a Great Seal, so called not only for its importance but for its size, three or more inches in diameter. The Great Seal in Plate A is that used by John in 1215 to attest to his acceptance of the Articles of the Barons during the negotiations preliminary to Magna Carta. Plate B, showing an authenticated copy of the Magna Carta of 1225, indicates how the wax seal, impressed on both sides, was suspended from the bottom of the document. The possession of the Great Seal and its use when instructed by the king were duties of the chancellor. The obvious importance of these functions made the chancellor, following the decline of the justiciar

PLATE A
The Great Seal of King John, obverse and reverse (by courtesy of the
Trustees of the British Museum).

PLATE B
Exemplification of King Henry III's reissue of Magna Carta, 1225 (by
courtesy of the Trustees of the British Museum).

PLATE C

Privy seal of Richard II (by permission of the Public Record Office, London).

after the loss of Normandy, the most important official of the royal government.

The creation and use of the privy seal (Plate C) as early as the reign of Henry II (1154–1189) indicate the enlargement of the royal government. Following the chancery's establishment at Westminster, the king still needed in his immediate household a means of authenticating documents. By the privy seal he could instruct the chancellor to use the Great Seal, or even bypass the Great Seal entirely. In the thirteenth and fourteenth centuries, especially in the reigns of Henry III (1216–1272) and Edward II (1307–1327), the barons endeavored, by gaining possession of the king's major officers and by controlling his council, to dominate his government. When they discovered that the king could by means of the privy seal circumvent the officers they controlled, specifically the chancellor, they attempted to make the keeper of the privy seal a public officer, just as was the chancellor. Richard II (1377–1399) later resorted to his yet more personal signet seal (Plate D), his ring kept by himself or later by his personal secretary. In the reign of Henry VIII (1509–1547), this household officer became the principal secretary, eclipsing the chancellor and becoming the original of the several secretaries of state of the modern cabinet.

The history of royal seals tells much about the origins and development of government, especially the household, the fertile breeding ground of royal servants who often became officers, and indeed offices, of the royal government.

PLATE D
Signet seal of Richard II (by permission of the Public Record Office,
London).

19

Statutes of Edward I: Gloucester (1278), Mortmain (1279), and Quia Emptores (1290)

When Edward I (1272–1307) became king, it had already been two centuries since the Conquest and the introduction of feudalism and one century since the beginning of the development of common law. The small council had recently, with the requirement that its members take a specified oath of office, become a distinct body with identifiable members. The great council was evolving into a parliament, consisting of elected representatives from the shires and boroughs as well as of the traditional great barons and churchmen. The statute was becoming distinct from the royal ordinance, the latter a minor or temporary order issued by the king and his small council, the former a permanent enactment or promulgation for which the king needed the support of a great council or parliament. Amidst this development and change, Edward saw the opportunity to refurbish and strengthen many features of his royal government and recognized the statute as the appropriate means.

The statutes reproduced below are typical of the many issued by Edward dealing with a wide range of matters from the promotion of trade (Statute of Acton Burnell, 1283) to the incorporation of the principality of Wales into the legal system of England (Statute of Rhuddlan, 1284). The Statute of Gloucestor, 1278, gave direction to the royal policy of retrieving the private

SOURCE. *Sources of English Constitutional History,* edited and translated by Carl Stephenson and Frederick George Marcham, pp. 169–170, 174. Copyright 1937 by Harper & Row, Publishers, Inc. Reprinted by permission of the publishers.

jurisdictions of vassals unable to show "by what warrant" they held them. The readiest warrant was of course a charter, but long-term possession was also acknowledged. In 1290 the term of possession was set at Richard I's coronation in 1189, a date soon recognized as the limit of legal memory beyond which no precedent need be traced. Mortmain, 1279, which means "dead hand," the dead hand by which the Church holds fast to its land, was an attempt to prevent vassals from subinfeudating or granting land to the Church by terms that would financially injure the lord. Quia Emptores, 1290, which means "whereas the buyers," attempted to prevent a lord's loss of reliefs and other feudal incidents by a vassal's careless or malicious subinfeudation. The solution, that the buyer (feoffee) should assume the place of the seller (feoffor) and that no new tenure be created, was a drastic remedy which, in fact, ended all the subinfeudation and proved an important step in the ultimate decline of the feudal system.

By means of statutes, Edward built a sounder administration and provided the foundation on which the common law would develop for the next five centuries. The statute, thus employed, became a powerful new instrument of governmental initiative, not only strengthening the hands of the king but enhancing the role of a developing parliament.

STATUTE OF GLOUCESTER (1278)

In the year of grace 1278, the sixth of the reign of King Edward, son of King Henry, at Gloucester in the month of August, the same king, having summoned the more discreet men of his kingdom, both greater and lesser, has made provision for the betterment of his kingdom and the fuller administration of justice, as is demanded by the kingly office. . . .

The sheriffs shall have it commonly proclaimed throughout their bailiwicks—that is to say, in cities, boroughs, trading towns, and elsewhere— that all those who claim to have any franchises by charters of the king's predecessors, kings of England, or by other title, shall come before the king or before the itinerant justices on a certain day and at a certain place to show what sort of franchises they claim to have, and by what warrant [they hold them]. . . . And if those who claim to have such franchises do not come on the day aforesaid, those franchises shall then be taken into the king's hand by the local sheriff in the name of distress; so that they shall not enjoy such franchises until they come to receive justice. . . .

STATUTE OF MORTMAIN (1279)

The king to his justices of the bench, greeting. Whereas it was formerly enacted that men of religion should not enter upon the fiefs of any persons without the consent and license of the principal lords from whom those fiefs were immediately held; and whereas since then men of religion have nevertheless entered upon the fiefs of others as well as their own—by appropriating them, buying them, and sometimes by receiving them through gifts of other men—whereby the services which are owed from fiefs of this sort, and which were originally established for the defence of the kingdom, are wrongfully withheld and the principal lords [are caused to] lose their escheats: [therefore] we, seeking in this connection to provide a suitable remedy for the good of the kingdom, by the counsel of the prelates, earls, and other faithful men of our kingdom who are members of our council, have enacted, established, and ordained that no man of religion or any other whatsoever shall buy or sell lands or tenements, or under colour of donation, lease, or other title of any sort shall receive them from any one, or presume artfully and craftily to appropriate them in any way whatsoever, whereby land and tenements of this sort may somehow come into mortmain— under pain of forfeiting the same [lands or tenements]. . . . And so we command you to have the aforesaid statute read in your presence and henceforth strictly held and observed.

STATUTE OF QUIA EMPTORES (1290)

Whereas the buyers of lands and tenements belonging to the fiefs of magnates and other men have in times past frequently entered upon their fiefs to the prejudice of the same [lords], because the freeholders of the same magnates and other men have sold their lands and tenements to such purchasers to be held in fee by themselves and their heirs of the feoffors and not of the principal lords of the fiefs, whereby those same principal lords have often lost the escheats, marriages, and wardships of lands and tenements belonging to their fiefs; and whereas this has seemed very hard and burdensome to those magnates and other lords, being in such cases manifest disinheritance: [therefore] the lord king in his parliament at Westminster [held] after Easter in the eighteenth year of his reign. . . , at the suggestion of the magnates of his realm, has granted, provided, and established that henceforth every freeman shall be permitted to sell his land or tenement, or a part of it, at pleasure; yet so that the feoffee shall hold that land or tenement of the same principal lord [of whom the feoffor held] and by the same services and customs by which the feoffor earlier held. . . .

20

Memorandum of Parliament (1306). Parliament's Membership and Activities

Parliament was initially not an institution, but an event, a meeting where men came together to talk—thus the word "parliament," from the French word *parler*, "to talk." More specifically, it was a meeting of the great council at which a number of functions were performed. It acted as a high court; it assisted in the formulation of statutes; not least, it approved grants of taxation. By the reign of John (1199–1216), it was occasionally useful to have knights of the shire meet with the great barons and churchmen. In 1265, at the climax of the troubles between Henry III and the barons, Simon de Montfort had in addition summoned representatives from boroughs to broaden support for the baronial party.

Edward I (1272–1307) inherited and exploited these constitutional experiments. In 1295 he summoned what has become known as the Model Parliament, containing all the elements of which parliament was ultimately to be composed: barons, prelates, and two representatives from each shire, city, and borough. In 1297, Edward promised in the Confirmation of the Charters to collect no taxes other than the three feudal aids "except by the common

SOURCE. *Sources of English Constitutional History,* edited and translated by Carl Stephenson and Frederick George Marcham, pp. 167–169. Copyright 1937 by Harper & Row, Publishers, Inc. Reprinted by permission of the publishers.

assent of the whole kingdom.'' Whatever the original intention of these words, they were soon interpreted to mean the consent of parliament with all the elements present.

It is an old argument whether a parliament in the early stage of its development was simply the king's small council temporarily made large or a completely different institution, the product of an ancient custom that the king must consult the kingdom. There is also debate over whether parliament's primary function was judicial, as a court of law, or legislative, as an assembly giving advice and granting taxation. Answers to these questions must come, at least in part, from study of the *Rotuli Parliamentorum,* the Parliament Rolls, on which parliamentary proceedings were recorded. The passage below, from the Memorandum for 1306, indicates that parliament was beginning to assume a definite membership and that taxation was an important item of its business. On the other hand, there is still no indication of a division into two houses, barons and prelates in one, and the commons in the other. In fact, the knights were still clearly associated with the barons, and the citizens and burgesses made their grant separately, almost as a separate estate.

Memorandum that, after the lord king had recently ordered that Edward, his first-born son, should be decorated with the belt of knighthood at the feast of Pentecost in the thirty-fourth year of his reign, mandates were issued for the archbishops, bishops, abbots, priors, earls, barons, and other magnates to come before the lord king and his council at Westminster on the morrow of Holy Trinity next following, in order to deliberate and ordain with regard to giving the king an aid for the knighting aforesaid and in order to consent to those matters which should further be ordained in the connection, or for them then and there to send procurators or attorneys with sufficient instructions to carry out the aforesaid matters in their place; also each of the sheriffs of England was commanded to cause two knights from his country to come to the said place at the said time, and from each city of his bailiwick two citizens and from each borough of the same bailiwick two burgesses or one, etc., in order to deliberate, ordain, and consent as aforesaid. . . . And when all the aforesaid persons had assembled before the aforesaid council of the king, and it had been explained to them by the same council on behalf of the king that by right of the royal crown aid should be given the lord king on the occasion aforesaid, and besides, that the lord king had incurred multifarious expenses and many other obligations toward suppressing the rebellion and malice of Robert Bruce, traitor to the same lord king, and of his adherents in the parts of Scotland, who were then presuming to make war against the king in those parts; the same prelates, earls, barons, and other magnates, as well as the knights of the shires, having discussed the matter with deliberation, and considering that aid was owed as aforesaid and that the king had incurred many obligations on account of the aforesaid war, at length unanimously granted to the lord king on behalf of themselves and the whole community of the land a thirtieth of all their movable temporal goods which they should happen to possess on Michaelmas next following, to be taken as a competent aid to the lord king for the knighting of his aforesaid son and also as an aid toward the expenditures that should be made in connection with the aforesaid war. This grant, however, [was made] on condition that it should in no way be held to their own prejudice or to that of their successors or heirs in future times, and that it should never be taken as a precedent in a case of this kind; also that in assessing the aforesaid goods all should be excepted which had been excepted in assessing the fifteenth granted by the community of the kingdom to the lord king in the eighteenth year of his reign for exiling the Jews. Moreover, the citizens and burgesses of the cities and boroughs aforesaid and others of the king's demesnes, being assembled and holding a discussion on the said matters, in consideration of the obligations incurred by the lord king as aforesaid, unanimously granted the lord king for the reasons aforesaid the twentieth of their movable goods, to be taken as aforesaid.

21

The Declaration of Arbroath (1320). Scottish Nationalism

This declaration, or diplomatic dispatch, was a product of the series of wars between the kingdoms of England and Scotland that began in the reign of Edward I (1272–1307) and continued until 1328, when England finally recognized Scotland's independence. By 1320, the date of the declaration, the Scots had survived several defeats and had, under the leadership of Robert Bruce (1306–1329), crushed the English decisively at Bannockburn in 1314 and driven them out of Scotland. England, by far the greater power, refused, however, to admit that the war was over as, indeed, in the border counties it was not. To achieve peace, Robert needed to maintain a solid political and military front in Scotland, and, more important, to bring outside pressure to bear on Edward II of England (1307–1327). This dispatch was Robert's attempt to enlist the help of Pope John XXII.

The interest of the document lies in its moving prose, in its expression of national feeling supported by the trappings of a national mythology, and in its breadth of popular support. Indeed, it enlists "the whole community of the realm." It remains a problem the extent to which such expressions of national sentiment should be taken literally rather than merely as diplomatic rhetoric. And to what extent does the seeming participation of the small freemen reflect their actual role in the royal government rather than simply the king's current need of such men's economic and military support in the wars against England?

It must not be forgotten that this is a Scottish—not an English—document. It is a valuable reminder to the English historian that evidence other than that found in English books and archives must often be consulted. Developments

SOURCE. Reproduced from "The Nation of Scots and the Declaration of Arbroath," by A. A. M. Duncan, published by the Historical Association, London, 1970, pp. 34–37.

in neighboring countries may also provide new insights into English developments. The "file copy" of the Declaration, written in Latin, is in the Scottish
Record Office, H. M. General Register House, Edinburgh.

To the most holy father and lord in Christ, lord John, by divine providence supreme pontiff of the holy Roman and universal church, his
humble and devout sons Duncan, earl of Fife, Thomas Randolph, earl of
Moray . . . and the other barons and freeholders and the whole community of the realm of Scotland send all manner of filial reverence, with
devout kisses of his blessed feet.

Most holy father and lord, we know, and we gather from the deeds and
books of the ancients, that among other distinguished nations our own
nation, namely of Scots, has been marked by many distinctions. It journeyed from Greater Scythia by the Tyrrhenian Sea and the Pillars of
Hercules, and dwelt for a long span of time in Spain among the most
savage peoples, but nowhere could it be subjugated by any people,
however barbarous. From there it came, twelve hundred years after the
people of Israel crossed the Red Sea and, having first driven out the
Britons and altogether destroyed the Picts, it acquired, with many victories and untold efforts, the places which it now holds, although often
assailed by Norwegians, Danes and English. As the histories of old time
bear witness, it has held them free of all servitude ever since. In their
kingdom one hundred and thirteen kings of their own royal stock have
reigned, the line unbroken by a single foreigner. Their high qualities
and merits, if they were not otherwise manifest, shine out sufficiently
from this: that the king of kings and lord of lords, our lord Jesus
Christ, after his passion and resurrection, called them, even though settled
in the uttermost ends of the earth, almost the first to his most holy faith.
Nor did he wish to confirm them in that faith by anyone but by the first
apostle by calling (though second or third in rank) —namely the most
gentle Andrew, the blessed Peter's brother, whom he wished to protect
them as their patron for ever.

The most holy fathers your predecessors gave careful heed to these
things and strengthened this same kingdom and people, as being the
special charge of the blessed Peter's brother by many favours and numerous privileges. Thus our people under their protection did heretofore
live in freedom and peace until that mighty prince Edward, king of the
English, father of the present one, when our kingdom had no head and
our people harboured no malice or treachery and were then unused to

wars or attacks, came in the guise of friend and ally to invade them as an enemy. His wrongs, killings, violence, pillage, arson, imprisonment of prelates, burning down of monasteries, despoiling and killing of religious, and yet other innumerable outrages, sparing neither age nor sex, religion nor order, no one could fully describe or fully understand unless experience had taught him.

But from these countless evils we have been set free, by the help of him who though he afflicts yet heals and restores, by our most valiant prince, king and lord, the lord Robert, who, that his people and his heritage might be delivered out of the hands of enemies, bore cheerfully toil and fatigue, hunger and danger, like another Maccabeus or Joshua. Divine providence, the succession to his right according to our laws and customs which we shall maintain to the death, and the due consent and assent of us all have made him our prince and king. We are bound to him for the maintaining of our freedom both by his rights and his merits, as to him by whom salvation has been wrought unto our people, and by him, come what may, we mean to stand. Yet if he should give up what he has begun, seeking to make us or our kingdom subject to the king of England or to the English, we would strive at once to drive him out as our enemy and a subverter of his own right and ours, and we would make some other man who was able to defend us our king; for, as long as a hundred of us remain alive, we will never on any conditions be subjected to the lordship of the English. For we fight not for glory, nor riches, nor honours, but for freedom alone, which no good man gives up except with his life.

Therefore it is, reverend father and lord, that we beseech your holiness . . . will look with paternal eyes on the troubles and anxieties brought by the English upon us and upon the church of God; that you will deign to admonish and exhort the king of the English, who ought to be satisfied with what he has, since England used once to be enough for seven kings or more, to leave in peace us Scots, who live in this poor little Scotland, beyond which there is no dwelling-place at all, and who desire nothing but our own. . . .

But if your Holiness giving too much credence to the tales of the English will not give sincere belief to all this, nor refrain from favouring them to our confusion, then the slaughter of bodies, the perdition of souls, and all the other misfortunes that will follow inflicted by them on us and by us on them, will, we believe, be imputed by the most high to you. . . .

Given at the monastery of Arbroath in Scotland on the sixth day of the month of April in the year of grace thirteen hundred and twenty and the fifteenth year of the reign of our aforesaid king.

22

Statute of York (1322). Assertion of Parliamentary Responsibility

In the decades that followed Magna Carta, the barons turned from attempting to restrain royal government by means of military force and a grievance committee to efforts to control the king's administration directly by gaining possession of the small council and the major offices. The first real effort in this direction, the Provisions of Oxford sponsored by Simon de Montfort in 1258, came to a violent end in 1265 in the battle of Evesham. A second attempt came when Edward II was forced to accept the Ordinances of 1311, by which the barons in parliament would dominate his royal government. This also failed. The barons, beset by disagreements among themselves and confronted by the king's greater reserve of power and authority, found that even by gaining direct control of the king's council they still could not control his government. The barons, the Lords Ordainers as they were called, were defeated in 1322 at the battle of Boroughbridge, and a few weeks later the Statute of York repealed the Ordinances of 1311, the basis of their attempted control of the government.

The Statute of York is highly controversial because of what it says, or seems to say, about parliament. There is, for instance, no consensus among scholars as to the meaning of the phrases, "the whole community of the realm" and "the commonalty of the kingdom." Do they refer to the commons, the representatives of the shires and boroughs, or to the kingdom in general? The intention of the last sentence of the statute is also unclear. Was it the establishment of a new and greater power of legislation for parliament? Was it a statement of what was already thought to be fact? Or was it simply a rhetorical flourish? Nevertheless, it is clear that the most important thing

SOURCE. B. Wilkinson, *Constitutional History of Medieval England, 1216–1399*, Volume II: *Politics and the Constitution, 1307–1399*, London: Longmans, Green and Co., 1952, pp. 155–156.

about the Statute of York is the simple fact of its existence. Edward used a parliamentary statute to sanction what had already been accomplished on the field of battle. Although parliament was used by the king against the barons in 1322, five years later the tables were turned, and it was then used by the barons to sanction Edward's abdication. The continued use of parliament to justify major governmental decisions, even those of dubious legality, strengthened it and made it a recognized part of the English constitution.

Our lord King Edward, son of King Edward, on March 16, in the third year of his reign, granted to the prelates, earls and barons of his realm . . . power to make ordinances. The archbishop of Canterbury, primate of all England, and the bishops, earls and barons chosen for the purpose, drew up certain ordinances . . . , which ordinances our said lord the king caused to be rehearsed and examined in his parliament at York three weeks after Easter in the fifteenth year of his reign. . . . Through that examination in the said parliament, it was found that, by the ordinances thus decreed, the royal power of our said lord the king was wrongfully limited in many respects, to the injury of his royal lordship and contrary to the estate of the crown. Furthermore, through such ordinances and provisions made by subjects in times past against the royal authority of our lord the king's ancestors, the kingdom has incurred troubles and wars, whereby the land has been imperilled. [Therefore] it is agreed, and established at the said parliament by our lord the king, by the said prelates and earls and barons, and by the whole community of the realm assembled in this parliament, that everything ordained by the said Ordainers and contained in the said ordinances shall henceforth and forever cease [to be valid], losing for the future all title, force, virtue, and effect; and that the statutes and establishment duly made by our lord the king and his ancestors prior to the said ordinances shall remain in force. And [it is decreed] that, henceforth and forever at all times, every kind of ordinance or provision made under any authority or commission whatsoever, by subjects of our lord the king or of his heirs, relative to the royal power of our lord the king or of his heirs, or contrary to the estate of the lord king or of his heirs or contrary to the estate of the crown, shall be null and shall have no validity or force whatever; but that matters which are to be determined for [i.e. favourable to] the estate of the king and of his heirs, and for the estate of the kingdom and of the people, shall be "treated," granted, and established in parliament by our lord the king and with the consent of the prelates, earls, and barons, and of the commonalty of the kingdom, as has been accustomed in times past.

23

Articles of the Spurriers (1345). Guilds in Medieval London

The growth of commerce and industry fostered in England, as elsewhere, the formation of guilds, organizations to protect the interests of certain mercantile groups. The most powerful were merchant guilds, made up of the important merchants in a town but, by the thirteenth century, strong craft or industrial guilds had also developed. In 1351 the most powerful craft guilds in London included the fishmongers, mercers, grocers, ironmongers, vinters, and woolmongers. There were also numerous smaller guilds, such as the glovers, cobblers, and spurriers, creating by 1422 a total of 111 organizations of this kind in London alone.

The craft guilds had useful functions. Initially, at least, they provided stability to the various trades and guaranteed the consumer a certain level of craftsmanship and honesty. They also established schools and charitable relief, maintained law and order in the absence of a regular police force, fought the frequent fires, and provided their members such special services as a dignified burial. In fact, some guilds began as religious or charitable organizations, resembling the friendly societies of the nineteenth century.

Guilds, however, which fell under the control of a few master craftsmen could easily become oppressive and monopolistic. For example, are the spurriers, in the regulations reprinted below, interested in protecting the consumer or are they simply using the excuse of quality control to restrict the

---

SOURCE.   *Memorials of London and London Life in the XIIIth, XIVth, and XVth Centuries,* ed. Henry Thomas Riley, London: Longmans, Green, and Co., 1868, pp. 226–228.

membership of their guild? The apprentice, finding it increasingly difficult to qualify as a master craftsman, often spent his entire life as a wage-earning journeyman. Eventually the journeymen were forced to form their own guilds or unions. As guilds became more powerful, they also sought, usually successfully, to dominate municipal government. Royal charters often permitted the mercantile oligarchy to become a self-perpetuating corporate body, controlling not only the social and economic life of a town but the political life as well. It is not surprising that guilds were criticized and that later generations viewed them as obstructing political liberty and economic progress.

Surviving guild records, like manorial records, are very numerous and widely scattered. Most of those relating to London are found in the Corporation of London Records Office and the Guildhall Library.

Be it remembered, that on Tuesday, the morrow of St. Peter's Chains [1 August], in the 19th year of the reign of King Edward the Third etc., the Articles underwritten were read before John Hamond, Mayor, Roger de Depham, Recorder, and the other Aldermen; and seeing that the same were deemed befitting, they were accepted and enrolled, in these words.—

"In the first place,—that no one of the trade of Spurriers shall work longer than from the beginning of the day until curfew rung out at the Church of St. Sepulchre, without Neugate; by reason that no man can work so neatly by night as by day. And many persons of the said trade, who compass how to practise deception in their work, desire to work by night rather than by day: and then they introduce false iron, and iron that has been cracked, for tin, and also, they put gilt on false copper, and cracked. And further,—many of the said trade are wandering about all day, without working at all at their trade; and then, when they have become drunk and frantic, they take to their work, to the annoyance of the sick and of all their neighbourhood, as well as by reason of the broils that arise between them and the strange folks who are dwelling among them. And then they blow up their fires so vigorously, that their forges begin all at once to blaze; to the great peril of themselves and of all the neighbourhood around. And then too, all the neighbours are much in dread of the sparks, which so vigorously issue forth in all directions from the mouths of the chimneys in their forges. By reason whereof, it seems unto them that working by night [should be put an end to,] in order such false work and such perils to avoid; and therefore, the Mayor and Aldermen do will, by assent of the good folks of the said trade, and for the common profit, that from henceforth such time for working, and such false work made in the trade, shall be forbidden. And if any person shall be found in the said trade to do the contrary hereof, let him be amerced, the first time in 40*d.*, one half thereof to go to the use of the Chamber of the Guildhall of London, and the other half to the use of the said trade; the second time, in half a mark, and the third time, in 10*s.*, to the use of the same Chamber and trade; and the fourth time, let him forswear the trade for ever.

"Also,—that no one of the said trade shall hang his spurs out on Sunday, or on other days that are Double Feasts; but only a sign indicating his business: and such spurs as they shall so sell, they are to shew and sell within their shops, without exposing them without, or opening the doors or windows of their shops, on the pain aforesaid.

"Also,—that no one of the said trade shall keep a house or shop to carry on his business, unless he is free of the City; and that no one shall cause to be sold, or exposed for sale, any manner of old spurs for new ones; or shall garnish them, or change them for new ones.

"Also,—that no one of the said trade shall take an apprentice for a less term than seven years; and such apprentice shall be enrolled, according to the usages of the said city.

"Also,—that if any one of the said trade, who is not a freeman, shall take an apprentice for a term of years, he shall be amerced, as aforesaid.

"Also,—that no one of the said trade shall receive the apprentice, serving-man, or journeyman, of another in the same trade, during the term agreed upon between his master and him; on the pain aforesaid.

"Also,—that no alien of another country, or foreigner of this country, shall follow or use the said trade, unless he is enfranchised before the Mayor, Aldermen, and Chamberlain; and that, by witness and surety of the good folks of the said trade, who will undertake for him as to his loyalty and his good behaviour.

"Also,—that no one of the said trade shall work on Saturdays, after None has been rung out in the City; and not from that hour until the Monday morning following."

24

Jean Froissart, *Chronicles.* The Battle of Crécy, 1346

Froissart is undoubtedly the most widely read medieval chronicler. A native of northern France, he went to England in 1361, becoming the secretary of Edward III's wife, Philippa of Hainault. Queen Philippa, a patron of the arts, encouraged Froissart to write his famous *Chronicles of England, France, Spain, etc.* Covering the period from 1307 to 1400, his chronicle is based largely on oral evidence gathered at the court of Edward III (1327–1377) and elsewhere. Froissart, despite his inaccuracies, has remained popular because of his forceful style and his preoccupation with the violence and pageantry of the Hundred Years' War (1337–1453). Better than any other writer, he captures the spirit of medieval feudalism; he is, as one recent historian has remarked, "a faithful echo of the feelings of chivalrous society."

It is ironic that Froissart's chronicle was written at a time when feudalism was declining. Although there were many reasons for the demise of feudalism, one important factor was the eclipse of the armored knight as the premier instrument of warfare. From Froissart's description of the battle of Crécy (1346), reprinted below, it is obvious that England's victory resulted not from the heroic exploits of her nobility but from the quiet efficiency of her lowborn archers. The Welsh longbow, used effectively for the first time in Edward I's Scottish campaigns, revolutionized medieval warfare. A good archer could fire 10 to 12 arrows a minute and had a maximum range of almost 400 yards. This increased firepower rendered the medieval knight obsolete. It was, however, very difficult for the nobility of England or France to accept the implications of Crécy. The question posed was simple. If a

SOURCE. Jean Froissart, *The Chronicles of England, France, Spain and the Adjoining Countries,* translated by Thomas Johnes, rev. ed., New York and London: The Cooperative Publication Society, 1901, pp. 39–41, 42, 44–45.

feudal elite trained for war was no longer a militarily necessity, how were knights to justify their existence, to say nothing of their special standing in society? The French nobility, refusing to accept its obsolescence, repeated the mistakes made at Crécy, and suffered the same disastrous results at the battles of Poitiers (1356) and Agincourt (1415). Only then did the nobility accept the inevitable. By the fifteenth century the military aspect of feudalism had become the pageantry of the tourney, and the place of the mounted knight in the royal arsenal had been taken not only by the longbowman but increasingly by the cannon and gunpowder.

There is no man, unless he had been present, that can imagine or describe truly the confusion of that day, especially the bad management and disorder of the French, whose troops were out of number. What I know, and shall relate in this book, I have learned chiefly from the English, and from those attached to Sir John of Hainault, who was always near the person of the King of France. The English, who, as I have said, were drawn up in three divisions, and seated on the ground, on seeing their enemies advance, rose up undauntedly, and fell into their ranks. The prince's battalion, whose archers were formed in the manner of a portcullis, and the men-at-arms in the rear, was the first to do so. The Earls of Northampton and Arundel, who commanded the second division, posted themselves in good order on the prince's wing to assist him if necessary.

You must know that the French troops did not advance in any regular order, and that as soon as their King came in sight of the English his blood began to boil, and he cried out to his marshals, "Order the Genoese forward and begin the battle in the name of God and St. Denis." There were about 15,000 Genoese cross-bow men; but they were quite fatigued, having marched on foot that day six leagues, completely armed and carrying their cross-bows, and accordingly they told the constable they were not in a condition to do any great thing in battle. The Earl of Alençon hearing this, said, "This is what one gets by employing such scoundrels, who fall off when there is any need for them." During this time a heavy rain fell, accompanied by thunder and a very terrible eclipse of the sun; and, before this rain, a great flight of crows hovered in the air over all the battalions, making a loud noise; shortly afterward it cleared up, and the sun shone very bright; but the French had it in their faces, and the English on their backs. When the Genoese were somewhat in order they approached the English and set up a loud shout, in order to frighten them; but the English remained quite quiet and did not seem to attend to it. They then set up a second shout, and advanced a little forward; the English never moved. Still they hooted a third time, advancing with their cross-bows presented, and began to shoot. The English archers then advanced one step forward, and shot their arrows with such force and quickness that it seemed as if it snowed. When the Genoese felt these arrows, which pierced through their armor, some of them cut the strings of their cross-bows, others flung them to the ground, and all turned about and retreated quite discomfited.

The French had a large body of men-at-arms on horseback to support the Genoese, and the King, seeing them thus fall back, cried out, "Kill me those scoundrels, for they stop up our road without any reason." The English continued shooting, and some of their arrows falling among the horsemen, drove them upon the Genoese, so that they were in such confusion they could never rally again.

In the English army there were some Cornish and Welsh men on foot, who had armed themselves with large knives; these advancing through the ranks of the men-at-arms and archers, who made way for them, came upon the French when they were in this danger, and falling upon earls, barons, knights, and squires, slew many, at which the King of England was exasperated. . . .

This battle, which was fought on Saturday, between La Broyes and Cressy, was murderous and cruel; and many gallant deeds of arms were performed that were never known; toward evening, many knights and squires of the French had lost their masters, and, wandering up and down the plain, attacked the English in small parties; but they were soon destroyed, for the English had determined that day to give no quarter, nor hear of ransom from anyone. . . .

This Saturday the English never quitted their ranks in pursuit of anyone, but remained on the field guarding their position and defending themselves against all who attacked them. The battle ended at the hour of vespers, when the King of England embraced his son and said to him, "Sweet son, God give you perseverance; you are my son; for most loyally have you acquitted yourself; you are worthy to be a sovereign." The prince bowed very low, giving all honor to the King, his father. The English during the night made frequent thanksgivings to the Lord for the happy issue of the day; and with them there was no rioting, for the King had expressly forbidden all riot or noise.

On the following day, which was Sunday, there were a few encounters with the French troops; however, they could not withstand the English, and soon either retreated or were put to the sword. When Edward was assured that there was no appearance of the French collecting another army, he sent to have the number and rank of the dead examined. This business was entrusted to Lord Reginald Cobham and Lord Stafford, assisted by three heralds to examine the arms, and two secretaries to write down the names. They passed the whole day upon the field of battle, and made a very circumstantial account of all they saw: according to their report it appeared that 80 banners, the bodies of 11 princes, 1,200 knights, and about 30,000 common men were found dead on the field. After this very successful engagement, Edward marched with his victorious army to Wisant, and having halted there one whole day, arrived on the following Thursday before the strong town of Calais, which he had determined to besiege.

25

Henry Knighton, *Chronicle.* The Black Death, 1348-1350

Little is known of the life of Henry Knighton except that he was a canon of St. Mary-of-the-Meadows Abbey, an Augustinian house at Leicester. Although noted neither for its style nor its analysis, his chronicle contains in its last part the most important contemporary narrative of the constitutional conflicts of the reign of Richard II (1377–1399). The earlier portion, based largely on well-known sources, also drew on local chronicles that have since been lost. Using these sources effectively, Knighton wrote what is regarded today as the best description of the Black Death and its effect on the population of England. Part of this is reprinted below.

The Black Death, a highly infectious form of the bubonic plague, struck England with great force in 1348 to 1349, returning in 1361 to 1362 and again in 1369. The death of approximately one third of the entire population could at the time be explained only in terms of God's wrath. Few historians, even

SOURCE. *The Peasants' Revolt of 1381,* ed. R. B. Dobson, London: Macmillan and Co., 1970, pp. 59–63. Reprinted by the permission of Macmillan, London and Basingstoke.

today, would argue that the social dislocation resulting from the plague was a "good thing," but it now seems likely that in the long run the plague did improve, if only slightly, the position of the English peasant. Surviving peasants took advantage of the labor shortage to bargain with the landlords for better terms. The attempt by the landed classes to freeze wages and to maintain their own status by a Statute of Labourers (1351) led to a number of local disturbances and eventually contributed to the Peasants' Revolt of 1381.

A Latin edition of the *Chronicon Henrici Knighton* was published in the Rolls Series, 1889 to 1895.

In this and the following year (1348–9) there was a general mortality among men throughout the whole world. It began first in India, and spread thence into Tharsis, thence to the Saracens, and at last to the Christians and Jews; so that in the space of a single year, namely from Easter to Easter, as it was rumored at the court of Rome, 8000 legions of men perished in those distant regions, besides Christians. . . .

Then the dreadful pestilence made its way along the coast by Southampton and reached Bristol, where almost the whole strength of the town perished, as it were surprised by sudden death; for few kept their beds more than two or three days, or even half a day. Then this cruel death spread on all sides, following the course of the sun. And there died at Leicester, in the small parish of St. Leonard's, more than 380 persons, in the parish of Holy Cross, 400, in the parish of St. Margaret's, Leicester, 700; and so in every parish, in a great multitude. Then the bishop of Lincoln sent notice throughout his whole diocese giving general power to all priests, both regulars and seculars, to hear confessions and give absolution with full episcopal authority to all persons, except only in case of debt. In such a case, the debtor was to pay the debt, if he were able, while he lived, or others were to be appointed to do so from his goods after his death. In the same way the Pope gave plenary remission of all sins (once only) to all receiving absolution at the point of death, and granted that this power should last until Easter next following, and that every one might choose his own confessor at will.

In the same year there was a great plague among sheep everywhere in the kingdom, so that in one place more than 5000 sheep died in a single pasture; and they rotted so much that neither bird not beast would touch them. . . . Sheep and oxen strayed at large through the fields and among the crops, and there were none to drive them off or herd them; but for lack of keepers they perished in remote by-ways and hedges in inestimable numbers throughout all districts, because there was such a great scarcity of servants that no one knew what he ought to do. For there was no recollection of so great and terrible a mortality since the time of Vortigern, king of the Britons, in whose day, as Bede testifies, in his book concerning the deeds of the English, the living did not suffice to bury the dead.

In the following autumn a reaper was not to be had for less than 8d, with his food, a mower for less than 12d, with food. Therefore many crops rotted in the fields for lack of men to gather them. But in the year of the pestilence, as has been said above of other things, there was so great an abundance of all kinds of corn that virtually no one cared for it. . . .

At this time there was everywhere so great a scarcity of priests that many churches were left destitute, without divine service, masses, matins, vespers or sacraments. A chaplain was scarcely to be had to serve any church for less than £10 or 10 marks; and whereas when there was an abundance of priests before the pestilence a chaplain could be had for 4, 5 or even 2 marks with his board, at this time there was scarcely one willing to accept any vicarage at £20 or 20 marks. . . .

Meanwhile the king sent notice into all counties of the realm that reapers and other labourers should not receive more than they used to take, under a penalty defined by statute; and he introduced a statute for this reason. But the labourers were so arrogant and hostile that they took no notice of the king's mandate; and if anyone wanted to employ them he was obliged to give them whatever they asked, and either to lose his fruits and crops, or satisfy at will the labourers' greed and arrogance. When it became known to him that they did not observe his ordinance and gave higher stipends to their labourers, the king levied heavy amercements upon abbots, priors, knights of greater and lesser degree, and others great and small throughout the countryside, taking 100s from some, 40s or 20s from others, according as they were able to pay. . . .

In the following winter there was such a shortage of servants for all sorts of labour as it was believed had never been before. For the sheep and cattle strayed in all directions without herdsmen, and all things were left with no one to care for them. Thus necessaries became so dear that what had previously been worth 1d was now worth 4d or 5d. Moreover the great men of the land and other lesser lords who had tenants, remitted the payment of their rents, lest their tenants should go away, on account of the scarcity of servants and the high price of all things—some half their rents, some more, some less, some for one, two, or three years according as they could come to an agreement with them. Similarly, those who had let lands on yearly labour-services to tenants as is the custom in the case of villeins, were obliged to relieve and remit these services, either excusing them entirely, or taking them on easier terms, in the form of a small rent, lest their houses should be irreparably ruined and the land should remain completely uncultivated. And all sorts of food and necessities became excessively dear.

26

John of Arderne, *Treatises of Fistula in Ano* (1376). A Surgeon's Code of Behavior

Medicine was by the fourteenth century a part of the curricula of many universities. Its study, however, had advanced little beyond the work of Galen, a second-century Roman physician. This was due, at least in part, to the reluctance of physicians to operate. Because surgery was manual labor and was inclined to be messy and even dangerous, doctors felt that it was beneath their dignity. As a result, most experimental work was done outside of the universities by "surgeons," who necessarily received their training at first as apprentices and then at the expense of their early patients. There were both ordinary surgeons, or barbers, who performed common treatments such as leeching and pulling teeth, and master surgeons, such as John of Arderne (1306–1390?), who specialized in more delicate operations. Competition for business led ultimately to the creation of rival professional organizations, the Barber Guilds and the Surgeon Guilds.

Little is known of John of Arderne's life. He apparently received a good education and then acquired his practical skills as a surgeon during the Hundred Years' War. In his most famous work, *Treatises of Fistula in Ano*

SOURCE. *English Historical Documents, Volume IV, 1327–1485*, edited by A. R. Myers, pp. 1184–1186. © Eyre and Spottiswoode, 1969. Reprinted by permission of Oxford University Press, Inc., and Eyre & Spottiswoode (Publishers) Ltd.

(1376), he broke new ground in the treatment of fistulas (abscesses) and gout and in the use of clysters (enemas). The large number of surviving translations of his Latin treatise indicates that his work was highly regarded. Although in advance of his colleagues, he was still a product of the fourteenth century, believing in astrology and, therefore, including in his book a section on the influence of the moon on surgery.

It is apparent from the following section that John of Arderne regarded medical practice as more than a matter of correct diagnosis and efficient treatment. He was concerned that surgeons maintain a code of conduct that would produce confidence in the patient's mind and money in the surgeon's pocket. The surgeon must always be aware of the social status of his patient. He must learn to set the correct fee. He must have a good bedside manner. And, he must be professionally responsible and not criticize his colleagues.

First, it behooves a surgeon who wishes to succeed in this craft always to put God first in all his doings, and always meekly to call with heart and mouth for his help, and sometimes give of his earnings to the poor, so that they by their prayers may gain him grace of the Holy Ghost. And he must not be found rash or boastful in his sayings or in his deeds; and he must abstain from much speech, especially among great men; and he must answer cautiously to all questions, so that he may not be trapped by his own words. For if his works are known to disagree often with his words and his promises, he will be held more unworthy, and he will tarnish his own good fame. . . . A surgeon should not laugh or joke too much; and as far as he can without harm, he should avoid the company of knaves and dishonest persons. He should be always occupied in things that belong to his craft, whether reading, studying, writing, or praying; the study of books is of great advantage to the surgeon, both by keeping him occupied and by making him wiser. Above all, it helps him much to be found always sober; for drunkenness destroys all wisdom and brings it to nought. In strange places he should be content with the meats and drinks which he finds there, using moderation in all things. . . . He must scorn no man. . . . If anyone talks to him about another surgeon, he must neither set him at nought nor praise nor commend him too much, but he may answer courteously thus: "I have no real knowledge of him, but I have neither learnt nor heard anything of him but what is good and honest." . . . A surgeon should not look too boldly at the lady or the daughters or other fair women in great men's houses, nor offer to kiss them, nor to touch them secretly or openly . . . lest he arouses the indignation of the lord or one of his household. . . . If sick men or any of their friends come to the surgeon to ask help or advice, let him be neither too brusque nor too familiar, but adjust his manner according to the character of the person; to some respectful, to some friendly. . . . Also it is a help for him to have excuses ready for not being able to undertake a case so that he does not hurt or anger some great man or friend, and does not interrupt some necessary work. Otherwise he could pretend to be hurt or ill or give some other likely excuse if he does not want to undertake a case. If he does undertake a case, he should make a clear agreement about payment and take the money in advance. But the surgeon should be sure not to make any definite pronouncement in any illness, unless he has first seen the sickness and the signs of it. When he has made an examination, even though he may think that the patient may be cured, he should warn the patient in his prognosis of the perils to come if treatment should be deferred. And if he sees that the patient is eager for the cure, then the surgeon must boldly adjust his fee to the man's status in life. But the surgeon should always beware of asking too little, for this is bad both for the market and the patient. Therefore for a case of fistula in ano, when it is curable, the surgeon may reasonably ask of a great man 100 marks or £40 with robes and fees to the value of 100 shillings each year for the rest of his life. From lesser men he may ask £40 or 40 marks without fees; but he must never take less than forty shillings. Never in my life have I taken less than 100 shillings for the cure of this disease; but of course every man must do what he thinks is right and most expedient. And if the patient or his friends and servants asks how long the cure will take, the surgeon had better always say twice as long as he really thinks; thus if a surgeon hopes to heal the patient in twenty weeks, which is the common period, let him add another twenty. For it is better to name a longer term for recovery than that the cure should drag on, a thing which might cause the patient to despair at the very time when confidence in the doctor is the greatest aid to recovery. For if the patient should later wonder or ask why the surgeon estimates so long for recovery when he was able to cure the patient in half the time, the surgeon should answer that it was because the patient had a strong heart and bore pain well and that he was of good complexion (that is, having such a combination of the four humours as would speed recovery) and that his flesh healed quickly; and he must think of other causes that would please the patient, for by such words are patients made proud and glad. And a surgeon should always be soberly dressed, not likening himself in clothing or bearing to minstrels, but rather after the manner of a clerk; for any discreet man clad in clerk's dress may sit at a gentleman's table. A surgeon must also have clean hands and well shaped nails, free from all blackness and dirt. And he should be courteous at the lord's table, and not displease the guests sitting by either

in word or deed; he should hear many things but speak only a few. . . . A
young doctor should also learn good proverbs relating to his craft to comfort his patients. . . . It is also expedient for the surgeon to be able to tell
good honest tales that may make the patient laugh, both from the Bible
and from other great books; and also any other stories that are not too
dubious which may make the patient more cheerful. A surgeon should
never betray inadvertently the confidences of his patients, either men or
women, nor belittle one to another, even if he should have cause . . . for
if men see that you can keep other men's confidences, they will have more
confidence in you.

27

Rolls of the Prior and Convent of Durham (1378). Life of the Medieval Peasant

The traditional, and most readily accessible, historical evidence dealing with
medieval England has one great failing: it ignores the peasants, who made
up the bulk of the population. Chroniclers seldom referred to the peasants
but concentrated instead on describing the activities of the secular and ecclesiastical leaders of society. Charters and related documents originating
in the royal chancery dealt almost exclusively with relations between the
king and his most important subjects. The popular literature of the period,
mostly in French, was written to please the lords and ladies, not their serfs

SOURCE.   English Historical Documents, Volume IV, 1327–1485, edited by
A. R. Myers, pp. 997–1000. © Eyre and Spottiswoode, 1969. Reprinted by
permission of Oxford University Press, Inc., and Eyre & Spottiswoode (Publishers) Ltd.

and hired laborers. Peasants, if depicted in these writings at all, appeared almost subhuman.

Today, historians recognize that a vast amount of evidence dealing with the lower classes actually does exist. The most important new material consists of manorial court proceedings, records of financial and land transactions between peasants and landlords, and inventories of the landholdings and property of manors. Most of this material is now deposited in county record offices. Although some of it is well organized and indexed, much of it is still difficult for the historian to use.

Items of evidence, such as the records of the manorial court of the Prior and Convent of Durham reprinted below, can give the historian a broader perspective on life in late medieval England. English history did not consist solely of endless feudal wars, developing legal institutions, and continuous constitutional conflicts, but of the lives of real people. To peasants life revolved around the seasons of the year and the village, not around events taking place in distant London. In 1378 John Akke was, for example, undoubtedly more concerned about keeping his dogs from chasing his lord's sheep and thus staying out of court than he was about the composition of the council of the new king Richard II.

At Bellyngham [Billingham] before the lords William Aslakbe, terrar, and Thomas Legat, bursar [i.e. officials of the convent] on Tuesday before the feast of the Purification of the Blessed Virgin Mary [28 January].

Billingham. . . . From all the tenants of the village because they did not repair the wethercot, as they were told to do in various halmotes— And they were ordered to repair the wethercot before the next meeting of the court on penalty of 40s. . . . All the tenants of the village were ordered not to follow an unjust path across the land called Litilmeres in the holding of Henry of the Neuraw, on penalty of 12d. It was ordered that everyone shall help to look after the pigs, and that everyone of them shall guard them, when his turn comes, until they have a common piggery, on penalty of 12d. It was ordered that none of them should dig in the high street in the village of Billyngham, on pain of 40d.

Neuton Vieuluve [Newton Beaulieu or Bewley].   Robert Smith came into court and took 1 cottage and 6 acres last in the tenure of John de Neuton, who lost it, because the aforesaid John was unwilling to stay there as he was ordered to do in several halmotes for the last three years. Robert is to have it for the term of his life, rendering for it the ancient rent. . . .

Acley. It was found by the oath of [8 jurors named] that John Clerk of Acley at the time when he killed Walter Tailliour had goods and chattels to the value of 26*s* 8*d* and they were given a day to show what goods and chattels of John came into the hands of John Tours the coroner and into whose hands the rest have come, within two weeks. The constable and all the tenants of the village were told not to let the chattels of felons or other fugitives be removed from the village; they were told to keep these chattels and cause them to be valued at their true value, until they should receive further orders from the prior and the bishop's official, on pain of 40*s*. It was ordered by common agreement that none of them should let any cattle trample down corn nor eat grass in any other place than is customary, on pain of half a mark.

Fery [Ferryhill]. All the tenants of the village and of the villages of East, West, and Mid Merrington and Chilton were ordered that none of them should play at ball [?football—*ad pilas*] henceforth on penalty of paying 40*s*.

West Merrington. A day was given to John de Heswell to make his law with six hands at the next court [i.e. to exonerate himself with six oath-helpers], that he does not owe John of Galleway, chaplain, 16*s* 6*d* for the corn, which he ought to have paid him for two years past, to the injury of John, 6*s* 8*d*. . . .

Jarrow. Thomas, son of Simon Fig of Jarrow, came into court and took 3 cottages and 36 acres of land last held by Agnes widow of John Hewet, of which land 12 acres belong to each cottage. He has them for the term of his life, to pay the ancient rent, and to do proper service and fulfil all the other burdens.

Suthwyk [Southwick]. A day was given to Thomas son of Alan [and eleven others] to inquire about the boundaries between the lands of the lord prior which John son of Adam junior holds and the free land, formerly of Thomas Ayer, which John de Thornton now holds and they are to place the boundary marks.

Wermouth [Wearmouth]. The jurors were told to inquire whether any cotter held more sheep than five as was ordained in the preceding court, on penalty of 40*d*.

Wyvestowe. The tenants of Wyvestow were told that they must get the mill pond repaired, each for his part as much as is needed, on penalty of 40*d* and also that they do not hold the way beyond Caldwelmedowe, on pain of 40*d*. . . .

Schelles [Shields]. From Thomas son of Henry, 6*d* John Hilton junior [6*d* pardoned by the terrar], John Akke [6*d* pardoned by the terrar] because his dogs chased the lord's sheep and bit them as is presented by the shepherd. . . .

Estraynton [East Rainton]. All the tenants of the village were told to make a well near the spring, on account of the shares of the ploughs breaking up the ground, so that the spring can be kept clean, on pain of paying 12*d* by the man who works at the forge, from anyone who is unwilling to do this.—Richard Widouson was chosen reeve of the village and swore to do what belongs to the office and John Freman will be the collector of the rents. . . .

Pittyngton [Pittington].   It was presented that Robert of the Kiln of Cokon took two hares, Ralph of Malteby took 1 hare; Thomas Menenyl took 1 hare. William Ayr of Houghton is a common poacher, also Alan Bouer and John Gray.

Mid-Merrington.   All the tenants of the village were told that no one should defame any other in words or deeds on pain of paying 40*s*. And a day was given for William Currour, John Smith, John de Fery, Roger Arowsmith, and William Byng, to inquire and present to the terrar at Durham who defamed Robert Robson and Mariot his wife and also night wanderers [i.e. presumably they were defamed of being night-wanderers and therefore suspect] on the Sunday next before Palm Sunday, on penalty of 20*s,* and also if John de Fery defamed the wife of John Doket calling her a whore and a thief.

Dalton.   All the tenants of the village were told that none of them must allow any of their beasts to enter gardens to trample down crops nor any other necessary things within the gardens of neighbors, on pain of paying 12*d*. . . .

Thomas Walsingham, *English History* (c. 1395). John Ball and the Peasants' Revolt, 1381

Thomas Walsingham (d. 1422?) was for many years the superintendent of the scriptorium of St. Albans, a Benedictine abbey long noted for its scholarship, especially in the writing of chronicles. His most famous work, *Historia Anglicana,* from which the passage below is taken, covers the period from 1372 to 1422. Although in places it follows the work of previous chroniclers, for the early years of Richard II's reign (1377–1399) it reflects Walsingham's original work.

The Peasants' Revolt of 1381, larger and more violent than earlier such disturbances, was the result of social dislocation caused by the plague, specific financial grievances such as the poll taxes levied by parliament and, as is revealed below, growing resentment at the privileges claimed by landlords. Although the revolt led by Wat Tyler and John Ball failed, its violence caused great fear and alarm among the propertied classes. In their search for a scapegoat, chroniclers like Walsingham gave prominence to the influence of John Ball, who is portrayed as a subversive seeking to "corrupt" the people by preaching "the perverse doctrines of the perfidious John Wycliffe."

This description of John Ball raises a number of interesting questions. How unique, for example, were Ball's ideas? Some recent scholars argue that his egalitarianism was fairly common in the fourteenth century. Also, was Ball a product of Lollardy or were the ecclesiastical chroniclers simply attempting to discredit Wycliffe by associating him with the social radicalism of Ball? Finally, since the chroniclers of this period were all biased against

SOURCE. *The Peasants' Revolt of 1381,* ed. R. B. Dobson, London: Macmillan and Co., 1970, pp. 373–375. Reprinted by the permission of Macmillan, London and Basingstoke.

the ideas of Ball and Tyler, how much of what they wrote about these two men can be accepted at face value?

All of Walsingham's manuscripts were published in the Rolls Series in the late nineteenth century.

Moreover, on that day [Saturday 13 July] the same Robert [Tresilian] sentenced John Balle, priest, after hearing of his scandalous and confessed crimes, to drawing, hanging, beheading, disembowelling and—to use the common words—quartering: he had been taken by the men of Coventry and on the previous day brought to St. Albans and into the presence of the king whose majesty he had insulted so gravely. His death was postponed until the following Monday [15 July] by the intervention of Lord William [Courtenay] bishop of London, who obtained a short deferment so that Balle could repent for the sake of his soul.

For twenty years and more Balle had been preaching continually in different places such things as he knew were pleasing to the people, speaking ill of both ecclesiastics and secular lords, and had rather won the goodwill of the common people than merit in the sight of God. For he instructed the people that tithes ought not to be paid to an incumbent unless he who should give them were richer than the rector or vicar who received them; and that tithes and offerings ought to be withheld if the parishioner were known to be a man of better life than his priest; and also that none were fit for the Kingdom of God who were not born in matrimony. He taught, moreover, the perverse doctrines of the perfidious John Wycliffe, and the insane opinions that he held, with many more that it would take long to recite. Therefore, being prohibited by the bishops from preaching in parishes and churches, he began to speak in streets and squares and in the open fields. Nor did he lack hearers among the common people, whom he always strove to entice to his sermons by pleasing words, and slander of the prelates. At last he was excommunicated as he would not desist and was thrown into prison, where he predicted that he would be set free by twenty thousand of his friends. This afterwards happened in the said disturbances, when the commons broke open all the prisons, and made the prisoners depart.

And when he had been delivered from prison, he followed them, egging them on to commit greater evils, and saying that such things must surely be done. And, to corrupt more people with his doctrine, at Blackheath, where two hundred thousand of the commons were gathered together, he began a sermon in this fashion:

> "Whan Adam dalf, and Eve span,
> Wo was thanne a gentilman?"

And continuing his sermon, he tried to prove by the words of the proverb that he had taken for his text, that from the beginning all men were created equal by nature, and that servitude had been introduced by the unjust and evil oppression of men, against the will of God, who, if it had pleased Him to create serfs, surely in the beginning of the world would have appointed who should be a serf and who a lord. Let them consider, therefore, that He had now appointed the time wherein, laying aside the yoke of long servitude, they might, if they wished, enjoy their liberty so long desired. Wherefore they must be prudent, hastening to act after the manner of a good husbandman, tilling his field, and uprooting the tares that are accustomed to destroy the grain; first killing the great lords of the realm, then slaying the lawyers, justices and jurors, and finally rooting out everyone whom they knew to be harmful to the community in future. So at last they would obtain peace and security, if, when the great ones had been removed, they maintained among themselves equality of liberty and nobility, as well as of dignity and power.

And when he had preached these and many other ravings, he was in such high favour with the common people that they cried out that he should be archbishop and Chancellor of the kingdom, and that he alone was worthy of the office, for the present archbishop was a traitor to the realm and the commons, and should be beheaded wherever he could be found.

William Langland, *Piers the Plowman* (c. 1390). A Description of English Society

William Langland (c. 1332–c. 1400) lived in obscure poverty. Despite a good education, he took only minor orders and, hence, never qualified for a lucrative position in the Church. He appears to have been something of a dreamer, spending much of his time writing unrhymed, alliterative poetry, a popular form of literature that had survived from the Anglo-Saxon period. *Piers the Plowman,* written and twice revised between about 1360 and 1390, is by far the best example of this type of poetry. It is a medieval allegory describing the visions of "William," presumably Langland himself. These visions, panoramas of fourteenth-century England, gradually reveal to William something of the nature of truth and righteousness.

Piers the Plowman is of importance to the social historian. The passage below, describing the various social classes, reveals Langland as an astute observer. Although not a revolutionary, he was certainly a social critic, being particularly hard on the higher clergy. The numerous surviving manuscripts indicate that Langland's work was highly regarded by his contemporaries, perhaps because it supported the social radicalism of the period.

Langland's poetry is also of value in studying the English language. The fourteenth century saw a renewed use of English by the government and in literature. Both *Piers the Plowman* and the statute of 1362 ordering the use of English in royal law courts are parts of the same movement away from French and Latin. The English used by Langland was, neither the Anglo-Saxon or Old English of *Beowulf* and "Maldon" nor the modern English of

SOURCE. William Langland, *Piers the Ploughman,* translated by J. F. Goodridge (Penguin Classics, 1966), pp. 25–28, 31. Copyright © J. F. Goodridge, 1959, 1966.

Shakespeare, but rather a "Middle English" descended from a mingling of Anglo-Saxon and French and still made up of a number of regional dialects. Langland actually used several dialects in his writings, the dominant one being that of the West Midlands, not that of London used by Geoffrey Chaucer.

Piers the Plowman remained popular through the turbulent fifteenth century. By the reign of Elizabeth I (1558–1603), however, English was becoming standardized, and people could no longer handle the dialects used by Langland. His work was increasingly dismissed as medieval allegory, and as such offensive to modern tastes. No new edition of *Piers the Plowman* appeared between 1561 and 1813, and only recently has Langland come to be recognized as one of the great literary talents of late medieval England.

One summer season, when the sun was warm, I rigged myself out in shaggy woollen clothes, as if I were a shepherd; and in the garb of an easy-living hermit I set out to roam far and wide through the world, hoping to hear of marvels. But on a morning in May, among the Malvern Hills, a strange thing happened to me, as though by magic. For I was tired out by my wanderings, and as I lay down to rest under a broad bank by the side of a stream, and leaned over gazing into the water, it sounded so pleasant that I fell asleep.

And I dreamt a marvellous dream: I was in a wilderness, I could not tell where, and looking Eastwards I saw a tower high up against the sun, and splendidly built on a top of a hill; and far beneath it was a great gulf, with a dungeon in it, surrounded by deep, dark pits, dreadful to see. But between the tower and the gulf I saw a smooth plain, thronged with all kinds of people, high and low together, moving busily about their wordly affairs.

Some laboured at ploughing and sowing, with no time for pleasure, sweating to produce food for the gluttons to waste. Others spent their lives in vanity, parading themselves in a show of fine clothes. But many, out of love for our Lord and in the hope of Heaven, led strict lives devoted to prayer and penance—for such are the hermits and anchorites who stay in their cells, and are not forever hankering to roam about, and pamper their bodies with sensual pleasures.

Others chose to live by trade, and were much better off—for in our worldly eyes such men seem to thrive. Then there were the professional entertainers, some of whom, I think, are harmless minstrels, making an honest living by their music; but others, babblers and vulgar jesters, are true Judas' children! They invent fantastic tales about themselves, and pose as half-wits, yet they show wits enough whenever it suits them, and could easily work for a living if they had to! I will not say all that St Paul says about them; it is enough to quote, "He who talks filth is a servant of the Devil."

And there were tramps and beggars hastening on their rounds, with their bellies and their packs crammed full of bread. They lived by their wits, and fought over their ale—for God knows, they go to bed glutted with food and drink, these brigands, and get up with foul language and filthy talk; and all day long, Sleep and shabby Sloth are at their heels.

And I saw pilgrims and palmers banding together to visit the shrines at Rome and Compostella. They went on their way full of clever talk, and took leave to tell fibs about it for the rest of their lives. And some I heard spinning such yarns of the shrines they had visited, you could tell by the way they talked that their tongues were more tuned to lying than telling the truth, no matter what tale they told.

Troops of hermits with their hooded staves were on their way to Walsingham, with their wenches following after. These great, long lubbers, who hated work, were got up in clerical gowns to distinguish them from laymen, and paraded as hermits for the sake of an easy life.

I saw the Friars there too—all four Orders of them—preaching to the people for what they could get. In their greed for fine clothes, they interpreted the Scriptures to suit themselves and their patrons. Many of these Doctors of Divinity can dress as handsomely as they please, for as their trade advances, so their profits increase. And now that Charity has gone into business, and become confessor-in-chief to wealthy lords, many strange things have happened in the last few years; unless the Friars and Holy Church mend their quarrel, the worst evil in the world will soon be upon us. . . .

Then there came into the field a king, guided by the knights. The powers of the Commons gave him his throne, and Common Sense provided men of learning to counsel him and to protect the people.

The king, with his nobles and counsellors, decided that the common people should provide them with resources; so the people devised different trades, and engaged ploughmen to labour and till the soil for the good of the whole community, as honest ploughmen should. Then the king and the people, helped by Common Sense, established law and order, so that every man might know his rights and duties. . . .

Besides all this, a hundred men in silk gowns stood swaying from side to side and making speeches. These were the lawyers who served at the bar, pleading their cases for as much money as they could get. Never once

did they open their mouths out of love for our Lord; indeed you could sooner measure the mist on the Malvern Hills, than get a sound out of them without first producing some cash!

I saw many more in this great concourse of people, as you shall hear presently: barons, burgesses, and peasants; bakers, brewers, and butchers; linen-weavers and tailors, tinkers and toll-collectors, masons and miners and many other tradesfolk. And all kinds of labourers suddenly appeared —shoddy workmen, who would while away their hours with bawdy songs —like "Dieu vous save, Dame Emme!"—while cooks with their boys cried, "Hot pies! Hot pies! Fat pigs and geese! Come and eat!" and inn-keepers were bawling, "White wine! Red wine! Gascon and Spanish! Wash down your meat with the finest Rhenish!"—

All this I saw in my dream, and a great deal more besides.

30

Statute of Praemunire (1393).
Anti-Papal Sentiment in Parliament

The long-standing rivalry between Rome and the English secular state was intensified by the conditions of the fourteenth century. The pope's transfer of residence from Rome to Avignon, adjacent to France, marked a decline in his prestige in England, especially after the outbreak of the Hundred Years' War in 1337.

Although popes had long claimed the right to make direct appointments —called provisions, the men thus appointed being called provisors—to English church offices, opposition to this remained slight or intermittent until it

SOURCE. *English Historical Documents, Volume IV, 1327–1485,* edited by A. R. Myers, pp. 661–662. © Eyre and Spottiswoode, 1969. Reprinted by permission of Oxford University Press, Inc., and Eyre & Spottiswoode (Publishers) Ltd.

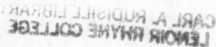

was taken up by parliament in the mid-fourteenth century. Provisors, often being foreigners and absentees, were thought to be a threat to English clerics seeking promotions and a drain on English money. The Statute of Provisors of 1351, based on the idea that the patronage of a church office was a property right protected by English courts, was designed to stop the pope's traffic in English ecclesiastical benefices. When the papacy persisted in issuing provisions and enforcing them in church courts, even with bulls of excommunication, parliament, in the Statute of Praemunire (1353), made it a crime to appeal to a foreign (meaning papal) court if an English court had jurisdiction. That these statutes were not readily heeded is indicated by the former's being renewed in stronger terms in 1390 and the latter's being renewed in 1365 and 1393. The act of 1393, reproduced below and often called the Great Statute of Praemunire, differed from earlier legislation in the breadth of its denial of papal jurisdiction in England and in the severity of its punishment.

To a great extent, the statutes were not enforced. The king generally ignored the powers the acts had given him and, instead, joined with the pope to make appointments agreeable to both of them. Nevertheless, in Praemunire's occasional use and, more important, in its claim that the "crown of England . . . has had no earthly lord," one recognizes a sense of national consciousness. The Great Statute of Praemunire is important as a reminder that medieval kings did not readily bow to the papacy when their own or their kingdom's interests were at stake. Henry VIII's later claims for himself and for England were not entirely without precedent.

Also, whereas the commons of the realm in this present parliament have shown to our redoubted lord the king, grievously complaining, that whereas the said lord our king and all his lieges ought of right, and were wont in olden time, to sue in the king's court, to recover their presentment to churches, prebends, and other benefices of holy church, to which they have a right to present, the cognisance of the plea of which suit belongs only to the king's court of the old right of his crown, used and approved in the time of all his forebears, kings of England; and when judgement shall be given in the same court on such a plea and presentment, the archbishops, bishops, and other spiritual persons who have institution of such benefices within their jurisdiction are bound to make and have made execution of such judgements by the king's commandments of all the time aforesaid without interruption, for no lay person may make such execution, and also are bound of right to make execution of many other of the king's commandments, of which right the crown of England has been peaceably seised, as well in the time of our lord the king that now is, as in the time of all his forebears till this day.

But now of late divers processes are made by the holy father the pope and censures of excommunication passed on certain bishops of England, because they have made execution of such commandments. . . . And also it is said, and a common clamour is made, that the said Bishop of Rome has ordained and proposed to translate some prelates of the realm, some out of the realm, and some from one bishopric to another within the realm, without the king's assent and knowledge, and without the assent of the prelates concerned, which prelates are very profitable and necessary to our said lord the king and to all his realm; by which translations, if they should be suffered, the statutes of the realm would be defeated and made void . . . and so the realm destitute as well of counsel as of wealth, to the final destruction of the realm; and so the crown of England, which has been so free at all times, that it has had no earthly lord, but is immediately subject to God in all matters touching the regality of the same crown, and to none other, would be subjected to the pope and the laws and statutes of the realm would be defeated by him . . . at his will. . . .

Whereupon our said lord the king, by the assent aforesaid, and at the request of his commons, has ordained and established, that if anyone should purchase or pursue, or cause to be purchased or pursued, in the court of Rome, or elsewhere, any such translations, processes and sentences of excommunication, bulls, instruments, or any other things whatsoever, which touch the king our lord, against him, his crown and his regality, or his realm, as is aforesaid, they, and those who bring such instruments into the realm, or receive them, or make thereof notification or any other execution whatsoever within the same realm or without, that they, their notaries, proctors, maintainers, abettors, favourers, and councillors, shall be put out of the king's protection and their lands and tenements, goods and chattels, be forfeit to our lord the king; and that they be attached by their bodies, if they may be found, and brought before that king and his council there to answer to the cases aforesaid, or that process shall be made against them by *praemunire facias,* in manner as it is ordained in other statutes of provisors, and others who sue in any other court in derogation of the regality of our lord the king.

Treaty of Troyes (1420). Henry V and the Hundred Years' War

To most English people in the late Middle Ages the central event was the Hundred Years' War (1337–1453). The war was a consequence of the English kings' possession of land in France and, more recently, of Edward III's claim to be the rightful king of France. The fortunes of war fluctuated. The initial phase, dominated by the English victories at Crécy (1346) and Poitiers (1356), ended with Edward III's holding several important French provinces. There followed a period of French success under Bertrand du Guesclin, and by 1400 England had lost most of her territory in France. The young king Henry V (1413–1422) renewed the contest, won the decisive battle of Agincourt (1415), and imposed on the French king the humiliating Treaty of Troyes. Following the death of Henry V, the French, at one time led by Joan of Arc and for a longer time inspired by her, gradually pushed the English out of France. When the war ended in 1453, only the port of Calais remained to console England for her past efforts.

The development of "nationalism" is frequently seen as a result of this long and otherwise barren conflict. Pride in being English was heightened by such national triumphs as Crécy, Poitiers, and Agincourt. French patriotism was strengthened by the victories and the memory of Joan of Arc. In view of this developing "nationalism," the Treaty of Troyes reads rather strangely. Instead of an accord between nations, it is an agreement between individuals, Henry V and the French king, Charles VI (1380–1422). Henry was immediately to become regent of France, governing on behalf of the frequently insane Charles. Following Charles's death, Henry was to become

SOURCE. *English Historical Documents, Volume IV, 1327–1485*, edited by A. R. Myers, pp. 225–226. © Eyre and Spottiswoode, 1969. Reprinted by permission of Oxford University Press, Inc., and Eyre & Spottiswoode (Publishers) Ltd.

king of France. To confirm these arrangements, Henry was to marry Charles's daughter, "our most dear and beloved Katherine." It is as if a family feud had been settled. Undoubtedly some people still viewed war in those terms, but many did not. There is, therefore, an absence of reality surrounding the terms of the Treaty of Troyes. The king of France could not, as it turned out, transfer his land and subjects to a foreign monarch by means of a piece of paper. Because the treaty was so flagrantly at odds with the spirit of the times, it was simply ignored: the French continued their war—not the king's war—to a successful conclusion.

Henry, by the grace of God, King of England, Heir and Regent of France, and Lord of Ireland, for perpetual remembrance, to all Christian people . . . we notify and declare that . . . we have taken a treaty with our father-in-law [Charles of France]; in the which treaty between our father and us, is concluded and agreed, in the form according to the following manner:

First, it is agreed between our said father of France and us, that for as much as by the bond of matrimony made for the good of peace between us and our most dear and most beloved Katherine, the daughter of our said father and of our most dear mother, Isabel his wife, those same Charles and Isabel are made our father and mother, therefore we shall regard them as our father and mother, and honour them as such, and as it fitteth such and so worthy a prince and princess, to be honoured especially before all other temporal princes of this world.

Also, that we will not disturb, distress, nor harass our said father; but he shall hold and possess, as long as he lives, as he holds and possesses at this time, the crown and the royal dignity of France, and the rents, fruits, and profits of the same, to the sustenance of his estate and the charges of the realm; and our foresaid mother shall also hold, as long as she lives, the estate and dignity of queen, according to the manner of the said realm, with a suitable and convenient part of the said rents and profits.

Also that the foresaid Katherine shall take and have dower in our realm of England as queens of England hitherto were wont to take and have, that is to say, to the sum of 40,000 crowns a year; of which two shall always be worth an English noble. . . .

Also, that after the death of our said father, and from thence forward, the crown and realm of France, with all their rights and appurtenances, shall remain and abide and belong to us and our heirs for evermore.

Also for as much as our said father is afflicted with various infirmities in such manner that he may not attend in his own person to arrange for the needs of the realm of France, therefore during the life of our said father the faculty and exercise of governance and disposition of the public good and common profit of the realm of France, with the counsel of nobles and wise men of the realm, . . . shall remain and abide with us, so that henceforward we may govern the same realm, both by ourself and also by others whom, with the counsel of the said nobles, we may be pleased to depute. . . .

Also that we will do our utmost to see that the court of the parlement of France be kept and observed in its authority and superiority, and in all that is due to it, in all manner of places that now, or in time to come, are, or shall be, subject to our said father.

Also that we diligently and truly to the utmost of our power, shall work and act so that justice may be administered and enforced in the realm of France, according to the laws, customs, and rights of the same realm without exception of persons. . . .

Also that we to the utmost of our strength and as soon as it may conveniently be done, shall labour to put into obedience to our father all manner of cities, towns, castles, places, countries, and persons, within the realm of France disobedient and rebellious to our said father, holding or belonging to the party commonly called Dauphin or Armagnac.

Also that all manner of conquests that shall be made by us in the realm of France over the said rebels, outside the duchy of Normandy, shall be done to the profit of the said father. . . .

Also by God's help when it shall happen to us to come to the crown of France, the duchy of Normandy and all other places conquered by us in the realm of France shall be under the commandment, obedience and monarchy of the crown of France.

Also that we will not impose any impositions or exactions, or cause them to be imposed, on the subjects of our said father without reasonable and necessary cause, nor otherwise than for the common good of the said realm of France, and according to the rules and demands of the reasonable and approved laws and customs of the realm.

Also that neither our father nor we nor our brother the Duke of Burgundy shall begin nor make with Charles, styling himself the Dauphin of Viennes, any treaty of peace or accord, except by the counsel and assent of all and each of us three and of the three estates of both of the aforesaid realms.

32

Jack Cade, Proclamation of June 4, 1450. Popular Discontent in the Fifteenth Century

In June 1450, England was approaching a crisis. The Hundred Years' War was coming to a weary and unsuccessful conclusion. Henry VI (1422–1461) was an ineffective king, leaning on and being exploited by various strongmen, such as the recently assassinated duke of Suffolk. And Kent, traditionally unruly and rebellious, was up in arms again.

The rebels of Kent in 1450 were unlike those of the Peasants' Revolt of 1381. They included not only peasants but yeomen, tradesmen, and a sprinkling of gentlemen. Their protest was not against agrarian conditions but the form and failure of the king's government, and their gathering at first was orderly and peaceful. Below is the declaration issued on their behalf by Jack Cade, their captain. They indicted the "false and unsuitable persons" that surrounded the king. For advice he should, instead, look to "men of his true blood from his royal realm," meaning Richard duke of York, the kingdom's greatest magnate and the heir to the throne. Particularly hateful were the extortioners who lined their own pockets and subverted justice—the sheriffs of Kent, the officers of the King's Bench, and those of the Exchequer, whose "green wax" sealed the writs used to enforce payments to the crown.

When the king fled, the rebels entered London and beheaded some royal advisers. The offer of pardon and the realization that they could not them-

SOURCE. B. Wilkinson, *Constitutional History of England in the Fifteenth Century (1399–1485) with illustrative documents,* London: Longmans, Green and Co., Ltd., 1964, pp. 82–86. Reprinted by permission of Longmans, Green and Co., Ltd.

selves form a government persuaded the rebels to return to their homes. King, magnates, and parliament joined to suppress the sporadic violence that continued, but they preserved the conditions that had provoked the rebels and which would eventually lead to the outbreak of the Wars of the Roses and the downfall of the Lancastrian dynasty.

The declaration and the rebellion of which it was a part illustrate the role of violence in the development of the English constitution. What made men believe that it was worthwhile to express their feelings against the government in this overt and potentially fatal fashion? And how were the officials of the government affected by the realization that they faced not only the legal censures of the constitution but the direct action of the popular will?

These are the points, causes, and discontents, relating to the gathering and assembly of us, the king's liege men of Kent, on the 3rd day of June, 1450, the twenty-ninth year of our sovereign lord the king. We trust to almighty God that with the help and grace of God and of our sovereign lord the king, and of the poor commons of England, we may find a remedy; if not, we shall die in the attempt.

We believe that the king our sovereign lord is betrayed by the insatiable covetousness and malicious purpose of certain false and unsuitable persons who are around his highness day and night. They duly inform him that good is evil and evil is good, as the Scriptures testify: *Woe to ye who say that good is bad and bad good.*

Also, they assert that at his pleasure our sovereign lord is above his laws, and that he may make them and break them as he pleases, without any distinction. The contrary is true. Otherwise, he would not have sworn to keep them. And we conceive it to be the highest point of treason for any subject to cause his prince to fall into perjury. . . .

Also, they say that the king should live upon his commons, and that their bodies and goods are the king's. The contrary is true, for if it were not, the king would never need parliament to sit, or have to ask for supplies from his commons. . . .

Also, we seek remedy for this: that the false traitors, will suffer no man to come to the king's presence for any reason, unless there is a bribe such as ought not to be; nor ought there to be any bribery about the king's person, but any man should have access to him to ask for his grace, or for his judgement in such cases as pertain to the king. . . .

Also, the law serves no other purpose in these days except to do wrong, for by virtue of the law almost no cause is heard except dishonest ones, through bribery, fear or favour; and so there is no wise remedy in the court of conscience.

Also, we say that our sovereign lord may understand this. His false council has lost his law; his merchandise is lost; his common people are destroyed; the sea is lost; France is lost. The king himself is so placed that he may not pay for his meat and drink. He owes more than ever any king of England ought. For daily, when anything should fall to him by his laws, immediately his traitors around him ask it from him. . . .

Also, we will have it known that we will not rob or thieve or steal; but that when the above wrongs have been amended, then we will go home. Wherefore, we exhort all the king's true liegemen to help and to support us. Whoever he be, who does not will that these wrongs be amended, he is falser than a Jew or a Saracen; and we shall as willingly live and die against him as against a Saracen or Jew. He who is against us in this cause, him shall we mark, for he is no true liegeman of the king.

Also, his true commons desire that the king will send away from him all the false progeny and affinity of the duke of Suffolk. These are openly known, and should be punished according to the law of the land. And the king should take about his noble person men of his true blood from his royal realm, that is to say, the high and mighty prince the duke of York, exiled from our sovereign lord's person by the suggestions of those false traitors the duke of Suffolk and his affinity. . . .

Also, they desire that all extortioners be laid low; that is to say the green wax which is falsely used to the perpetual hurt and destruction of the commons of Kent; and also the extortioners of the King's Bench, which is a heavy charge on all the commons without any provision for this made by our sovereign lord and his true council.

Also, the taking of wheat and other grains which is an unbearable injury to the commons, without any provision for it by our sovereign lord and his true council; for his commons may no longer bear it.

Also, the Statute of Labourers and the great extortioners of Kent, that is to say, Slegge, Crowmer, Isle and Robert Est.

Also, we move and desire that the same true justice may be sent into Kent, by certain true lords and knights, who will enquire regarding all such bribers and traitors. The justices are to do true judgement upon them, whosoever they may be. . . .

Also, when these defaults have been duly remedied, from henceforth no person about the king's person shall take any manner of bribe, upon pain of death, for speeding or hindering any bill or petition or cause. Thus, our sovereign lord shall reign and rule with great honour, and have the love of God and of his people. For he shall have such great love of his people that he shall, with God's help, conquer where he will. As for us, we shall always be ready to defend our country from all nations with our own goods, and to go with our sovereign lord, as his true liegeman, wherever he will command.

33

The *Paston Letters* (1448-1455). Political Disorder and the Wars of the Roses

The collection of letters and related documents known today as the *Paston Letters* is one of the most valuable historical sources for the study of England in the late Middle Ages. The Pastons were an old Norfolk family which, through good marriages and important political and economic contacts, achieved some prosperity and social standing in the middle of the fifteenth century. The thousand or so letters written by or to members of this remarkable family are unique in their scope and, of course, in the fact that they have survived into modern times.

The *Paston Letters* touch on many aspects of English life in the fifteenth century. Education, marriage and the position of women in general, household management, and the difficulties involved in protecting property rights are all prominently mentioned. Many of the letters also provide insight into the political instability of the period. The letters reprinted below deal with several aspects of the violence and disorder resulting from the weakness of Henry VI's government—the need to defend one's home against belligerent neighbors, the constant threat of piracy and kidnapping, and the beginnings of that institutionalized violence known as the Wars of the Roses.

The first edited collection of Paston letters, most of the originals of which

SOURCE. *Selections from the Paston Letters,* ed. Alice Drayton Greenwood, London: G. Bell & Sons, Ltd., 1920, pp. 12–13, 36–37, 79–80.

are now deposited in the British Museum, was begun in 1787 by a Norfolk antiquarian named John Fenn. Many other editions have since appeared, the most famous being that of James Gairdner in six volumes (1904).

Margaret Paston to John Paston, April 1448

RIGHT worshipful husband, I recommend me to you, and pray you to get some Cross Bows and Wyndacs to bind them with and Quarrels, for your houses here be so low that there may none man shoot out with no long bow, though we had never so much need.

I suppose ye should have such things of Sir John Fastolf, if ye would send to him; and also I would ye should get two or three short Pole-axes to keep with doors, and as many Jacks, and ye may.

Partrich and his fellowship are sore afraid that ye would enter again upon them, and they have made great ordnance within the house, and it is told me they have made bars to bar the doors cross wise, and they have made wickets on every quarter of the house to shoot out at, both with bows and with hand-guns; and the holes that be made for hand-guns they be scarce knee high from the plancher (*floor*) and of such holes be made five, there can none man shoot out at them with no hand-bows.

Purry fell in fellowship with William Hasard at Quarles's, and told him that he would come and drink with Partrich and with him, and he said he should be welcome, and after noon he went thither for to espy what they did and what fellowship they had with them; and when he came thither the doors were fast sparred and there were none folks with them but Mariott, and Capron and his wife, and Quarles's wife, and another man in a black, went somewhat halting, I suppose by his words that it was Norfolk at Gimmingham; and the said Purry espied all these foresaid things.

And Mariott and his fellowship had much great language that shall be told you when ye come home.

I pray you that ye will vouchsafe to do buy for me one lb. of Almonds and one lb. of sugar, that ye will do buy some frieze to make of your child his gowns, ye shall have best cheap, and best choice of Hay's wife, as it is told me. And that ye will buy a yard of broad cloth of black for one hood for me of 44*d*. or four Shillings a yard, for there is neither good cloth nor good frieze in this town. As for the child his gowns and I have them, I will do them maken (*have them made*).

The Trinity have you in his keeping, and send you good speed in all your matters.

Agnes Paston to John Paston, 12 March 1450

SON, I greet you, and send you God's blessing and mine; as for my daughter your wife she fareth well, blessed be God! as a woman in her plight may do, and all your Sons and Daughters.

And for as much as ye will send me no tidings, I send you such as be in this Country; Richard Lynsted came this day from Paston and let me weet, that on Saturday last past, Dravell, half-brother to Warren Harman, was taken with enemies, walking by the Sea side, and have him forth with them, and they took two Pilgrims, a man and a woman, and they robbed the woman and let her go, and led the man to the Sea; and when they knew he was a Pilgrim they gave him money, and set him again on the land; and they have this week taken four Vessels of Winterton, and Happisborough and Eccles.

Men be sore afraid for taking of men, for there be ten great Vessels of the Enemy's; God give grace that the sea may be better kept than it is now, or else it shall be a perilous dwelling by the sea coast. . . .

Written at Norwich, the Wednesday next before Saint Gregory. . . .

John Crane to John Paston, 25 May 1455

RIGHT worshipful and entirely well beloved Sir, I recommend me unto you, desiring heartily to hear of your welfare.

Furthermore letting you weet, as for such Tidings as we have here, these three Lords be dead, the Duke of Somerset, the Earl of Northumberland, and the Lord Clifford; and as for any other men of name, I know none, save only Cotton of Cambridgeshire.

As for any other Lords, many of them be hurt, and as for Fylongley he liveth, and fareth well, as far as I can enquire, &c.

And as for any great Multitude of people that there was, as we can tell, there was at most slain six score; and as for the Lords that were with the King, they and their men were pilled and spoiled out of all their Harness and Horses; and as for what Rule we shall have yet I weet not, save only there be made new certain Officers.

My Lord of York, Constable of England; my Lord of Warwick is made Captain of Calais; my Lord Bourchier is made Treasurer of England; and as yet other Tidings have I none.

And as for Our Sovereign Lord, thanked be God, he hath no great harm.

No more to you at this time, but I pray you send this Letter to my

Mistress Paston, when ye have seen it; praying you to remember my Sister Margaret against the time that she shall be made a Nun.

Written at Lamehith (*Lambeth*) on Whitsunday, &c.

By your Cousin,

34

Thomas More, *Utopia* (1516). Description of Tudor England

Sir Thomas More (1478–1535), known to his contemporaries as Henry VIII's lord chancellor and a martyr for Roman Catholicism, is best remembered today as the author of *Utopia*. Created by More out of Greek words, the title means "Noplace." The book is a dialogue between More and a world traveler named Raphael Hythloday—Dispenser of Nonsense. Raphael contrasts favorably the wise and rational institutions and practices of Utopia with those of Christian Europe. Before discussing Utopia, however, he recalls a conversation he once had in the house of Archbishop Morton, Henry VII's lord chancellor. This affords him the opportunity to describe the condition of things in England; part of that description is reproduced below.

Being a humanist, More consciously patterned his writing and thinking after that of the ancients, writing the purest Latin and using Plato's *Republic* as the model for his *Utopia*. As he was English and Northern European, his humanism had a Christian flavor, harking back to the writings and virtues of the Church Fathers and the New Testament as well as to those of pagan Greeks and Romans. His interest in humanity and his criticism of the

SOURCE.   St. Thomas More, *Utopia,* edited by Edward Surtz, S. J. and J. H. Hexter, pp. 61, 63, 65, 67, 69, 71. Copyright © 1965 by Yale University. Reprinted by permission of Yale University Press.

foolishness he saw about him were thus in the name of both reason and Christianity.

In the dialogue, Raphael is outspoken in his praise and criticism; More is subdued and defensive. It remains a problem to know the extent to which he is, in fact, speaking for More, the author, and to know just how literally anything is to be taken in this half-serious, half-jesting, satire of Europe in the sixteenth century.

Utopia, originally published in Latin in 1516, has been translated into English many times as well as into all major languages.

"It happened one day that I was at his table when a layman, learned in the laws of your country, was present. Availing himself of some opportunity or other, he began to speak punctiliously of the strict justice which was then dealt out to thieves. They were everywhere executed, he reported, as many as twenty at a time being hanged on one gallows, and added that he wondered all the more, though so few escaped execution, by what bad luck the whole country was still infested with them. I dared be free in expressing my opinions without reserve at the Cardinal's table, so I said to him:

" 'You need not wonder, for this manner of punishing thieves goes beyond justice and is not for the public good. It is too harsh a penalty for theft and yet is not a sufficient deterrent. Theft alone is not a grave offense that ought to be punished with death, and no penalty that can be devised is sufficient to restrain from acts of robbery those who have no other means of getting a livelihood. In this respect not your country alone but a great part of our world resembles bad schoolmasters, who would rather beat than teach their scholars. You ordain grievous and terrible punishments for a thief when it would have been much better to provide some means of getting a living, that no one should be under this terrible necessity first of stealing and then of dying for it.' . . .

" 'Now there is the great number of noblemen who not only live idle themselves like drones on the labors of others, as for instance the tenants of their estates whom they fleece to the utmost by increasing the returns (for that is the only economy they know of, being otherwise so extravagant as to bring themselves to beggary!) but who also carry about with them a huge crowd of idle attendants who have never learned a trade for a livelihood. As soon as their master dies or they themselves fall sick, these men are turned out at once, for the idle are maintained more readily than the sick, and often the heir is not able to support as large a household as his father did, at any rate at first.

" 'In the meantime the fellows devote all their energies to starving, if they do not to robbing. Indeed what can they do? . . .

" 'Yet this is not the only situation that makes thieving necessary. There is another which, as I believe, is more special to you Englishmen.'

" 'What is that?' asked the Cardinal.

" 'Your sheep,' I answered, 'which are usually so tame and so cheaply fed, begin now, according to report, to be so greedy and wild that they devour human beings themselves and devastate and depopulate fields, houses, and towns. In all those parts of the realm where the finest and therefore costliest wool is produced, there are noblemen, gentlemen, and even some abbots, though otherwise holy men, who are not satisfied with the annual revenues and profits which their predecessors used to derive from their estates. They are not content, by leading an idle and sumptuous life, to do no good to their country; they must also do it positive harm. They leave no ground to be tilled; they enclose every bit of land for pasture; they pull down houses and destroy towns, leaving only the church to pen the sheep in. And, as if enough English land were not wasted on ranges and preserves of game, those good fellows turn all human habitations and all cultivated lands into a wilderness.

" 'Consequently, in order that one insatiable glutton and accursed plague of his native land may join field to field and surround many thousand acres with one fence, tenants are evicted. Some of them, either circumvented by fraud or overwhelmed by violence, are stripped even of their own property, or else, wearied by unjust acts, are driven to sell. By hook or by crook the poor wretches are compelled to leave their homes—men and women, husbands and wives, orphans and widows, parents with little children and a household not rich but numerous, since farm work requires many hands. Away they must go, I say, from the only homes familiar and known to them, and they find no shelter to go to. All their household goods which would not fetch a great price if they could wait for a purchaser, since they must be thrust out, they sell for a trifle.

" 'After they have soon spent that trifle in wandering from place to place, what remains for them but to steal and be hanged—justly, you may say!—or to wander and beg. And yet even in the latter case they are cast into prison as vagrants for going about idle when, though they most eagerly offer their labor, there is no one to hire them. For there is no farm work, to which they have been trained, to be had, when there is no land for plowing left. A single shepherd or herdsman is sufficient for grazing livestock on that land for whose cultivation many hands were once required to make it raise crops.

" 'A result of this situation is that the price of food has risen steeply in many localities. Indeed, the price of raw wools has climbed so high that the English poor who used to make cloth cannot possibly buy them, and so great numbers are driven from work into idleness. One reason is that, after the great increase in pasture land, a plague carried off a vast multitude of sheep as though God were punishing greed by sending upon the sheep a murrain—which should have fallen on the owners' heads more justly! But, however much the number of sheep increases, their price does not decrease a farthing because, though you cannot brand that a monopoly which is a sale by more than one person, yet their sale is certainly an oligopoly, for all sheep have come into the hands of a few men, and those already rich, who are not obliged to sell before they wish and who do not wish until they get the price they ask. . . .

" 'Thus, the unscrupulous greed of a few is ruining the very thing by virtue of which your island was once counted fortunate in the extreme. For the high price of food is causing everyone to get rid of as many of his household as possible, and what, I ask, have they to do but to beg, or—a course more readily embraced by men of mettle—to become robbers?

" 'In addition, alongside this wretched need and poverty you find ill-timed luxury. Not only the servants of noblemen but the craftsmen and almost the clodhoppers themselves, in fact all classes alike, are given to much ostentatious sumptuousness of dress and to excessive indulgence at table. Do not dives, brothels, and those other places as bad as brothels, to wit, wine shops and alehouses—do not all those crooked games of chance, dice, cards, backgammon, ball, bowling, and quoits, soon drain the purses of their votaries and send them off to rob someone?

" 'Cast out these ruinous plagues. Make laws that the destroyers of farmsteads and country villages should either restore them or hand them over to people who will restore them and who are ready to build. Restrict this right to rich individuals to buy up everything and this license to exercise a kind of monopoly for themselves. Let fewer be brought up in idleness. Let farming be resumed and let cloth-working be restored once more that there may be honest jobs to employ usefully that idle throng, whether those whom hitherto pauperism has made thieves or those who, now being vagrants or lazy servants, in either case are likely to turn out thieves. Assuredly, unless you remedy these evils, it is useless for you to boast of the justice you execute in the punishment of theft. Such justice is more showy than really just or beneficial. When you allow your youths to be badly brought up and their characters, even from early years, to become more and more corrupt, to be punished, of course, when, as grown-up men, they commit the crimes which from boyhood they have shown every prospect of committing, what else, I ask, do you do but first create thieves and then become the very agents of their punishment?' "

35

An Act Concerning Punishment of Beggars and Vagabonds (1531)

The sixteenth century was a period of rapid and far-reaching economic and social change. Enterprising men, such as the farmers who enclosed land and the Merchant Adventurers who traded in woolen cloth with the Netherlands, had the opportunity of acquiring great wealth. But others, especially those displaced by enclosures, were less fortunate. Many became the beggars and vagabonds, who were a concern of Thomas More in his *Utopia* and of the English government as well.

The statute below is parliament's attempted solution to this problem in 1531. Its basic character is indicated in the title, "An Act Concerning Punishment of Beggars and Vagabonds." Nevertheless, parliament had sufficient vision to differentiate "aged poor and impotent persons" from "persons being whole and mighty in body and able to labour." The former were authorized to beg within their local communities; the latter were to be whipped and sent back to their own parishes, there to live as "a true man ought to do." This act was the most harsh and punitive of the poor laws passed during the Tudor period. Later acts, beginning in 1536 and finally assuming definitive form in 1598 and 1601, stipulated that the honest poor were to be assisted by a tax levied on the parish. Sturdy beggars, although still to be whipped and sent home if caught outside their own parish, were to be provided with parish-sponsored work.

SOURCE.   J. R. Tanner, *Tudor Constitutional Documents, A.D. 1485–1603, with an Historical Commentary*, Cambridge: At the University Press, 1940, pp. 475–479. Reprinted by permission of Cambridge University Press.

Such legislation expanded the duties of the already busy justices of the peace and helped to create the parish as a subunit of county government with the primary responsibility for the oversight of the poor. Equally important, the poor laws, harsh though they might appear, marked the beginning of the attempt by the royal government to solve problems that had formerly been left to the Church and to local charity. Its attempts at providing for the commonwealth, the commonweal or the common good, reveal the beginning of the national government's assumption of responsibility for the social and economic welfare of the people.

Where in all places throughout this realm of England vagabonds and beggars have of long time increased and daily do increase in great and excessive numbers, by the occasion of idleness, mother and root of all vices, whereby hath insurged and sprung and daily insurgeth and springeth continual thefts, murders, and other heinous offences and great enormities, to the high displeasure of God, the inquietation and damage of the King's people, and to the marvellous disturbance of the common weal of this realm. . . . Be it therefore enacted . . . That the Justices of the Peace . . . shall make diligent search and enquiry of all aged, poor, and impotent persons which live or of necessity be compelled to live by alms of the charity of the people that be or shall be hereafter abiding . . . within the limits of their division, and after and upon such search made the said Justices . . . shall have power and authority by their discretions to enable to beg, within such . . . limits as they shall appoint, such of the said impotent persons which they shall find and think most convenient within the limits of their division to live of the charity and alms of the people, and to give in commandment to every such aged and impotent beggar (by them enabled) that none of them shall beg without the limits to them so appointed, and shall also register and write the names of every such impotent beggar (by them appointed) in a bill or roll indented, the one part thereof to remain with themselves and the other part by them to be certified before the Justices of Peace at the next Sessions after such search . . . there to remain under the keeping of the Custos Rotulorum; And that the said Justices of Peace . . . shall make and deliver to every such impotent person by them enabled to beg, a letter containing the name of such impotent person and witnessing that he is authorised to beg and the limits within which he is appointed to beg, the same letter to be sealed with such . . . seals as shall be engraved with the name of the limit wherein such impotent person shall be appointed to beg in, and to be subscribed with the name of one of the said Justices. . . . And if any such impotent person so authorised to beg do beg in any other place than within such limits that he shall be assigned unto, that then the Justices of Peace . . . shall by their discretions punish all such persons by imprisonment in the stocks by the space of 2 days and 2 nights, giving them but only bread and water, and after that cause every such impotent person to be sworn to return again without delay to the [*limits* . . .] where they be authorised to beg in.

III.   And be it further enacted . . . That if any person or persons being whole and mighty in body and able to labour, . . . or if any man or woman being whole and mighty in body and able to labour having no land, master, nor using any lawful merchandise, craft, or mystery, whereby he might get his living . . . be vagrant and can give none reckoning how he doth lawfully get his living, that then it shall be lawful to the constables and all other the King's officers, ministers, and subjects of every town, parish, and hamlet to arrest the said vagabonds and idle persons and them to bring to any of the Justices of Peace of the same shire or liberty . . . and that every such Justice of Peace . . . shall cause every such idle person so to him brought to be had to the next market town or other place where the said Justices of Peace . . . shall think most convenient, . . . and there to be tied to the end of a cart naked and be beaten with whips throughout the same market town or other place till his body be bloody by reason of such whipping; and after such punishment and whipping had, the person so punished . . . shall be enjoined upon his oath to return forthwith without delay in the next and straight way to the place where he was born, or where he last dwelled before the same punishment by the space of 3 years, and there put himself to labour like as a true man oweth to do. . . .

IV.   And be it enacted . . . That scholars of the Universities of Oxford and Cambridge that go about begging, not being authorised under the seal of the said Universities . . . and all and singular shipment pretending losses of their ships and goods of the sea going about the country begging without sufficient authority witnessing the same, shall be punished and ordered in manner and form as is above rehearsed of strong beggars . . . and all other idle persons going about in any countries or abiding in any city, borough, or town, some of them using divers and subtile crafty and unlawful games and plays, and some of them feigning themselves to have knowledge in physic, physnamy, palmistry, or other crafty sciences, whereby they bear the people in hand that they can tell their destinies, deceases, and fortunes, and such other like fantastical imaginations, to the great deceit of the King's subjects, shall upon examination had before two Justices of Peace, whereof the one shall be of the Quorum, if he by provable witness be found guilty of any such deceits, be punished by whipping at two days together after the manner above rehearsed: And if he eftsoons offend in the said offence or any like offence, then to be scourged two days and the third day to be put upon the pillory from 9 of the clock till 11 before noon of the same day, and to have one of his ears cut off; and if he offend the third time, to have like punishment with whipping, standing on the pillory, and to have his other ear cut off.

36

Reformation Statutes: Act in Restraint of Appeals (1533), Act of Supremacy (1534)

Henry VIII (1509–1547) called the Reformation Parliament in 1529, when it became apparent that his chancellor, Cardinal Wolsey, could not obtain from Rome the annulment of Henry's marriage to Catherine of Aragon. Henry's patience had run out; he would have a legitimate heir and that by Ann Boleyn. He hoped that parliament could succeed where Wolsey had failed, frightening the pope into thinking England might follow the example of Lutheran Germany. Henry, however, had to wait another three and one-half years before he was free of Catherine and able to marry Ann. The Act in Restraint of Appeals, the instrument by which this was made possible, shows the influence of his new adviser, Thomas Cromwell. Though the act may seem long and convoluted, it was, in fact, very simple. Its effect was to stop all appeals to Rome, a thoroughgoing application of the idea set forth in the Statute of Praemunire. Thus Henry's divorce from Catherine also began his reformation of the Church, both accomplished simply by a juris-

SOURCE. J. R. Tanner, *Tudor Constitutional Documents, A.D. 1485–1603, with an Historical Commentary,* Cambridge: At the University Press, 1940, pp. 41–45, 47–48. Reprinted by permission of Cambridge University Press.

dictional break with Rome. The following year, 1534, the Act of Supremacy recognized Henry as "Supreme Head of the Church of England." Five years later, the Act of Six Articles affirmed that the doctrine and practice of the English church should remain Catholic.

It should be noted in the acts reprinted below that parliament still retained its medieval reticence openly to legislate or to change the law, holding that the law was too sacred and eternal simply to be made. Thus the really significant things are declared in the preambles, "that this realm of England is an empire" (i.e., a sovereign nation-state), and that "the King's Majesty justly and rightfully is . . . the supreme head of the Church of England." The strictly legislative parts of the statutes confirm what is already taken for granted in the preambles, work out useful consequences, and provide punishment for violations. Although parliament's power is thus limited in concept, the fact remains that the Reformation Parliament sat over a period of seven years, enacted more important statutes than had any previous parliament, provided many men with legislative experience, and accustomed people to parliament's participation in the making of important decisions. Parliament, eclipsed by the Yorkist kings (1461–1485) and until now by the Tudors, began a new stage of its development, a development made all the more significant by the suppression of representative institutions by absolute monarchs on the continent.

AN ACT THAT THE APPEALS IN SUCH CASES AS HAVE BEEN USED TO BE PURSUED TO THE SEE OF ROME SHALL NOT BE FROM HENCEFORTH HAD NOR USED BUT WITHIN THIS REALM

Where by divers sundry old authentic histories and chronicles it is manifestly declared and expressed that this realm of England is an empire, and so hath been accepted in the world, governed by one Supreme Head and King having the dignity and royal estate of the imperial Crown of the same, unto whom a body politic, compact of all sorts and degrees of people divided in terms and by names of Spiritualty and Temporalty, be bounden and owe to bear next to God a natural and humble obedience; he being also institute and furnished by the goodness and sufferance of Almighty God with plenary, whole, and entire power, preeminence, authority, prerogative, and jurisdiction to render and yield justice and final determination to all manner of folk residents or subjects within this his realm, in all causes, matters, debates, and contentions happening to occur, insurge, or begin within the limits thereof, without restraint or provocation to any foreign princes or protentates of the world: the body spiritual whereof having power when any cause of the law divine happened to come in question or of spiritual learning, then it was declared, interpreted, and shewed by that part of the said body politic called the Spiritualty, now being usually called the English Church, which always hath been reputed and also found of that sort that both for knowledge, integrity, and sufficiency of number, it hath been always thought and is also at this hour sufficient and meet of itself, without the intermeddling of any exterior person or persons, to declare and determine all such doubts and to administer all such offices and duties as to their rooms spiritual doth appertain; For the due administration whereof and to keep them from corruption and sinister affection the King's most noble progenitors, and the antecessors of the nobles of this realm, have sufficiently endowed the said Church both with honour and possessions: And the laws temporal for trial of propiety of lands and goods, and for the conservation of the people of this realm in unity and peace without ravin or spoil, was and yet is administered, adjudged, and executed by sundry judges and administers of the other part of the said body politic called the Temporalty, and both their authorities and jurisdictions do conjoin together in the due administration of justice the one to help the other: And whereas the King his most noble progenitors, and the Nobility and Commons of this said realm, at divers and sundry Parliaments as well in the time of King Edward the First, Edward the Third, Richard the Second, Henry the Fourth, and other noble kings of this realm, made sundry ordinances, laws, statutes, and provisions for the entire and sure conservation of the prerogatives . . . to keep it from the annoyance as well of the see of Rome as from the authority of other foreign potentates attempting the diminution or violation thereof. . . . And notwithstanding the said good estatutes and ordinances made in the time of the King's most noble progenitors . . . divers and sundry inconveniences and dangers not provided for plainly by the said former acts, statutes, and ordinances have risen and sprung by reason of appeals sued out of this realm to the see of Rome . . . not only to the great inquietation, vexation, trouble, costs, and charges of the King's Highness and many of his subjects and residents in this his realm, but also to the great delay and let to the true and speedy determination of the said causes. . . . In consideration whereof the King's Highness, his Nobles and Commons . . . doth therefore by his royal assent and by the assent of the Lords spiritual and temporal and the Commons . . . enact, establish, and ordain that all causes testamentary, causes of matrimony and divorces, rights of tithes, oblations, and obventions . . . shall be from henceforth heard, examined, discussed, clearly finally and definitively adjudged and determined, within the King's jurisdiction and authority and not elsewhere, . . . any foreign inhibitions, appeals . . . or any other process or impediments of what natures, names, qualities, or conditions soever they be, from the see of Rome or any other foreign courts or potentates of the world . . . notwithstanding. . . . As also that all spiritual prelates, pastors, ministers, and curates within this realm and the dominions of the same shall and may use, minister, execute, and do, or cause to be used, ministered, executed, and done, all sacraments, sacramentals, divine services, and all other things within the said realm and dominions unto all the subjects of the same as Catholic and Christian men owe to do; Any foreign citations . . . from or to the see of Rome or any other foreign prince . . . notwithstanding. And if any of the said spiritual persons, by the occasion of the said fulminations of any of the same interdictions . . . do at any time hereafter refuse to minister or to cause to be ministered the said sacraments and sacramentals and other divine services in form as is aforesaid, shall for every such time or times that they or any of them do refuse so to do or to cause to be done, have one year's imprisonment and to make fine and ransom at the King's pleasure.

II. And it is further enacted . . . that if any person or persons . . . do attempt, move, purchase, or procure, from or to the see of Rome or from or to any other foreign court or courts out of this realm, any manner foreign process . . . or judgments, of what nature, kind, or quality soever they be, or execute any of the same process . . . that then every person or persons so doing . . . being convict of the same, for every such default shall incur and run in the same pains, penalties, and forfeitures ordained and provided by the statute of provision and praemunire made in the sixteenth year of the reign of . . . King Richard the Second.

AN ACT CONCERNING THE KING'S HIGHNESS TO BE SUPREME HEAD OF THE CHURCH OF ENGLAND AND TO HAVE AUTHORITY TO REFORM AND REDRESS ALL ERRORS, HERESIES, AND ABUSES IN THE SAME

Albeit the King's Majesty justly and rightfully is and ought to be the Supreme Head of the Church of England, and so is recognised by the clergy of this realm in their Convocations; yet neverthless for corroboration and confirmation thereof, and for increase of virtue in Christ's religion within this realm of England, and to repress and extirp all errors, heresies, and other enormities and abuses heretofore used in the same, Be it enacted by authority of this present Parliament that the King our Sovereign Lord, his heirs and successors kings of this realm, shall be taken, accepted, and reputed the only Supreme Head in earth of the Church of England called *Anglicana Ecclesia,* and shall have and enjoy annexed and united to the imperial Crown of this realm as well the title and style thereof, as all honours, dignities, preeminences, jurisdictions, privileges, authorities, immunities, profits, and commodities, to the said dignity of Supreme Head of the same Church belonging and appertaining: And that our said Sovereign Lord, his heirs and successors kings of this realm, shall have full power and authority from time to time to visit, repress, redress, reform, order, correct, restrain, and amend all such errors, heresies, abuses, offences, contempts, and enormities, whatsoever they be, which by any manner spiritual authority or jurisdiction ought or may lawfully be reformed, repressed, ordered, redressed, corrected, restrained, or amended, most to the pleasure of Almighty God, the increase of virtue in Christ's religion, and for the conservation of the peace, unity, and tranquillity of this realm: any usage, custom, foreign laws, foreign authority, prescription, or any other thing or things to the contrary hereof notwithstanding.

37

Royal Proclamation Announcing New Coinage (1551)

A royal proclamation was an ordinance issued by the king with the advice of his council and authenticated by the Great Seal. Such proclamations dealt with many matters of concern to the government, from coinage as in that of October 30, 1551, reproduced below, to religion, monopolies, and land enclosures. More than anything else, proclamations reveal a vigorous royal administration dealing with the practical problems of government.

SOURCE.   Paul L. Hughes and James F. Larkin, eds., *Tudor Royal Proclamations*, Volume I: *The Early Tudors (1485–1553)*, New Haven and London: Yale University Press, 1964, pp. 535–536. Reprinted by permission of Yale University Press.

5s. Piece

2s. 6d. Piece

Sterling shilling

6d. Piece

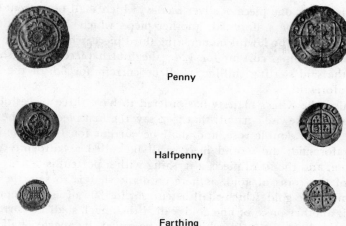

Penny

Halfpenny

Farthing

PLATE A
(by courtesy of the Trustees of the British Museum).

One of the most serious problems was how to respond to the dramatic price rise. Whereas prices had remained relatively stable during the fifteenth century, now they spurted upwards, more than doubling in the first half of the sixteenth. This was due to a growing population and also to a quickening of the European economy. By mid century, England suffered from uncontrolled inflation, hastened along first by Henry VIII's war spending and then by successive devaluations of the English coinage. Although England's coinage was not restored to its traditional soundness until early in the reign of Elizabeth I (1558–1603), this proclamation of Edward VI (1547–1553) was an attempt to move in that direction.

The proclamation gives an insight into the problem of obtaining a stable currency during a time of runaway inflation. It shows already in existence several of the English coins that remained standard throughout the next four centuries and did not disappear until only recently—for example, the penny, halfpenny, and farthing, the shilling of 12 pence, and the half shilling or sixpence (see Plate A). Finally, the proclamation is interesting as an instrument of royal prerogative. Its frequent use raises the question of its relationship to a parliamentary statute, usually considered the supreme instrument of the sovereign Tudor state.

The king's majesty hath ordered and established to be made within his mints these several coins, as well of silver in fineness of the standard sterling, as also of gold, as hereafter ensueth:

That is to say, one piece of silver money, which shall be current for 5s. of the lawful moneys aforesaid; another piece, which shall be called the piece of 2s. 6d. of the lawful moneys; the third piece, which shall be called the sterling shilling, current for 12d.; the fourth piece, which shall be half of the said sterling shilling, shall be current for 6d. of the lawful moneys aforesaid.

And also, the King's majesty has ordered to have three pieces of small moneys made likewise current: that is to say, the first piece shall be called a penny with a double rose, and shall be current for 1d. of the lawful moneys aforesaid; the second piece shall be called a halfpenny with a single rose; and the third piece, a farthing with a portcullis.

And of the coins of gold, as here ensueth: that is to say, the whole sovereign of fine gold, which shall be current for 30s. of lawful moneys of England; another piece of fine gold, called the angel, shall be current for 10s.; the third piece of gold, which shall be called the angelet, half of the angel, current for 5s. of lawful moneys aforesaid;

And further, a whole sovereign, of crown gold, shall be current for 20s.; the second piece of crown gold, which shall be called the half-sovereign, shall be current for 10s.; and the third piece of crown gold, which shall be called a crown, current for 5s.; the fourth piece of crown gold, which shall be called the half-crown, which shall be current for 2s. 6d. of the lawful moneys aforesaid;

Straightly charg[ing] and command[ing] all manner of persons within his realms and dominions to receive and pay the said several pieces of moneys, as well of silver as of gold, at the several rates before rehearsed; under pain of the King's high displeasure, and to be further punished as his highness shall think convenient.

And his express commandment is that all such base moneys which his majesty did lately by his several proclamations reduce to the value of a lower rate shall pass and go current in payment in like manner and sort as his highness' last proclamation did declare, until such time as his majesty's mints may with diligence convert the same into the said new coins, which his majesty mindeth to have done with all possible expedition.

And his majesty signifieth to all his loving subjects that, if they do bring in any quantity of money now current into his grace's mints within the Tower of London, they shall have the same received there by tale at the value as they be now current upon bills; and they shall, in as convenient time as may, be repaid for the said moneys now current by tale in other the King's majesty's new moneys afore declared.

John Foxe, *Acts and Monuments* (1563). The Burning of Archbishop Cranmer, 1556

Thomas Cranmer (1489–1556) was the central figure of the English Reformation. Upon becoming Archbishop of Canterbury in 1533, he nullified Henry VIII's marriage to Catherine of Aragon. He wrote the prayer books of 1549 and 1552 by which the ceremony of the English church became Protestant. He suffered martyrdom under Bloody Mary. Yet, he was a retiring and scholarly man, little interested in politics save for his adherence to the king's position as supreme head of the Church of England. He remained faithful to Henry's Anglo-Catholicism, although his personal inclination toward Protestantism enabled him to adapt to the religious settlements of Edward VI (1547–1553).

The accession of Mary (1553–1558) placed Cranmer in a dilemma, caught between his belief in Mary's right to determine England's religion and his own adherence to Protestantism. His high position in the Church and his past actions made Mary and the Catholic Church determined to have the example of his returning to orthodoxy. Cranmer's difficulties were intensified by his having not a resolute heart but an overcareful mind, which could see the merits of both sides of a question and which realized the tentativeness of truth and the difficulty of attaining it. Perhaps this caused him to sign the six recantations admitting his former errors. Or was it the fires that certainly awaited him if he refused? At the last moment, however, just as his examiners were expecting his public confession, he changed his mind again and by a seventh recantation voided the previous six. The Catholics were

SOURCE. John Foxe, *The Acts and Monuments of John Foxe*, ed. Stephen Reed Cattley, Vol. VIII, London: R. B. Seeley and W. Burnside, 1839, pp. 88–90.

dashed, and Protestants rejoiced and took strength from his glorious martyrdom.

Cranmer's death at the stake and that of almost 300 others made a vivid impression on the people of England, an impression intensified and kept alive by John Foxe's *Acts and Monuments* (1563). Better known as Foxe's *Book of Martyrs,* it recounted and by its woodcuts depicted the sufferings and heroic martyrdoms of those who died in England for their Protestant faith. Below is its account of Thomas Cranmer.

Foxe's *Book of Martyrs* became after the Bible easily the most popular and influential book in England. It justified England's hatred of Rome, helping to make it a permanent part of her national consciousness, to this day not yet extinguished. Furthermore, by glorifying England's steadfastness in the face of persecution, it fostered in the English a sense of their special association with God's purpose and, in the words of John Milton, even of God's regarding them as "his Englishmen."

¶ The burning of the Archbishop of Canturbury Doctor Thomas *Cranmer, in the Towneditch at Oxford, with his hand first thrust into the* fire, wherewith he subscribed before.

PLATE A

The burning of Cranmer (by permission of the Folger Shakespeare Library).

Cranmer. ". . . And now I come to the great thing, which so much troubleth my conscience, more than any thing that ever I did or said in my whole life, and that is the setting abroad of a writing contrary to the truth; which now here I renounce and refuse, as things written for fear of death, and to save my life if it might be; and that is, all such bills and papers which I have written or signed with my hand since my degradation; wherein I have written many things untrue. And forasmuch as my hand offended, writing contrary to my heart, my hand shall first be punished there-for; for, may I come to the fire, it shall be first burned.

"And as for the pope, I refuse him, as Christ's enemy, and antichrist, with all his false doctrine.

"And as for the sacrament, I believe as I have taught in my book against the bishop of Winchester, the which my book teacheth so true a doctrine of the sacrament, that it shall stand at the last day before the judgment of God, where the papistical doctrine contrary thereto shall be ashamed to show her face."

Here the standers-by were all astonied, marvelled, were amazed, did look one upon another, whose expectation he had so notably deceived. Some began to admonish him of his recantation, and to accuse him of falsehood. Briefly, it was a world to see the doctors beguiled of so great a hope. I think there was never cruelty more notably or better in time deluded and deceived; for it is not to be doubted but they looked for a glorious victory and a perpetual triumph by this man's retractation; who, as soon as they heard these things, began to let down their ears, to rage, fret, and fume; and so much the more, because they could not revenge their grief—for they could now no longer threaten or hurt him. For the most miserable man in the world can die but once; and whereas of necessity he must needs die that day, though the papists had been never so well pleased, now, being never so much offended with him, yet could he not be twice killed of them. And so, when they could do nothing else unto him, yet, lest they should say nothing, they ceased not to object unto him his falsehood and dissimulation.

Unto which accusation he answered, "Ah! my masters," quoth he, "do not you take it so. Always since I lived hitherto, I have been a hater of falsehood, and a lover of simplicity, and never before this time have I dissembled:" and in saying this, all the tears that remained in his body appeared in his eyes. And when he began to speak more of the sacrament and of the papacy, some of them began to cry out, yelp, and bawl, and specially Cole cried out upon him, "Stop the heretic's mouth, and take him away."

And then Cranmer being pulled down from the stage, was led to the fire, accompanied with those friars, vexing, troubling, and threatening him most cruelly. "What madness," say they, "hath brought thee again into this error, by which thou wilt draw innumerable souls with thee into hell? To whom he answered nothing, but directed all his talk to the people, saving that to one troubling him in the way, he spake, and exhorted him to get him home to his study, and apply his book diligently; saying, if he did diligently call upon God, by reading more he should get knowledge.

But the other Spanish barker, raging and foaming was almost out of his wits, always having this in his mouth, "Non fecisti?" "Didst thou it not?"

But when he came to the place where the holy bishops and martrys of God, Hugh Latimer and Nicholas Ridley, were burnt before him for the confession of the truth, kneeling down, he prayed to God; and not long tarrying in his prayers, putting off his garments to his shirt, he prepared himself to death. His shirt was made long, down to his feet. His feet were bare; likewise his head, when both his caps were off, was so bare, that one hair could not be seen upon it. His beard was long and thick, covering his face with marvellous gravity. Such a countenance of gravity moved the hearts both of his friends and of his enemies. . . .

Then was an iron chain tied about Cranmer, whom when they perceived to be more steadfast than that he could be moved from his sentence, they commanded the fire to be set unto him.

And when the wood was kindled, and the fire began to burn near him, stretching out his arm, he put his right hand into the flame, which he held so steadfast and immovable (saving that once with the same hand he wiped his face), that all men might see his hand burned before his body was touched. His body did so abide the burning of the flame with such constancy and steadfastness, that standing always in one place without moving his body, he seemed to move no more than the stake to which he was bound; his eyes were lifted up into heaven, and oftentimes he repeated "his unworthy right hand," so long as his voice would suffer him; and using often the words of Stephen, "Lord Jesus, receive my spirit," in the greatness of the flame he gave up the ghost. . . .

And this was the end of this learned archbishop, whom, lest by evilsubscribing he should have perished, by well-recanting God preserved; and lest he should have lived longer with shame and re-proof, it pleased God rather to take him away, to the glory of his name and profit of his church. . . . But especially he had to rejoice, that dying in such a cause, he was to be numbered amongst Christ's martyrs, much more worthy the name of St. Thomas of Canterbury, than he whom the pope falsely before did canonize.

And thus have you the full story concerning the life and death of this reverend archbishop and martyr of God, Thomas Cranmer, and also of divers other the learned sort of Christ's martyrs burned in queen Mary's time, of whom this archbishop was the last, being burnt about the very middle time of the reign of that queen, and almost the very middle man of all the martyrs which were burned in all her reign besides.

39

Sir Thomas Smith, *De Republica Anglorum* (1583). Descriptions of Parliament and Star Chamber

Sir Thomas Smith (1513–1577), a scholar and a government official, is today remembered as the author of *De Republica Anglorum: The maner of Governement or policie of the Realm of England.* Written between 1562 and 1566 while Smith was Elizabeth's ambassador to France, although not published until 1583, *De Republica Anglorum* is the best contemporary description of the form and procedures of Tudor government.

The historian can use such descriptions to learn how the English viewed their constitution at various points in its development. It is noteworthy that Smith stresses the breadth and authority of parliament's statute-making power and the idea that in parliament's consent "is taken to be everie mans consent." However, in this collective sovereignty there is as yet no hint of an impending split between the two parts, that the crown-in-parliament of the sixteenth century would become the crown or parliament of the seventeenth.

Smith's great respect for the force and authority of the court of Star Chamber is indicative of Tudor, not Stuart, attitudes. Originally, the Star Chamber had been the king's council sitting in a judicial capacity, but Thomas

SOURCE. Sir Thomas Smith, *De Republica Anglorum: A Discourse on the Commonwealth of England,* ed. L. Alston, Cambridge: At the University Press, 1906, pp. 48–49, 115–118. Reprinted by permission of Cambridge University Press.

Cromwell, by his administrative reforms of the 1530s, made it a separate body, although its basic membership remained that of the Privy Council. Its jurisdiction over riot was broadly defined to include almost any breach of the peace. Although a prerogative court, the Star Chamber was limited to administering the common law and was unable to inflict the death penalty. Its exalted membership and unfettered procedures made it, nevertheless, efficient and formidable. Not limited to formal indictments of grand juries, it could proceed on the basis of a plaintiff's bill or on information from the attorney general. Nor did it depend on trial juries or procedural technicalities that could be exploited by overmighty subjects. Thus came its prestige and usefulness as seen by Smith, but at a later day its reputation as an instrument of an oppressive royal government.

By the end of the seventeenth century, *De Republica Anglorum* had gone through eleven English editions, four in Latin translation, one in German, and a partial translation into Dutch, a testimonial to the importance accorded Smith as a constitutional analyst.

OF THE PARLIAMENT AND THE AUTHORITIE THEREOF

The most high and absolute power of the realme of Englande, consisteth in the Parliament. For as in warre where the king himselfe in person, the nobilitie, the rest of the gentilitie, and the yeomanrie are, is the force and power of Englande: so in peace and consultation where the Prince is to give life, and the last and highest commaundement, the Baronie for the nobilitie and higher, the knightes, esquiers, gentlemen and commons for the lower part of the common wealth, the bishoppes for the clergie bee present to advertise, consult and shew what is good and necessarie for the common wealth, and to consult together, and upon mature deliberation everie bill or lawe being thrise reade and disputed uppon in either house, the other two partes first each a part, and after the Prince himselfe in presence of both the parties doeth consent unto and alloweth. That is the Princes and whole realmes deede: whereupon justlie no man can complaine, but must accommodate himselfe to finde it good and obey it.

That which is doone by this consent is called firme, stable, and *sanctum,* and is taken for lawe. The Parliament abrogateth olde lawes, maketh newe, giveth orders for thinges past, and for thinges hereafter to be followed, changeth rightes, and possessions of private men, legittimateth bastards, establisheth formes of religion, altereth weightes and measures, giveth formes of succession to the crowne, defineth of doubtfull rightes, whereof is no lawe alreadie made, appointeth subsidies, tailes, taxes, and impositions, giveth most free pardons and absolutions, restoreth in bloud and name as the highest court, condemneth or absolveth them whom the Prince will put to that triall: And to be short, all that ever the people of Rome might do either in *Centuriatis comitijs* or *tributis,* the same may be doone by the parliament of Englande, which representeth and hath the power of the whole realme both the head and the bodie. For everie Englishman is entended to bee there present, either in person or by procuration and attornies, of what preheminence, state, dignitie, or qualitie soever he be, from the Prince (be he King or Queene) to the lowest person of Englande. And the consent of the Parliament is taken to be everie mans consent.

OF THE COURT OF STARRE CHAMBER

There is yet in Englande an other court, of the which that I can understand there is not the like in any other Countrie. In the Terme time every weeke once at the least, (which is commonly on Fridaies, and Wednesdaies, and the next day after that the terme doeth ende,) the Lorde Chauncellor, and the Lordes and other of the privie Counsell, so many as will, and other Lordes and Barons which be not of the Privie Counsell, and be in the towne, and the Judges of England, specially the two chiefe Judges, from ix. of the clocke till it be xj. doe sit in a place which is called the starre chamber, either because it is full of windowes, or because at the first all the roofe thereof was decked with images of starres gilted. There is plaints hear of riots. Riot is called in our English terme or speache, where any number is assembled with force to doe any thing: and it had the beginning, because that our being much accustomed either in foreine wars, in Fraunce, Scotland, or Ireland, or being overmuch exercised with civill warres within the Realme (which is the fault that falleth ordinarily amongest bellicous nations) whereby men of warre, Captaines and souldiers become plentifull: which when they have no externe service wherewith to occupie their buisie heads and handes accustomed to fight and quarell, must needes seeke quarels and contentions amongest themselves, and become so readie to oppresse right among their neighbours, as they were woont before with praise of manhoode, to be in resisting iniurie offered by their enemies. So that our nation used hereunto, and upon that more insolent at home, and not easie to be governed by Lawe and politike order, men of power beginning many fraies, and the stronger by factions and parties offering too much injurie to the weaker, were occasions of making good Lawes. First of reteiners, that no man should have above a number in his

Liverie or retinue: then of the enquirie of routs and riots at everie Sessions, and of the lawe whereby it is provided that if any by force or by riot enter upon any possessions, the Justices of the peace shal assemble themselves and remoove the force, and within certain time enquire thereof. And further, because such things are not commonlie done by meane men, but such as be of power and force, and be not to be dealt withal of everie man, nor of meane Gentlemen: if the riot be found and certified to the Kings Counsell, or if otherwise it be complained of, the partie is sent for, and he must appeare in this starre chamber, where seeing (except the presence of the Prince onely) as it were the maiestie of the whole Realme before him, being never so stoute, he will be abashed: and being called to aunswere (as he must come of what degree soever he be) he shall be so charged with such gravitie, with such reason and remonstrance, and of those chiefe personages of Englande, one after an other handeling him on that sort, that what courage soever he hath, his heart will fall to the grounde, and so much the more, when if he make not his aunswere the better, as seldome he can so in open violence, he shalbe commaunded to the Fleete, where he shall be kept in prison in such sort as these Judges shall appoint him, lie there till he be wearie aswell of the restraint of his libertie, as of the great expences, which he must there sustaine, and for a time be forgotten, whiles after long suite of his friendes, he will be glad to be ordered by reason. Sometime as his deserts be, he payeth a great fine to the Prince, besides great costs and dammages to the partie, and yet the matter wherefore he attempteth this riot and violence is remitted to the common lawe. For that is the effect of this Court to bridle such stoute noble men, or Gentlemen which would offer wrong by force to any manner men, and cannot be content to demaund or defend the right by order of lawe. This court began long before, but tooke great augmentation and authoritie at that time that Cardinall *Wolsey* Archbishop of Yorke was Chauncellor of Englande, who of some was thought to have first devised the Court, because that he after some intermission by negligence of time, augmented the authoritie of it, which was at that time marvellous necessary to doe, to re-presse the insolencie of the noble men and gentlemen of the North partes of Englande, who being farre from the King and the seate of iustice made almost as it were an ordinarie warre among themselves, and made their force their Lawe.

40

Peter Wentworth, Speech in Commons (1576). Parliamentary Privilege

Peter Wentworth (1530?–1596) was both a Puritan and a parliament man. As a Puritan he rejoiced in Elizabeth's break with Rome in 1559, but he agonized that the Church had not banished the traditional priestly vestments and all other dregs of popery. Unable to find justification for these things in the Bible, the Puritans rejected them and denounced the bishops who enforced them. They turned to parliament for help.

Throughout the early 1570s, Peter Wentworth brooded over the state of the Church and the failure of parliament seriously to entertain its reform. The product of his brooding was the speech that he delivered in the House of Commons on February 8, 1576; it is reproduced in part below. In Wentworth's blazing sincerity and moral self-confidence and in his fear of naught save God alone, one sees the hallmarks of a Puritan, though more typical of the seventeenth century than of the sixteenth. In his regard for parliament's right to debate freely any topic it chose, he was equally representative of a seventeenth-century parliament man. It is not surprising that his fellow members of the Commons recognized that they as well as the queen and her ministers were being chastised. Astonished and horrified, they halted him in mid course and, after deliberation, packed him off to the Tower, feeling it safer to dispose of him themselves than to await the wrath of the queen. Although what Elizabeth thought is uncertain, two days before the session ended she granted Wentworth his release.

SOURCE. Sir Simonds D'Ewes, ed., *The Journals of All the Parliaments During the Reign of Queen Elizabeth, Both of the House of Lords and House of Commons,* London: Printed for John Starkey at the Mitre in Fleetstreet near Temple-Bar, 1682, pp. 236–239.

Wentworth was returned to the Tower in 1587 following another outburst concerning the liberties of the House of Commons, and again in the following decade for reviving the question of the succession to the throne. On the last occasion, in 1593, he refused to obtain his release by promising to cease his agitation, and thus he remained imprisoned until his death in 1597, a martyr not only to his own crotchety stubbornness but for causes that he believed were more important than his own liberty. Although his agitation accomplished little in his own day, he did raise a legitimate question of parliamentary privileges, and he became a part of the long tradition of personal protest by which the rights and liberties of Englishmen were forged and defended.

The official Journals of the House of Lords and the House of Commons, as printed in the nineteenth century by the Record Commission, commence in 1509 and 1547, respectively. However, for much of Elizabeth's reign, private *Journals* edited by Sir Symonds D'Ewes (1602–1650) and published in 1682 are the most complete record and the source of Wentworth's speech.

Mr Speaker, I find written in a little Volume these words in effect: Sweet is the name of Liberty, but the thing it self a value beyond all inestimable Treasure. So much the more it behoveth us to take care lest we contenting our selves with the sweetness of the name, lose and forgo the thing, being of the greatest value that can come unto this noble Realm. The inestimable Treasure is the use of it in this House. . . .

Sometime it happeneth that a good man will in this place (for Argument sake) prefer an evil cause, both for that he would have a doubtful truth to be opened and manifested, and also the evil prevented; so that to this point I conclude, that in this House which is termed a place of free Speech, there is nothing so necessary for the preservation of the Prince and State as free Speech, and without it is a scorn and mockery to call it a Parliament House, for in truth it is none, but a very School of Flattery and Dissimulation, and so a fit place to serve the Devil and his Angels in, and not to glorify God and benefit the Common-Wealth. . . .

Amongst other, Mr Speaker, Two things do great hurt in this place, of the which I do mean to speak: the one is a rumour which runneth about the House and this it is, take heed what you do, the Queens Majesty liketh not such a matter, whosoever preferreth it, she will be offended with him; or the contrary, Her Majesty liketh of such a matter, whosoever speaketh against it she will be much offended with him.

The other: sometimes a Message is brought into the House either of Commanding or Inhibiting, very injurious to the freedom of Speech and Consultation, I would to God, Mr Speaker, that these two were Buried in Hell, I mean rumours and Messages; for wicked undoubtedly they are, the reason is, the Devil was the first Author of them, from whom proceedeth nothing but wickedness. . . .

Now the other was a Message Mr Speaker brought the last Sessions into the House, that we should not deal in any matters of Religion, but first to receive from the Bishops: Surely this was a doleful Message, for it was as much as to say, Sirs, ye shall not deal in Gods Causes, no, ye shall in no wise seek to advance his Glory. . . . Yet truly I assure you Mr Speaker, there were divers of this House that said with grievous hearts, immediately upon the Message, that God of his Justice could not prosper the Session. . . . God . . . was the last Session shut out of Doors; but what fell out of it forsooth? his great indignation was therefore poured upon this House, for he did put into the Queens Majesties Heart to refuse good and wholesome Laws for her own Preservation, the which caused many faithful hearts for grief to burst out with sorrowful tears, and moved all Papists Traytors to God and her Majesty . . . in their Sleeves to laugh all the whole Parliament House to scorn; and shall I pass over this weighty matter so slightly? Nay, I will discharge my Conscience and Duties to God, My Prince and Country. So certain it is Mr Speaker that none is without fault, no not our Noble Queen, sith then her Majesty hath committed great fault, yea dangerous faults to her self.

Love, even perfect love void of Dissimulation, will not suffer me to hide them, to her Majesties peril, but to utter them to her Majesties Safety: and these they are, it is a dangerous thing in a Prince unkindly to abuse his or her Nobility and People, and it is a dangerous thing in a Prince to oppose or bend her self against her Nobility and People, yea against most loving and faithful Nobility and People. And how could any Prince more unkindly intreat, abuse, oppose her self against her Nobility and People, than her Majesty did the last Parliament? . . . And will not this her Majesties handling think you, Mr Speaker, make cold dealing in any of her Majesties Subjects toward her again? I fear it will. . . . And I beseech . . . God to endue her Majesty with his Wisdom, whereby she may discern faithful advice from traiterous sugared Speeches, and to send her Majesty a melting yielding heart unto sound Counsel, that Will may not stand for a Reason: and then her Majesty will stand when her Enemies are fallen, for no Estate can stand where the Prince will not be governed by advice.

41

The Several Facts of Witchcraft (1585)

Elizabethan England, although often viewed as a golden age of cultural and literary sophistication, retained many beliefs that the twentieth century regards as mere superstition. Astrology was a recognized science. Elves, fairies, and ghosts shared the world with humans. Charms, amulets, and spells were essential guarantees for earthly success. The most sinister aspect of this supernatural environment was the witch who, according to the respected master of the common law, Sir Edward Coke, was "a person who hath conference with the Devil, to consult with him or to do some act." This belief in the power of witches, although strongest among the lower classes, extended to all elements in the English population. In 1563 parliament made witchcraft a crime punishable by death, and as late as the reign of George I (1714–1727) witches were still executed.

Elizabethan interest in witchcraft is reflected in the large number of surviving chap-books dealing with witches and their crimes. These inexpensive pamphlets, one of which is reproduced in part below, appealed to a wide audience and warned the population of the dangers witches posed to society. From these accounts a number of interesting questions arise. Why were most accused witches socially undesirable members of the lower class? Why did witchcraft increase during times of social and political turmoil, such as the late 1640s following parliament's victory over Charles I? Why were witches women? The obvious importance of the supernatural to the people of Tudor-Stuart England has made demonology a topic of continuing study and controversy.

SOURCE. William Huse Dunham, Jr., and Stanley Pargellis, eds., *Complaint and Reform in England, 1436–1714,* New York: Oxford University Press, 1938, pp. 191–194.

On Wednesday being the seventh day of February last past Anno 1585, Margaret Harkett of the Town of Stanmore, in the County of Middlesex widow about threescore years of age, was arraigned, examined, found guilty and condemned at the Sessions of Gaol Delivery, for the City of London and Middlesex: at the Sessions house in the Old Bailey, where by the several oaths of sundry honest persons, these matters were proved, *videlicet*. That she came to a close in the same town of Stanmore, belonging to one Joan Frynde, whose pease being ripe and ready to gather, she (without the consent of the said Joan Frynde or any other household) did gather a basket full, and filled her apron also with the said pease, and when she was ready to depart, this Joan Frynde who owned the close came, and demanded why she did gather those pease without leave, wherefore she willed her to deliver her the pease that were in her basket, and those that were in her lap she would give her.

But this ungodly woman did fling the pease down on the ground, saying, if you make so much ado for a few pease, take them all, the next year I will have enough of my own, and you shall have few enough. So she cursed the same ground and stamped on it and went her ways, and never since that time that the woman could have any pease grow in her ground or any other corn would grow in the same place.

William Frynde's wife, of the said Town of Stanmore, brought home a child to nurse from Westminster where the parents dwelt: who brought the child and showed it to her husband, but he said unless he knew the parents of the child, he would not suffer her to keep it: this witch being at her house the same time, owing her a grudge, said, what will you do with a nurse child, you will but starve it, sure I will warrant you the child shall not prosper: and the child shortly after did fall sick, and consumed to the death in most strange manner, so that in three weeks following the child died, and was consumed and parched like a green leaf that had been hanged to dry in a chimney.

She came to the house of one William Goodwin of the same town for the yeast, the servants denied that there was any in the house: notwithstanding, the stand was new filled, and the servants were loath to take of the yeast. Whereat this witch said you shall have less, and so went her ways, and the next day following, though none of the house did draw out any drink out of the same stand, yet was it found dry without drink or yeast, except a few hard dried dregs.

She came thither also another time for oat-meal, and they would give her none: and forthwith a lamb (which was kept in the same house), being in the room where the witch was, fell down and died presently. . . .

She came to one of her neighbours to borrow a horse, knowing him to have four very good indifferent geldings, the worst worth four marks:

and he denied her thereof, but she said she would be even with him, and shortly after all his four geldings were dead, and died suddenly one after another.

She came to one John Frynde, of the age of twenty years, the son of Thomas Frynde being of the same town, and offered him a pair of shoes to sell, her price was ten pence, and he offered her six pence and would give her no more. Whereat she was sore vexed, because at that time she had need of money: this was in the latter end of summer, so the fellow thinking nothing, went to gathering of pears from off the tree, and upon a sudden fell down to the ground, and did hurt his cods with the said fall, so that he was constrained to keep in the house. But this witch did openly make report in the town, that he was burned with a whore, and that he came to her and desired to have his pleasure of her: which speeches came to the fellow's ear, who a quarter of a year after he was recovered did meet this witch in the town: where he asked why she gave out such lewd speeches of him, being most unjust, demanding of her, if ever he spake to her in any such sort, but she answered that he knew best: then he charged her that he thought his harm came by her means, I, said she, I have not done with thee yet: so he went about his business and being come home, he complained of his back and his belly, saying assuredly that he thought she had bewitched him: so his pain increased more and more, and he began to grow into a consumption, and wasted away like as the child before mentioned, like a parched or withered leaf, hanged up in the smoke of a chimney, and died three months after, and before he died his side did burst, and his guts and backbone was rotted in sunder, so that his guts and bowels being rotten did issue forth of his belly: and died hereof in most pitiful and grievous manner, the said party taking it upon his death, that her witchcraft and sorcery was the cause of his death.

After whose death the townsmen made complaint of her dealing to the justice, who commanded one Master Norwood, a gentleman in the town, to go search her house: this gentleman went thither and did search her house, yet desired the justice not to apprehend her, until there were some further trial made of her. But she promised for their searching, she would requite them shortly: and forthwith, the next morning one of the gentleman's best milch kine, which was worth four mark, being well over night, was found dead. The gentleman fearing some greater injury by her, did then command his servants that they should give her nothing if she came thither to crave anything, so within two days after she came for buttermilk, but they denied her thereof: and after that they could never make cheese or butter since.

Then was she apprehended and brought before the justice, by whom she was examined, and by him committed to the gaol of Newgate, where she remained until the sessions, held for gaol delivery of London and Middlesex: And then by twelve honest substantial men for the causes aforesaid, was found guilty and worthy of death: where she had judgment and was executed accordingly.

42

Aerial Photographs

Archeologists in Britain have traditionally concentrated on the study of pre-historic and Roman Britain, periods on which there is little written evidence. Recently, however, the physical remains of medieval England have been subjected to intensive study. This new archeology has been assisted by aerial photography, a technique suggested by the air force surveys of World War II and later regularized by the surveys undertaken by Cambridge University. Because of their unique perspective and their comprehensive view, aerial photographs have proved useful in clarifying ground observations and also in suggesting new areas of investigation.

The following photographs illustrate some of the uses of this new approach to the study of medieval England. Plate A is a Tudor diagram of the village of Toddington, showing such dominant features as the central market place, the church, and the moat and what remains of the medieval castle. Its similarity to Plate B, a recent photograph, shows the village's physical continuity into modern times and suggests that few radical changes occurred in the lives of its people. Some towns outgrew their medieval limits, as is shown by the photograph (Plate C) of the Welsh town of Caernarvon. Sometimes villages disappear altogether; Plate D shows the remains of Ditchford. Aerial photography can fix the sites of these deserted villages and can tell the historian much about the population distribution of medieval England.

Finally, aerial photography can reveal the location of the open fields, divided into numerous narrow strips and shared by several families. Some

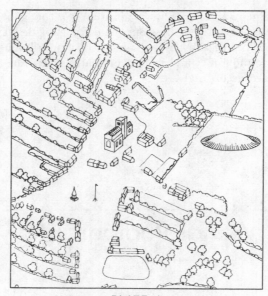

PLATE A
Toddington in 1581, after Ralph Agas (Cambridge University Collection, copyright reserved).

PLATE B
Toddington (Cambridge University Collection, copyright reserved).

PLATE C
Caernarvon (Cambridge University Collection, copyright reserved).

PLATE D
Ditchford (Cambridge University Collection, copyright reserved).

PLATE E
Isle of Portland (Cambridge University Collection, copyright reserved).

of these open fields remained in cultivation until recently, as is illustrated by the 1948 photo (Plate E) of the Isle of Portland in Dorset. Plate F clearly indicates the breakup of the open fields by the enclosure movement. It shows the fences built after 1795 across the fields around the village of Padbury. The ridges in these fields were the result of the strip farming of the manorial system.

PLATE F
Padbury (Cambridge University Collection, copyright reserved)

Historians are constantly seeking new sources of evidence to help answer old questions. The use of aerial photography to study the landscape and man's influence on it is a product of this never-ending search.

43

Robert Carey, *Memoirs.*
The Spanish Armada, 1588

England's defeat of the Spanish Armada was the high point of a conflict which had begun as a confrontation of two aggressive powers—each getting more and more in each other's way. As England and Spain became respectively the champions of the Protestant and Catholic camps, their quarrel attained a cosmic level, almost a judicial duel to determine the judgment of God. The English victory in 1588 was not the end of the war, which continued until 1604, nor of the Spanish navy, which better defended Spanish treasure fleets after 1588 than it had before, nor of Spain's attempt to conquer England. Nevertheless, the outcome did demonstrate that England would not quickly be defeated nor Protestantism in Europe easily vanquished. And it fed the English myth, already alive in Foxe's *Book of Martyrs,* that England was favored by God and that the English were his chosen people.

Sir Robert Carey (c. 1560–1639) was the grandson of Mary Boleyn, the sister of Queen Elizabeth's mother. Although the youngest of 10 sons, he managed to follow in his father's footsteps, as near relative and a courtier to the queen. He never attained the importance of Sir Walter Ralegh, or the earl of Essex, but Elizabeth took note of his marriage and was annoyed. Late in life, probably in 1626, he wrote his memoirs, which however were not published until 1759. Although his recollections are brief (only 2045 lines in the modern edition) and obviously from some distance, Carey nevertheless presents a vivid account of the principal events in which he participated, the foiling of Spain's attempt to invade England, reproduced below, his madcap race to be the first to inform James VI of Scotland of his accession to the English throne, and his joining Prince Charles in Madrid, whence he had gone in 1623 to woo the Spanish Infanta. Writing as an old

SOURCE. *The Memoirs of Robert Carey,* ed. F. H. Mares, pp. 9–11. © 1972 Oxford University Press. By permission of The Clarendon Press, Oxford.

man in the reign of Charles I, Carey gives the somber impression of one
who realizes that his own youth is passed and that England's heroic age is
gone as well.

The next year (1588) the King of Spain's great Armada came upon
our coast, thinking to devour us all. Upon the news sent to court from
Plymouth of their certain arrival, my Lord Cumberland and myself took
post horse, and rode straight to Portsmouth, where we found a frigate
that carried us to sea; and having sought for the fleets a whole day, the
night after we fell amongst them: where it was our fortune to light first
upon the Spanish fleet; and finding ourselves in the wrong, we tacked
about, and in short time got to our own fleet, which was not far from
the other. At our coming aboard our admiral, we stayed there awhile;
but finding the ship much pestered, and scant of cabins, we left the
admiral, and went aboard Captain Reyman, where we stayed, and were
very welcome, and much made of. It was on Thursday that we came to
the fleet. All that day we followed close the Spanish Armada, and nothing
was attempted on either side: the same course we held all Friday and
Saturday, by which time the Spanish fleet cast anchor just before Calais.
We likewise did the same, a very small distance behind them, and so
continued till Monday morning about two of the clock; in which time
our council of war had provided six old hulks, and stuffed them full of all
combustible matter fit for burning, and on Monday at two in the morning
they were let loose, with each of them a man in her to direct them. The
tide serving, they brought them very near the Spanish fleet, so that they
could not miss to come amongst the midst of them: then they set fire
on them, and came off themselves, having each of them a little boat to
bring him off. The ships set on fire, came so directly to the Spanish fleet,
as they had no way to avoid them, but to cut all their hawsers, and so
escape; and their haste was such that they left one of their four great
galeasses on ground before Calais, which our men took and had the spoil
of, where many of the Spaniards were slain with the governor thereof,
but most of them were saved with wading ashore to Calais. They being
in this disorder, we made ready to follow them, where began a cruel
fight, and we had such advantage, both of wind and tide, as we had a
glorious day of them; continuing fight from four o'clock in the morning,
till almost five or six at night, where they lost a dozen or fourteen of
their best ships, some sunk, and the rest ran ashore in divers parts to
keep themselves from sinking. After God had given us this great victory,

they made all the haste they could away, and we followed them Tuesday and Wednesday, by which time they were gotten as far as Flamborough Head. It was resolved on Wednesday at night, that by four o'clock on Thursday, we should have a new fight with them for a farewell; but by two in the morning, there was a flag of council hung out in our vice admiral, when it was found that in the whole fleet there was not munition sufficient to make half a fight; and therefore it was there concluded that we should let them pass, and our fleet to return to the Downs. That night we parted with them, we had a mighty storm. Our fleet cast anchor, and endured it: but the Spanish fleet, wanting their anchors, were many of them cast ashore on the west of Ireland, where they had all their throats cut by the Kerns; and some of them on Scotland, where they were no better used: and the rest (with much ado) got into Spain again. Thus did God bless us, and gave victory over this invincible navy: the sea calmed, and all our ships came to the Downs on Friday in safety.

On Saturday my Lord of Cumberland and myself came on shore, and took post horse, and found the Queen in her army at Tilbury camp, where I fell sick of a burning fever, and was carried in a litter to London. I should have been then sent ambassador to the King of Scots, but could not by reason of my sickness.

44

Richard Hakluyt, *The Principal Navigations* (1589)

Richard Hakluyt (1551–1616) was a scholar, a historian, who recorded but who also influenced the course of English history. He was educated at Oxford and ordained in 1578. Although he remained a clergyman of the

SOURCE. Richard Hakluyt, *The Principal Navigations, Voyages, Traffiques, & Discoveries of the English Nation,* 8 vols., London: J. M. Dent and Sons, 1907, I, 1–5. Reprinted by permission of W. & R. Holmes (Books).

Church of England until his death, his interest in geography and exploration became the dominant influence in his life, as is revealed in the following selection from the "Epistle Dedicatorie" to the first edition of his *The Principal Navigations, Voyages, Traffiques, and Discoveries of the English Nation.* Hakluyt was the first man to lecture at Oxford on cosmography (geography). In addition, he was an adviser to the Muscovy Company, a supporter of Sir Humphrey Gilbert's colonization plans, and a publicist for Sir Walter Ralegh. In 1584, he presented to Queen Elizabeth *A Discourse of Western Planting,* one of the first systematic treatments of the benefits to be gained by colonizing the Western Hemisphere: England would spread the true religion, relieve the problems of pauperism and overpopulation and, especially, by expanding her commerce, forestall Spain.

Hakluyt spent most of his life researching and writing his great work, *The Principal Navigations.* Although at first sight it appears to be a random collection of narratives dealing with voyages of discovery, it does have a theme—the important role of England in early exploration and the need for her to remember, glorify, and continue this tradition. Throughout the 1590s, he traveled widely interviewing survivors of early voyages, and in 1598 to 1600 he published a second and expanded edition in three large volumes.

The Principal Navigations was immediately popular. The general public found it exciting reading, and it provided valuable information to the businessman and the potential colonist. Hakluyt's reputation was such that when he died in 1616 he was honored by burial in Westminster Abbey. Today his memory is preserved by the Hakluyt Society, a scholarly organization begun in 1846 which sponsors the editing and publication of old manuscripts related to exploration.

THE EPISTLE DEDICATORIE IN THE FIRST EDITION, 1589

To the Right Honorable Sir Francis Walsingham Knight, Principall Secretarie to her Majestie, Chancellor of the Duchie of Lancaster, and one of her Majesties most honourable Privie Councell.

RIGHT HONORABLE, I do remember that being a youth, and one of her Majesties scholars at Westminster that fruitful nurserie, it was my happe to visit the chamber of M. Richard Hakluyt my cosin, a Gentleman of the Middle Temple, well knowen unto you, at a time when I found lying open upon his boord certeine bookes of Cosmographie, with an universall Mappe: he seeing me somewhat curious in the view therof, began to instruct my ignorance, by shewing me the division of the earth into three parts after the olde account, and then according to the latter, & better distribution, into more : he pointed with his wand to all the knowen Seas, Gulfs, Bayes, Straights, Capes, Rivers, Empires, Kingdomes, Dukedomes, and Territories of ech part, with declaration also of their speciall commodities, & particular wants, which by the benefit of traffike, & entercourse of merchants, are plentifully supplied. From the Mappe he brought me to the Bible, and turning to the 107 Psalme, directed mee to the 23 & 24 verses, where I read, that they which go downe to the sea in ships, and occupy by the great waters, they see the works of the Lord, and his woonders in the deepe, &c. Which words of the Prophet together with my cousins discourse (things of high and rare delight to my yong nature) tooke in me to deepe an impression, that I constantly resolved, if ever I were preferred to the University, where better time, and more convenient place might be ministred for these studies, I would by Gods assistance prosecute that knowledge and kinde of literature, the doores whereof (after a sort) were so happily opened before me.

According to which my resolution, when, not long after, I was removed to Christ-church in Oxford, my exercises of duety first performed, I fell to my intended course, and by degrees read over whatsoever printed or written discoveries and voyages I found extant either in the Greeke, Latine, Italian, Spanish, Portugall, French, or English languages, and in my publike lectures was the first, that produced and shewed both the olde imperfectly composed, and the new lately reformed Mappes, Globes, Spheares, and other instruments of this Art for demonstration in the common schooles, to the singular pleasure, and generall contentment of my auditory. In continuance of time, and by reason principally of my insight in this study, I grew familiarly acquainted with the chiefest Captaines at sea, the greatest Merchants, and the best Mariners of our nation: by which meanes having gotten somewhat more then common knowledge, I passed at length the narrow seas into France with sir Edward Stafford, her Majesties careful and discreet Ligier, where during my five yeeres aboad with him in his dangerous and chargeable residencie in her Highnes service, I both heard in speech, and read in books other nations miraculously extolled for their discoveries and notable enterprises by sea, but the English of all others for their sluggish security, and continuall neglect of the like attempts especially in so long and happy a time of peace, either ignominiously reported, or exceedingly condemned: . . . Thus both hearing, and reading the obloquie of our nation, and finding few or none of our owne men able to replie heerin: and further, not seeing any man to have care to recommend to the world, the industrious labors, and painefull travels of our countrey men: for stopping the mouthes of the reprochers, my selfe being the last winter returned from France with the honorable the Lady Sheffield, for her passing good behavior highly esteemed in all the French court, determined notwithstanding all difficulties, to undertake the burden of that worke wherin all others pretended either ignorance, or lacke of leasure, or want of sufficient argument, whereas (to speake truely) the huge toile, and the small profit to insue, were the chiefe causes of the refusall. I call the worke a burden, in consideration that these voyages lay so dispersed, scattered, and hidden in severall hucksters hands, that I now woonder of my selfe, so see how I was able to endure the delayes, curiosity, and backwardnesse of many from whom I was to receive my originals: . . .

To harpe no longer upon this string, & to speake a word of that just commendation which our nation doe indeed deserve: it can not be denied, but as in all former ages, they have bene men full of activity, stirrers abroad, and searchers of the remote parts of the world, so in this most famous and peerlesse governement of her most excellent Majesty, her subjects through the speciall assistance, and blessing of God, in searching the most opposite corners and quarters of the world, and to speake plainly, in compassing the vaste globe of the earth more then once, have excelled all the nations and people of the earth. For, which of the kings of this land before her Majesty, had theyr banners ever seene in the Caspian sea? which of them hath ever dealt with the Emperor of Persia, as her Majesty hath done, and obteined for her merchants large & loving privileges? who ever saw before this regiment, an English Ligier in the stately porch of the Grand Signor at Constantinople? who ever found English Consuls & Agents at Tripolis in Syria, at Aleppo, at Babylon, at Balsara, and which is more, who ever heard of Englishman at Goa before now? what English shippes did heeretofore ever anker in the mighty river of Plate? passe and repasse the unpassable (in former opinion) straight of Magellan, range along the coast of Chili, Peru, and all the backside of Nova Hispania, further then any Christian ever passed, travers the mighty bredth of the South sea, land upon the Luzones in despight of the enemy, enter into alliance, amity, and traffike with the princes of the Moluccaes, & the Isle of Java, double the famous Cape of Bona Speranza, arive at the Isle of Santa Helena, & last of al returne home most richly laden with the commodities of China, as the subjects of this now flourishing monarchy have done?

Lucius Florus in the very end of his historie de gestis Romanorum recordeth as a wonderfull miracle, that the Seres, (which I take to be the people of Cathay, or China) sent Ambassadors to Rome, to intreate frindship, as moved with the fame of the majesty of the Romane Empire. And have not we as good cause to admire, that the Kings of the Moluccaes, and Java major, have desired the favour of her majestie, and the commerce & traffike of her people? Is it not as strange that the borne naturalles of Japan, and the Philippinaes are here to be seene, agreeing with our climate, speaking our language, and informing us of the state of their Easterne habitations? For mine owne part, I take it as a pledge of Gods further favour both unto us and them: to them especially, unto whose doores I doubt not in time shalbe by us caried the incomparable treasure of the trueth of Christianity, and of the Gospell, while we use and exercise common trade with their marchants. . . .

Now wheras I have always noted your wisdome to have a speciall care of the honor of her Majesty, the good reputation of our country, & the advancing of navigation, the very walles of this our Island, as the oracle is reported to have spoken of the sea forces of Athens: and whereas I acknowledge in all dutiful sort how honorably both by your letter and speech I have bene animated in this and other my travels, I see my selfe bound to make presentment of this worke to your selfe, as the fruits of your owne incouragements, & the manifestation both of my unfained service to my prince and country, and of my particular duty to your honour: . . .

And thus beseeching God, the giver of all true honor & wisdome to increase both these blessings in you, with continuance of health, strength, happinesse, and whatsoever good things els your selfe can wish, I humbly take my leave. London the 17 of November.

Your honors most humble alwayes to be
commanded RICHARD HAKLUYT.

45

Elizabeth I, "Golden Speech" (1601)

The lack of serious conflict between crown and parliament in the late Tudor period was due in part to the consummate political skill of Elizabeth I. Peter Wentworth's outbursts revealed an isolated member's growing consciousness of parliament's rights, but his fate showed even more vividly the determination of parliament to avoid a clash with the queen. The danger of Rome and

SOURCE.   J. E. Neale, *Elizabeth I and her Parliaments, 1584–1601*, London: Jonathan Cape, Ltd., 1953, pp. 388–391. Reprinted by permission of Jonathan Cape Ltd.

Spain was generally enough to bring these would-be rivals together.

Toward the end of Elizabeth's reign, however, when the fear of Rome and Spain had subsided, an issue arose that revealed a potential chasm between the crown and the House of Commons. The issue was royal monopolies. These monopolies, or patents, were sometimes legitimate attempts to protect copyrights or inventions. However, in her dire need for revenue, Elizabeth granted to individuals and groups monopolies over the manufacture and distribution of all sorts of everyday commodities, such as tin, steel, salt, and playing cards. These monopolies removed competition and reduced supplies, thus raising prices and giving the House of Commons a broad popular complaint. Their previous petition having been ignored, many members of parliament were ready in 1601 to draft legislation forbidding the queen to grant monopolies and thus raising the fundamental question of the limits of the royal prerogative.

Elizabeth, correctly sensing the gravity of the situation, promised to withdraw the hated monopolies and sent the Commons a gracious message, thanking it for its attention to her needs and to the welfare of the kingdom. A few days later, the queen received a large deputation from the Commons to hear its reply to her message and to deliver what she perhaps realized might be her valedictory to her last parliament. This speech, as reconstructed below, illustrates clearly the love affair between Elizabeth and her people and the exquisite political grasp of England's greatest queen. From the seriousness of the issue raised and then avoided and from the grace and charm of Elizabeth's reply can be gauged something of the difficulties that would face the less skillful and less fortunate Stuart kings.

The audience took place in the Council Chamber at Whitehall at about 3 p.m. on November 30th. Speaker Croke was but meanly endowed with eloquence, yet his heart spoke the abundant gratitude of the Commons: "They come not as one of ten to give thanks, and the rest to depart unthankful; but they come, all in all, and these for all, to be thankful . . . for gracious favours bestowed of your gracious mere motion and of late published by your Majesty's most royal proclamation." For this and for all else, "they give glory first unto God, that hath in mercy towards them placed so gracious and benign a prince over them, praying to the same God to grant them continuance of your so blessed and happy government over them, even to the end of the world."

"Mr. Speaker," began Elizabeth, in reply, "We have heard your declaration and perceive your care of our estate, by falling into a consideration of a grateful acknowledgement of such benefits as you have received; and that your coming is to present thanks to us, which I accept with no less joy than your loves can have desire to offer such a present.

"I do assure you there is no prince that loves his subjects better, or whose love can countervail our love. There is no jewel, be it of never so rich a price, which I set before this jewel: I mean your love. For I do esteem it more than any treasure or riches; for that we know how to prize, but love and thanks I count unvaluable. And, though God hath raised me high, yet this I count the glory of my crown, that I have reigned with your loves. This makes me that I do not so much rejoice that God hath made me to be a Queen, as to be a Queen over so thankful a people. Therefore, I have cause to wish nothing more than to content the subject; and that is a duty which I owe. Neither do I desire to live longer days than I may see your prosperity; and that is my only desire. And as I am that person that still yet under God hath delivered you, so I trust, by the almighty power of God, that I shall be His instrument to preserve you from every peril, dishonour, shame, tyranny and oppression; partly by means of your intended helps [the subsidies they were granting] which we take very acceptably, because it manifesteth the largeness of your good loves and loyalties unto your sovereign.

"Of myself I must say this: I never was any greedy, scraping grasper, nor a strait, fast-holding Prince, nor yet a waster. My heart was never set on any worldly goods, but only for my subjects' good. What you bestow on me, I will not hoard it up, but receive it to bestow on you again. Yea, mine own properties I account yours, to be expended for your good; and your eyes shall see the bestowing of all for your good. Therefore, render unto them, I beseech you, Mr. Speaker, such thanks as you imagine my heart yieldeth, but my tongue cannot express."

Hitherto, the Commons had been kneeling, but now her Majesty said: "Mr. Speaker, I would wish you and the rest to stand up, for I shall yet trouble you with longer speech." Thereupon they all stood up, and she continued:

"Mr. Speaker, you give me thanks, but I doubt me I have a greater cause to give you thanks than you me, and I charge you to thank them of the Lower House from me. For, had I not received a knowledge from you, I might have fallen into the lapse of an error, only for lack of true information.

"Since I was Queen, yet did I never put my pen to any grant but that, upon pretext and semblance made unto me, it was both good and beneficial to the subject in general, though a private profit to some of my ancient servants who had deserved well at my hands. But the contrary being found by experience, I am exceedingly beholding to such subjects as would move the same at the first. And I am not so simple to suppose, but that there be some of the Lower House whom these grievances never touched: and for them, I think they spake out of zeal to their countries, and not out of spleen or malevolent affection as being parties grieved; and I take it exceeding gratefully from them, because it gives us to know that no respects or interest had moved them, other than the minds they have to suffer no diminution of our honour and our subjects' love unto us. The zeal of which affection, tending to ease my people and knit their hearts unto me, I embrace with a princely care, for above all earthly treasure I esteem my people's love, more than which I desire not to merit.

"That my grants should be grievous to my people and oppressions privileged under colour of our patents, our kingly dignity shall not suffer it. Yea, when I heard it, I could give no rest unto my thoughts until I had reformed it. Shall they, think you, escape unpunished that have thus oppressed you, and have been respectless of their duty, and regardless of our honour? No, I assure you, Mr. Speaker, were it not more for con-science' sake than for any glory or increase of love that I desire, these errors, troubles, vexations and oppressions, done by these varlets and lewd persons, not worthy the name of subjects, should not escape without condign punishment. But I perceive they dealt with me like physicians who, ministering a drug, make it more acceptable by giving it a good aromatical savour, or when they give pills do gild them all over.

"I have ever used to set the Last-Judgment Day before mine eyes, and so to rule as I shall be judged to answer before a higher Judge, to whose judgment seat I do appeal, that never thought was cherished in my heart that tended not unto my people's good. And now, if my kingly bounties have been abused, and my grants turned to the hurt of my people, contrary to my will and meaning, and if any in authority under me have neglected or perverted what I have committed to them, I hope God will not lay their culps and offences to my charge; who, though there were danger in repealing our grants, yet what danger would I not rather incur for your good, than I would suffer them still to continue?

"I know the title of a King is a glorious title; but assure yourself that the shining glory of princely authority hath not so dazzled the eyes of our understanding, but that we well know and remember that we also are to yield an account of our actions before the great Judge. To be a King and wear a crown is a thing more glorious to them that see it, than it is pleasant to them that bear it. For myself, I was never so much enticed with the glorious name of a King or royal authority of a Queen, as delighted that God hath made me His instrument to maintain His truth and glory, and to defend this Kingdom (as I said) from peril, dishonour, tyranny and oppression.

"There will never Queen sit in my seat with more zeal to my country, care for my subjects, and that will sooner with willingness venture her life for your good and safety, than myself. For it is my desire to live nor reign no longer than my life and reign shall be for your good. And though you have had and may have many princes more mighty and wise sitting in this seat, yet you never had nor shall have any that will be more careful and loving.

"Shall I ascribe anything to myself and my sexly weakness? I were not worthy to live then; and, of all, most unworthy of the mercies I have had from God, who hath given me a heart that yet never feared any foreign or home enemy. And I speak it to give God the praise, as a testimony before you, and not to attribute anything to myself. For I, oh Lord! what am I, whom practices and perils past should not fear? Or what can I do? ["These words," says our diarist, "she spake with a great emphasis"]. That I should speak for any glory, God forbid.

"This, Mr. Speaker, I pray you deliver unto the House, to whom heartily recommend me. And so I commit you all to your best fortunes and further counsels. And I pray you, Mr. Comptroller, Mr. Secretary, and you of my Council, that before these gentlemen go into their countries, you bring them all to kiss my hand."

46

William Shakespeare, *Richard II* (1595) and *Henry V* (1599). English Nationalism

William Shakespeare (1564–1616) is without question the premier figure in English literature. Although little is known of his personal life, this somehow seems irrelevant. His work possesses a timelessness that has captivated successive generations, appealing to different people in different ways. Part of Shakespeare's attraction lies in the unprecedented range of his

SOURCE. *The Life of Henry the Fifth,* ed. Robert D. French, New Haven: Yale University Press, 1918, pp. 82–84; *The Tragedy of King Richard the Second,* ed. Llewellyn M. Buell, New Haven: Yale University Press, 1921, pp. 26–28. Reprinted by permission of Yale University Press.

plays, including histories, tragedies, romances, and comedies. His powers of characterization are almost without equal, creating such enduring figures as Hamlet, Othello, Macbeth, and Falstaff. Finally, the consistent excellence of his style, be it the cleverly constructed dialogue or the philosophical soliloquy, has never been surpassed.

To his contemporaries, the men who crowded the Globe Theatre to heckle and applaud the actors, Shakespeare had yet another quality that is today largely overlooked. He was a historian who during the great war with Spain presented the past in the light of England's developing nationalism. In the following selections from *Richard II (1595)* and *Henry V* (1599), Shakespeare's pride in England is obvious. John of Gaunt, dismayed at the evils that have befallen England under Richard II, has, nevertheless, little doubt that England, "this blessed plot," will survive to enjoy a more glorious future. Similarly, Henry V in his speech before the battle of Agincourt contemplates the glories to be won by his army, "we band of brothers." Neither man is likely to have uttered such words, but the fact that Shakespeare places them in their mouths tells a great deal about what sentiments were acceptable to Elizabethan audiences. This distortion should alert the reader to the fact that Shakespeare was first a dramatist and only secondly a historian. This is well illustrated in his treatment of Richard III (1483–1485). For dramatic effect, to say nothing of political expediency, Shakespeare portrayed the last Yorkist king as odious and deformed, the personification of evil. Recent scholars have attempted to present Richard in a more favorable light, but their efforts have largely been frustrated by Shakespeare's wider audience and dramatic appeal.

RICHARD II

    Gaunt. Methinks I am a prophet new inspir'd,
And thus expiring do foretell of him:
His rash fierce blaze of riot cannot last,
For violent fires soon burn out themselves;
Small showers last long, but suddent storms are short;
He tires betimes that spurs too fast betimes;
With eager feeding food doth choke the feeder:
Light vanity, insatiate cormorant,
Consuming means, soon preys upon itself.
This royal throne of kings, this scepter'd isle,
This earth of majesty, this seat of Mars,
This other Eden, demi-paradise,
This fortress built by Nature for herself

Against infection and the hand of war,
This happy breed of men, this little world,
This precious stone set in the silver sea,
Which serves it in the office of a wall,
Or as a moat defensive to a house,
Against the envy of less happier lands,
This blessed plot, this earth, this realm, this England,
This nurse, this teeming womb of royal kings,
Fear'd by their breed and famous by their birth,
Renowned for their deeds as far from home,—
For Christian service and true chivalry,—
As is the sepulchre in stubborn Jewry
Of the world's ransom, blessed Mary's Son:
This land of such dear souls, this dear, dear land,
Dear for her reputation through the world,
Is now leas'd out,—I die pronouncing it,—
Like to a tenement, or pelting farm:
England, bound in with the triumphant sea,
Whose rocky shore beats back the envious siege
Of watery Neptune, is now bound in with shame,
With inky blots, and rotten parchment bonds:
That England, that was wont to conquer others,
Hath made a shameful conquest of itself.
Ah! would the scandal vanish with my life,
How happy then were my ensuing death.

HENRY V

    K. Henry.   What's he that wishes so?
My cousin Westmoreland? No, my fair cousin:
If we are mark'd to die, we are enow
To do our country loss; and if to live,
The fewer men, the greater share of honour.
God's will! I pray thee, wish not one man more.
By Jove, I am not covetous for gold,
Nor care I who doth feed upon my cost;
It yearns me not if men my garments wear;
Such outward things dwell not in my desires:
But if it be a sin to covet honour,
I am the most offending soul alive.
No, faith, my coz, wish not a man from England:

God's peace! I would not lose so great an houour
As one man more, methinks, would share from me,
For the best hope I have. O! do not wish one more:
Rather proclaim it, Westmoreland, through my host,
That he which hath no stomach to this fight,
Let him depart; his passport shall be made,
And crowns for convoy put into his purse:
We would not die in that man's company
That fears his fellowship to die with us.
This day is call'd the feast of Crispian:
He that outlives this day, and comes safe home,
Will stand a tip-toe when this day is nam'd,
And rouse him at the name of Crispian.
He that shall live this day, and see old age,
Will yearly on the vigil feast his neighbours,
And say, "To-morrow is Saint Crispian";
Then will he strip his sleeve and show his scars,
And say, "These wounds I had on Crispin's day."
Old men forget: yet all shall be forgot,
But he'll remember with advantages
What feats he did that day. Then shall our names,
Familiar in his mouth as household words,
Harry the king, Bedford and Exeter,
Warwick and Talbot, Salisbury and Gloucester,
Be in their flowing cups freshly remember'd.
This story shall the good man teach his son;
And Crispin Chrispian shall ne'er go by,
From this day to the ending of the world,
But we in it shall be remembered;
We few, we happy few, we band of brothers;
For he to-day that sheds his blood with me
Shall be my brother; be he ne'er so vile,
This day shall gentle his condition:
And gentlemen in England, now a-bed,
Shall think themselves accurs'd they were not here,
And hold their manhoods cheap whiles any speaks
That fought with us upon Saint Crispin's day.

Sir Edward Coke, *Reports.*
Defense of the Common Law, 1607

The problem of the limits of the royal prerogative, raised briefly in 1601 regarding monopolies, returned a few years later. This time, however, the protagonist was not parliament but the common law, in the person of Sir Edward Coke (1552–1634), its greatest champion and the symbol of its reviving stature. The prerogative courts, especially the Star Chamber lauded by Sir Thomas Smith and the High Commission, had been created and sustained largely by royal prerogative. Although once viewed as a valuable supplement to the common law courts, they were now seen more as an illegal and dangerous encroachment. One weapon the common law used, especially against the High Commission, was the writ of prohibition, whereby a common law court could halt any action until it was satisfied that its own jurisdiction was not being infringed upon.

Sir Edward Coke, who in 1606 became chief justice of the court of common pleas, was avid in issuing these writs and in defending them against the arguments of Archbishop Richard Bancroft. Bancroft appealed to James I's absolute authority by divine right, but Coke based his position simply on "the law and custom of England," which was not only "a measure to try the causes of the subjects," but also "protected the king in safety and peace." When James protested that Coke's view placed him under the law, Coke repeated the often-quoted words of Henry Bracton, the great legal writer of the thirteenth century, "The king is subject not to men but to God and the law." This was, however, only the beginning of Coke's confrontations with the king. Ultimately, in 1616, James removed Coke when he would not agree to halt court proceedings to hear James's special interests. Coke's

---

SOURCE.   J. P. Kenyon, ed., *The Stuart Constitution, 1603–1688: Documents and Commentary,* Cambridge University Press, 1966, pp. 180–181. Reprinted by permission of Cambridge University Press.

reply was, "when that case should be, he would do what should be fit for a judge to do."

Released from the bench, Coke threw his weight and that of the common law onto the side of parliament in its continuing struggle with the king. Coke is famous for his personal stand against the king and for his career in parliament, but equally for his writings on the law. His *Institutes of the Laws of England* and his *Reports* on the cases of his own day, including the discussion concerning prohibitions reproduced below, are among the most important books ever written on the English law.

Note, upon Sunday the 10th of November in this same term the King, upon complaint made to him by Bancroft, archbishop of Canterbury, concerning prohibitions, the King was informed that when the question was made of what matters the ecclesiastical judges have cognisance, either upon the exposition of the statute concerning tithes, or any other thing ecclesiastical, or upon the statute 1 Eliz. concerning the High Commission, or in any other case in which there is not express authority in law, the King himself may decide it in his royal person, and that the judges are but the delegates of the King, and that the King may take what causes he shall please to determine from the determination of the judges, and may determine them himself. And the archbishop said that this was clear in divinity, that such authority belongs to the King by the world of God in the Scripture.

To which it was answered by me, in the presence and with the clear consent of all the judges of England and barons of the exchequer, that the King in his own person cannot adjudge any case, either criminal (as treason, felony, &c.) or betwixt party and party, concerning his inheritance, chattels or goods, &c., but this ought to be determined and adjudged in some court of justice according to the law and custom of England. And always judgements are given, *ideo consideratum est per curiam,* so that the court gives the judgement; and the King hath his court, viz., in the Upper House of Parliament, in which he with his Lords is the supreme judge over all other judges; for if error be in the Common Pleas, that may be reversed in the King's Bench; and if the Court of King's Bench err, that may be reversed in the Upper House of Parliament, by the King with the assent of the Lords spiritual and temporal, without the Commons, and in this respect the King is called the Chief Justice. . . . And it appears in our books that the King may sit in the Star Chamber, but this was to consult with the justices upon certain questions proposed to them, and not *in judicio*; so in the King's Bench he may sit, but the court gives the judgement, and it is commonly said in our books that the King is always present in court in the judgement of law, and upon this he cannot be nonsuit[ed]; but the judgements are always given *per curiam* and the judges are sworn to execute justice according to law and the custom of England. . . . And the judges informed the King that no king after the Conquest assumed to himself to give any judgement in any cause whatsoever which concerned the administration of justice within this realm, but these were solely determined in the courts of justice . . . , and it was greatly marvelled that the archbishop durst inform the King that such absolute power and authority, as is aforesaid, belonged to the King by the word of God. . . .

Then the King said, that he thought the law was founded upon reason, and that he and others had reason, as well as the judges. To which it was answered by me, that true it was that God had endowed his Majesty with excellent science and great endowments of nature, but his Majesty was not learned in the laws of his realm of England, and causes which concern the life, or inheritance, or goods, or fortunes of his subjects are not to be decided by natural reason but by the artificial reason and judgement of law, which law is an act which requires long study and experience before that a man can attain to the cognisance of it, and that the law was the golden mete-wand and measure to try the causes of the subjects, and which protected his Majesty in safety and peace. With which the King was greatly offended, and said, that then he should be under the law, which [it] was treason to affirm, as he said. To which I said, that Bracton saith, *quod rex non debet esse sub homine, sed sub Deo et lege.*

48

The King James Bible (1611).
"The Epistle Dedicatory"

The King James Version, published in 1611, was not the first English translation of the Bible. To find that, one must go back to fragments translated into Anglo-Saxon or, for a complete translation, to the fourteenth-century efforts of the followers of John Wycliffe. Modern English translations began with William Tyndale's New Testament, published in 1526. Tyndale's work was completed by Miles Coverdale in 1535, and this became the basis of the Matthew Bible of 1537 and the Great Bible of 1539. The Geneva Bible, produced in 1560 by Marian exiles in Geneva, was the first English Bible to receive wide circulation and popular usage, especially among those enclined toward Puritanism. The Bishops' Bible (1568) was the official response to its popularity and Puritan inclinations. Catholic exiles in 1582 produced the Rheims New Testament and in 1609 to 1610 the Douai Old Testament. The culmination of all this work, at least of the Protestant efforts, was the King James Version of 1611.

The immediate impetus for a new translation of the Bible was the suggestion of a Puritan member of the Hampton Court Conference of 1604. Although James I (1603–1625) took offense at other things said, this suggestion hit a responsive chord. He had translated parts of the Bible himself, and now gave the project not only his enthusiasm but valuable suggestions, such as the omission of the marginal comments that had encumbered the Geneva Bible. The final product, representing the collective work of 47 scholars, leaned heavily on Tyndale and was far superior to previous English versions. The tradition of calling it the "Authorized Version" is of uncertain origin and perhaps comes simply from the designation on the title page, "Appointed to be read in Churches." Its simple yet dignified style, avoiding

SOURCE. *The Holy Bible . . . Authorized King James Version.* Reprinted by permission of Eyre & Spottiswoode (Publishers), Ltd., H. M. Printers.

the classical terminology and ornate flourishes that often corrupted contemporary prose, made it a literary masterpiece and suitable reading for
all who were literate. It intensified the popular inclination toward Bible reading and helped to pattern English speech and writing habits for centuries
to come.

"The Epistle Dedicatory," which is reproduced below, is interesting and
revealing. The thankfulness for the peaceful accession of James and for
the safe retention of the Protestant settlement is apparent, indicative of the
intensity of those concerns during the long reign of Elizabeth. And there is
the recognition that the English church occupied a central position between
"Popish Persons" on one hand and "selfconceited Brethren" on the other.

TO THE MOST HIGH AND MIGHTY PRINCE JAMES, BY THE GRACE OF GOD, KING OF GREAT BRITAIN, FRANCE, AND IRELAND, DEFENDER OF THE FAITH, ETC., THE TRANSLATORS OF THE BIBLE WISH GRACE, MERCY, AND PEACE, THROUGH JESUS CHRIST OUR LORD

GREAT and manifold were the blessings, most dread Sovereign, which
Almighty God, the Father of all mercies, bestowed upon us the people of
England, when first he sent Your Majesty's Royal Person to rule and reign
over us. For whereas it was the expectation of many, who wished not
well unto our *Sion*, that upon the setting of that bright *Occidental Star*,
Queen *Elizabeth* of most happy memory, some thick and palpable clouds
of darkness would so have overshadowed this Land, that men should
have been in doubt which way they were to walk; and that it should
hardly be known, who was to direct the unsettled State; the appearance
of Your Majesty, as of the *Sun* in his strength, instantly dispelled those
supposed and surmised mists, and gave unto all that were well affected
exceeding cause of comfort; especially when we beheld the Government
established in Your Highness, and Your hopeful Seed, by an undoubted
Title, and this also accompanied with peace and tranquility at home
and abroad.

But among all our joys, there was no one that more filled our hearts,
than the blessed continuance of the preaching of God's sacred Word
among us; which is that inestimable treasure, which excelleth all the
riches of the earth; because the fruit thereof extendeth itself, not only
to the time spent in this transitory world, but directeth and disposeth
men unto that eternal happiness which is above in heaven.

Then not to suffer this to fall to the ground, but rather to take it up,
and to continue it in that state, wherein the famous Predecessor of Your

Highness did leave it: nay, to go forward with the confidence and resolution of a Man in maintaining the truth of Christ, and propagating it far and near, is that which hath so bound and firmly knit the hearts of all Your Majesty's loyal and religious people unto You, that Your very name is precious among them: their eye doth behold You with comfort, and they bless You in their hearts, as that sanctified Person, who, under God, is the immediate Author of their true happiness. And this their contentment doth not diminish or decay, but every day increaseth and taketh strength, when they observe, that the zeal of Your Majesty toward the house of God doth not slack or go backward, but is more and more kindled, manifesting itself abroad in the farthest parts of *Christendom,* by writing in defence of the Truth, (which hath given such a blow unto that man of sin, as will not be healed,) and every day at home, by religious and learned discourse, by frequenting the house of God, by hearing the Word preached, by cherishing the Teachers thereof, by caring for the Church, as a most tender and loving nursing Father.

There are infinite arguments of this right christian and religious affection in Your Majesty; but none is more forcible to declare it to others than the vehement and perpetuated desire of accomplishing and publishing of this work, which now with all humility we present unto Your Majesty. For when Your Highness had once out of deep judgment apprehended how convenient it was, that out of the Original Sacred Tongues, together with comparing of the labours, both in our own, and other foreign Languages, of many worthy men who went before us, there should be one more exact Translation of the holy Scriptures into the *English Tongue;* Your Majesty did never desist to urge and to excite those to whom it was commended, that the work might be hastened, and that the business might be expedited in so decent a manner, as a matter of such importance might justly require.

And now at last, by the mercy of God, and the continuance of our labours, it being brought unto such conclusion, as that we have great hopes that the Church of *England* shall reap good fruit thereby; we hold it our duty to offer it to Your Majesty, not only as to our King and Sovereign, but as to the principal Mover and Author of the work: humbly craving of Your most Sacred Majesty, that since things of this quality have ever been subject to the censures of illmeaning and discontented persons, it may receive approbation and patronage from so learned and judicious a Prince as Your Highness is, whose allowance and acceptance of our labours shall more honour and encourage us, than all the calumniations and hard interpretations of other men shall dismay us. So that if, on the one side, we shall be traduced by Popish Persons at home or abroad, who therefore will malign us, because we are poor instruments to make God's holy Truth to be yet more and more known

unto the people, whom they desire still to keep in ignorance and darkness; or if, on the other side, we shall be maligned by selfconceited
Brethren, who run their own ways, and give liking unto nothing, but
what is framed by themselves, and hammered on their anvil; we may
rest secure, supported within by the truth and innocency of a good
conscience, having walked the ways of simplicity and integrity, as before
the Lord; and sustained without by the powerful protection of Your
Majesty's grace and favour, which will ever give countenance to honest
and christian endeavours against bitter censures and uncharitable imputa-
tions.

The Lord of heaven and earth bless Your Majesty with many and
happy days, that, as his heavenly hand hath enriched Your Highness
with many singular and extraordinary graces, so You may be the
wonder of the world in this latter age for happiness and true felicity,
to the honour of that great GOD, and the good of his Church,
through Jesus Christ our Lord and only Saviour.

49

Sir Francis Bacon, *Novum Organum* (1620). The Scientific Method

Sir Francis Bacon (1561–1626) was one of the great men of his time. A son
of Elizabeth's Lord Keeper of the Great Seal, he became a lawyer, a member of parliament, a civil servant, and finally in 1618 Lord Chancellor. As a
lawyer he championed the absolute authority of the king, in opposition to Sir
Edward Coke. When the latter helped revive impeachment in 1621, Bacon
was one of its first victims, admitting he had accepted money from litigants

SOURCE. *The Works of Francis Bacon,* collected and edited by James
Spedding, Robert Leslie Ellis, and Douglas.Denon Heath, Vol. IV, London:
Longman and Co. et al., 1860, pp. 39–42, 47–51, 115, 247–248.

whose cases were pending before his court. Bacon was, and remains, more famous as the author of *Essays* (1597, 1625), a *History of Henry the Seventh* (1622), and several important works on philosophy and the scientific method. Even as a student at Trinity College, Cambridge, he had noted the sterility of contemporary scholarship, especially in natural science, where men still slavishly followed the logic and conclusions of Aristotle rather than emulating his example of examining things first hand. Bacon envisioned a "Great Instauration," a great restoration or repairing, of men's approach to the investigation and exploitation of nature. In the *New Organon, or True Directions Concerning the Interpretation of Nature,* written in Latin in 1620, he emphasized the need to liberate science from the restraints of theology and from its bondage to the logic, or *Organon,* of Aristotle. What was needed was a new organon, a new method, a rigorous induction from observed fact and experiment to sound general laws and principles.

Bacon was not a great scientist or experimenter himself, although he is reputed to have died of a cold caught in a snowbank while trying to determine whether a dressed chicken could be preserved by packing it in ice. Also, he had little appreciation for the importance of mathematics or for the best scientists of his day—men such as William Gilbert, who experimented with the magnet, and Galileo, who discovered the science of mechanics. Nevertheless, by separating the study of nature from theology and by pronouncing it not only agreeable to God but useful to mankind, Bacon became an important propagandist and an inspiration for the advancement of science. The Royal Society of London for Improving Natural Knowledge, founded in 1660, acknowledged its debt to him, as can be seen from these lines of Abraham Cowley (1618–1667):

> Bacon, like Moses, led us forth at last,
> The barren wilderness he past,
> Did on the very border stand
> Of the blest promis'd land
> And from the mountain's top of his exalted wit
> Saw it himself, and shew'd us it.

PREFACE

Those who have taken upon them to lay down the law of nature as a thing already searched out and understood, whether they have spoken in simple assurance or professional affection, have therein done philosophy and the sciences great injury. . . . Those on the other hand who have taken a contrary course, and asserted that absolutely nothing can be known,—whether it were from hatred of the ancient sophists, or from uncertainty and fluctuation of mind, or even from a kind of fulness of learning, that they fell upon this opinion,—have certainly advanced reasons for it that are not to be despised; but yet they have neither started from true principles nor rested in the just conclusion, zeal and affectation having carried them much too far. . . .

Now my method, though hard to practise, is easy to explain; and it is this. I propose to establish progressive stages of certainty. The evidence of the sense, helped and guarded by a certain process of correction, I retain. But the mental operation which follows the act of sense I for the most part reject; and instead of it I open and lay out a new and certain path for the mind to proceed in, starting directly from the simple sensuous perception. . . . There remains but one course for the recovery of a sound and healthy condition,—namely, that the entire work of the understanding be commenced afresh, and the mind itself be from the very outset not left to take its own course, but guided at every step; and the business be done as if by machinery. . . .

Upon these premises two things occur to me of which, that they may not be overlooked, I would have men reminded. First it falls out fortunately as I think for the allaying of contradictions and heart-burnings, that the honour and reverence due to the ancients remains untouched and undiminished; while I may carry out my designs and at the same time reap the fruit of my modesty. For if I should profess that I, going the same road as the ancients, have something better to produce, there must needs have been some comparison or rivalry between us (not to be avoided by any art of words) in respect of excellency or ability of wit; and though in this there would be nothing unlawful or new (for if there be anything misapprehended by them, or falsely laid down, why may not I, using a liberty common to all, take exception to it?) yet the contest, however just and allowable, would have been an unequal one perhaps, in respect of the measure of my own powers. . . . The other point of which I would have men reminded relates to the matter itself.

Be it remembered then that I am far from wishing to interfere with the philosophy which now flourishes, or with any other philosophy more correct and complete than this which has been or may hereafter be propounded. For I do not object to the use of this received philosophy, or others like it, for supplying matter for disputations or ornaments for discourse,—for the professor's lecture and for the business of life. Nay more, I declare openly that for these uses the philosophy which I bring forward will not be much available. It does not lie in the way. It cannot be caught up in passage. It does not flatter the understanding by conformity with preconceived notions. Nor will it come down to the apprehension of the vulgar except by its utility and effects.

Let there be therefore (and may it be for the benefit of both) two streams and two dispensations of knowledge; and in like manner two tribes or kindreds of students in philosophy—tribes not hostile or alien to each other, but bound together by mutual services;—let there in short be one methed for the cultivation, another for the invention, of knowledge.

APHORISMS CONCERNING THE INTERPRETATION OF NATURE AND THE KINGDOM OF MAN.

APHORISM

I.

Man, being the servant and interpreter of Nature, can do and understand so much and so much only as he has observed in fact or in thought of the course of nature: beyond this he neither knows anything nor can do anything.

XI.

As the sciences which we now have do not help us in finding out new works, so neither does the logic which we now have help us in finding out new sciences.

XII.

The logic now in use serves rather to fix and give stability to the errors which have their foundation in commonly received notions than to help the search after truth. So it does more harm than good.

XIII.

The syllogism is not applied to the first principles of sciences, and is applied in vain to intermediate axioms; being no match for the subtlety of nature. It commands assent therefore to the proposition, but does not take hold of the thing.

XIV.

The syllogism consists of propositions, propositions consist of words, words are symbols of notions. Therefore if the notions themselves (which is the root of the matter) are confused and over-hastily abstracted from the facts, there can be no firmness in the superstructure. Our only hope therefore lies in a true induction.

XIX.

There are and can be only two ways of searching into and discovering truth. The one flies from the senses and particulars to the most general axioms, and from these principles, the truth of which it takes for settled and immoveable, proceeds to judgment and to the discovery of middle axioms. And this way is now in fashion. The other derives axioms from the senses and particulars, rising by a gradual and unbroken ascent, so that it arrives at the most general axioms last of all. This is the true way, but as yet untried.

XXIV.

It cannot be that axioms established by argumentation should avail for the discovery of new works; since the subtlety of nature is greater many times over than the subtlety of argument. But axioms duly and orderly formed from particulars easily discover the way to new particulars, and thus render sciences active.

CXXIX.

Only let the human race recover that right over nature which belongs to it by divine bequest, and let power be given it; the exercise thereof will be governed by sound reason and true religion.

LII.

. . . There cannot but follow an improvement in man's estate, and an enlargement of his power over nature. For man by the fall fell at the same time from his state of innocency and from his dominion over creation. Both of these losses however can even in this life be in some part repaired; the former by religion and faith, the latter by arts and sciences. For creation was not by the curse made altogether and for ever a rebel, but in virtue of that charter "In the sweat of thy face shalt thou eat bread," it is now by various labours (not certainly by disputations or idle magical ceremonies, but by various labours) at length and in some measure subdued to the supplying of man with bread; that is, to the uses of human life.

William Bradford, *Of Plymouth Plantation, 1606-1646*. Puritanism and the New World

Puritanism, an important movement within the Church of England in the late sixteenth century, agitated for further reform. It is difficult to define these Puritans, for the term included both the moderate reformers, who sought to purify the established church of its Roman traditions, and the separatists, who left the Church of England to form separate congregations. Most Puritans, however, supported certain general principles. As Bradford points out below, they wanted a church "according to the simplicitie of the gospel," responsive to its members' interpretation of Scripture and less tied to the maintenance of "episcopall dignitie (affter the popish manner)." The church should also be the active enforcer of personal and public morality. Critics have traditionally stressed the last aspect of Puritanism, as is indicated in these satirical lines written about 1640.

> A puritan, is he, that when he prays,
>   his rowling eyes up to the heavens doth raise.
> A puritan, is he, that cannot dine,
>   nor sup, without a double grace divine.
> A puritan, is he, that through the year,
>   two Lords-day sermons doth either preach or hear.
> A puritan, is he, whose austere life,
>   will not admit a mistress and a wife.
> That when his betters swear, doth bite the lip,
>   nor will be drunken for good-fellowship.

SOURCE. William Bradford, *Of Plymouth Plantation, 1620–1647*, ed. Samuel Eliot Morison, New York: Alfred A. Knopf, 1952, pp. 5–10, 23, 25, 28, 75–76. Reprinted by permission of Alfred A. Knopf, Inc.

Of Plymouth Plantation is William Bradford's story of the separatists from the village of Scrooby. Bradford describes their persecution in England, their flight to Holland in 1608 and, eventually, their voyage to America, where they hoped to preserve both their religious belief and their English culture. Bradford was well qualified to write such a history. A member of the Scrooby congregation and a prosperous weaver during the exile in Holland, he helped in 1620 to organize the voyage of the *Mayflower* and later served for more than 30 years as governor of Plymouth Colony.

The history of Bradford's manuscript provides an interesting commentary on relations between old England and the new England that Bradford helped to create in America. Finished about 1646, *Of Plymouth Plantation* remained unprinted for over two centuries. During the seventeenth and early eighteenth centuries, it was used by other historians, some of whom corrected portions of it. The manuscript disappeared from the Old South Church of Boston during the American Revolution, but reappeared mysteriously 70 years later in the library of the bishop of London. Although it was copied and in 1856 published, the original remained in London despite numerous private and official efforts to persuade the British to return it. Its presentation to the Commonwealth of Massachusetts in 1897 may be viewed symbolically as the end of the Anglo-American schism within the British community and the beginning of a new era of understanding and cooperation.

Mr. Foxe recordeth how that besids those worthy martires and confessors which were burned in queene Marys days and otherwise tormented, *many (both students and others) fled out of the land, to the number of 800. And became severall congregations.* . . . Amongst whom (but especialy those at Frankford) begane that bitter warr of contention and persecution aboute the ceremonies, and servisebooke, and other popish and antichristian stuffe, the plague of England to this day. . . .

The one side laboured to have the right worship of God and discipline of Christ established in the church, according to the simplicitie of the gospell, without the mixture of mens inventions, and to have and to be ruled by the laws of Gods word, dispensed in those offices, and by those officers of Pastors, Teachers, and Elders, etc. according to the Scripturs. The other partie, though under many colours and pretences, endevored to have the episcopall dignitie (affter the popish manner) with their large power and jurisdiction still retained; with all those courts, cannons, and ceremonies, togeather with all such livings, revenues, and subordinate officers, with other such means as formerly upheld their antichristian greatnes, and enabled them with lordly and tyranous power to persecute the poore servants of God. . . .

And this contention dyed not with queene Mary, nor was left beyonde the seas, but at her death these people returning into England under gracious queene Elizabeth, many of them being preferred to bishopricks and other promotions, according to their aimes and desires, that inveterate hatered against the holy discipline of Christ in his church hath continued to this day. . . . And many the like, to stop the mouthes of the more godly, to bring them over to yeeld to one ceremoney after another, and one corruption after another; by these wyles begyleing some and corrupting others till at length they begane to persecute all the zealous professors in the land . . . both by word and deed, if they would not submitte to their ceremonies, and became slaves to them and their popish trash, which have no ground in the word of God, but are relikes of that man of sine. . . . And to cast contempte the more upon the sincere servants of God, they opprobriously and most injuriously gave unto, and imposed upon them, that name of Puritans. . . .

But that I may come more near my intendmente; when as by the travell and diligence of some godly and zealous preachers, and Gods blessing on their labours, as in other places of the land, so in the North parts, many became inlightened by the word of God, and had their ignorance and sins discovered unto them, and begane by his grace to reforme their lives, and make conscience of their wayes, the worke of God was no sooner manifest in them, but presently they were both scoffed and scorned by the prophane multitude, and the ministers urged with the yoak of subscription, or els must be silenced; and the poore people were so vexed with apparators, and pursuants, and the comissarie courts, as truly their affliction was not smale; which, notwithstanding, they bore sundrie years with much patience, till they were occasioned (by the continuance and encrease of these troubles, and other means which the Lord raised up in those days) to see further into things by the light of the word of God. How not only these base and beggerly ceremonies were unlawfull, but also that the lordly and tiranous power of the prelats ought not to be submitted unto; which thus, contrary to the freedome of the gospell, would load and burden mens consciences, and by their compulsive power make a phophane mixture of persons and things in the worship of God. And that their offices and calings, courts and cannons, etc. were unlawfull and antichristian; being such as have no warrante in the word of God; but the same that were used in poperie, and still retained. . . .

So many therfore of these proffessors as saw the evill of these things, in thes parts, and whose harts the Lord had touched with heavenly zeale for his trueth, they shooke of this yoake of antichristian bondage, and as the Lords free people, joyned them selves (by a covenant of the Lord) into a church estate, in the felowship of the gospell, to walke in all his wayes, made known, or to be made known unto them, according to their best endeavours, whatsoever it should cost them, the Lord assisting them. And that it cost them something this ensewing historie will declare. . . .

But after these things they could not long continue in any peaceable conditon, but were hunted and persecuted on every side, so as their former afflictions were but as fleabitings in comparison of these which now came upon them. For some were taken and clapt up in prison, others had their houses besett and watcht night and day, and hardly escaped their hands; and the most were faine to flie and leave their howses and habitations, and the means of their livelehood. Yet these and many other sharper things which affterward befell them, were no other then they looked for, and therfore were the better prepared to bear them by the assistance of Gods grace and spirite. Yet seeing them selves thus molested, and that ther was no hope of their continuance ther, by a joynte consente they resolved to goe into the Low-Countries, wher they heard was freedome of Religion for all men. . . .

AFTER . . . about some 11. or 12. years, . . . and sundrie of them were taken away by death, and many others begane to be well striken in years, the grave mistris Experience haveing taught them many things, those prudent governours with sundrie of the sagest members begane both deeply to apprehend their present dangers, and wisely to foresee the future, and thinke of timly remedy. In the agitation of their thoughts, and much discours of things hear aboute, at length they began to incline to this conclusion, of remoovall to some other place. . . .

The place they had thoughts on was some of those vast and unpeopled countries of America. . . .

Some (and none of the meanest) had thoughts and were ernest for Guiana, or some of those fertill places in those hott climats; others were for some parts of Virginia, wher the English had all ready made enterance, and begining. . . .

I SHALL a litle returne backe and begine with a combination made by them before they came ashore, being the first foundation of their govermente in this place; occasioned partly by the discontented and mutinous speeches that some of the strangers amongst them had let fall from them in the ship—That when they came a shore they would use their owne libertie; for none had power to command them, the patente they had being for Virginia, and not for New-england, which belonged to an other Goverment, with which the Virginia Company had nothing to doe. And partly that shuch an acte by them done (this their condition considered) might be as firme as any patent, and in some respects more sure.

The forme was as followeth.

"In the name of God, Amen. We whose names are under-writen, the loyall subjects of our dread soveraigne Lord, King James, by the grace of God, of Great Britaine, Franc, and Ireland king, defender of the faith, etc., haveing undertaken, for the glorie of God, and advancemente of the Christian faith, and honour of our king and countrie, a voyage to plant the first colonie in the Northerne parts of Virginia, doe by these presents solemnly and mutualy in the presence of God, and one of another, covenant and combine our selves togeather into a civill body politick, for our better ordering and preservation and furtherance of the ends aforesaid; and by vertue hearof to enacte, constitute, and frame such just and equall lawes, ordinances, acts, constitutions, and offices, from time to time, as shall be thought most meete and convenient for the generall good of the Colonie, unto which we promise all due submission and obedience. In witnes wherof we have hereunder subscribed our names at Cap-Codd the 11. of November, in the year of the raigne of our soveraigne lord, King James, of England, France, and Ireland the eighteenth, and of Scotland the fiftie fourth. An°: Dom. 1620.

After this they chose, or rather confirmed, Mr. John Carver (a man godly and well approved amongst them) their Governour for that year. And after they had provided a place for their goods, or comone store, (which were long in unlading for want of boats, foulnes of winter weather, and sicknes of diverce,) and begune some small cottages for their habitation, as time would admitte, they mette and consulted of lawes and orders, both for their civill and military Govermente, as the necessitie of their condition did require, still adding therunto as urgent occasion in severall times, and as cases did require.

51

The Petition of Right (1628)

The king's need for money was always the weakest point in the armor defending his prerogative, and parliament's control over taxation was ever its strongest weapon. Parliament had thus through the centuries forged its privileges and defended individual rights. Such a coinciding of royal needs and parliamentary concern occurred in 1628, a result of Charles I's and the Duke of Buckingham's insistence on fighting an ill-conceived war with France and Spain. The outcome was the Petition of Right, England's most important constitutional document since Magna Carta.

The document's form, a petition by which the king was asked to confirm existing rights, was due to the legal genius of Sir Edward Coke. In a statute these rights would have seemed a new creation requiring the king's approval. What Coke and the others wanted was a recognition of traditional rights. As the House of Commons had asserted in its Apology of 1604, "we most truly avouch that our privileges and liberties are our rights and due inheritance no less than our very lands and goods."

The similarity of the Petition of Right to Magna Carta was not accidental. Like Magna Carta, it listed a number of infringements of the ancient rights of Englishmen. The king's acknowledgment of such rights—not to be taxed without parliamentary consent, not to be imprisoned arbitrarily, not to have soldiers billeted in private houses without consent or compensation, not to have martial law imposed—placed them on a more solid and defensible foundation. Behind the specifics, however, was the unspoken but undoubted affirmation of the principle that the king was indeed beneath the law. As Coke said in the debate on the Petition: "Magna Carta is such a fellow that he will have no 'sovereign.' "

The English constitution is singularly devoid of broad, theoretical state-

SOURCE. J. P. Kenyon, ed., *The Stuart Constitution, 1603–1688: Documents and Commentary,* Cambridge University Press, 1966, pp. 82–85. Reprinted by permission of Cambridge University Press.

ments of the people's rights. Its great documents deal with specific rights arising out of immediate problems of one time and place. It is the understanding behind them that is the real constitution of England. Being unwritten it has been able to grow with time and circumstance, but without vigilance and effort it could as easily have been neglected and lost. Thus, again in the words of the Apology of the House of Commons: "The prerogatives of princes may easily and do daily grow; the privileges of the subject are for the most part at an everlasting stand. They may be by good providence and care preserved; but being once lost are not recovered but with much disquiet."

The Petition exhibited to his Majesty by the Lords Spiritual and Temporal and Commons in this present Parliament assembled concerning divers rights and liberties of the subject.

To the King's Most Excellent Majesty

Humbly show unto our Sovereign Lord the King the Lords Spiritual and Temporal and Commons in Parliament assembled, that whereas it is declared and enacted by a statute made in the time of the reign of King Edward the First commonly called Statutum de Tallagio non Concedendo . . . and by authority of Parliament holden in the five and twentieth year of the reign of King Edward the Third . . . and by other laws of this realm it is provided that . . . your subjects have inherited this freedom, that they should not be compelled to contribute to any tax, tallage, aid or other like charge not set by common consent in Parliament.

II. Yet, nevertheless of late . . . your people have been in divers places assembled and required to lend certain sums of money unto your Majesty, and many of them upon their refusal so to do have . . . been constrained to become bound to make appearance and give attendance before your Privy Council and in other places; and others of them have been therefore imprisoned, confined, and sundry other ways molested and disquieted. . . .

III. And where also by the statute called the Great Charter of the Liberties of England it is declared and enacted, that no freeman may be taken or imprisoned or be disseised of his freehold or liberties or his free customs or be outlawed or exiled or in any manner destroyed, but by the lawful judgement of his peers or by the law of the land.

V. Nevertheless against the tenor of the said statutes and other the good laws and statutes of your realm to that end provided, divers of your subjects have of late been imprisoned without any cause shown; and when for their deliverance they were brought before your justices by your Majesty's writ of habeas corpus there to undergo and receive as the Court should order, and their Keepers commanded to certify the causes of their detainer, no cause was certified, but that they were detained by your Majesty's special command signified by the Lords of your Privy Council, and yet were returned back to several prisons without being charged with any thing to which they might make answer according to the law.

VI. And whereas of late great companies of soldiers and mariners have been dispersed into divers counties of the realm, and the inhabitants against their will have been compelled to receive them into their houses, and there to suffer them to sojourn against the laws and customs of this realm and to the great grievance and vexation of the people.

VII. And whereas also by authority of Parliament in the five and twentieth year of the reign of King Edward the Third it is declared and enacted that no man should be forejudged of life and limb against the form of the Great Charter and the law of the land; and by the said Great Charter, and other the laws and statutes of this your realm, no man ought to be adjudged to death but by the laws established in this your realm, either by the customs of the same realm or by Act of Parliament . . . nevertheless of late time divers commissions under your Majesty's great seal have issued forth, by which certain persons have been assigned and appointed commissioners with power and authority to proceed within the land according to the justice of martial law . . . and by such summary course and order as is agreeable to martial law and as is used in armies in time of war to proceed to the trial and condemnation of such offenders, and them to cause to be executed and put to death according to the law martial.

By pretext whereof some of your Majesty's subjects have been by some of the said commissioners put to death. . . .

And also sundry grievous offenders by colour thereof claiming an exemption have escaped the punishments due to them by the laws and statutes of this your realm . . . upon pretence that the said offenders were punishable only by martial law. . . .

VIII. They do therefore humbly pray your most excellent Majesty that no man hereafter be compelled to make or yield any gift, loan, benevolence, tax or such like charge without common consent by Act of Parliament, and that none be called to make answer or take such oath or to give attendance or be confined or otherwise molested or disquieted concerning the same or for refusal thereof. And that no freeman in any such manner as is before mentioned be imprisoned or detained. And that your Majesty would be pleased to remove the said soldiers and mariners, and that your people may not be so burdened in time to come. And that the aforesaid commissions for proceeding by marital law may be revoked and annulled.

And that hereafter no commissions of like nature may issue forth to any person or persons whatsoever to be executed as aforesaid, lest by colour of them any of your Majesty's subjects be destroyed or put to death contrary to the laws and franchises of the land.

All of which they most humbly pray of your excellent Majesty as their rights and liberties according to the laws and statutes of this realm, and that your Majesty would also vouchsafe to declare that the awards, doings, and proceedings to the prejudice of your people in any of the premises shall not be drawn hereafter into consequence or example. And that your Majesty would be also graciously pleased for the further comfort and safety of your people to declare your royal will and pleasure, that in the thing aforesaid all your officers and ministers shall serve you according to the laws and statutes of this realm as they tender the honour of your Majesty and the prosperity of this kingdom.

52

John Milton, *Areopagitica* (1644). Freedom of the Press

The desire of Puritanism to reform the English church led to the belief that preachers should be allowed freely to preach, for only then could the word of God work its act of reformation. This, it turned out, was a dynamic beyond anything the Puritans envisioned. After the Star Chamber was abolished in 1641 and with it the state's control over the press, there was a flood of literature expressing all sorts of radical ideas regarding the church, state, and society. Not surprisingly, the presbyterian majority in parliament in 1643 ordered printing once more to be licensed and restricted. The reformation had gone far enough, and the expression of radical ideas should be halted.

SOURCE. John Milton, *Complete Prose Works of John Milton*, gen. eds. Douglas Bush et al., Vol. II (1643–1648), New Haven: Yale University Press, 1959, pp. 492–493, 561. Reprinted by permission of Yale University Press.

John Milton (1608–1674), scholarly and independent of mind, was both a Puritan and a humanist. The poetry he had already written was the earnest of the greatness yet to come, and his polemical pamphlets denouncing bishops and justifying divorce were as perceptive as they were controversial. The budding presbyterian settlement of 1643, which included the Solemn League and Covenant with the Scots and the new restrictions on printing, he denounced as "New Presbyter is but old Priest writ large." His motive in writing *Areopagitica* (1644) may have been to safeguard his own writings, but more likely it was to defend a principle in which he believed deeply. *Areopagitica* is in the form of a classical oration, having the same name as one Isocrates directed at the Athenian *areopagus* or assembly. The passage below remains one of the most forceful justifications of liberty.

Like the presbyterians, Milton also reached a point beyond which he could not go. Further along in *Areopagitica,* he added, "I mean not tolerated popery, and open superstition, which as it extirpats all religions and civil supremacies, so itself should be extirpat." Milton thus raised perhaps the greatest of all questions regarding liberty: should it be extended even to those who want to destroy it? Can truth really take care of itself, or must it ever be circumscribed within safe limits? If the latter, what are the limits and who defines them?

I deny not, but that it is of greatest concernment in the Church and Commonwealth, to have a vigilant eye how Bookes demeane themselves, as well as men; and thereafter to confine, imprison, and do sharpest justice on them as malefactors: For Books are not absolutely dead things, but doe contain a potencie of life in them to be as active as that soule whose progeny they are; nay they do preserve as in a violl the purest efficacie and extraction of that living intellect that bred them. I know they are as lively, and as vigorously productive, as those fabulous Dragons teeth; and being sown up and down, may chance to spring up armed men. And yet on the other hand unlesse warinesse be us'd, as good almost kill a Man as kill a good Book; who kills a Man kills a reasonable creature, Gods Image; but hee who destroyes a good Booke, kills reason it selfe, kills the Image of God, as it were in the eye. Many a man lives a burden to the Earth; but a good Booke is the pretious life-blood of a master spirit, imbalm'd and treasur'd up on purpose to a life beyond life. 'Tis true, no age can restore a life, whereof perhaps there is no great losse; and revolutions of ages doe not oft recover the losse of a rejected truth, for the want of which whole Nations fare the worse. We should be wary therefore what persecution we raise against the living labours of publick men; how we spill that season'd life of man preserv'd and stor'd up in Books; since we see a kinde of homicide may be thus committed, sometimes a martyrdome, and if it extend to the whole impression, a kinde of massacre, whereof the execution ends not in the slaying of an elementall life, but strikes at that ethereall and fift essence, the breath of reason it selfe, slaies an immortality rather then a life. . . . And though all the windes of doctrin were let loose to play upon the earth, so Truth be in the field, we do injuriously by licencing and prohibiting to misdoubt her strength. Let her and Falshood grapple; who ever knew Truth put to the wors, in a free and open encounter.

53

The Putney Debates. Radicalism in the New Model Army, 1647

The importance of the English Revolution (1640–1660) is partly in the actions taken, culminating in 1649 in the public trial and execution of Charles I for treason, and partly in the new political ideas expressed. In both deed and thought, the Revolution was thereafter an example for political thinkers and practitioners to contemplate and to follow or avoid.

Some of the Revolution's most serious political thought and discussion took place in the New Model Army, which had by 1647 begun to consider itself a political as well as a military body. It seized the king from parliament and proceeded itself to negotiate with him. There were, however, in the army two points of view, that of the Independents, as represented by

SOURCE. A. S. P. Woodhouse, ed., *Puritanism and Liberty: Being the Army Debates (1647–9) from the Clarke Manuscripts*, Chicago: The University of Chicago Press, 1951, pp. 7, 24–27, 33, 53–58, 65–66. Reprinted by permission of the University of Chicago Press and J. M. Dent, Ltd.

Lieutenant General Oliver Cromwell and his son-in-law, Commissary General Henry Ireton, and that of the more radical representatives of the regiments, such men as John Wildman and Thomas Rainborough, who can best be described as Levellers. The basic issue was the nature of England's political settlement. Should it be based on the moderate "Heads of the Proposals" written by Ireton or the Levellers' radical "Agreement of the People"? As is shown below, the issues were raised to the highest theoretical level: Is justice "that which is just according to the foundation of justice between man and man"? or is "the justice of the thing" gauged by a higher, abstract law that can even determine "that an unjust engagement is rather to be broken than kept"? And who should have a political voice in the kingdom, only those with a "permanent interest," "the persons in whom the land lies, and those in corporations in whom all trading lies," or "every man born in England"?

The debates achieved nothing, except to convince Cromwell that it was dangerous to allow them to continue. He and the other generals reasserted their authority, ending all participation in politics or army decisions by "Agitators" elected from the ranks. The Putney Debates are valuable for the light that they shed on the activities of the army during a period of intense and unprecedented political activity and on the difficult relationship between Puritanism and radical political thought and action.

These debates, held at Putney near London on October 28 and 29 and November 1, 1647, were recorded in shorthand by William Clarke, a clerk of the New Model Army. They were probably not written out in "a fair hand" until after the Restoration. Though these "Clarke Papers" were given to Worcester College, Oxford, by Clarke's son in 1736, they went unnoticed until they were mentioned in a catalogue of manuscripts in 1852. They were edited for the Camden Society by Charles Firth in 1891. The dialogue below is taken from the edition of A. S. P. Woodhouse. The state of the manuscript required Woodhouse to add the words in square backets in order to make speeches and sentences intelligible.

Cromwell: Truly this paper does contain in it very great alterations of the very government of the kingdom. . . . And what the consequences of such an alteration as this would be . . . wise men and godly men ought to consider. . . . How do we know if, whilst we are disputing these things, another company of men shall [not] gather together, and put out a paper as plausible perhaps as this? . . . And not only another, and another, but many of this kind. And if so, what do you think the consequence of that would be? Would it not be confusion? Would it not be utter confusion? . . .

Wildman: And whereas it is desired that engagements may be considered, I shall desire that only the justice of the thing that is proposed may be considered. [I would know] whether the chief thing in the Agreement, the intent of it, be not this, to secure the rights of the people in their Parliaments. . . . I shall make that motion to be the thing considered: Whether the thing be just, or the people's due? And then there can be no engagement to bind from it.

Ireton: . . . when we talk of just, it is not so much of what is sinful before God . . . but . . . that which is just according to the foundation of justice between man and man. And for my part I account that the great foundation of justice . . . that we should keep covenant one with another. . . . What right hath any man to anything if you lay not [down] that principle, that we are to keep covenant? If you will resort only to the Law of Nature, by the Law of Nature you have no more right to this land, or anything else, than I have. I have as much right to take hold of anything that is for my sustenance, [to] take hold of anything that I have a desire to for my satisfaction, as you. . . .

Wildman: Our [sense] was, that an unjust engagement is rather to be broken than kept. . . . I make a question whether any engagement can be [binding] to an unjust thing. . . . I do apply this to the case in hand: that it might be considered whether it be unjust to bring in the King in such a way as he may be in a capacity to destroy the people. . . .

Rainborough: Is it not an argument, if a pilot run his ship upon a rock, or [if] a general mount his cannon against his army, he is to be resisted? I think that this [is] as clear[ly] the very case as anything in the world. . . . For really I think that the poorest he that is in England hath a life to live, as the greatest he; and therefore truly, sir, I think it's clear, that every man that is to live under a government ought first by his own consent to put himself under that government; and I do think that the poorest man in England is not at all bound in a strict sense to that government that he hath not had a voice to put himself under. . . .

Ireton: Give me leave to tell you, that if you make this the rule I think you must fly for refuge to an absolute natural right, and you must deny all civil right. . . . We talk of birthright. Truly [by] birthright there is thus much claim. Men may justly have by birthright, by their very being born in England, that we should not seclude them out of England, that we should not refuse to give them air and place and ground, and the freedom of the highways and other things, to live amongst us—not any man that is born here, though by his birth there come nothing at all (that is part of the permanent interest of this kingdom) to him. That I think is due to a man by birth. But that by a man's being born here he shall have a share in that power that shall dispose of the lands here, and of all things here, I do not think it a sufficient ground. I am sure if we look upon that which is the utmost (within [any] man's view) of what was originally the constitution of this kingdom, upon that which is most radical and fundamental, and which if you take away, there is no man hath any land, any goods, [or] any civil interest, that is this: that those that choose the representers for the making of laws by which this state and kingdom are to be governed, are the persons who, taken together, do comprehend the local interest of this kingdom; that is, the persons in whom all land lies, and those in corporations in whom all trading lies. . . .

Rainborough: Truly, sir, I am of the same opinion I was, and am resolved to keep it till I know reason why I should not. . . . I do hear nothing at all that can convince me, why any man that is born in England ought not to have his voice in election of burgesses. It is said that if a man have not a permanent interest, he can have no claim; and [that] we must be no freer than the laws will let us be, and that there is no [law in any] chronicle will let us be freer than that we [now] enjoy. . . . And therefore I say, that either it must be the Law of God or the law of man that must prohibit the meanest man in the kingdom to have this benefit as well as the greatest. I do not find anything in the Law of God, that a lord shall choose twenty burgesses, and a gentleman but two, or a poor man shall choose none: I find no such thing in the Law of Nature, nor in the Law of Nations. But I do find that all Englishmen must be subject to English laws, and I do verily believe that there is no man but will say that the foundation of all law lies in the people. . . . A man, when he hath an estate, hath an interest in making laws, [but] when he hath none, he hath no power in it; so that a man cannot lose that which he hath for the maintenance of his family but he must [also] lose that which God and nature hath given him! And therefore I do [think], and am still of the same opinion, that every man born in England cannot, ought not, neither by the Law of God nor the Law of Nature, to be exempted from the choice of those who are to make laws for him to live under, and for him, for aught I know, to lose his life under. . . .

Ireton: All the main thing that I speak for, is because I would have an eye to property. . . . let every man consider with himself that he do not go that way to take away all property. For here is the case of the most fundamental part of the constitution of the kingdom, which if you take away, you take away all by that. Here men of this and this quality are determined to be the electors of men to the Parliament, and they are all those who have any permanent interest in the kingdom, and who, taken together, do comprehend the whole [permanent, local] interest of the kingdom. . . . Now I wish we may all consider of what right you will challenge that all the people should have right to elections. Is it by the right of nature? If you will hold forth that as your ground, then I think you must deny all property too, and this is my reason. For thus: by that same right of nature (whatever it be) that you pretend, by which you can say, one man hath an equal right with another to the choosing of him that shall govern him—by the same right of nature, he hath the same [equal] right in any goods he sees—meat, drink, clothes—to take and use them for his sustenance. He hath a freedom to the land, [to take] the ground, to exercise it, till it; he hath the [same] freedom to anything that any one doth account himself to have any propriety in. . . .

Wildman: Our case is to be considered thus, that we have been under slavery. That's acknowledged by all. Our very laws were made by our conquerors; and whereas it's spoken much of chronicles, I conceive there is no credit to be given to any of them; and the reason is because those that were our lords, and made us their vassals, would suffer nothing else to be chronicled. We are now engaged for our freedom. That's the end of Parliaments; not to constitute what is already [established, but to act] according to the just rules of government. Every person in England hath as clear a right to elect his representative as the greatest person in England. I conceive that's the undeniable maxim of government: that all government is in the free consent of the people. . . . And therefore I should humbly move, that if the question be stated—which would soonest bring things to an issue—it might rather be thus: Whether any person can justly be bound by law, who doth not give his consent that such persons shall make laws for him?

John Rushworth, *Historical Collections.* The Trial of Charles I, 1649

Charles I (1625–1649) was a most exasperating man, as the Scots, then parliament, and finally the New Model Army discovered following the First Civil War. His escape in November 1647 and his subsequent Engagement with the Scots inaugurating a Second Civil War turned exasperation into complete disillusion and hatred. Parliament decided it would make no further attempts to negotiate with him, and William Goffe, at an army prayer meeting on May 1, 1648, spoke for the army when he resolved "to call Charles Stuart, that man of blood, to an account for that blood he had shed and the mischief he had done." Victory in the field was to the army proof that God favored its cause and approved its intentions. The army purged a hesitant parliament of its 140 presbyterian members, leaving a Rump of 50 or 60 members whose opinions matched those of the army. The Rump then appointed the court that tried the king. The court's sentence, reproduced in part below, was delivered on January 27, 1649. The king's speech was delivered on the scaffold just before his execution on January 30.

Whether Charles was in fact "a Tyrant, Traitor, and Murderer, and publick Enemy to the Commonwealth," as charged and sentenced, or "the Martyr of the People," as he claimed in his speech, each historian after much study and thought must decide for himself. Certainly, Charles's interpretation was the one accepted by the mass of the people at the time, and Charles dead proved as troublesome to his enemies as ever he had alive. The revolutionaries, having destroyed the old government, were unable to replace it

SOURCE. John Rushworth, *Historical Collections,* Vol. VII, The Second Edition, London: Printed for J. Walthoe et al., 1721, pp. 1418–1419, 1429–1430.

with another acceptable to the people, their more exalted view of government notwithstanding. In the end the monarchy was restored in the person of Charles II (1660–1685), and the whole interlude of civil wars and Interregnum was officially forgotten. Nevertheless, the king was alerted to the danger of exasperating his subjects, and subjects were made cautious by the certain knowledge that desperate means might well doom worthy objectives to failure.

John Rushworth (1612?–1690) held various government and army positions throughout the period of the revolution. The notes he kept and the papers he gathered were later published in eight large folio volumes (1659–1701).

Whereas the Commons of England assembled in Parliament, have by their late Act . . . Authorised and constituted us an High Court of Justice. . . .

By virtue whereof the said Charles Stuart . . . was charged, That he the said Charles Stuart, being admitted King of England, and therein trusted with a limited Power to govern by and according to the Law of the Land, and not otherwise; and by his Trust, Oath, and Office, being obliged to use the Power committed to him, for the good and benefit of the People, and for the preservation of their Rights and Liberties; yet nevertheless out of a wicked design to erect and uphold in himself an unlimited and tyrannical Power to rule according to his Will and to overthrow the Rights and Liberties of the People, and to take away and make void the foundations thereof, and of all redress and remedy of misgovernment, which by the fundamental Constitutions of this Kingdom were reserved on the Peoples behalf in the Right and Power of frequent and successive Parliaments, or national Meetings in Council; he the said Charles Stuart, for accomplishment of such his Designs, and for the Protecting of himself and his Adherents in his and their wicked Practices, to the same end, hath traitorously and maliciously levyed War against the present Parliament, and People therein represented . . . and that he hath thereby caused and procured many thousands of the free People of this Nation to be slain; and by Divisions, Parties, and Insurrections within this Land, by Invasions from foreign Parts, endeavoured and procured by him, and by many other evil ways and means, he the said Charles Stuart hath not only maintained and carried on the said War both by Sea and Land, but also hath renewed, or caused to be renewed, the said War against the Parliament and good People of this Nation to this present year 1648. . . . And that by the said cruel and unnatural War so levyed, continued and renewed, much innocent Blood of the free People of this Nation hath been spilt; many Families undone; the publick Treasure wasted; Trade obstructed, and miserably decaed; vast expence and damage to the Nation incurred, and many parts of the Land spoiled, some of them even to Desolation; and that he still continues his Commission to his said Son, and other Rebels and Revolters . . . and that all the said wicked Designs, Wars, and evil Practices of him the said Charles Stuart, were still carried on for the advancement and upholding of the personal Interest of Will, Power, and pretended Prerogative to himself and his Family, against the publick Interest, Common Right, Liberty, Justice and Peace of the People of this Nation: And that he thereby hath been and is the Occasioner, Author, and Continuer of the said unnatural, cruel and bloody Wars, and therein guilty of all the Treasons, Murders, Rapines, Burnings, Spoils, Desolations, Damage, and Mischief to this Nation, acted and committed in the said Wars, or occasioned thereby; whereupon the Proceedings and Judgments of this Court were prayed against him, as a Tyrant, Traitor, and Murderer, and publick Enemy to the Commonwealth.

Now therefore upon serious and mature Deliberation of the Premises, and Consideration had of the notoriety of the matters of fact charged upon him as aforesaid, this Court is in Judgment and Conscience satisfied that he the said Charles Stuart is guilty of levying War against the said Parliament and People, and maintaining and continuing the same; . . . and by the general Course of his Government, Counsels and Practices, before and since this Parliament began . . . that he has been and is guilty of the wicked Designs and Endeavours in the said Charge set forth; and that the said War hath been levyed, maintained and continued by him as aforesaid, in prosecution and for accomplishment of the said Designs; and that he hath been and is the Occasioner, Author, and Continuer of the said unnatural, cruel, and bloody Wars, and therein guilty of High Treason, and of the Murders, Rapines, Burnings, Spoils, Desolations, Damage and Mischief to this Nation acted and committed in the said War, and occasioned thereby. For all which Treasons and Crimes this Court doth adjudg, That he the said Charles Stuart, as a Tyrant, Traitor, Murderer and a publick Enemy to the good People of this Nation, shall be put to death by severing of his Head from his Body.

The King

"I could hold my peace very well, if I did not think that holding my Peace would make some Men think that I did submit to the Guilt, as well as to the Punishment. But I think it is my Duty to God first, and to my Country, for to clear my self both as an honest Man, a good King, and a good Christian. I shall begin first with my Innocency: In troth, I think it not very needful for me to insist upon this, for all the World knows I never did begin the War with the two Houses of Parliament; and I call God to witness (to whom I must shortly make an account) that I never did intend to incroach upon their Privileges. They began upon me: It is the Militia they began upon; they confess that the Militia was mine, but they thought it fit to have it from me: . . . yet for all this God forbid that I should be so ill a Christian, as not to say that God's Judgments are just upon me; many times he does pay Justice by an unjust Sentence, that is ordinarily: I only say this, that an unjust Sentence (meaning Strafford) that I suffered to take effect, is punished now by an unjust Sentence upon me; that is, so far I have said to shew you that I am an innocent Man. . . . Now, Sirs . . . you will never do right, nor God will never prosper you, until you give him his due, the King his due (that is, my Successors) and the People their due, I am as much for them as any of you: You must give God his due, by regulating rightly his Church. . . . As for the King, the Laws of the Land will clearly instruct you for that. . . .

"For the People: And truly I desire their Liberty and Freedom, as much as any Body whomsoever; but I must tell you, That their Liberty and Freedom consists in having of Government, those Laws by which their Life and their Goods may be most their own. It is not for having share in government (Sirs) that is nothing pertaining to them. A Subject and a Sovereign are clean different things; and therefore until they do that, I mean, That you do put the People in that Liberty as I say, certainly they will never enjoy themselves. Sirs, it was for this now that I am come here. If I would have given way to an Arbitrary Way, for to have all Laws changed according to the Power of the Sword, I needed not to have come here; and therefore I tell you (and I pray God it be not laid to your Charge) that I am the Martyr of the People."

55

Oliver Cromwell, Letter (September 17, 1649). The Capture of Drogheda

Oliver Cromwell (1599–1658) personified the English Revolution. Although not prominent in parliament at the beginning, once war broke out his aptitude for organization and for military strategy and tactics soon pushed him to the fore. His cavalry regiment, the "Ironsides," was the key element in parliament's victory at Marston Moor in 1644 and the nucleus of the New Model Army created in 1645. By 1649, Cromwell had become the dominant force not only in the army but in all of England. More than anyone else, he determined the trial and execution of Charles I, the creation of the Commonwealth, and the destruction of its enemies.

The Commonwealth's first concern was Ireland, of which England had lost control following the rebellion of 1641 and the massacre of Protestants in Ulster. Cromwell in August 1649 embarked for Ireland with a well equipped army of 12,000 to suppress the eight-year-old rebellion and to prevent Ireland's becoming the staging ground for Prince Charles's attempt to regain the throne of his father. Cromwell's first military action, which he described in the letter below, was the brief siege and capture of the fortress town of Drogheda.

The massacres at Drogheda and at Wexford a month later, if they do not display Cromwell's military genius, certainly indicate his efficiency. That his purpose was served is indicated by the royalist earl of Ormonde's assessment of his action: "It is not to be imagined how great the terror is that those successes and the power of the rebels have struck into this

---

SOURCE. Wilbur Cortez Abbott, *The Writings and Speeches of Oliver Cromwell*, Vol. II: *The Commonwealth, 1649–1653,* Cambridge: Harvard University Press, 1939, pp. 125–128. By permission of Harvard University Press.

people." By tradition an army was justified in using such harshness when forced to suffer casualties in storming a fortress. Cromwell's conviction that the victory was the "righteous judgment of God upon these barbarous wretches" reflected a common English assessment of the Irish and the Puritan view of success as indicative of God's approval. Nevertheless, Cromwell's enthusiasm in attributing the success of his bloody deeds to God has always seemed to a degree unnatural, something his apologists have felt they must explain and his detractors have pointed to as proof of his excess and unbalance. The political consequences of Drogheda and its effect on Cromwell's reputation were in the long run questionable. A priest who claimed to have witnessed and escaped from the slaughter at Wexford denounced Cromwell as "that English pest of hell," a judgment the Irish have retained to this day, just as they have remembered Drogheda as England's greatest crime against them.

For the Honourable William Lenthall, Esquire, Speaker of the Parliament of England: These

SIR,

Your Army came before the town upon Monday following, where having pitched, as speedy course was taken as could be to frame our batteries, which took up the more time because divers of the battering guns were on shipboard. Upon Monday the 9th of this instant, the batteries began to play. Whereupon I sent Sir Arthur Ashton, the then Governor, a summons to deliver the town to the use of the Parliament of England. To the which I received no satisfactory answer, but proceeded that day to beat down the steeple of the church on the south side of the town, and to beat down a tower not far from the same place. . . .

Upon Tuesday the 10th of this instant, about five o'clock in the evening, we began the storm, and after some hot dispute we entered about seven or eight hundred men, the enemy disputing it very stiffly with us. And indeed, through the advantages of the place, and the courage God was pleased to give the defenders, our men were forced to retreat quite out of the breach, not without some considerable loss. . . .

Although our men that stormed the breaches were forced to recoil, as before is expressed, yet, being encouraged to recover their loss, they made a second attempt, wherein God was pleased [so] to animate them that they got ground of the enemy, and by the goodness of God, forced him to quit his entrenchments. And after a very hot dispute . . . our men became masters both of their retrenchments and the church; which . . . proved of excellent use to us. . . .

The enemy retreated, divers of them, into the Mill-Mount; a place very strong and of difficult access, being exceedingly high, having a good graft, and strongly palisadoed. The Governor, Sir Arthur Ashton, and divers considerable Officers being there, our men getting up to them, were ordered by me to put them all to the sword. And indeed, being in the heat of action, I forbade them to spare any that were in arms in the town, and, I think, that night they put to the sword about 2,000 men, divers of the officers and soldiers being fled over the Bridge into the other part of the Town, where about one hundred of them possessed St. Peter's church-steeple, some the west gate, and others a strong round tower next the gate called St. Sunday's. These being summoned to yield to mercy, refused, whereupon I ordered the steeple of St. Peter's Church to be fired, where one of them was heard to say in the midst of the flames: "God damn me, God confound me; I burn, I burn."

The next day, the other two towers were summoned, in one of which was about six or seven score; but they refused to yield themselves, and we knowing that hunger must compel them, set only good guards to secure them from running away until their stomach were come down. From one of the said towers, notwithstanding their condition, they killed and wounded some of our men. When they submitted, their officers were knocked on the head, and every tenth man of the soldiers killed, and the rest shipped for the Barbadoes. The soldiers in the other tower were all spared, as to their lives only, and shipped likewise for the Barbadoes.

I am persuaded that this is a righteous judgment of God upon these barbarous wretches, who have imbrued their hands in so much innocent blood; and that it will tend to prevent the effusion of blood for the future, which are the satisfactory grounds to such actions, which otherwise cannot but work remorse and regret. . . .

And now give me leave to say how it comes to pass that this work is wrought. It was set upon some of our hearts, That a great thing should be done, not by power or might, but by the Spirit of God. And is it not so clear? That which caused your men to storm so courageously, it was the Spirit of God, who gave your men courage, and took it away again; and gave the enemy courage, and took it away again; and gave your men courage again, and therewith this happy success. And therefore it is good that God alone have all the glory.

It is remarkable that these people, at the first, set up the mass in some places of the town that had been monasteries; but afterwards grew up so insolent that, the last Lord's day before the storm, the Protestants were thrust out of the great Church called St. Peter's, and they had public mass there: and in this very place near one thousand of them were put to the sword, fleeing thither for safety. I believe all their friars were knocked on the head promiscuously but two; the one of which was Father Peter Taaff, (brother to the Lord Taaff), whom the soldiers took, the next day, and made an end of; the other was taken in the round tower, under the repute of lieutenant, and when he understood that the officers in that tower had no quarter, he confessed he was a friar; but that did not save him. . . .

Your most humble servant,
OLIVER CROMWELL.
Dublin,
Sept. 17, 1649.

56

Thomas Mun, *England's Treasure by Forraign Trade* (1664)

England's greatest mercantile endeavor of the seventeenth century was the East India Company, chartered by the crown in 1600 to promote commerce with the east. Despite its success, the company was constantly criticized by the general public. Some viewed it as just another royal monopoly restricting commerce for the benefit of a few fortunate merchants. Other critics saw the company's exchange of specie for spices as economically damaging to England. To these "bullionists," gold and silver represented wealth and power, whose shipment to India weakened England. The East India Company had, of course, numerous defenders, the most able being Thomas Mun (1571–1641), a wealthy merchant who became a director of the company. His most famous pamphlet was *England's Treasure by Forraign Trade*, written about 1630 but not published until 1664.

SOURCE. Thomas Mun, *England's Treasure by Forraign Trade*, Oxford: Basil Blackwell, 1949, pp. 1, 5, 71–73, 80–82, 88. Reprinted by permission of Basil Blackwell, Ltd.

In his defense of the company, Mun presents a number of interesting ideas. In the following selection, he develops the concept of the balance of trade; England must always "sell more to strangers yearly than wee consume of theirs in value." He did not, however, believe in restricting the export of specie. The gold and silver sent to India represented seed from which you reaped a crop of greater value. He was also insistent that England's future rested largely on the shoulders of her merchants. The English must cease "besotting" themselves with "pipe and pot" and work to develop England's economic potential. Finally, it is significant that Mun at a relatively early date (1630) considered Holland, not France or Spain, as the greatest threat to England, a remarkably astute observation as evidenced by the great commercial wars with the Dutch in the 1650s and 1660s.

The love and service of our Country consisteth not so much in the knowledge of those duties which are to be performed by others, as in the skilful practice of that which is done by our selves; and therefore (my Son) it is now fit that I say something of the Merchant, which I hope in due time shall be thy Vocation: Yet herein are my thoughts free from all Ambition, although I rank thee in a place of so high estimation; for the Merchant is worthily called *The Steward of the Kingdoms Stock,* by way of Commerce with other Nations; a work of no less *Reputation* than *Trust,* which ought to be performed with great skill and conscience, that so the private gain may ever accompany the publique good. . . .

Although a Kingdom may be enriched by gifts received, or by purchase taken from some other Nations, yet these are things uncertain and of small consideration when they happen. The ordinary means therefore to encrease our wealth and treasure is by *Forraign Trade,* wherein wee must ever observe this rule; to sell more to strangers yearly than wee consume of theirs in value. For suppose that when this Kingdom is plentifully served with the Cloth, Lead, Tinn, Iron, Fish and other native commodities, we doe yearly export the overplus to forraign Countries to the value of twenty two hundred thousand pounds; by which means we are enabled beyond the Seas to buy and bring in forraign wares for our use and Consumptions, to the value of twenty hundred thousand pounds; By this order duly kept in our trading, we may rest assured that the Kingdom shall be enriched yearly two hundred thousand pounds, which must be brought to us in so much Treasure; because that part of our stock which is not returned to us in wares must necessarily be brought home in treasure. . . .

If we duly consider *Englands* Largeness, Beauty, Fertility, Strength, both by Sea and Land, in multitude of warlike People, Horses, Ships, Ammunition, advantagious situation for Defence and Trade, number of Sea-ports and Harbours, which are of difficult access to Enemies, and of easie outlet to the Inhabitants wealth by excellent Fleece-wools, Iron, Lead, Tynn, Saffron, Corn, Victuals, Hides, Wax, and other natural Endowments; we shall find this Kingdome capable to sit as master of a Monarchy. For what greater glory and advantage can any powerful Nation have, than to be thus richly and naturally possessed of all things needful for Food, Rayment, War, and Peace, not onely for its own plentiful use, but also to supply the wants of other Nations, in such a measure, that much money may be thereby gotten yearly, to make the happiness compleat. For experience telleth us, that notwithstanding that excessive Consumption of this Kingdome alone, to say nothing of *Scotland,* there is exported *communibus annis* of our own native commodities for the value of twenty two hundred thousand pounds *Sterling,* or somewhat more; so that if we were not too much affected to Pride, monstrous Fashions, and Riot, above all other Nations, one million and an half of pounds might plentifully supply our unnecessary wants (as I may term them) of Silks, Sugars, Spices, Fruits, and all others; so that seven hundred thousand pounds might be yearly treasur'd up in money to make the Kingdome exceeding rich and powerful in short time. But this great plenty which we enjoy, makes us a people not only *vicious* and *excessive,* wastful of the means we have, but also improvident & careless of much other wealth that shamefully we lose, which is, the Fishing in his Majesty's Seas of *England, Scotland,* and *Ireland,* being of no less consequence than all our other riches which we export and vent to Strangers, whilest in the mean time (through lewd idleness) great multitudes of our people cheat, roar, rob, hang, beg, cant, pine and perish, which by this means and maintenance might be much encreased, to the further wealth and strength of these Kingdomes, especially by Sea, for our own safety, and terrour of our enemies. The endeavours of the industrious Dutch do give sufficient testimony of this truth, to *our great shame, and no less perill,* if it have not a timely prevention: for, whilest we leave our wonted honourable exercises and studies, following our pleasures, and of late years besotting our selves with pipe and pot, in a beastly manner, sucking smoak, and drinking healths, until death stares many in the face; the said Dutch have well-neer left this swinish vice, and taken up our wonted valour, which we have often so well performed both by Sea and Land, and particularly in their defence, although they are not now so thankful as to acknowledge the same. The summ of all is this, that the general leprosie of our Piping, Potting, Feasting, Fashions, and mis-spending of our time in Idleness and Pleasure (contrary to the Law of God, and the use of other Nations) hath made us effeminate in our bodies, weak in our knowledg, poor in our Treasure, declined in our Valour, unfortunate in our Enterprises, and contemned by our Enemies. I write the more of these exeses, because they do so greatly wast our wealth, which is the main subject of this whole Books discourse: and indeed our wealth might be a rare discourse for all *Christendome* to admire and fear, if we would but add *Art* to *Nature,* our *labour* to our *natural means*; the neglect whereof hath given a notable advantage to other *nations,* & especially to the *Hollanders,* whereof I will briefly say something in the next place. . . .

I have heard some Italians wisely and worthily discourse of the natural Strength and Wealth of *England,* which they make to be matchless, if we should (but in part) apply our selves to such policies and endeavours as are very commonly used in some other Countreys of *Europe*; and much they have admired, that our thoughts and jealousies attend only upon the Spanish and French greatness, never once suspecting, but constantly embracing the Netherlanders as our best Friends and Allies; when in truth (as they well observe) there are no people in Christendome who do more undermine, hurt, and eclipse us daily in our Navigation and Trades, both abroad and at home; and this not only in the rich Fishing in his Majesty's Seas (whereof we have already written) but also in our Inland trades between City and City, in the Manufactures of Silk, Woolls, and the like, made here in this Kingdom, wherein they never give employment or education in their Arts to the English, but ever (according to the custome of the Jewes, where they abide in *Turkey,* and divers places of Christendome) they live wholly to themselves in their own Tribes. So that we may truly say of the Dutch, that although they are amongst us, yet certainly they are not of us, no not they who are born and bred here in our own Countrey, for stil they will be Dutch, not having so much as one drop of English bloud in their hearts.

More might be written of these Netherlanders pride and ambitious endeavours, whereby they hope in time to grow mighty, if they be not prevented, and much more may be said of their cruel and unjust violence used (especially to their best friends, the English) in matters of bloud, trade, and other profits, where they have had advantage and power to perform it: but these things are already published in print to the view and admiration of the world; wherefore I will conclude, and the summ of all is this, that the United Provinces, which now are so great a trouble, if not a terrour to the Spaniard, were heretofore little better than a charge to them in their possession, and would be so again in the like occasion, the reasons whereof I might yet further enlarge; but they are not pertinent to this discourse, more than is already declared, to shew the different effects between *Natural and Artificial Wealth:* The first of which, as it is most noble and advantagious, being always ready and certain, so doth it make the people careless, proud, and given to all excesses; whereas the second enforceth Vigilancy, Literature, Arts and Policy. My wishes therefore are, that as *England* doth plentifully enjoy the one, and is fully capable of the other, that our endeavours might as worthily conjoyn them both together, to the reformation of our vicious idleness, and greater glory of these famous Kingdomes. . . .

Behold then the true form and worth of forraign Trade, which is, *The great Revenue of the King, The honour of the Kingdom, The Noble profession of the Merchant, The School of our Arts, The supply of our wants, The employment of our poor, The improvement of our Lands, The Nurcery of our Mariners, The walls of the Kingdoms, The means of our Treasure, The Sinnews of our wars, The terror of our Enemies.* For all which great and weighty reasons, do so many well governed States highly countenance the profession, and carefully cherish the action, not only with Policy to encrease it, but also with power to protect it from all forraign injuries: because they know it is a Principal in Reason of State to maintain and defend that which doth Support them and their estates.

57

Samuel Pepys, *Diary.* Great Fire of London, 1666

Samuel Pepys (1633–1703) was one of the most able administrators of the seventeenth century. Although born poor, he was fortunate in his family connections, being related to Edward Montagu, a naval commander under Oliver Cromwell and later the first earl of Sandwich. Through Montagu's influence, Pepys obtained a clerkship in the Navy Office. Eventually, in 1673 he became Secretary of the Admiralty, a position he held off and on until

SOURCE. *The Diary of Samuel Pepys*, ed. Henry B. Wheatley, London: G. Bell and Sons Ltd., 1962, V, 392–400, 403.

the Glorious Revolution. While at the Admiralty, he did much to streamline procurement procedures and to make the navy a more efficient fighting force.

Today Pepys is best known for his diary, which covers the years from 1660 to 1669. Being a bureaucrat and a Londoner, Pepys provides valuable insight into the life-style of the urban middle class in Restoration England. Not only does he discuss the new fads in sport, etiquette, and literature, but he vividly describes the great events that he witnessed, the restoration of Charles II, the plague of 1665 to 1666, and the great fire of September 1666. The historian can only regret that failing eyesight forced Pepys in 1669 to discontinue his diary, thereby denying future generations his comments on the great constitutional struggles of the 1670s and 1680s.

Pepys wrote his diary in shorthand, probably never intending it for publication. The original manuscript of 3000 pages bound by Pepys in six volumes was given by his heirs to Magdalene College, Cambridge. The first published edition did not appear until 1825. The candor and grace of his writing made it immediately popular, and countless other editions, usually abridged, have appeared since. A diarist can aspire to no greater honor than to be the "Pepys" to his generation.

2nd (Lord's day).   Some of our mayds sitting up late last night to get things ready against our feast to-day, Jane called us up about three in the morning, to tell us of a great fire they saw in the City. So I rose and slipped on my night-gowne, and went to her window, and thought it to be on the back-side of Marke-lane at the farthest; but, being unused to such fires as followed, I thought it far enough off; and so went to bed again and to sleep. About seven rose again to dress myself, and there looked out at the window, and saw the fire not so much as it was and further off. So to my closett to set things to rights after yesterday's cleaning. By and by Jane comes and tells me that she hears that above 300 houses have been burned down to-night by the fire we saw, and that it is now burning down all Fish-street, by London Bridge. So I made myself ready presently, and walked to the Tower, and there got up upon one of the high places, Sir J. Robinson's little son going up with me; and there I did see the houses at that end of the bridge all on fire, and an infinite great fire on this and the other side the end of the bridge. . . . So down, with my heart full of trouble, to the Lieutenant of the Tower, who tells me that it begun this morning in the King's baker's house in Pudding-lane, and that it hath burned St. Magnus's Church and most part of Fish-street already. So I down to the water-side, and there got a boat and through bridge, and there saw a lamentable fire. . . . Having staid, and in an hour's time seen the fire rage every way, and nobody to my sight, endeavouring to quench it, but to remove their goods, and leave all to the fire, and having seen it get as far as the Steele-yard, and the wind mighty high and driving it into the City; and every thing, after so long a drought, proving combustible, even the very stones of churches, and among other things the poor steeple . . . whereof my old schoolfellow Elborough is parson, taken fire in the very top, and there burned till it fell down: I to White Hall . . . where people come about me, and I did give them an account dismayed them all, and word was carried in to the King. So I was called for, and did tell the King and Duke of Yorke what I saw, and that unless his Majesty did command houses to be pulled down nothing could stop the fire. They seemed much troubled, and the King commanded me to go to my Lord Mayor from him, and command him to spare no houses, but to pull down before the fire every way. . . . At last met my Lord Mayor in Canning-street, like a man spent, with a handkercher about his neck. To the King's message he cried, like a fainting woman, "Lord! what can I do? I am spent: people will not obey me. I have been pulling down houses; but the fire overtakes us faster than we can do it." . . . So he left me, and I him, and walked home, seeing people all almost distracted, and no manner of means used to quench the fire. The houses, too, so very thick thereabouts, and full of matter for burning, as pitch and tarr, in Thames-street; and warehouses of oyle, and wines, and brandy, and other things. . . . Having seen as much as I could now, I away to White Hall by appointment, and there walked to St. James's Parke, and there met my wife and Creed and Wood and his wife, and walked to my boat; and there upon the water again, and to the fire up and down, it still encreasing, and the wind great. So near the fire as we could for smoke; and all over the Thames, with one's face in the wind, you were almost burned with a shower of fire-drops. . . . When we could endure no more upon the water, we to a little ale-house on the Bankside, over against the Three Cranes, and there staid till it was dark almost, and saw the fire grow; and, as it grew darker, appeared more and more, and in corners and upon steeples, and between churchs and houses, as far as we could see up the hill of the City, in a most horrid malicious bloody flame, not like the fine flame of an ordinary fire. . . . We staid till, it being darkish, we saw the fire as only one entire arch of fire from this to the other side the bridge, and in a bow up the hill for an arch of above a mile long: it made me weep to see it. The churches, houses, and all on fire and flaming at once; and a horrid noise the flames made, and the cracking of houses at their ruine. So home with a sad heart, . . . and did by moonshine it being brave dry, and moonshine, and warm weather carry much of my goods into the garden, . . . and I did remove my money and iron chests into my cellar, as thinking that the safest place. And got my bags of gold into my office, ready to carry away, and my chief papers of accounts also there, and my tallys into a box by themselves. . . .

3rd. About four o'clock in the morning, my Lady Batten sent me a cart to carry away all my money, and plate, and best things, to Sir W. Rider's at Bednall-greene. Which I did, riding myself in my night-gowne in the cart; and, Lord! to see how the streets and the highways are crowded with people running and riding, and getting of carts at any rate to fetch away things. . . .

4th. Up by break of day to get away the remainder of my things; which I did by a lighter at the Iron gate: and my hands so few, that it was the afternoon before we could get them all away. Sir W. Pen and I to Tower-streete, and there met the fire burning three or four doors beyond Mr. Howell's whose goods, poor man, his trayes, and dishes, shovells, &c., were flung all along Tower-street in the kennels, and people working therewith from one end to the other; the fire coming on in that narrow streete, on both sides, with infinite fury. Sir W. Batten not knowing how to remove his wine, did dig a pit in the garden, and laid it in there; and I took the opportunity of laying all the papers of my office that I could not otherwise dispose of. And in the evening Sir W. Pen and I did dig another, and put our wine in it; and I my Parmazan cheese, as well as my wine and some other things. . . . I after supper walked in the darke down to Tower-streete, and there saw it all on fire, at the Trinity House on that side, and the Dolphin Taverne on this side, which was very near us; and the fire with extraordinary vehemence. Now begins the practice of blowing up of houses in Tower-streete, those next the Tower, which at first did frighten people more than any thing; but it stopped the fire where it was done, it bringing down the houses to the ground in the same places they stood, and then it was easy to quench what little fire was in it, though it kindled nothing almost.

5th. I lay down in the office again upon W. Hewer's quilt, being mighty weary, and sore in my feet with going till I was hardly able to stand. About two in the morning my wife calls me up and tells me of new cryes of fire, it being come to Barkeing Church, which is the bottom of our lane. I up, and finding it so, resolved presently to take her away, and did, and took my gold, which was about £2,350, . . . but, Lord! what a sad sight it was by moone-light to see the whole City almost on fire, that you might see it plain at Woolwich, as if you were by it. There, when I come, I find the gates shut, but no guard kept at all, which troubled me, because of discourse now begun, that there is plot in it, and that the French had done it. I got the gates open, and to Mr. Shelden's, where I locked up my gold, and charged my wife and W. Hewer never to leave the room without one of them in it, night or day.

7th. Up by five o'clock; and, blessed be God! find all well; and by water to Paul's Wharfe. Walked thence, and saw all the towne burned, and a miserable sight of Paul's church, with all the roofs fallen, and the body of the quire fallen into St. Fayth's; Paul's school also, Ludgate, and Fleet-street, my father's house, and the church, and a good part of the Temple the like. So to Creed's lodging, near the New Exchange, and there find him laid down upon a bed; the house all unfurnished, there being fears of the fire's coming to them. There borrowed a shirt of him, and washed. To Sir W. Coventry, at St. James's, who lay without curtains, having removed all his goods; as the King at White Hall, and every body had done, and was doing. He hopes we shall have no publique distractions upon this fire, which is what every body fears, because of the talke of the French having a hand in it. And it is a proper time for discontents; but all men's minds are full of care to protect themselves, and save their goods: the militia is in armes every where.

58

An Anonymous Account of the Popish Plot (1678)

There were undoubtedly people in 1678 who would have welcomed and encouraged England's return to Roman Catholicism. Nevertheless, the Popish Plot that came to light then was largely the product of the fertile and unscrupulous imaginations of Titus Oates (1649–1705) and his crony, Dr. Israel Tonge (1621–1680). That the ground on which their lies and rumors fell gave them mushroom growth indicates English attitudes, still colored by John Foxe's *Book of Martyrs* and displaying a willingness to see a Catholic plot behind every national misfortune. The English people uniformly believed

SOURCE. Historical Manuscripts Commission, Fourteenth Report, Appendix, Part VI, *The Manuscripts of Lord Kenyon,* London: Printed for Her Majesty's Stationery Office by Eyre and Spottiswoode, 1894, pp. 105–108.

what Oates said or, for purposes of policy, acted as if they did. It was a case of mass hysteria, but with such grave consequences as the fall of Lord Danby, the attempted exclusion of James, Duke of York, from accession to the throne and, not least, the judicial murder of 35 people.

It was more than two years before those passions were extinguished and England began to see Oates for the liar and scoundrel he was. Under James II (1685–1688), he was brought to trial for perjury, was found guilty, and was sentenced to successive floggings that were surely intended to kill him. He survived, however, being released from prison and given a government pension at the time of the Glorious Revolution. He became a member of a Baptist congregation, but in 1701 was expelled for being "a disorderly person and a hypocrite."

The extreme passions of the time and the proven unreliability of central participants make it difficult to know precisely what happened. The death of Sir Edmund Berry Godfrey has never been explained satisfactorily. The account below came to light in the nineteenth century as a result of the work of the Historical Manuscripts Commission, created in 1869 by Queen Victoria. The Commission's purpose was to save from loss or destruction manuscripts and papers of general and public interest that were in the hands of private families and institutions and to make them available for scholarly use. Its numerous reports, like that describing and reproducing in part the manuscripts of Lord Kenyon of Gredington Hall, have opened up a vast new source of evidence for historical investigation.

This anonymous account of the Popish Plot presents much of Oates's fabrication and indicates the panic that was developing. However, since the author and the exact circumstances of the writing are unknown, the historian must take great care neither to overrate nor to undervalue its significance.

1678, October 31.—Since my last, wherein I discovered to you the first account of this horrible plott, greate hath beene the diligence boeth of the Councell and Parliament in bringing the same to light, wherein their endeavours have beene soe happy that they are now arrived to the bottome of it, and it lies now before boeth houses in its owne monstrous shape; it being noe lesse then the murder of the King, the subversion of our religion, lawes, and properties, the introduceing of popery and a tyrannicall arbitrary government by an army, our common and statute laws to be abolished and anihilated, and a mixture of military and civil law introduced, where counsell of warr should supply this place of our courts of justice, and the racke for the jury, with many such differences too tediouse to expresse here; but I hope, by this tymely and miraculouse discovery, we may be able to distroy this cochatrice in the egge which will yet certainely devoure us if hee bee hatcht. The manner of proceedings have beene thus:—One Mr. Oates, being a minister in Sussex, by reason of some lawe suites with persons which were too powerfull for him, hee was forced to quitt his parish and, comeing into London, fell into acquaintance with Mr. Tonge, a minister who hath beene many yeares a diligent inquirer into the practices and principals of the Jesuites and had published severall bookes against them. This man findeing Oates, by reason of poverty, enclined to travell to seeke a livelyhood amongst the papists abroad, endeavoured to divert him by giveing him full information of theire wicked principles and practices. Whereupon Oates resolves to try the trueth, and promised, if hee found it to bee as Tonge informed, hee would renounce that religion and retorne againe to the Protestant Church. Oates thereupon, some yeares since, goes and enters himselfe a Noviciat in the College of the Jesuites in St. Omer's, where behaveing himselfe with great zeale, diligence, and demonstrateing his abilities, hee was soone taken notice of and thought a fitt instrument to convey the intelligence and correspondency of this hellish plott to most of the Courts in christendome. In acting whereof, by opening letters and packquetts entrusted with him and thereby gaineing some light, soe insinuated himselfe whereever hee came, that in time hee came to the depth and counsells of the designe. Whereby, about Aprill last, understanding the execution of this horrid villany to bee att hand and that comissions were signed by the Pope for all bishops and other clergy, for the officers of state and of theire armies, hee began to feare it would be executed before hee should find meanes to discover it. And being ready to lay hould of all oppertunities to come for England to doe it, it fell out that a booke called *the Jesuites' Moralls,* which Tonge had translated came to their handes, for which upon consultation it was agreed Tonge should bee killed, but a fitt person was wanting to doe it. Whereupon Oates offered to undertake it and . . . prepares for the journey . . . but in the interim, underhand resortes to Tonge and acquaints him with the whole designe, of which haveing drawne a short relation, hee desires Tonge to give it privately to the King and offer to make it good if his Majesty would conceale the thing and appoynt a counsell to sitt and heare it. . . . The matter thus settled, Tonge severall tymes presses the Treasurer, but noething done in 6 weekes; though the 2nd of September, whereon the King was to bee murdered, was past; whereon Tonge doubting some future trouble in case Oates should be killed or recant, causes Oates to draw an exact narrative containeing 15 or 16 sheetes and to sweare it before Sir Edmundbury Godfrey. . . . I say noe more, but Godfrey . . . was murdered soone after, being, as appeared plainely, strangled, and after carryed and layd in a ditch near Primrose

Hill and his owne sword runne through him, noething missing but his band and pockett booke wherein were his noates concerning this affaire. His murder raised a great spiritt in the people, which could not bee outfaced by the partie and theire adherents that murdered him, though there wanted neither diligence nor impudence in that party in all places to make it appeare hee murdered himselfe. Tomorrow hee is to bee buried from the Hall of Bridewell where I believe thousands will appeare to attend his corps to St. Martins. But to retorne to the plott.

Godfrey, haveing taken the information, was forced then to bring it to counsell about the end of September 1678, where Oates appeared and made it good beyond all scruple. . . . Since the sitting of the Parliament, Oates hath beene every day examined before them, speakeing 5 or 6 hours at a tyme, giveing particuler demonstration of the whole affaire, wherein hee hath clearly proved the manner and designe of the fire of London, Southerwarke, and many other fires, with the intended massacre in the fire of London, the designe of raiseing the Blackheath Army, with the reasons and occations of the severall Dutch warrs in order to this designe, the raiseing of the present army and the generall peace to ensue for the compleateing the worke, the raiseing and maintaineing privately 20,000 men att this tyme, with the generall and all other officers, all which are now in readinesse to joyne with the army, the greatest part whereof they thought themselves sure of, and in Ireland they had likewise a generall and army ready, and Scotland the same. The manner to put it in execution was thus:—One Conyers, a Jesuite, with foure Irish ruffaines, undertooke to murder the King att Windsor, 21 September last, and thereupon a great cry was to bee made that the phanatiques had murdered the King, an alarume presently thereupon to bee given to the whole army, being then about 16,000, quartered in and neare London, whereof two regiments of 4,000 men, consisting all of Irish, Scotts and French papists, were about a month before brought out of France and quartered about Barnet, Enfeild, St. Albans, Ware, &c. were imediately to march to London to assist the proclaimeing the Duke of York, and under that pretence to fall upon and massacre and slaughter the people, under the notion of phanatiques who had murdered the King, and then to have assisted the papists all over the kingdom to doe the like. The Duke of Yorke was to take the Crowne by gift from the Pope, and least any opposition should bee made, the French were to bee ready with an army and fleete to seize upon our fleete, burne and destroy such as opposed, and take the rest, and then the whole nation to bee shared among this crew (viz) the ancient church lands amongst the clergy, the murdered protestants' lands amongst the great officers, boeth civill and military, and the plunder of citties and townes amongst the soldiers and rabble of Irish and French papists. This is the substance of what is collected from the severall informations, proofes, and papers which have beene seized and made out.

Things thus appeareing, the Commons lockt themselves up for many hours, sent for Chiefe Justice Scroggs to them, who yssued out at one tyme, 40 or 50 warrants against noblemen and others. The high constables were sent for allsoe into the House and the warrants there delivered to them, and the House kept still shutt to prevent intelligence, and that night and next day, six lords and diverse persons of lesse quality were seized and comitted to the Tower, King's Bench, Newgate Gatehouse, and other prisons. . . .

Things thus standing, some intimation was brought to the Lord Mayor and Aldermen, on Saturday last, that on Sunday in sermon tyme some attempt would bee made upon the Citty, whereupon they ordered stronge double watches to bee sett, of house keepers in person, and the lights to bee renewed att 12 aclock att night; the gates to bee shutt all Sunday, and the watches to continue till releived att night, which was performed.

59

The Exclusion Bill (1680).
The Origin of Political Parties

It is not surprising that the Popish Plot prompted parliament to limit the political activity of Roman Catholics. Having already been excluded from holding office in the royal government by the Test Act of 1673, Catholics were now forbidden in 1678 to sit in either house of parliament, a disability not removed until 1829. Of greater importance were the exclusion bills designed to prevent James, Duke of York, from succeeding to the throne on the death of his brother Charles II (1660–1685). Their interest lies not so much in their religious bias as in what they reveal of the origin of political parties.

SOURCE.   J. P. Kenyon, ed., *The Stuart Constitution, 1603–1688: Documents and Commentary*, Cambridge University Press, 1966, pp. 469–471. Reprinted by permission of Cambridge University Press.

The earl of Danby, Charles's chief minister from 1674 to 1679, had, in putting together a block of political support for the king, created the beginnings of the Tory party. Upholding the old Cavalier idea of royal prerogative and supporting the established church, it espoused the principles of nonresistance and divine-right succession to the throne. In opposition was the earl of Shaftesbury and the equally embryonic Whig party, whose principles were parliamentary supremacy and a loud "no popery." The exclusion bills, introduced and discussed between 1678 and 1681, turned these political interests into actual political parties and gave them their names. The Tories, resisting the anti-Catholic enthusiasm of the Whigs, were given the name of Irish Catholic outlaws. The Whigs, in turn, were named after roughly equivalent Scottish presbyterians.

The exclusion bills clearly illustrate the Whig position that parliament can alter the royal succession. The bill of 1680, reproduced below, is also interesting for the fuzziness of the last paragraph, regarding who should inherit the throne, assuming "James, Duke of York, were naturally dead." Shaftesbury purposely left the way open for the accession of Charles's illegitimate son, the duke of Monmouth, who would be more pliable to parliament and to Shaftesbury than would be the capable William of Orange, the husband of James's daughter Mary. The failure of this bill in the House of Lords and the king's control of the next parliament in 1681 moved the Whigs to madcap schemes of violent revolution and then to hiding in exile. Their return to power by the Glorious Revolution and the vindication of their principle of parliamentary supremacy were due less to themselves than to the excesses of the King James whom they would, if given the chance, have excluded.

Whereas James, duke of York, is notoriously known to have been perverted from the Protestant to the Popish religion, whereby not only great encouragement hath been given to the Popish party to enter into and carry on most devilish and horrid plots and conspiracies for the destruction of his Majesty's sacred person and government, and for the extirpation of the true Protestant religion, but also if the said duke should succeed to the imperial crown of this realm, nothing is more manifest than that a total change of religion within these kingdoms would ensue.

For the prevention whereof, be it therefore enacted by and with the advice and consent of the Lords spiritual and temporal and the Commons in this present parliament assembled, and by the authority of the same, that the said James, duke of York, shall be and is by authority of the present parliament excluded and made for ever incapable to inherit, possess or enjoy the imperial crown of this realm and of the kingdom of Ireland and the dominions and territories to them or either of them belonging, or to have, exercise or enjoy any dominion, power, jurisdiction or authority within the same. . . .

[2.] And be it further enacted by the authority aforesaid that if the said James, duke of York, shall at any time hereafter challenge, claim, or attempt to possess or enjoy, or shall take upon him to use or exercise any dominion, power, authority or jurisdiction within the said kingdoms . . . as king or chief magistrate of the same, that then he, the said James, duke of York, for every such offence shall be deemed and adjudged guilty of high treason, and shall suffer the pains, penalties and forfeitures as in cases of high treason; and further, that if any person or persons whatsoever shall assist, aid, maintain, abet, or willingly adhere unto the said James, duke of York, in such his challenge, claim or attempt, or shall of themselves attempt or endeavour to put or bring the said James, duke of York, into the possession or exercise of any regal power, jurisdiction or authority within the kingdoms or dominions aforesaid, or shall by writing or preaching advisedly publish, maintain or declare that he hath any right, title or authority to exercise the office of king or chief magistrate . . . , that then every such person shall be deemed and adjudged guilty of high treason. . . .

[3.] And be it further enacted . . . that if the said James, duke of York, shall at any time from and after the fifth day of November in the year of our Lord God 1680 return or come into or within any of the kingdoms or dominions aforesaid, that then he . . . shall be deemed and adjudged guilty of high treason. . . . And further, that if any person or persons whatsoever shall be aiding or assisting unto such return of the said James, duke of York, that then every such person shall be deemed and adjudged guilty of high treason. . . .

[5.] And be it further enacted and declared . . . that it shall and may be lawful to and for all magistrates, officers and other subjects whatsoever . . . to apprehend and secure the said James, duke of York, and every other person offending in the premises, and with him or them in case of resistance to fight and him or them by force to subdue, for all which actings and for so doing they are and shall be by virtue of this Act saved harmless and indemnified.

[6.] Provided . . . that nothing in this Act contained shall be construed, deemed or adjudged to disable any person from inheriting or enjoying the imperial crown of the realms and dominions aforesaid . . . , but that in case the said James, duke of York, shall survive his now Majesty and the heirs of his Majesty's body, the said imperial crown shall descend to and be enjoyed by such person and persons successively during the lifetime of the said James, duke of York, as should have inherited and enjoyed the same in case the said James, duke of York, were naturally dead, anything in this Act contained to the contrary notwithstanding.

60

A Medley of Nursery Rhymes

Oral evidence, usually personal interviews, is to the contemporary historian of obvious importance. In the study of the earlier periods in English history, however, such evidence is insignificant. Unlike some societies, such as those in parts of Africa, the English possessed few oral traditions that were passed from generation to generation. The existence in England of a literate class from a relatively early date made this unnecessary. Why train someone to memorize the royal genealogy if you can simply write it down? Except perhaps for folks songs, the closest that the English have come to an oral tradition is the nursery rhyme. That this term, "nursery rhyme," was first used in the 1820s, shows that until then few of these rhymes were specifically designed for children.

Although nursery rhymes have been subjected to intense analysis, considerable debate still surrounds their origin and historical significance. Some have a medieval origin. "Baa, baa, black sheep" apparently refers to a 1275 export tax on wool. Only about 25 percent of the common rhymes, however, date from before 1600, and only about 2 percent of them can be found in a written form before that date. Thus care must be taken not to attribute antiquity to what may in reality be a product of the eighteenth or nineteenth century. Caution must also be exercised in attributing to a nursery rhyme a historical significance. Some have an obvious historical meaning:

SOURCE. Iona and Peter Opie, eds., *The Oxford Dictionary of Nursery Rhymes,* Oxford: Clarendon Press, 1952, pp. 61, 88, 115–116, 152, 185, 269, 310, 394, 424. By permission of The Clarendon Press, Oxford.

"The lion and the unicorn," refers to the struggle between England and Scotland during the Stuart period; "William and Mary, George and Anne," describes the overthrow of James II; "Over the water and over the lea," deals with Bonnie Prince Charles; and "Little General Monk," ridicules the duke of Albermarle. Unfortunately, the historical meaning of most nursery rhymes is uncertain. For example, does "Sing a song of sixpence" refer to Henry VIII's counting of the money obtained from the dissolved monasteries or is there another, forgotten historical reference? Does "Hark, hark" suggest the general problem of beggars in Tudor England or does it refer to the Dutch "beggars" brought to England by William III? It would help in this case to know exactly how old the rhyme actually is. Is "Georgie Porgie" really George I? Finally, is the baby "on the tree top" James II's son, who falls because the wind in 1688 blew William's fleet to England?

The first important collection of nursery rhymes appeared in 1744, *Tommy Thumb's Pretty Song Book*. The more famous *Mother Goose's Melody* (1760) was reprinted several times and inspired numerous similar collections in the nineteenth century. Today, the best edition of nursery rhymes, complete with a discussion of their possible origins, is *The Oxford Dictionary of Nursery Rhymes*.

Baa, baa, black sheep,
   Have you any wool?
Yes, sir, yes, sir,
   Three bags full;
One for the master,
   And one for the dame,
And one for the little boy
   Who lives down the lane.

The lion and the unicorn
   Were fighting for the crown;
The lion beat the unicorn
   All round about the town.

Some gave them white bread,
   And some gave them brown;
Some gave them plumb cake
   And drummed them out of town.

William and Mary, George and Anne,
Four such children had never a man:
They put their father to flight and shame,
And called their brother a shocking bad name.

Over the water and over the lea,
    And over the water to Charley.
Charley loves good ale and wine,
    And Charley loves good brandy,
And Charley loves a pretty girl
    As sweet as sugar candy.

Over the water and over the lea,
    And over the water to Charley.
I'll have none of your nasty beef,
    Nor I'll have none of your barley;
But I'll have some of your very best flour
    To make a white cake for my Charley.

Little General Monk
Sat upon a trunk,
Eating a crust of bread;
There fell a hot coal
And burnt in his clothes a hole,
Now little General Monk is dead.

Sing a song of sixpence,
    A pocket full of rye;
Four and twenty blackbirds,
    Baked in a pie.

When the pie was opened,
    The birds began to sing;
Was not that a dainty dish,
    To set before the king?

The king was in his counting-house,
    Counting out his money;
The queen was in the parlour,
    Eating bread and honey.

The maid was in the garden,
    Hanging out the clothes,
There came a little blackbird,
    And snapped off her nose.

            Hark, hark,
            The dogs do bark,
The beggars are coming to town;
            Some in rags,
            And some in jags,
And one in a velvet gown.

Georgie Porgie, pudding and pie,
Kissed the girls and made them cry;
When the boys came out to play,
Georgie Porgie ran away.

Hush-a-bye, baby, on the tree top,
When the wind blows the cradle will rock;
When the bough breaks the cradle will fall,
Down will come baby, cradle, and all.

61

Sir John Reresby, *Memoirs.* His Quarrels and Duels, 1660-1683

Sir John Reresby (1634–1689) was not an important figure in Stuart England. Rather, he was typical of the country gentlemen who filled the benches of the House of Commons and ran local government. He served as high sheriff of Yorkshire in 1667 and entered parliament in 1673, where he quickly became a supporter of Charles II. For this support he was rewarded in 1682 with the governorship of York. Like many Tories, however, Reresby could not abide the follies of James II, especially his appointment of Roman Catholics to high office.

During middle age, Reresby decided to write his memoirs. For the edification of posterity he recalled the exploits of his youth. These memoirs, written in diary form largely in 1679, were first published in 1734. The Tories, then engaged in a political struggle with the Whig prime minister, Sir Robert Walpole, wanted an account of the Tory role in the Revolution of 1688 to combat the popular Whig version of Bishop Gilbert Burnet. Reresby's memoirs proved very popular, and they were consequently published in a number of editions during the eighteenth century. Most historians today regard his memoirs as valuable in portraying the life of the country gentleman, whom one scholar has referred to as the "backbone of English society." This aspect of England was omitted from the more famous diaries of John Evelyn and Samuel Pepys simply because they were unfamiliar with it. The passage below, in which Reresby discussed his frequent quarrels and duels, is a vivid reminder that Restoration England, although often praised for its growing cultural and social sophistication, remained a violent age.

SOURCE. *Memoirs of Sir John Reresby,* ed. Andrew Browning, Glasgow: Jackson, Son & Co., 1936, pp. 33–34, 46, 188–189, 317–318.

10 September 1660

I came into Yorkshire, and after some short stay at my own hous at
Thriberge went for Yorke by the way of Selby, wher a quarrell hapning
between my company and some others about first going into the boat, I
was struck over the head with a cudgill, which provouked me to wound
one or two with my sword. This gave soe great an alarme to the country
people ther met togather upon the occasion of the markit that I was en-
compassed, and two gentlemen with me and our servants, and after a
long defence pulled off my hors, and had certainly been knocked on the
head had I not been rescued by my Moor, who gott hould of the man's
arm that had me down, as he was going to give the blowe. Being gott up
again, I defended myselfe till I gott into the hous of an honest man, that
gave us protection till the rabble was appeased.

From Yorke I went to Mauton, a famous fair for horses, wher with
other gentlemen I was invited to dinner at Sir Thomas Norclifs, who had
severall hansome daughters, especially one who was to be speedily married
to a yong gentleman with whom I had a quarrell about his mistriss which
had near spoiled the match. We should have fought the next day, but
considering better of it he submitted (though it was he that had received
the affront, for I threw a glass of wine in his face), and soe we were
reconcild. . . .

12 July 1663

Sir Henry Bellasis sent to invite me to dinner to the Bear at the bridge
foot, wher on Mack de Mar, an Irish gentleman, was to give him a venison
pasty. After dinner he provoaked me to give him some language, which
he soe farr resented that he demanded satisfaction, either by my denying
that I meant any injury to him by the saying of the words, and asking his
pardon, or by fighting with him. I denyed the first, and soe being chal-
lenged was obliged to fight him that afternoon in Hide Parke, which I
did, an Irish gentleman that he met by the way being his secound, and
Sir Henry Belasis mine. At the first pass I hurt him slightly on the sword
hand, and at the same time he closeing with me we both fell to the
ground (he haveing hould of my sword and I of his). Sir Henry and his
man were fighting at the same time close by, and Sir Henry had gott the
better, wounded the other in the belly and disarmed him, and was
comming in to us as we were both risen and I had gott his sword out of
his hand, which I took home with me, but sent it to him the next day.
The secound to Mac de Mar was in danger of death by his wound for
some weeks, which made us abscond. I was with the Duke of Buckingham
the best part of this time at Wallinford Hous. But at last it pleased God
he recovered. . . .

22 Septmber 1679

Was the day named to poule at Pontefract. My friends that went in with me stayed for me at Rigstone Hill a little longer than ordinary.

That day Sir John Jackson of Hickleton (the last of his family, and the fourth heir from its first being raised) came to me at Pontefract (ther haveing been some coolness between us before) and tould me I had affronted him in bringing in his tenents with me to voat for Sir John Kay, when he designed to bring them in himselfe. I answered that I writt to all (or sent to them) that I thought qualified to voat to come in, without reguarding who was their landlords, but if he took that ill in his own perticular I was a man to give him what satisfaction he required. But I found him not much inclined to fight, for after severall words he tould me that he neither desired to court my friendship nor enmity. Then I tould him we were very equall in that particular, for I thought his friendship was very little to be valued or enmity to be feared; and soe we parted. . . .

23 October 1683

The Sunday following, being in the Minster, I found the cussin which used to be in my seat remooved into the next, wher Sir John Brook was to sitt (a person that I had thought fitt, with other deputy lieutenants, to disarm in our late search for arms). This gentleman riseing at the psalmes, I took up the cussin and replaced it in my seat. Service being ended, Sir John asked me if I had the same commission to take his cussin that I had to take his arms. I said I took it as my own, as I should always doe when I see it misplaced; and if he took his being disarmed ill from me he made choice of an ill place to quarrell in, and that hee durst not say thos things in any other.

The next day I expected to hear from him, he seeming very much disturbed with this treatment; but not sending to me for reparation, the next morning I sent the captain that then commanded a company in Yorke to tell him that I had stayed some time at home, thinkeing to hear from him, and believed the reason why I did not to be the character I bore in that citty, and did therefore now send to him to tell him that if he had any ressentment either for my takeing his cussin or arms, I was ready to give him satisfaction as a private person. He returned me this answer, that he was most concerned at my takeing away the cussin, bycaus it did prevent his giveing it to me, which he intended; but that for satisfaction he thought what had passed between us did not oblige him to aske it in his circumstances, and was willing to be quiett. Soe that the substance of this matter was this, that he foolishly owned himselfe under such circumstances as to own himselfe affronted, but not to see himselfe righted. I could have been very well content that noe occasion of such disputes had offered themselves, but when they doe I have found that the best way to prevent them for the future is not to seem too backward in seeking reparation.

62

The Bill of Rights (1689)

The Glorious Revolution of 1688 to 1689 was both the culmination of a century-long constitutional struggle between crown and parliament and the consequence of specific actions of James II (1685–1688). Seldom has any king so quickly and so thoroughly alienated his subjects. At the beginning of his reign they were favorably inclined toward him, but three years later not even the Tories and Anglicans, who believed in nonresistance and indefeasible divine right, would lift a finger to save him. Increasingly the English people saw James's active Roman Catholicism and his inclination to tyranny as related dangers. This departure from English practice was their justification for abandoning their sworn allegiance to their king.

The heart of the revolutionary settlement was the Bill of Rights, parliament's official confirmation of the original Declaration of Rights written by the Convention Parliament of February 1689 and presented to William and Mary as the terms of their invitation to become king and queen. Like Magna Carta and the Petition of Right, the Bill of Rights was a statement of specific violations of the law and the promise that in the future the law would be obeyed. This conservative pretense was, however, not always accurate. The statement on "raising or keeping a standing army" reflects more a fear and complaint than an established law or custom. Although the Revolution was accomplished by the cooperation of both political parties, the terms of the settlement were, in fact, more Whig than Tory. Specifically, the throne was recognized as vacant, and it was then granted not to Mary, the sole legal heir (ignoring James's son, the Old Pretender, born in June 1688), but to William and Mary jointly. Also, limitations on the succession, specifically regarding religion, were firmly established. Parliament was not actually proclaimed to be sovereign, but by its actions there could be no doubt that it

---

SOURCE. *Statutes of the Realm,* VI, 142–144 (1 William and Mary, Sess. 2, c. 2).

was. The Revolution was a wedding of Whig principles with Tory pragmatism, more a practical than a logical triumph.

AN ACT DECLAREING THE RIGHTS AND LIBERTIES OF THE SUBJECT AND SETLEING THE SUCCESSION OF THE CROWNE

Whereas the Lords Spirituall and Temporall and Comõns assembled at Westminster lawfully fully and freely representing all the Estates of the People of this Realme did upon the thirteenth day of February in the yeare of our Lord one thousand six hundred eighty eight present unto their Majesties then called and known by the Names and Stile of William and Mary Prince and Princesse of Orange being present in their proper Persons a certaine Declaration in Writeing made by the said Lords and Comõns in the Words following viz

Whereas the late King James the Second by the Assistance of diverse evill Councellors Judges and Ministers imployed by him did endeavour to subvert and extirpate the Protestant Religion and the Lawes and Liberties of this Kingdome . . .

All which are utterly and directly contrary to the knowne Lawes and Statutes and Freedome of this Realme.

And whereas the said late King James the Second haveing Abdicated the Government and the Throne being thereby Vacant His [Highnesse] the Prince of Orange (whome it hath pleased Almighty God to make the glorious Instrument of Delivering this Kingdome from Popery and Arbitrary Power) did (by the Advice of the Lords Spirituall and Temporall and diverse principall Persons of the Commons) cause Letters to be written to the Lords Spirituall and Temporall being Protestants and other Letters to the severall Countyes Cityes Universities Burroughs and Cinque Ports for the Choosing of such Persons to represent them as were of right to be sent to Parlyament to meete and sitt at Westminster upon the two and twentyeth day of January in this Yeare one thousand six hundred eighty and eight in order to such an Establishment as that their Religion Lawes and Liberties might not againe be in danger of being Subverted, Upon which Letters Elections haveing beene accordingly made.

And thereupon the said Lords Spirituall and Temporall and Commons pursuant to their respective Letters and Elections being now assembled in a full and free Representative of this Nation takeing into their most serious Consideration the best meanes for attaining the Ends aforesaid Doe in the first place (as their Auncestors in like Case have usually done) for the Vindicating and Asserting their auntient Rights and Liberties, Declare

That the pretended Power of Suspending of Laws or the Execution of Laws by Regall Authority without Consent of Parlyament is illegall.

That the pretended Power of Dispensing with Laws or the Execution of Laws by Regall Authoritie as it hath beene assumed and exercised of late is illegall.

That the Commission for erecting the late Court of Commissioners for Ecclesiasticall Causes and all other Commissions and Courts of like nature are Illegall and Pernicious.

That levying Money for or to the Use of the Crowne by pretence of Prerogative without Grant of Parlyament for longer time or in other manner then the same is or shall be granted is Illegall.

That it is the Right of the Subjects to petition the King and all Commitments and Prosecutions for such Petitioning are Illegall.

That the raising or keeping a standing Army within the Kingdome in time of Peace unlesse it be with Consent of Parlyament is against Law.

That the Subjects which are Protestants may have Arms for their Defence suitable to their Conditions and as allowed by Law.

That Election of Members of Parlyament ought to be free.

That the Freedome of Speech and Debates or Proceedings in Parlyament ought not to be impeached or questioned in any Court or Place out of Parlyament.

That excessive Baile ought not be required nor excessive Fines imposed nor cruell and unusuall Punishments inflicted.

That Jurors ought to be duely impannelled and returned and Jurors which passe upon Men in Trialls for High Treason ought to be Freeholders.

That all Grants and Promises of Fines and Forfeitures of particular persons before Conviction are illegall and void.

And that for Redresse of all Grievances and for the amending strengthening and preserveing of the Lawes Parlyaments ought to be held frequently.

And they doe Claime Demand and Insist upon all and singular the Premises as their undoubted Rights and Liberties and that noe Declarations Judgements Doeings or Proceedings to the Prejudice of the People in any of the said Premisses ought in any wise to be drawne hereafter into Consequence or Example. To which Demand of their Rights they are particularly encouraged by the Declaration of his Highnesse the Prince of Orange as being the onely meanes for obtaining a full Redresse and Remedy therein. Haveing therefore an intire Confidence That his said Highnesse the Prince of Orange will perfect the Deliverance soe farr advanced by him and will still preserve them from the Violation of their Rights which they have here asserted and from all other Attempts upon their Religion Rights and Liberties, The said Lords Spirituall and Temporall and Commons assembled at Westminster doe Resolve That William and Mary Prince and Princesse of Orange be and be declared King and Queene of England France and Ireland and the Dominions thereunto belonging to hold the Crowne and Royall Dignity of the said Kingdomes and Dominions to them the said Prince and Princesse dureing their Lives and the Life of the Survivour of them And that the sole and full Exercise of the Regall Power to be onely in and executed by the said Prince of Orange in the Names of the said Prince and Princesse dureing their joynt Lives And after their Deceases the said Crowne and Royall Dignitie of the said Kingdoms and Dominions to be to the Heires of the Body of the said Princesse And for default of such Issue to the Princesse Anne of Denmarke and the Heires of her Body And for default of such Issue to the Heires of the Body of the said Prince of Orange. And the Lords Spirituall and Temporall and Commons doe pray the said Prince and Princesse to accept the same accordingly. . . . And whereas it hath beene found by Experience that it is inconsistent with the Safety and Welfare of this Protestant Kingdome to be governed by a Popish Prince or by any King or Queene marrying a Papist the said Lords Spirituall and Temporall and Commons doe further pray that it may be enacted That all and every person and persons that is are or shall be reconciled to or shall hold Communion with the See or Church of Rome or shall professe the Popish Religion or shall marry a Papist shall be excluded and be for ever uncapeable to inherit possesse or enjoy the Crowne and Government of this Realme and Ireland and the Dominions thereunto belonging or any part of the same or to have use or exercise any Regall Power Authoritie or Jurisdiction within the same [And in all and every such Case or Cases the People of these Realmes shall be and are hereby absolved of their Allegiance] And the said Crowne and Government shall from time to time descend to and be enjoyed by such person or persons being Protestants as should have inherited and enjoyed the same in case the said person or persons soe reconciled holding Communion or Professing or Marrying as aforesaid were naturally dead.

John Locke, *Two Treatises*
of Government (1690)

The Glorious Revolution was vindicated not only by the solid facts of its immediate success and of England's ensuing prosperity, but by the common-
sense arguments of England's most influential political pamphlet. In 1690
appeared anonymously John Locke's *Two Treatises of Government: In the
Former, the False Principles and Foundations of Sir Robert Filmer, And His
Followers, are Detected and Overthrown. The Latter is an Essay concerning
The True Original, Extent, and End of Civil-Government.* The first treatise,
seldom read today, is a refutation of Filmer's Biblical justification of the
patriarchal authority of absolute monarchs. In the second treatise, a passage
of which is reproduced below, Locke gives his own understanding of the
basis of government. It is a contract between the people and their government, the people retaining the right to recall the legislature and the executive
if they violate the trust given them. All the people are alike subject to the
law of nature, which they can discern by their reason. They are understood to
enter society and to set up a government—a legislature and an executive—
to avoid certain inconveniences inherent in an otherwise felicitous state of
nature. Their chief concern "is the preservation of property," which is understood to be not only lands and material goods but more widely "the Lives,
Liberties, and Estates of the People." Despite Locke, however, it has remained a concern whether lives and liberties should take primacy over
estates, or indeed whether they can be separated.

The *Two Treatises* is in reality a single work. Locke wrote in his preface,
"Thou hast here the Beginning and End of a Discourse," "the Papers that

SOURCE. John Locke, *Two Treatises of Government: A Critical Edition with
an Introduction and Apparatus Criticus,* by Peter Laslett, Second Edition,
Cambridge: At the University Press, 1967, pp. 430–432. Reprinted by permission of Cambridge University Press.

should have filled up the middle, and were more than all the rest," having
been lost. Although published in 1690, it was probably written between 1679
and 1681, and certainly before 1683. Thus Locke wrote during the Exclusion
Crisis, to justify what the earl of Shaftesbury, his friend and patron, was
attempting, and not in 1689 and 1690, to justify what had already been
accomplished. As such, Locke's ideas were potentially dangerous. This helps
to explain his exile from 1683 till 1689 and his extreme care in not acknowl-
edging his authorship of the *Two Treatises* until a few days before his death.

It was Locke's genius to combine the radical ideas of the Puritan revolution with tradition and common sense, making them palatable and useful,
even if not always consistent and logical. In all respects, the *Two Treatises*
was the intellectual counterpart of the Glorious Revolution, owing its success
to the Revolution even more than the Revolution owed its justification to the
Two Treatises. Its primary importance in the long run may have been that it
put English ideas and practice in a packaged form available for export. In
the eighteenth century England began to eclipse the once-mighty France,
and French thinkers and politicians looked to England, and preeminently to
Locke, for an alternative to absolute monarchy.

The Reason why Men enter into Society, is the preservation of their
Property; and the end why they chuse and authorize a Legislative, is,
that there may be Laws made, and Rules set as Guards and Fences to the
Properties of all the Members of the Society, to limit the Power, and
moderate the Dominion of every Part and Member of the Society. For
since it can never be supposed to be the Will of the Society, that the Legislative should have a Power to destroy that, which every one designs to
secure, by entering into Society, and for which the People submitted
themselves to the Legislators of their own making; whenever the *Legislators endeavour to take away, and destroy the Property of the People,* or
to reduce them to Slavery under Arbitrary Power, they put themselves
into a state of War with the People, who are thereupon absolved from
any farther Obedience, and are left to the common Refuge, which God
hath provided for all Men, against Force and Violence. Whensoever
therefore the *Legislative* shall transgress this fundamental Rule of Society;
and either by Ambition, Fear, Folly or Corruption, *endeavour to grasp*
themselves, *or put into the hands of any other an Absolute Power* over the
Lives, Liberties, and Estates of the People; By this breach of Trust they
forfeit the Power, the People had put into their hands, for quite contrary
ends, and it devolves to the People, who have a Right to resume their

original Liberty, and, by the Establishment of a new Legislative (such as they shall think fit) provide for their own Safety and Security, which is the end for which they are in Society. What I have said here, concerning the Legislative, in general, holds true also concerning the *supreame Executor,* who having a double trust put in him, both to have a part in the Legislative, and the supreme Execution of the Law, Acts against both, when he goes about to set up his own Arbitrary Will, as the Law of the Society. He *acts* also *contrary to his Trust,* when he either imploys the Force, Treasure, and Offices of the Society, to corrupt the *Representatives,* and gain them to his purposes: or openly pre-ingages the *Electors,* and prescribes to their choice, such, whom he has by Sollicitations, Threats, Promises, or otherwise won to his designs; and imploys them to bring in such, who have promised before-hand, what to Vote, and what to Enact. Thus to regulate Candidates and *Electors,* and new model the ways of *Election,* what is it but to cut up the Government by the Roots, and poison the very Fountain of publick Security? For the People having reserved to themselves the Choice of their *Representatives,* as the Fence to their Properties, could do it for no other end, but that they might always be freely chosen, and so chosen, freely act and advise, as the necessity of the Commonwealth, and the publick Good should, upon examination, and mature debate, be judged to require. . . . What Power they ought to have in the Society, who thus imploy it contrary to the trust went along with it in its first Institution, is easie to determine; and one cannot but see, that he, who has once attempted any such thing as this, cannot any longer be trusted.

To this perhaps it will be said, that the People being ignorant, and always discontented, to lay the Foundation of Government in the unsteady Opinion, and uncertain Humour of the People, is to expose it to certain ruine; And *no Government will be able long to subsist,* if the People may set up a new Legislative, whenever they take offence at the old one. To this, I Answer: Quite the contrary. People are not so easily got out of their old Forms, as some are apt to suggest. They are hardly to be prevailed with to amend the acknowledg'd Faults, in the Frame they have been accustom'd to. And if there be any Original defects, or adventitious ones introduced by time, or corruption; 'tis not an easie thing to get them changed, even when all the World sees there is an opportunity for it. This slowness and aversion in the People to quit their old Constitutions, has, in the many Revolutions which have been seen in this Kingdom, in this and former Ages, still kept us to, or, after some interval of fruitless attempts, still brought us back again to our old Legislative of King, Lords and Commons: And whatever provocations have made the Crown be taken from some of our Princes Heads, they never carried the People so far, as to place it in another Line.

64

The Riot Act (1715). The Maintenance of Law and Order

The Act of Settlement (1701) confirmed the exclusion of the Catholic Stuarts from the throne and designated Electress Sophia of Hanover and her heirs as the royal successors to William III and Princess Anne. Although this satisfied Whigs and Protestants, many, specifically Roman Catholics and die-hard legitimists, remained Jacobites, drinking toasts to the king over the water (James III, the Pretender who was in France). In 1714 Sophia's son, George I, peacefully succeeded Queen Anne. Jacobites and others besides soon found George and his Hanoverian retinue to be unattractive and very German. Tumultuous assemblies and riots occurred in several parts of England, and an invasion by the Pretender was anticipated. The Whig government, firmly in control of parliament but not confident of its control of the kingdom, passed the Riot Act of 1715.

The lapse in 1603 of the riot acts passed in the Tudor period and the abolition of Star Chamber in 1641 had left no settled means of dealing with crowds that either threatened to get out of control or actually did. Toward the end of the Stuart period, efforts, largely unsuccessful, had been made to include riot within the scope of treason. The Riot Act of 1715, reviving the terms of the Tudor acts, gave magistrates greater authority to enforce order. One hour after the "reading of the Riot Act" the mere presence of 12 or more people became a felony, and those acting to suppress it were indemnified against charges that might be brought against them by injured rioters. Some doubt remained, however, regarding the enforcement of the law in the intervening hour and the extent of the force that might be used thereafter. The act illustrates both the tumultuous condition of England in the eighteenth century and the absence of an effective system of law enforcement.

SOURCE. *The Statutes At Large,* XIII, 142–144 (1 George I. c. 5).

AN ACT FOR PREVENTING TUMULTS AND RIOTOUS ASSEMBLIES AND FOR THE MORE SPEEDY AND EFFECTUAL PUNISHING THE RIOTERS

I. Whereas *of late many rebellious riots and tumults have been in divers parts of this kingdom, to the disturbance of the publick peace, and the endangering of his Majesty's person and government, and the same are yet continued and fomented by persons disaffected to his Majesty, presuming so to do, for that the punishments provided by the laws now in being are not adequate to such heinous offences; and by such rioters his Majesty and his administration have been most maliciously and falsly traduced, with an intent to raise divisions, and to alienate the affections of the people from his Majesty: therefore for the preventing and suppressing of such riots and tumults, and for the more speedy and effectual punishing the offenders therein;* be it enacted. . . That if any persons to the number of twelve or more, being unlawfully, riotously, and tumultously assembled together, to the disturbance of the publick peace . . . and being required or commanded by any one or more justice or justices of the peace, or by the sheriff of the county, or his under-sheriff, or by the mayor, bailiff or bailiffs, or other head-officer, or justice of the peace of any city or town corporate . . . by proclamation to be made in the King's name, in the form herein after directed, to disperse themselves, and peaceably to depart to their habitations, or to their lawful business, shall . . . unlawfully, riotously, and tumultuously remain or continue together by the space of one hour after such command or request . . . that then such continuing together . . . shall be adjudged felony without benefit of clergy, and the offenders therein shall be adjudged felons, and shall suffer death as in case of felony without benefit of clergy.

II. And be it further enacted by the authority aforesaid, That the order and form of the proclamation . . . shall be as hereafter followeth (that is to say) the justice of the peace, or other person authorized by this act to make the said proclamation shall, among the said rioters, or as near to them as he can safely come, with a loud voice command, or cause to be commanded silence to be, while proclamation is making, and after that, shall openly and with loud voice make or cause to be made proclamation in these words, or like in effect:

> Our sovereign Lord the King chargeth and commandeth all persons, being assembled, immediately to disperse themselves, and peaceably to depart to their habitations, or to their lawful business, upon the pains contained in the act made in the first year of King George, for preventing tumults and riotous assemblies.

> God save the King.

III. And be it further enacted by the authority aforesaid, That if such persons . . . shall continue together and not disperse themselves within one hour, That then it shall and may be lawful to and for every justice of the peace . . . and other peace-officer . . . and for such other . . . persons as shall be commanded to be assisting unto any such justice of the peace . . . or other head-officer aforesaid . . . to seize and apprehend, and they are hereby required to seize and apprehend such persons so unlawfully, riotously and tumultuously continuing together after proclamation made, as aforesaid, and forthwith to carry the persons so apprehended before one or more of his Majesty's justices of the peace . . . in order to their being proceeded against for such their offences according to law; and that if the persons so unlawfully, riotously and tumultuously assembled, or any of them, shall happen to be killed, maimed or hurt . . . by reason of their resisting the persons so dispersing, seizing or apprehending, or endeavouring to disperse, seize or apprehend them, that then every such justice of the peace . . . or other peace-officer, and all and singular persons, being aiding and assisting to them . . . shall be free, discharged and indemnified . . . of, for, or concerning the killing, maiming, or hurting of any such person or persons.

65

Jonathan Swift, A Modest Proposal (1729). A Radical Solution to the Problems of Ireland

Jonathan Swift is known primarily for one book, Gulliver's Travels, a satire on the period of Robert Walpole but erroneously regarded by many today as a children's story. Swift was, to his contemporaries, one of a small group of

SOURCE.   Carl Van Doren, ed., The Portable Swift, New York: The Viking Press, 1948, pp. 549, 551–553, 555–556, 559.

eminent essayists and satirists, including Richard Steele, Joseph Addison, and Daniel Defoe. These men used their pens alternately to promote and to subvert the governments of the early eighteenth century. Historians use their pamphlets and essays, still widely read today because of their style, to study the major problems of late Stuart and Hanoverian England and to understand the attitudes of the educated class to which they were addressed.

Swift (1667–1745), an ambitious and arrogant man, never achieved the political prominence and influence he so desperately sought. Because he had used his literary talents in support of the Tories and their anti-war policies during the reign of Queen Anne (1702–1714), the accession of George I and the resulting ascendancy of the Whigs forced him to retire to Dublin, where he served until his death in 1745 as the Dean of St. Patrick's Cathedral.

Swift's mission in later life was to expose the harshness and injustice of British rule in Ireland, specifically the political, religious, and economic plight of the Roman Catholic peasantry. To this end he published a number of pamphlets, the most famous being *A Modest Proposal for Preventing the Children of Poor People from Being a Burthen to Their Parents or Country, and for Making Them Beneficial to the Public.* Although a member of the Protestant establishment, Swift was for this effort given the freedom of the the City of Dublin and recognized as one of the ablest defenders of Irish liberties. The obvious savageness of his satire reflects the intensity both of his personal frustrations and of his sincere abhorrence of England's policies in Ireland.

A Modest Proposal first appeared in Dublin in October 1729. It was immediately reprinted several times, achieving a popularity lasting to the present time.

It is a melancholy object to those who walk through this great town, or travel in the country, when they see the streets, the roads, and cabin-doors crowded with beggars of the female sex, followed by three, four, or six children, *all in rags,* and importuning every passenger for an alms. These mothers, instead of being able to work for their honest livelihood, are forced to employ all their time in strolling, to beg sustenance for their helpless infants, who, as they grow up, either turn thieves for want of work, or leave their dear Native Country to fight for the Pretender in Spain, or sell themselves to the Barbadoes.

I think it is agreed by all parties that this prodigious number of children, in the arms, or on the backs, or at the heels of their mothers, and frequently their fathers, is in the present deplorable state of the kingdom a very great additional grievance; and therefore whoever could find out a fair, cheap, and easy method of making these children sound useful members of the commonwealth would deserve so well of the public as to have his statue set up for a preserver of the nation. . . .

I shall now therefore humbly propose my own thoughts, which I hope will not be liable to the least objection.

I have been assured by a very knowing American of my acquaintance in London, that a young healthy child well nursed is at a year old a most delicious, nourishing, and wholesome food, whether stewed, roasted, baked, or broiled, and I make no doubt that it will equally serve in a fricassee, or a ragout.

I do therefore humbly offer it to public consideration, that of the hundred and twenty thousand children already computed, twenty thousand may be reserved for breed, whereof only one fourth part to be males, which is more than we allow to sheep, black-cattle, or swine, and my reason is that these children are seldom the fruits of marriage, a circumstance not much regarded by our savages, therefore one male will be sufficient to serve four females. That the remaining hundred thousand may at a year old be offered in sale to the persons of quality, and fortune, through the kingdom, always advising the mother to let them suck plentifully in the last month, so as to render them plump, and fat for a good table. A child will make two dishes at an entertainment for friends, and when the family dines alone, the fore or hind quarter will make a reasonable dish, and seasoned with a little pepper or salt will be very good boiled on the fourth day, especially in winter.

I have reckoned upon a medium, that a child just born will weigh 12 pounds, and in a solar year if tolerably nursed increaseth to 28 pounds.

I grant this food will be somewhat dear, and therefore very proper for landlords, who, as they have already devoured most of the parents, seem to have the best title to the children. . . .

I have already computed the charge of nursing a beggar's child (in which list I reckon all cottagers, labourers, and four-fifths of the farmers) to be about two shillings *per annum,* rags included, and I believe no gentleman would repine to give ten shillings for the carcass of a good fat child, which, as I have said, will make four dishes of excellent nutritive meat, when he hath only some particular friend or his own family to dine with him. Thus the Squire will learn to be a good landlord, and grow popular among his tenants, the mother will have eight shillings net profit, and be fit for work till she produces another child.

Those who are more thrifty (as I must confess the times require) may flay the carcass; the skin of which, artificially dressed, will make admirable gloves for ladies, and summer boots for fine gentlemen. . . . I think the advantages by the proposal which I have made are obvious and many, as well as of the highest importance.

For first, as I have already observed, it would greatly lessen the number of Papists, with whom we are yearly over-run, being the principal breeders of the nation, as well as our most dangerous enemies. . . .

Secondly, The poorer tenants will have something valuable of their own, which by law be made liable to distress, and help to pay their land-lord's rent, their corn and cattle being already seized, and *money a thing unknown.* . . .

Sixthly, This would be a great inducement to marriage, which all wise nations have either encouraged by rewards, or enforced by laws and penalties. It would increase the care and tenderness of mothers toward their children, when they were sure of a settlement for life, to the poor babes, provided in some sort by the public to their annual profit instead of expense. We should see an honest emulation among the married women, which of them could bring the fattest child to the market, men would become as fond of their wives, during the time of their pregnancy, as they are now of their mares in foal, their cows in calf, or sows when they are ready to farrow, nor offer to beat or kick them (as it is too frequent a practice) for fear of a miscarriage. . . .

I profess in the sincerity of my heart that I have not the least personal interest in endeavouring to promote this necessary work, having no other motive than the *public good of my country, by advancing our trade, providing for infants, relieving the poor, and giving some pleasure to the rich.* I have no children by which I can propose to get a single penny; the youngest being nine years old, and my wife past child-bearing.

66

The Hat Act (1732) and the Iron Act (1750). Mercantilistic Regulation of Trade

To the mercantilist of the eighteenth century, it was self-evident that political units were not created with equal economic rights. Colonies had been founded, and were now defended, because of their economic value to the "mother country," meaning among other things that they were supposed to provide a market for manufactured goods. The British naturally attempted to restrict manufacturing in the colonies, particularly when it competed with established industries in England. Skilled artisans were discouraged from going to America. Colonial legislation favorable to manufacturing interests was often vetoed. Finally, and most visibly, parliament at Westminster passed legislation restricting certain colonial industries, the most famous being the Hat Act (1732) and the Iron Act (1750). Although both acts are restrictive, there is an important difference between them. The Hat Act prohibited the export of all hats made in the plantations, but the Iron Act actually encouraged the production and export of iron, as long as it was in pig or bar form.

The effectiveness of this legislation in obstructing the growth of American industry has often been debated. Today, most historians would argue that its importance has been exaggerated. Much of this legislation, including the Iron Act, was ignored by the colonists and the British officials. In addition, other industries, including shipbuilding and shoe and paper manufacturing, were never regulated even in theory, while still others, such as the production of naval stores (turpentine, tar, and pitch), were actively encouraged. In most instances, when an industry failed to develop in the colonies, it was due

SOURCE. *The Statutes At Large*, XVI, 304–305, 307 (5 George II. c. 22); XX, 97, 99–100 (23 George II. c. 29).

to its inefficiency and its inability to compete with the more mature British industry. The lack of capital and the high cost of labor probably did more to retard American industrial growth than all of Britain's mercantilistic legislation combined. Perhaps the most significant consequence of the Hat Act and the Iron Act was their exploitation after 1763 as political grievances.

AN ACT TO PREVENT THE EXPORTATION OF HATS OUT OF ANY OF HIS MAJESTY'S COLONIES OR PLANTATIONS IN AMERICA AND TO RESTRAIN THE NUMBER OF APPRENTICES TAKEN BY THE HAT-MAKERS IN THE SAID COLONIES OR PLANTATIONS, AND FOR THE BETTER ENCOURAGING THE MAKING HATS IN GREAT BRITAIN

Whereas *the art and mystery of making hats in* Great Britain *hath arrived to great perfection, and considerable quantities of hats manufactured in this kingdom have heretofore been exported to his Majesty's plantations or colonies in* America, *who have been wholly supplied with hats from Great Britain; and whereas great quantities of hats have of late years been made, and the said manufacture is daily increasing in the* British *plantations in* America, *and is from thence exported to foreign markets, which were heretofore supplied from Great Britain, and the hat-makers in the said plantations take many apprentices for very small terms, to the discouragement of the said trade, and debasing the said manufacture:* wherefore for preventing the said ill practices for the future, and for promoting and encouraging the trade of making hats in *Great Britain,* be it enacted . . . That . . . no hats or felts whatsoever, dyed or undyed, finished or unfinished, shall be shipt, loaden or put on board any ship or vessel in any place or parts within any of the *British* plantations . . . and also that no hats or felts, either dyed or undyed, finished or unfinished, shall be loaden upon any horse, cart or other carriage, to the intent or purpose to be exported, transported, shipped off, carried or conveyed out of any of the said *British* plantations to any other of the *British* plantations, or to any other place whatsover, by any person or persons whatsoever.

VII. And it is hereby further enacted by the authority aforesaid, That no person residing in any of his Majesty's plantations in *America* shall . . . make or cause to be made, any felt or hat of or with any wool or stuff whatsoever, unless he shall have first served as an apprentice in the trade or art of felt-making during the space of seven years at the least; neither shall any felt-maker or hat-maker in any of the said plantations imploy, retain or set to work, in the said art or trade, any person as a journeyman or hired servant, other than such as shall have lawfully served an apprenticeship in the said trade for the space of seven years; nor shall any felt-maker or hat-maker in any of the said plantations have, take or keep above the number of two apprentices at one time, or take any apprentice for any less term than seven years, upon pain to forfeit and pay the sum of five pounds for every month that he shall continue offending in the premisses contrary to the true meaning of this act. . . .

VIII. And be it further enacted by the authority aforesaid, That no person or persons inhabiting in the said plantations . . . shall retain or set on work, in the said art of felt making, any black or negro, upon pain to forfeit and pay the sum of five pounds for every month wherein such person or persons shall so offend, contrary to the meaning of this act.

AN ACT TO ENCOURAGE THE IMPORTATION OF PIG AND BAR IRON FROM HIS MAJESTY'S COLONIES IN AMERICA; AND TO PREVENT THE ERECTION OF ANY MILL OR OTHER ENGINE FOR SLITTING OR ROLLING OF IRON; OR ANY PLATEING FORGE TO WORK WITH A TILT HAMMER; OR ANY FURNACE FOR MAKING STEEL IN ANY OF THE SAID COLONIES

Whereas *the importation of bar iron from his Majesty's colonies in* America, *into the port of* London, *and the importation of pig iron from the said colonies, into any port of* Great Britain, *and the manufacture of such bar and pig iron in* Great Britain, *will be a great advantage not only to the said colonies, but also to this kingdom, by furnishing the manufacturers of iron with a supply of that useful and necessary commodity, and by means thereof large sums of money, now annually paid for iron to foreigners, will be saved to this kingdom, and a greater quantity of the woollen, and other manufactures of* Great Britain, *will be exported to* America, *in exchange for such iron so imported;* be it therefore enacted . . . That . . . the several and respective subsidies, customs, impositions, rates, and duties, now payable on pig iron, made in and imported from his Majesty's colonies in *America,* into any port of *Great Britain,* shall cease . . . and that . . . no subsidy, custom, imposition, rate, or duty whatsoever, shall be payable upon bar iron made in and imported from the said colonies into the port of *London*; any law, statute, or usage to the contrary thereof in any wise notwithstanding.

IX. And, that pig and bar iron made in his Majesty's colonies in *America* may be further manufactured in this kingdom, be it further enacted

... That ... no mill or other engine for slitting or rolling of iron, or any plateing-forge to work with a tilt hammer, or any furnace for making steel, shall be erected, or after such erection, continued, in any of his Majesty's colonies in *America*; and if any person or persons shall erect, or cause to be erected, or after such erection, continue, or cause to be continued, in any of the said colonies, any such mill, engine, forge, or furnace, every person or persons so offending, shall, for every such mill, engine, forge, or furnace, forfeit the sum of two hundred pounds of lawful money of *Great Britain*.

67

John Wesley, *Journal.*
The Methodist Revival (1738)

John Wesley was a reluctant revolutionary, forced against his will to take action against an established church. Anglicanism, he felt, had become overly intellectual and callous to the needs of the general population, specifically the residents of the new industrial cities. While at Oxford, Wesley and his younger brother, Charles, formed the Holy Club; ignoring charges of being "enthusiasts" and "methodists," they devoted much of their time to social work. On his return to England in 1738 after two frustrating years in James Oglethorpe's debtor colony of Georgia, John Wesley experienced a spiritual crisis. His failures in Georgia undoubtedly contributed to his fear that, by emphasizing "good works," he was also failing God. His Aldersgate experience, reproduced below from his *Journal,* finally brought him peace of mind. His acceptance of salvation by faith alone, by a "true trust and confidence of the mercy of God through our Lord Jesus Christ," launched his great career as an evangelist.

SOURCE. *The Journal of John Wesley,* ed. Nehemiah Curnock, New York: Capricorn Books, 1963, pp. 49–52.

During the next 50 years, Wesley traveled approximately 250,000 miles, mostly on horseback, and delivered an estimated 40,000 sermons. He was a strange revivalist, however. His university training made him uncomfortable with the enthusiasm generated at some of his outdoor meetings. He was also very reluctant to break with the Church of England, remaining an Anglican priest until his death in 1791. Only gradually did "Pope John," as he was called by some, come to exercise control over a de facto religious denomination, Methodism. Unlike some revolutionaries, he lived to see his movement become socially respectable. He accepted this development rationally although, one senses, with a certain amount of regret. "I do not see how it is possible in the nature of things for a religious revival to last long. For religion must necessarily produce industry and frugality. And these cannot but produce riches. But as Riches increase, so will Pride and love of the world in all of its branches."

Another interesting aspect of the Wesleyan Movement is its relationship to the other reform movements of the eighteenth century. Although Wesley's early career confirms Methodism's obvious social dimension, social or secular reform was never his primary concern. Politically he was a Tory, opposed to the ideas of John Wilkes and of Continental Congresses; religiously he was intolerant, opposed to Roman Catholic emancipation; socially he opposed government regulation of business, preferring child labor to the idleness of play. His career illustrates the conflict of priorities present in many religions: to stress the spiritual salvation of one's own soul or to show concern for the material welfare of one's fellow man?

The Journal of John Wesley consists of almost daily comments written during most of his adult life. Most of the entries are much briefer than those given below and describe simply a sermon preached and the congregation's response. The standard edition, in eight volumes, was edited by Nehemiah Curnock.

24 May 1738. . . . All the time I was at Savannah I was thus beating the air. Being ignorant of the righteousness of Christ, which, by a living faith in Him, bringeth salvation "to every one that believeth," I sought to establish my own rightousness; and so laboured in the fire all my days. I was now properly "under the law"; I knew that "the law" of God was "spiritual; I consented to it, that it was good." Yea, "I delighted in it, after the inner man." Yet was I "carnal, sold under sin." Every day was I constrained to cry out, "What I do, I allow not: for what I would, I do not; but what I hate, that I do. . . ."

In this vile, abject state of bondage to sin, I was indeed fighting continually, but not conquering. Before, I had willingly served sin; now it was unwillingly; but still I served it. I fell, and rose, and fell again. Sometimes I was overcome, and in heaviness: sometimes I overcame, and was in joy. For as in the former state I had some foretastes of the terrors of the law, so had I in this, of the comforts of the gospel. . . .

On my return to England, January, 1738, being in imminent danger of death, and very uneasy on that account, I was strongly convinced that the cause of that uneasiness was unbelief; and that the gaining a true, living faith was the "one thing needful" for me. But still I fixed not this faith on its right object: I meant only faith in God, not faith in or through Christ. Again, I knew not that I was wholly void of this faith; but only thought I had not enough of it. So that when Peter Böhler, whom God prepared for me as soon as I came to London, affirmed of true faith in Christ (which is but one), that it had those two fruits inseparably attending it, "dominion over sin, and constant peace from a sense of forgiveness," I was quite amazed, and looked upon it as a new gospel. If this was so, it was clear I had not faith. But I was not willing to be convinced of this. . . .

When I met Peter Böhler again, he consented to put the dispute upon the issue which I desired, namely, Scripture and experience. I first consulted the Scripture. But when I set aside the glosses of men, and simply considered the words of God, comparing them together, endeavouring to illustrate the obscure by the plainer passages; I found they all made against me, and was forced to retreat to my last hold, "that experience would never agree with the literal interpretation of those scriptures. Nor could I therefore allow it to be true, till I found some living witnesses of it." He replied, he could show me such any time; if I desired it, the next day. And accordingly, the next day he came again with three others, all of whom testified, of their own personal experience, that a true, living faith in Christ is inseparable from a sense of pardon for all past, and freedom from all present, sins. They added with one mouth, that this faith was the gift, the free gift, of God; and that He would surely bestow it upon every soul who earnestly and perseveringly sought it. I was now thoroughly convinced; and by the grace of God, I resolved to seek it unto the end: 1. By absolutely renouncing all dependence, in whole or in part, upon my own works or righteousness; on which I had really grounded my hope of salvation, though I knew it not, from my youth up. 2. By adding to the constant use of all the other means of grace, continual prayer for this very thing, justifying, saving faith, a full reliance on the blood of Christ shed for me; a trust in Him as my Christ, as my sole justification, sanctification, and redemption.

I continued thus to seek it (though with strange indifference, dulness, and coldness, and unusually frequent relapses into sin), till Wednesday, May 24. . . .

In the evening I went very unwillingly to a society in Aldersgate Street, where one was reading Luther's preface to the Epistle to the Romans. About a quarter before nine, while he was describing the change which God works in the heart through faith in Christ, I felt my heart strangely warmed. I felt I did trust in Christ, Christ alone, for salvation: and an assurance was given me, that He had taken away my sins, even mine, and saved me from the law of sin and death.

I began to pray with all my might for those who had in a more especial manner despitefully used me and persecuted me. I then testified openly to all there, what I now first felt in my heart. But it was not long before the enemy suggested, "This cannot be faith; for where is thy joy?" Then was I taught, that peace and victory over sin are essential to faith in the Captain of our salvation; but that, as to the transports of joy that usually attend the beginning of it, especially in those who have mourned deeply, God sometimes giveth, sometimes withholdeth them, according to the counsels of His own will.

After my return home, I was much buffeted with temptations; but cried out, and they fled away. They returned again and again. I as often lifted up my eyes, and He "sent me help from His holy place." And herein I found the difference between this and my former state chiefly consisted. I was striving, yea, fighting with all my might under the law, as well as under grace. But then I was sometimes, if not often, conquered; now I was always conqueror.

25 May 1738. The moment I awaked, "Jesus, Master," was in my heart and in my mouth; and I found all my strength lay in keeping my eye fixed upon Him, and my soul waiting on Him continually. Being again at St Paul's in the afternoon, I could taste the good word of God, in the anthem, which began, "My song shall be always of the loving-kindness of the Lord: with my mouth will I ever be showing forth Thy truth from one generation to another." Yet the enemy injected a fear, "If thou dost believe, why is there not a more sensible change?" I answered (yet not I), "That I know not. But this I know, I have 'now peace with God.' And I sin not to-day, and Jesus my Master has forbid me to take thought for the morrow."

"But is not any sort of fear," continued the tempter, "a proof that thou dost not believe?" I desired my Master to answer for me; and opened His Book upon those words of St. Paul, "Without were fightings, within were fears." Then, inferred I, well may fears be within me; but I must go on, and tread them under my feet.

68

Samuel Sandys and Sir Robert Walpole, Debate in the House of Commons (1741). The Office of Prime Minister

Despite parliament's preeminence after 1688, the king remained the chief executive and possessed vast areas of independence in the day-to-day running of the government. His most important prerogative was the power to appoint his own advisers. Parliament could remove these ministers through impeachment, bringing criminal charges against them, or by refusing to vote the funds necessary for the implementation of their policies. It lacked, however, the practical ability of influencing their routine activities on behalf of the king's government. The ultimate solution to the problem of controlling the executive was the development of the office of prime minister, the head of a cabinet, all of whose members were jointly responsible to the House of Commons and capable of removal by a simple majority vote. This system of responsible government, worked out during the eighteenth and nineteenth centuries, seems so natural and obvious that one must make an effort to keep from seeing some constitutional architect plotting its development from the beginning.

Although kings throughout England's history had chief, or prime, ministers, the evolution of the present office of that name began in the early eighteenth century. This was due first to the weakness of Queen Anne (1702–1714) and then to the disinclination of George I (1714–1727) and George II (1727–1760) to attend the meetings of their ministers. The first modern prime

---

SOURCE. William Cobbett, *Parliamentary History of England,* 36 vols., London, 1806–1820, XI, 1223–1224, 1229–1230, 1232, 1241–1242, 1284, 1287, 1295–1296.

minister—who presides over and dominates the cabinet, who through his personality or other influence manages the House of Commons, and who is the king's "prime minister"—was Sir Robert Walpole, who held this position from 1721 to 1742. The debate in Commons reproduced below reveals the frustration and outrage felt by opposition members at the extended dominance of Walpole. The charges of Sandys and the reply of Walpole show that their understanding of the office of prime minister was at best embryonic.

William Cobbett (1762–1835), who had begun publishing the *Parliamentary Debates* in 1803, complemented his project by reconstructing the debates for the period prior to 1803. The 36 large volumes that he produced between 1806 and 1820 provide the historian with a ready source of evidence on the workings of parliament, evidence that previously had to be obtained from many different sources.

DEBATE IN THE COMMONS ON MR. SANDYS'S MOTION FOR THE REMOVAL OF SIR ROBERT WALPOLE

Mr. Sandys: Sir . . . I believe, there is not a gentleman of this House, who is not sensible, that both the foreign and domestic measures of our government, for several years past, have been dissatisfactory to a great majority of the nation, I may say to almost every man in the nation, who has not been concerned in advising or carrying them on. I believe, there is not a gentleman in this House, if he will freely declare his sentiments, who is not sensible, that one single person in the administration has not only been thought to be, but has actually been the chief, if not the sole adviser and promoter of all those measures. . . . As I am only to propose an Address to remove him from his majesty's counsels, I have no occasion to accuse him of any crime; the people's being generally dissatisfied with him and suspicious of his conduct, is a sufficient foundation for such an Address, and a sufficient cause for his majesty's removing him from his counsels; because, no sovereign of these kingdoms ought to employ a minister, who is become disagreeable to the generality of the people; and when any minister happens to become so, it is our duty to inform his majesty of it, that he may give satisfaction to his people, by the removal of such a minister. . . .

According to our constitution, we can have no sole and prime minister: we ought always to have several prime ministers or officers of state: every such officer has his own proper department; and no officer ought to meddle in the affairs belonging to the department of another. But it is publicly known, that this minister, having obtained a sole influence over all our public counsels, has not only assumed the sole direction of all public affairs, but has got every officer of state removed that would not follow his direction, even in the affairs belonging to his own proper department. By this means he hath monopolized all the favours of the crown, and engrossed the sole disposal of all places, pensions, titles, and ribbons, as well as of all preferments, civil, military, or ecclesiastical.

This, Sir, is of itself a most heinous offence against our constitution: but he has greatly aggravated the heinousness of his crime; for, having thus monopolized all the favours of the crown, he has made a blind submission to his direction at elections and in parliament, the only ground to hope for any honours or preferments, and the only tenure by which any gentleman could preserve what he had. This is so notoriously known, that it can stand in need of no proof. . . .

But farther, Sir, suppose this minister had never been guilty of any crime, error, or oversight in his public conduct; suppose the people had all along been perfectly pleased with his administration, yet the very length of it is, in a free country, sufficient cause for removing him. It is a most dangerous thing in a free government, to allow any man to continue too long in the possession of great power: most common-wealths have been overturned by this very oversight; and in this country, we know how difficult it has often proved, for our parliament to draw an old favourite from behind the throne, even when he has been guilty of the most heinous crimes. I wish this may not be our case at present; for though I shall not say, nor have I at present any occasion for shewing, that the favourite I am now complaining of has been guilty of heinous crimes, yet I will say, that there is a very general suspicion against him, that this suspicion is justified by the present situation of our affairs both at home and abroad, and that it is ridiculous to expect, that any proper discovery should be made, as long as he is in possession of all the proofs, and has the distribution of all the penalties the crown can inflict, as well as of all the favours the crown can bestow. Remove him from the king's counsels and presence; remove him from those high offices and power he is now possessed of; if he has been guilty of any crimes, the proof may then be come at, and the witnesses against him will not be afraid to appear: till you do this, it is impossible to determine, whether he is guilty or innocent; and, considering the universal clamour against him, it is high time to reduce him to such a condition, as that he may be brought to a fair, an impartial, and a strict account. If he were conscious of his being entirely innocent, and had a due regard to the security and glory of his master and sovereign, he would have chose to have put himself into this condition long before this time: since he has not thought fit to do so, it is our duty to endeavour to do it for him; and therefore I shall conclude with moving,

"That an humble address be presented to his majesty, that he will be graciously pleased to remove the right hon. sir Robert Walpole, knight of the most noble order of the garter, first commissioner for executing the office of treasurer of the exchequer, chancellor and under-treasurer of the exchequer, and one of his majesty's most honourable privy council, from his majesty's presence and counsels for ever."

Sir Robert Walpole: Sir, it has been observed by several gentlemen in vindication of this motion, that if it should be carried, neither my life, liberty, or estate will be affected. But do the honourable gentlemen consider my character and reputation as of no moment? . . . As I am conscious of no crime, my own experience convinces me, that none can be justly imputed. I must therefore ask the gentlemen, from whence does this attack proceed? From the passions and prejudices of the parties combined against me. . . .

I am called repeatedly and insidiously prime and sole minister. . . .

Have gentlemen produced one instance of this exorbitant power of the influence which I extend to all parts of the nation, of the tyranny with which I oppress those who oppose, and the liberality with which I reward those who support me? But having first invested me with a kind of mock dignity, and styled me a prime minister, they impute to me an unpardonable abuse of that chimerical authority which they only have created and conferred. If they are really persuaded that the army is annually established by me, that I have the sole disposal of posts and honours, that I employ this power in the destruction of liberty, and the diminution of commerce, let me awaken them from their delusion. Let me expose to their view the real condition of the public weal; let me shew them that the crown has made no encroachments, that all supplies have been granted by parliament, that all questions have been debated with the same freedom as before the fatal period, in which my counsels are said to have gained the ascendancy. . . .

But while I unequivocally deny that I am sole and prime minister, and that to my influence and direction all the measures of government must be attributed, yet I will not shrink from the responsibility which attaches to the post I have the honour to hold; and should, during the long period in which I have sat upon this bench, any one step taken by government be proved to be either disgraceful or disadvantageous to the nation, I am ready to hold myself accountable.

To conclude, Sir, though I shall always be proud of the honour of any trust or confidence from his majesty, yet I shall always be ready to remove from his counsels and presence, when he thinks fit; and therefore I should think myself very little concerned in the event of the present question, if it were not for the encroachment that will thereby be made upon the prerogatives of the crown. But I must think, that an address to his majesty to remove one of his servants, without so much as alleging any particular crime against him, is one of the greatest encroachments that was ever made upon the prerogatives of the crown; and therefore, for the sake of my master, without any regard for my own, I hope all those that have a due regard for our constitution, and for the rights and prerogatives of the crown, without which our constitution cannot be preserved, will be against this motion.

69

William Hogarth, Prints (1725-1763). The Artist as Social Critic

William Hogarth (1697–1764) is today recognized as one of England's greatest artists. His art, unique for the eighteenth century, reflected what he saw in everyday life. This explains why his paintings and prints never appealed to the wealthy English connoisseurs, who, Hogarth complained, preferred "shiploads of dead Christs, Madonnas, and Holy Families." He disliked this pretentious art of the continent and agreed with Dr. Samuel Johnson, who once stated: "I had rather see the portrait of a dog I know than all the allegories you can show me." Hogarth gloried in his Englishness, visiting France only once in his lifetime and disliking the experience. He was also a social critic and a moralist. He felt that art should do more than entertain; it should "improve the mind" and be "of public utility." Hogarth's sense of morality, which was that of the rising middle class, was best expressed in his famous progresses: "The Harlot's Progress" (1732), "The Rake's Progress" (1735), "Marriage-à-la-Mode" (1745), and "Industry and Idleness" (1747). Because these paintings were later engraved, the prints being sold to subscribers, Hogarth's work reached a far wider audience than that of any other eighteenth-century artist.

Hogarth's social criticism is clearly visible in the prints reproduced below. "The Sleeping Congregation" (Plate A) is a jab at the vitality of the Church of England. Plate B, "Chairing the Members," is the fourth and final of his

PLATE A

"The Sleeping Congregation" (by courtesy of the Trustees of the British Museum).

"Election" prints, ridiculing the process by which members are elected to parliament. Plate C, "Inhabitants of the Moon," points an accusing finger at the corruption of the establishment—the monarchy, the church, and the law. "Gin Lane" (Plate D), perhaps Hogarth's most famous print, illustrates

PLATE B

"Chairing the Members" (by courtesy of the Trustees of the British Museum).

the evils of the unregulated traffic in cheap gin, which destroys society but profits the pawnbroker. Hogarth's simple solution in Plate E, "Beer Street," is to encourage people to consumer beer.

> Beer, happy Produce of our Isle
> Can sinewy Strength impart,
> And wearied with Fatigue and Toil
> Can chear each manly Heart.

Finally, Hogarth's talent at caricature, evident in "John Wilkes, Esquire" (Plate F), served as an example for such later political cartoonists and satirists as James Gillray and Thomas Rowlandson.

The art of any era can provide insight into the tastes and general attitudes of the people. Hogarth's prints, by dealing largely with social problems and by appealing to a large audience, are more valuable in this regard than the works of any other English artist. His paintings and etchings are widely scattered, the most complete collection being in the British Museum.

PLATE C

"Inhabitants of the Moon" (by courtesy of the Trustees of the British Museum).

PLATE D
"Gin Lane" (by courtesy of the Trustees of the British Museum).

PLATE E
"Beer Street" (by courtesy of the Trustees of the British Museum).

John Wilkes Esq.

Drawn from the Life and Etch'd in Aquafortis by W.ᵐ Hogarth.

Price 1 Shilling.   Publish'd according to Act of Parliament May y.ᵉ 16. 1763.

PLATE F
"John Wilkes, Esquire" (by courtesy of the Trustees of the British Museum).

Horace Walpole, Letters.
The 1745 Jacobite Rebellion

Horace Walpole (1717–1797), the fourth son of prime minister Sir Robert Walpole, was a member of parliament from 1741 to 1767. His life revolved, however, around Strawberry Hill, his house at Twickenham, which had the appearance of a small castle and contained his private printing press, from which he produced, among other things, his own Gothic novel, *The Castle of Otranto* (1764). Quite literally, he was a scholar and a gentleman. He was a member of society, he traveled abroad, he was acquainted with everyone, he knew everything that was happening. His thousands of letters were filled with his astute, witty, and even scandalous observations on people and events. Although often an annoyance to his contemporaries, Walpole is through his letters one of the historian's brightest windows into the eighteenth century.

In the letters reproduced below he describes to Horace Mann, one of his chief correspondents and the British envoy to Florence from 1740 to 1784, the course of the Jacobite uprising of 1745. From them can be determined the outline of the attempt of Bonnie Prince Charlie to regain the throne for his father, the Old Pretender—his routing of General Sir John Cope's forces at Prestonpans on September 21, his march into England as far as Derby, a mere 80 miles from London, his turning back on December 6, when England did not rise on his behalf, his retreat into the Highlands but not before defeating another English army at Falkirk on January 17, 1746, and, finally,

---

SOURCE. *Horace Walpole's Correspondence with Sir Horace Mann,* Vol. III, eds. W. S. Lewis, Warren Hunting Smith, and George L. Lam (*The Yale Edition of Horace Walpole's Correspondence,* ed. W. S. Lewis, Vol. XIX), New Haven: Yale University Press, 1954, pp. 101–103, 116–118, 178–180, 185, 188–189, 246–249. Copyright 1954 by Yale University Press.

his utter defeat by the duke of Cumberland and the demise of the Jacobite threat at Culloden on April 16. It must be remembered, however, that Walpole's account is not firsthand; his information is no better than the source from which he obtained it, which is uncertain. On the other hand, his keen observations of feelings and reactions in England were his own and should be taken very seriously. He is at his reportorial and entertaining best when giving his impression of parliament's reception of the news that Hessian mercenaries had been hired and when he observes that London has been reduced "to a state of Presbyterian dullness," relieved only by the marriage of the duchess of Bridgwater.

A volume of Walpole's letters was included in his works published in 1798, the year after his death. Since then, longer and fuller editions have succeeded one after another, the latest complete edition, not yet finished, being projected to run to about 50 volumes.

September 6, 1745

The confusion I have found, and the danger we are in, prevent my talking of anything else. The young Pretender, at the head of three thousand men, has got a march on General Cope, who is not eighteen hundred strong; and when the last accounts came away, was fifty miles nearer Edinburgh than Cope; and by this time is there. The clans will not rise for the government: the Dukes of Argyle and Athol are come post to town, not having been able to raise a man. . . .

I look upon Scotland as gone! I think of what King William said to Duke Hamilton, when he was extolling Scotland; "My Lord, I only wish it was an hundred thousand miles off, and that you was king of it."

There are two manifestos published, signed Charles Prince, Regent for his father, King of Scotland, England, France and Ireland. By one, he promises to preserve everybody in their just rights; and orders all persons who have public moneys in their hands to bring it to him; and by the other dissolves the Union between England and Scotland.—But all this is not the worst! Notice came yesterday, that there are ten thousand men, thirty transports and ten men of war at Dunkirk. Against this force, we have—I don't know what—scarce fears! Three thousand Dutch we hope are by this time landed in Scotland; three more are coming hither: we have sent for ten regiments from Flanders, which may be here in a week, and we have fifteen men of war in the Downs.

September 27, 1745

I can't doubt but the joy of the Jacobites has reached Florence before this letter—Your two or three Irish priests, I forget their names, will have set out to take possession of abbey lands here. I feel for what you will feel, and for the insulting things that will be said to you upon the battle we have lost in Scotland—but all this is nothing to what it prefaces. The express came hither on Tuesday morning, but the Papists knew it on Sunday night. Cope lay in face of the rebels all Friday, he scarce two thousand strong; they vastly superior, though we don't know their numbers. The military people say that he should have attacked them. However we are sadly convinced that they are not such raw ragamuffins as they represented. . . . One does not hear the boy's personal valour cried up, by which, I concluded he was not in the action. Our dragoons most shamefully fled without striking a blow, and are with Cope, who escaped in a boat to Berwick. . . . This defeat has frightened everybody, but those it rejoices, and those it should frighten most; but my Lord Granville still buoys up the King's spirits, and persuades him it is nothing. He uses his ministers as ill as possible, and discourages everybody that would risk their lives and fortunes with him. Marshal Wade is marching against the rebels; but the King will not let him take above eight thousand men; so that if they come into England, another battle, with no advantage on our side, may determine our fate. . . .

Prince Charles has called a Parliament in Scotland for the 7th of October; ours does not meet till the 17th so that even in the show of liberty and laws, they are beforehand with us. With all this, we hear of no men of quality or fortune having joined him, but Lord Elcho, whom you have seen at Florence; and the Duke of Perth, a silly racehorsing boy, who is said to be killed in this battle. But I gather no confidence from hence: my father always said, "If you see them come again, they will begin by their lowest people; their chiefs will not appear till the end." His prophecies verify every day!

December 9th 1745

I am glad I did not write to you last post as I intended; I should have sent you an account that would have alarmed you; and the danger would have been over before the letter had crossed the sea. The Duke, from some strange want of intelligence, lay last week for four and twenty hours under arms at Stone in Staffordshire, expecting the rebels every moment, while they were marching in all haste to Derby. The news of this threw the town into great consternation; but his Royal Highness repaired his mistake, and got to Northampton between the Highlanders and London. . . . They must either go to North Wales, where they will probably all perish, or to Scotland, with great loss. We dread them no longer. We are threatened with great preparations for a French invasion, but the coast is exceedingly guarded; and for the people, the spirit against the rebels increases every day: though they have marched thus into the heart of the kingdom, there has not been the least symptom of a rising, not even in the great towns of which they possessed themselves. They have got no recruits since their first entry into England, except one genleman in Lancashire, one hundred and fifty common men and two parsons at Manchester, and a physician from York. But here in London the aversion to them is amazing: on some thoughts of the King's going to an encampment at Finchley, the weavers not only offered him a thousand men but the whole body of the law formed themselves into a little army under the command of Lord Chief Justice Willes, and were to have done duty at St James's, to guard the royal family in the King's absence.

December 20, 1745

We have at last got a springtide of good luck. The rebels turned back from Derby; and have ever since been flying with the greatest precipitation. . . . Into England I scarce believe the Highlanders will be drawn again—To have come as far as Derby; to have found no rising in their favour, and to find themselves not strong enough to fight either army, will make lasting impressions! . . .

We had yesterday a very remarkable day in the House: the King notified his having sent for six thousand Hessians into Scotland. Mr Pelham for an address of thanks. Lord Cornbury (indeed an exceedingly honest man) was for thanking for the notice, not for the sending for the troops; and proposed to add a representation of the national being the only constitutional troops; and to hope we should be exonerated of these foreigners as soon as possible. Pitt, and that clan joined him; but the voice of the House, and the desires of the whole kingdom for all the troops we can get, were so strong, that on the division we were 190 to 44: I think and hope this will produce some Hanoverians too. . . .

In the midst of our political distresses, which I assure you have reduced the town to a state of Presbyterian dullness, we have been entertained with the marriage of the Duchess of Bridgwater and Dick Lyttelton; she, forty, plain, very rich, and with five children; he six and twenty, handsome, poor, and proper to get her five more.

April 25th 1746

You have bid me for some time send you good news—well! I think, I will. . . .

On the 16th the Duke by forced marches came up with the rebels a little on this side Inverness—by the way, the battle is not christened yet; I only know that neither Prestonpans nor Falkirk are to be godfathers. The rebels, who fled from him after their victory, and durst not attack him when so much exposed to them at his passage of the Spay, now stood him, they seven thousand, he ten. They broke through Barril's regiment, and killed Lord Robert Kerr, a handsome young gentleman, who was cut to pieces with above thirty wounds; but they were soon repulsed and fled; the whole engagement not lasting above a quarter of an hour. The young Pretender escaped; Mr Conway says, he hears, wounded; he certainly was in the rear. They have lost above a thousand men in the engagement and pursuit; and six hundred were already taken. . . . The defeat is reckoned total, and the dispersion general; and all their artillery is taken. 'Tis a brave young Duke! The town is all blazing round me, as I write, with fireworks and illuminations: I have some inclination to lap up half a dozen skyrockets to make you drink the Duke's health. Mr Doddington, on the first report, came out with a very pretty illumination; so pretty, that I believe he had it by him, ready for *any* occasion.

71

Earl of Chesterfield, *Letters* (1748). The Education of a Gentleman

Like many historical figures, Philip Dormer Stanhope, fourth earl of Chester-field (1694–1773), has today a different significance than when he was alive. To the eighteenth century, he was an ambassador, a lord-lieutenant of Ire-

SOURCE.   *The Letters of Philip Dormer Stanhope, 4th Earl of Chesterfield,* ed. Bonamy Dobrée, 6 vols., New York: AMS Reprint, 1968, IV, 1205–1211.

land, and a politician of considerable importance. Today his reputation rests on his letters; from a man of politics he has been transformed into a man of literature.

The writing of letters was then considered an art. Chesterfield, Horace Walpole, Samuel Johnson, and many others exercised great care to insure that their correspondence was informative, coherent, and, hopefully, even entertaining. Much private correspondence has survived, aiding the historian in his study of all aspects of English life. Today, the telephone is rapidly replacing the letter, destroying in the process a traditional and valuable form of historical evidence.

Chesterfield's most famous letters are those written to his illegitimate son, Philip, to assist him in acquiring the graces necesary for social and political advancement. Collectively these letters constitute a gentleman's book of etiquette. One, reproduced below, details the proper conduct toward women. These letters have always been controversial. To Chesterfield's numerous critics, the letters are wicked, because they substitute manners for morality; one need not be a gentleman, he only need appear to be one. To prove their point, critics never fail to stress that the letters were addressed to a product of one of his numerous social indiscretions. Also, Chesterfield, with his biting wit and arrogance, was not the logical person to turn to for advice on winning friends and influencing people. For example, in Chesterfield's society the most important person to please was the king, but George II (1727–1760) looked upon Chesterfield as nothing more than "a little tea-table scoundrel."

The originals of Chesterfield's letters, almost all of which have been published, are scattered among various local repositories, the British Museum, and the Public Record Office. The first edition of his letters was published in 1774, the year following his death.

London, 5 September O.S. 1748

Dear Boy,

I have received yours, with the inclosed German letter to Mr. Grevenkop, which he assures me is extremely well written, considering the little time that you have applied yourself to that language. As you have now got over the most difficult part, pray go on diligently, and make yourself absolutely master of the rest. . . .

St. Thomas's day now draws near, when you are to leave Saxony and go to Berlin; and I take it for granted, that if anything is yet wanting to complete your knowledge of the state of that Electorate, you will not fail to procure it before you go away. . . . You will there be in more company than you have yet been; manners and attentions will therefore be more necessary. Pleasing in company is the only way of being pleased in it yourself. Sense and knowledge are the first and necessary foundations for pleasing in company; but they will by no means do alone, and they will never be perfectly welcome if they are not accompanied with manners and attentions. You will best acquire these by frequenting the companies of people of fashion; but then you must resolve to acquire them in those companies by proper care and observation; for I have known people who, though they have frequented good company all their lifetime, have done it in so inattentive and unobserving a manner as to be never the better for it, and to remain as disagreeable, as awkward, and as vulgar, as if they had never seen any person of fashion. When you go into good company (by good company is meant the people of the first fashion of the place) observe carefully their turn, their manners, their address, and conform your own to them. But this is not all, neither; go deeper still; observe their characters, and pry, as far as you can, into both their hearts and their heads. Seek for their particular merit, their predominant passion, or their prevailing weakness; and you will then know what to bait your hook with to catch them. . . .

As women are a considerable, or at least a pretty numerous part, of company; and as their suffrages go a great way towards establishing a man's character in the fashionable part of the world (which is of great importance to the fortune and figure he proposes to make in it), it is necessary to please them. I will therefore, upon this subject, let you into certain *arcana*, that will be very useful for you to know, but which you must, with the utmost care, conceal, and never seem to know. Women, then, are only children of a larger growth; they have an entertaining tattle and sometimes wit; but for solid, reasoning good-sense, I never in my life knew one that had it, or who reasoned or acted consequentially for four-and-twenty hours together. . . . A man of sense only trifles with them, plays with them, humours and flatters them, as he does with a sprightly, forward child; but he neither consults them about, nor trusts them with, serious matters; though he often makes them believe that he does both; which is the thing in the world that they are proud of; for they love mightily to be dabbling in business (which, by the way, they always spoil); and being justly distrustful that men in general look upon them in a triffling light, they almost adore that man who talks more seriously to them, and who seems to consult and trust them; I say, who seems, for weak men really do, but wise ones only seem to do it. No flattery is either too high or too low for them. They will greedily swallow the highest, and gratefully accept of the lowest; and you may safely flatter any woman, from her understanding down to the exquisite taste of her fan. Women, who are either indisputably beautiful, or indisputably ugly, are best flattered upon the score of their understandings; but those who are in a state of mediocrity, are best flattered upon their beauty, or at least their graces; for every woman who is not absolutely ugly, thinks herself handsome; but, not hearing often that she is so, is the more grateful and the more obliged to the few who tell her so; whereas a decided and conscious beauty looks upon every tribute paid to her beauty, only as her due; but wants to shine, and to be considered on the side of her understanding; and a woman who is ugly enough to know that she is so, knows that she has nothing left for her but her understanding, which is consequently (and probably in more senses than one) her weak side. . . . It is, therefore, absolutely necessary to manage, please, and flatter them; and never to discover the least marks of contempt, which is what they never forgive; but in this they are not singular, for it is the same with men; who will much sooner forgive an injustice than an insult. Every man is not ambitious, or covetous, or passionate; but every man has pride enough in his composition to feel and resent the least slight and contempt. Remember, therefore, most carefully to conceal your contempt, however just, wherever you would not make an implacable enemy. Men are much more unwilling to have their weaknesses and their imperfections known, than their crimes; and, if you hint to a man that you think him silly, ignorant, or even illbred or awkward, he will hate you more, and longer, than if you tell him plainly that you think him a rogue. . . .

These are some of the hints which my long experience in the great world enables me to give you; and which, if you attend to them, may prove useful to you in your journey through it. I wish it may be a prosperous one; at least, I am sure that it must be your own fault if it is not.

Make my compliments to Mr. Harte, who, I am very sorry to hear, is not well. I hope by this time he is recovered.

Adieu!

Samuel Johnson, *A Dictionary of the English Language* (1755)

Samuel Johnson (1709–1784) was in the eighteenth century England's dominant literary personality. He spent years as an anonymous denizen of Grub Street (see definition below), writing for various journals and sometimes reporting illegally the debates of the House of Commons, of which he said he was careful to see that "the Whig dogs should not have the best of it." His *Dictionary* in 1755 suddenly made him famous. This plus his helping to found the Literary Club in 1764, his editing of Shakespeare's plays in 1765, and his receiving LL.D. degrees from Dublin and Oxford in 1765 and 1775, respectively, made him the respected Dr. Johnson, the literary lion and archcritic who ruled the kingdom of letters throughout the remainder of his lifetime and beyond. James Boswell (1740–1795), an enterprising and intrepid Scot who initiated his long association with Johnson in 1763, produced in 1791 a massive *Life of Samuel Johnson*. He described Johnson's endearing foibles as well as his genius, confirming his reputation, and establishing him as a figure somewhat larger than life.

Although English dictionaries had appeared before that of Johnson, none was very satisfactory. The widely varying spellings in the earlier documents in this book illustrate well the writers' freedom and lack of direction. Johnson's two large folio volumes in 1755 and an abridgement a year later changed all this, raising the lexicographer's art to new levels of excellence and producing a practical guide to spelling and usage that was not superseded for nearly a century. The short passage from Johnson's preface and

SOURCE. *Johnson's Dictionary: A Modern Selection,* eds. E. L. McAdam, Jr., and George Milne, New York: Pantheon Books, A Division of Random House, 1963, pp. 4, 24, 71, 73, 74, 85, 103, 131, 158, 176, 193, 199, 202, 222, 225, 233, 268, 293, 303, 304, 420, 449. Reprinted by permission of Random House.

the definition of lexicographer, reproduced below, reveal his insight into his task. Though at first thinking that he might be able to "fix our language," to make it standard for all time, he soon concluded what folly it was for any-one to "imagine that his dictionary can enbalm his language." The defini-tions below, besides their individual interest, reveal something of Johnson's character. Although obviously a Tory and in many respects a conservative, he was not afraid of using words or of making honest and forthright judg-ments. Little of the blunt Anglo-Saxon of popular speech found its way into his dictionary, but what did, along with the frankness of his definitions and comments, reveals in him, and in the eighteenth century in general, a lack of inhibition and an earthy sense of humor.

When I took the first survey of my undertaking, I found our speech copious without order, and energetick without rules: wherever I turned my view, there was perplexity to be disentangled, and confusion to be regulated; choice was to be made out of boundless variety, without any established principle of selection; adulterations were to be detected, with-out a settled test of purity; and modes of expressions to be rejected or received, without the suffrages of any writers of classical reputation or acknowledged authority. . . .

Of the event of this work, for which, having laboured it with so much application, I cannot but have some degree of parental fondness, it is natural to form conjectures. Those who have been persuaded to think well of my design, require that it should fix our language, and put a stop to those alterations which time and chance have hitherto been suffered to make in it without opposition. With this consequence I will confess that I flattered myself for a while; but now begin to fear that I have in-dulged expectation which neither reason nor experience can justify. When we see men grow old and die at a certain time one after another, from century to century, we laugh at the elixir that promises to prolong life to a thousand years; and with equal justice may the lexicographer be derided, who being able to produce no example of a nation that has pre-served their words and phrases from mutability, shall imagine that his dictionary can embalm his language, and secure it from corruption and decay, that it is in his power to change sublunary nature, or clear the world at once from folly, vanity, and affectation.

assie'nto. (In Spanish a contract or bargain.) A contract or convention between the king of Spain and other powers, for furnishing the Spanish dominions in America with negro slaves. This contract was transferred from the French to the English South-Sea company, by the treaty of 1713, for thirty years; who were likewise permitted to send a register ship, of 500 tuns, yearly to the Spanish settlements, with European goods. Chambers.

athle′tick. (2) Strong of body; vigorous; lusty; robust.

Science distinguishes a man of honour from one of those *athletick* brutes, whom undeservedly we call heroes. Dryden.

a′tom. (1) Such a small particle as cannot be physically divided: and these are the first rudiments, or the component parts of all bodies. Quincy.

to ba′rbecue. A term used in the West-Indies for dressing a hog whole; which, being split to the backbone, is laid flat upon a large gridiron, raised about two foot above a charcoal fire, with which it is surrounded.

> Oldfield, with more than harpy throat endu'd,
> Cries, send me, gods, a whole hog *barbecu'd*. Pope.

bo′oby. (A word of no certain etymology; Henshaw thinks it a corruption of *bull-beef* ridiculously; Skinner imagines it to be derived from *bobo,* foolish, Span. Junius finds *bowbard* to be an old Scottish word for a *coward,* a *contemptible fellow*; from which he naturally deduces *booby*; but the original of *bowbard* is not known.) A dull, heavy, stupid fellow; a lubber.

> Young master next must rise to fill him wine,
> And starve himself to see the *booby* dine. King.

corn. (1) The seeds which grow in ears, not in pods; such as are made into bread.

(4) An excrescence on the feet, hard and painful; probably so called from its form, though by some supposed to be denominated from its *corneous* or horny substance.

> Even in men, aches and hurts and *corns* do engrieve
> either towards rain or towards frost. Bacon's *Natural History.*

dri′nkmoney. Money given to buy liquor.

Peg's servants were always asking for *drinkmoney*. Arbuthnot.

to fart. To break wind behind.

> As when we a gun discharge,
> Although the bore be ne'er so large,
> Before the flame from muzzle burst,
> Just at the breech it flashes first;
> So from my lord his passion broke,
> He *farted* first, and then he spoke. Swift.

gaol. A prison; a place of confinement. It is always pronounced and too often written *jail*, and sometimes *goal*.

gas. (A word invented by the chymists.) It is used by Van Helmont, and seems designed to signify, in general, a spirit not capable of being coagulated: but he uses it loosely in many senses, and very unintelligibly and inconsistently. Harris.

go′speller. A name of the followers of Wicklif, who first attempted a reformation from popery, given them by the Papists in reproach, from their professing to follow and preach only the gospel.

go′ssip. (1) One who answers for the child in baptism.
(2) A tippling companion.
(3) One who runs about tattling like women at a lying-in.

gru′bstreet. Originally the name of a street in Moorfields in London, much inhabited by writers of small histories, dictionaries, and temporary poems; whence any mean production is called grubstreet.

jail. A gaol; a prison; a place where criminals are confined. See *gaol*. It is written either way; but commonly by latter writers *jail*.

to ke′elhale. To punish in the seamens way, by dragging the criminal under water on one side of the ship and up again on the other.

lexico′grapher. A writer of dictionaries; a harmless drudge, that busies himself in tracing the original, and detailing the signification of words.

oats. A grain, which in England is generally given to horses, but in Scotland supports the people.

pi′epowder court. A court held in fairs for redress of all disorders committed therein.

pota′to. (I suppose an American word.) An esculent root.

> Leek to the Welch, to Dutchmen butter's dear,
> Of Irish swains *potatoe* is the chear;
> Oats for their feasts the Scottish shepherds grind,
> Sweet turnips are the food of Blouzelind;
> While she loves turnips, butter I'll despise,
> Nor leeks, nor oatmeal nor *potatoe* prize. Gay.

potva′liant. Heated with courage by strong drink.

pou′ndage. (1) A certain sum deducted from a pound; a sum paid by the trader to the servant that pays the money, or to the person who procures him customers.

to′ry. (A cant term, derived, I suppose, from an Irish word signifying a savage.) One who adheres to the antient constitution of the state, and the apostolical hierarchy of the church of England, opposed to a whig.

The knight is more a *tory* in the country than the town,
because it more advances his interest. Addison.

whig.   (2) The name of a faction.

The southwest counties of Scotland have seldom corn enough to serve them round the year; and the northern parts producing more than they need, those in the west come in the summer to buy at Leith the stores that come from the north; and from a word, whiggam, used in driving their horses, all that drove were called the whiggamors, and shorter the *whiggs*. Now in that year before the news came down of duke Hamilton's defeat, the ministers animated their people to rise and march to Edinburgh; and they came up marching on the head of their parishes with an unheard-of fury, praying and preaching all the way as they came. The marquis of Argyle and his party came and headed them, they being about six thousand. This was called the whiggamor's inroad; and ever after that, all that opposed the court came in contempt to be called *whigs:* and from Scotland the word was brought into England, where it is now one of our unhappy terms of disunion. Burnet.

Whoever has a true value for church and state, should avoid the extremes of *whig* for the sake of the former, and the extremes of tory on the account of the latter. Swift.

73

Wilkes v. *Wood* (1763) and *Leach* v. *Money* (1765). John Wilkes and General Warrants

The English judiciary, intimidated and dominated by the Stuart kings, became independent in 1701, when the Act of Settlement confirmed and established William III's practice of appointing judges for life. Henceforth, judges could not be influenced by threats to alter their salaries or be removed except by an address of both houses of parliament. The eighteenth century was characterized by outstanding justices, who used this independence to extend the rights of individuals and thereby added luster to the common law. Their decisions affirmed what William Blackstone wrote in his *Commentaries* (1765–1769) that in an independent judiciary "consists one main preservative of the public liberty."

One of the most famous and important issues dealt with involved the legality of general warrants, ordering the arrest of unnamed persons and authorizing the seizure of a man's private papers. The general warrant reproduced below was issued on April 30, 1763, for the arrest of "the authors, printers and publishers" of *The North Briton,* No. 45, "together with their papers," thus satisfying both conditions. One of the 49 men arrested by the warrant was John Wilkes (1727–1797), a wild and wealthy young man, a member of parliament as well as of the Hell Fire Club, and a founder of *The North Briton.* Number 45 had been especially harsh in its criticism of the king and his ministers. Wilkes quickly obtained his release on the grounds that he was a member of parliament, and then in a suit against Robert Wood, an undersecretary of state, he was awarded damages for the rifling of his papers. Lord Chief Justice of Common Pleas Sir Charles Pratt de-

---

SOURCE. T. B. Howell, ed., *A Complete Collection of State Trials and Proceedings for High Treason and Other Crimes and Misdemeanors,* Vol. XIX, London, 1816, pp. 881, 1167–1168, 1026–1027.

clared that such seizures were "totally subversive of the liberty of the subject." Two years later, in the case of *Leach* v. *Money*, Lord Chief Justice Mansfield joined with other judges in declaring the invalidity of a warrant, "upon the single objection of the incertainty of the person, being neither named or described." The illegality of general warrants was confirmed by Justice Pratt (now Lord Camden) in the case of *Entick* v. *Carrington* in 1765 and by parliamentary resolution in 1766.

Wilkes's career was a curious, but significant one. Besides his wealth and his keen sense of the ridiculous, he had little to support the fame that he attained as a champion of liberty, first in the matter of general warrants, then in his bid for election to parliament in 1768 and 1769, and finally in 1771 for championing the right to publish the debates of parliament. His entering these struggles demonstrated his flair for publicity and his intrepidity in the face of restrictions on his liberty. When he grew older he became conservative and respectable, but for a decade "Wilkes and Liberty" (see Plate F, p. 247) was a popular cry among the common people. His career as a radical illustrates both the dilapidation of the political system of the 1760s and the dawning realization that repairs needed to be made.

The General Warrant, April 30, 1763

George Montague Dunk, earl of Halifax, viscount Sunbury and baron Halifax, one of the lords of his majesty's most honourable privy council, lieutenant general of his majesty's forces, and principal secretary of state: these are in his majesty's name to authorize and require you (taking a constable to your assistance) to make strict and diligent search for the authors, printers and publishers of a seditious and treasonable paper, intitled, The North Briton, N° 45, Saturday April 23, 1763, printed for G. Kearsley in Ludgate-street, London, and them, or any of them, having found, to apprehend and seize, together with their papers, and to bring in safe custody before me, to be examined concerning the premises, and further dealt with according to law: and in the due execution thereof, all mayors, sheriffs, justices of the peace, constables, and all other his majesty's officers civil and military, and loving subjects whom it may concern, are to be aiding and assisting to you, as there shall be occasion; and for so doing this shall be your warrant. Given at St. James's the 26th day of April, in the third year of his majesty's reign.

DUNK HALIFAX

To Nathan Carrington, John Money, James Watson, and Robert Blackmore, four of his majesty's messengers in ordinary.

Wilkes v. *Wood,* December 6, 1763

His lordship then went upon the warrant, which he declared was a point of the greatest consequence he had ever met with in his whole practice. The defendants claimed a right, under precedents, to force persons' houses, break open escrutores, seize their papers, &c. upon a general warrant, where no inventory is made of the things thus taken away, and where no offenders' names are specified in the warrant, and therefore a discretionary power given to messengers to search wherever their suspicions may chance to fall. If such a power is truly invested in a secretary of state, and he can delegate this power, it certainly may affect the person and property of every man in this kingdom, and is totally subversive of the liberty of the subject.

And as for the precedents, will that be esteemed law in a secretary of state which is not law in any other magistrate of this kingdom? If they should be found to be legal, they are certainly of the most dangerous consequences; if not legal, must aggravate damages. Notwithstanding what Mr. Solicitor General has said, I have formerly delivered it as my opinion on another occasion, and I still continue of the same mind, that a jury have it in their power to give damages for more than the injury received. Damages are designed not only as a satisfaction to the injured person, but likewise as a punishment to the guilty, to deter from any such proceeding for the future, and as a proof of the detestation of the jury to the action itself.

As to the proof of what papers were taken away, the plaintiff could have no account of them; and those who were able to have given an account (which might have been an extenuation of their guilt) have produced none. It lays upon the jury to allow what weight they think proper to that part of the evidence. It is my opinion the office precedents, which had been produced since the Revolution, are no justification of a practice in itself illegal, and contrary to the fundamental principles of the constitution; though its having been the constant practice of the office, might fairly be pleaded in mitigation of damages.

The Jury, after withdrawing for near half an hour, returned, and found a general verdict upon both issues for the plaintiff, with a thousand pounds damages.

Leach v. *Money,* June 18, 1765

Lord *Mansfield* . . . At present—as to the validity of the warrant, upon the single objection of the incertainty of the person, being neither named nor described—the common law, in many cases, gives authority to arrest without warrant; more especially, where taken in the very act: and there are many cases where particular acts of parliament have given authority to apprehend, under general warrants; as in the case of writs of assistance, or warrants to take up loose, idle, and disorderly people. But here, it is not contended, that the common law gave the officer authority to apprehend; nor that there is any act of parliament which warrants this case.

Therefore it must stand upon principles of common law.

It is not fit, that the receiving or judging of the information should be left to the discretion of the officer. The magistrate ought to judge; and should give certain directions to the officer. This is so, upon reason and convenience.

Then as to authorities—Hale and all others hold such an uncertain warrant void: and there is no case or book to the contrary. . . .

Mr. Justice *Wilmot* declared, that he had no doubt, nor ever had, upon these warrants: he thought them illegal and void.

Neither had the two other judges, Mr. Justice Yates, and Mr. Justice Aston, any doubt (upon this first argument) of the illegality of them: for no degree of antiquity can give sanction to a usage bad in itself. And they esteemed this usage to be so. They were clear and unanimous in opinion, that this warrant was illegal and bad.

74

William Pitt, Speech in Commons (1766). American Taxation

Britain's victory in the Seven Years' War (1756–1763) established her pre-eminence as a world power, but it left her with serious problems: a heavy burden of debt; political unrest as evidenced by the commotions caused by John Wilkes; and, not least, increasingly difficult relations with her American colonies. After decades of benign neglect, the colonies began to attract the attention of the British government. To mitigate the Indian problem on

SOURCE.   William Cobbett, *Parliamentary History of England,* 36 vols., London, 1806–1820, XVI, 98–100, 103–104, 107.

the western frontier, the Proclamation of 1763 forbade settlement west of the Appalachians. To enforce a coherent economic policy within the empire, the Sugar Act of 1764 reduced colonial tariffs but provided the machinery for their collection. And to relieve the British taxpayer of the cost of the defense and administration of the enlarged empire, the Stamp Act of 1765 imposed on the American colonies a tax on newspapers, advertisements, and legal documents. The British government viewed these actions as parts of a unified and rational imperial policy. The American colonists, however, regarded them as infringements of their lawful rights and liberties.

The colonists' successful resistance, especially in getting the Stamp Act repealed in 1766, was due in part to the support that they received from members of the British parliament, especially those Whigs who felt that the Americans' problems were related to the general complaints they themselves had against the government of George III (1760–1820). One of the most outspoken champions of the Americans' right to resist "taxation without representation" was William Pitt the Elder (1708–1778), later the earl of Chatham. Today, Pitt is recognized as England's premier statesman of the mid-eighteenth century and, with the possible exception of Winston Churchill, her greatest wartime leader of the modern era. In a crisis he was a superb leader, as in the Seven Years' War when he saved the British Empire. On specific issues requiring insight and bold, forthright judgment, he invariably spoke out for the true interests of England and for the maintenance of the principles of the Glorious Revolution. From the excerpt below from Pitt's speech of January 14, 1766, one can sense the power and the passion of his oratory and can appreciate the similarity of arguments for political reform on both sides of the Atlantic.

I hope a day may be soon appointed to consider the state of the nation with respect to America. . . . A subject of greater importance than ever engaged the attention of this House! that subject only excepted, when near a century ago, it was the question whether you yourselves were to be bound, or free. . . . It is my opinion, that this kingdom has no right to lay a tax upon the colonies. At the same time, I assert the authority of this kingdom over the colonies, to be sovereign and supreme, in every circumstance of government and legislation whatsoever. They are the subjects of this kingdom, equally entitled with yourselves to all the natural rights of mankind and the peculiar privileges of Englishmen. Equally bound by its laws, and equally participating of the constitution of this free country. The Americans are the sons, not the bastards, of England. Taxation is no part of the governing or legislative power. The taxes are a voluntary gift and grant of the Commons alone. In legislation the three estates of the realm are alike concerned, but the concurrence of the peers and the crown to a tax, is only necessary to close with the form of a law. The gift and grant is of the Commons alone. In ancient days, the crown, the barons, and the clergy possessed the lands. In those days, the barons and the clergy gave and granted to the crown. They gave and granted what was their own. At present, since the discovery of America, and other circumstances permitting, the Commons are become the proprietors of the land. The crown has divested itself of its great estates. The church (God bless it) has but a pittance. The property of the Lords, compared with that of the Commons, is as a drop of water in the ocean: and this House represents those Commons, the proprietors of the lands; and those proprietors virtually represent the rest of the inhabitants. When, therefore, in this House we give and grant, we give and grant what is our own. But in an American tax, what do we do? We, your Majesty's Commons of Great Britain, give and grant to your Majesty, what? Our own property? No. We give and grant to your Majesty, the property of your Majesty's commons of America. It is an absurdity in terms.

The distinction between legislation and taxation is essentially necessary to liberty. The Crown, the Peers, are equally legislative powers with the Commons. If taxation be a part of simple legislation, the Crown, the Peers, have rights in taxation as well as yourselves: rights which they will claim, which they will exercise, whenever the principle can be supported by power.

There is an idea in some, that the colonies are virtually represented in this House. I would fain know by whom an American is represented here? Is he represented by any knight of the shire, in any county in this kingdom? Would to God that respectable representation was augmented to a greater number! Or will you tell him, that he is represented by any representative of a borough—a borough, which perhaps, its own representative never saw. This is what is called, "the rotten part of the constitution." It cannot continue the century; if it does not drop, it must be amputated. The idea of a virtual representation of America in this House, is the most contemptible idea that ever entered into the head of a man; it does not deserve a serious refutation.

The Commons of America, represented in their several assemblies, have ever been in possession of the exercise of this, their constitutional right, of giving and granting their own money. They would have been slaves if they had not enjoyed it. At the same time, this kingdom, as the supreme governing and legislative power, has always bound the colonies by her laws, by her regulations, and restrictions in trade, in navigation, in manufactures, in every thing, except that of taking their money out of their pockets without their consent.

Here I would draw the line. . . .

I have been charged with giving birth to sedition in America. They have spoken their sentiments with freedom, against this unhappy act, and that freedom has become their crime. . . . The gentleman tells us, America is obstinate; America is almost in open rebellion. I rejoice that America has resisted. Three millions of people, so dead to all the feelings of liberty, as voluntarily to submit to be slaves, would have been fit instruments to make slaves of the rest. . . .

A great deal has been said without doors, of the power, of the strength of America. It is a topic that ought to be cautiously meddled with. In a good cause, on a sound bottom, the force of this country can crush America to atoms. . . . But on this ground, on the Stamp Act, when so many here will think it a crying injustice, I am one who will lift up my hands against it.

In such a cause, your success would be hazardous. America, if she fell, would fall like a strong man. She would embrace the pillars of the state, and pull down the constitution along with her. Is this your boasted peace? Not to sheath the sword in its scabbard, but to sheath it in the bowels of your countrymen?

75

Oliver Goldsmith, "The Deserted Village" (1770)

Oliver Goldsmith (c. 1730–1774) was one of England's most versatile writers. He was an essayist (The Citizen of the World, 1762), a novelist (The Vicar of Wakefield, 1766), a poet ("The Deserted Village," 1770), and a playwright (She Stoops to Conquer, 1773).

SOURCE. The Complete Poetical Works of Oliver Goldsmith, ed. Austin Dobson, London: Oxford University Press, 1906, pp. 24–25, 33, 36–37. Reprinted by the permission of Oxford University Press.

Goldsmith's early life was not directed toward a career in literature. Born in a small Irish village, the fifth child of a poor rector, he spent his youth searching for a profession. While a student at Trinity College, Dublin, he was once forced to flee because of his participation in a student riot, and on another occasion he was imprisoned on suspicion of recruiting Scots for the French army. After considering several careers, including the church, law, and medicine, in 1756 he arrived destitute in London. There, befriended by Samuel Johnson, he became an original member of the Literary Club; he had found his calling.

In much of Goldsmith's writing there is a personal element, as is obvious in "The Deserted Village." In describing the misfortunes of the small farmer forced off the land because of enclosure, he is recalling the plight of the cottagers in his boyhood village. He also deplores the blatant materialism of the mercantile London he observed in later life. His portrayal of the effects of enclosure are, however, open to criticism. Some scholars argue that the individual misery resulting from enclosure was necessary to increase agricultural production and, in the long run, to raise the general standard of living. Also, was life in the small village the idyllic and noble existence described by Goldsmith or something existing only in his imagination; a reflection of the anti-urban bias that remained so prevelant in England and later in the United States?

> Sweet smiling village, loveliest of the lawn,
> Thy sports are fled, and all thy charms withdrawn;
> Amidst thy bowers the tyrant's hand is seen,
> And desolation saddens all thy green:
> One only master grasps the whole domain,
> And half a tillage stints thy smiling plain:
> No more thy glassy brook reflects the day,
> But chok'd with sedges, works its weedy way.
> Along thy glades, a solitary guest,
> The hollow-sounding bittern guards its nest;
> Amidst thy desert walks the lapwing flies,
> And tires their echoes with unvaried cries.
> Sunk are thy bowers in shapeless ruin all,
> And the long grass o'ertops the mould'ring wall;
> And trembling, shrinking from the spoiler's hand,
> Far, far away, thy children leave the land.

Ill fares the land, to hast'ning ills a prey,
Where wealth accumulates, and men decay:
Princes and lords may flourish, or may fade;
A breath can make them, as a breath has made;
But a bold peasantry, their country's pride,
When once destroy'd, can never be supplied.

A time there was, ere England's griefs began,
When every rood of ground maintain'd its man;
For him light labour spread her wholesome store,
Just gave what life requir'd, but gave no more:
His best companions, innocence and health;
And his best riches, ignorance of wealth.

But times are alter'd; trade's unfeeling train
Usurp the land and dispossess the swain;
Along the lawn, where scatter'd hamlets rose,
Unwieldy wealth, and cumbrous pomp repose;
And every want to opulence allied,
And every pang that folly pays to pride.
Those gentle hours that plenty bade to bloom,
Those calm desires that ask'd but little room,
Those healthful sports that grac'd the peaceful scene,
Liv'd in each look, and brighten'd all the green;
These, far departing, seek a kinder shore,
And rural mirth and manners are no more.

·   ·   ·

Where then, ah! where, shall poverty reside,
To 'scape the pressure of contiguous pride?
If to some common's fenceless limits stray'd,
He drives his flock to pick the scanty blade,
Those fenceless fields the sons of wealth divide,
And e'en the bare-worn common is denied.

If to the city sped—What waits him there?
To see profusion that he must not share;
To see ten thousand baneful arts combin'd
To pamper luxury, and thin mankind;
To see those joys the sons of pleasure know
Extorted from his fellow creature's woe.
Here, while the courtier glitters in brocade,
There the pale artist plies the sickly trade;
Here, while the proud their long-drawn pomps display,
There the black gibbet glooms beside the way.

·   ·   ·

E'en now the devastation is begun,
And half the business of destruction done;
E'en now, methinks, as pond'ring here I stand,
I see the rural virtues leave the land:
Down where yon anchoring vessel spreads the sail,
That idly waiting flaps with ev'ry gale,
Downward they move, a melancholy band,
Pass from the shore, and darken all the strand.

. . .

Teach erring man to spurn the rage of gain;
Teach him, that states of native strength possess'd,
Though very poor, may still be very bless'd;
That trade's proud empire hastes to swift decay,
As ocean sweeps the labour'd mole away;
While self-dependent power can time defy,
As rocks resist the billows and the sky.

76

The Unanimous Declaration of the Thirteen United States of America (1776)

The British government learned little from the failure of the Stamp Act; it simply devised subtler means to tax and more overt means to control. The Americans, for their part, learned that protest did produce results and that their liberties were respected by many who sat in the parliament at West-

SOURCE.   Carl L. Becker, *The Declaration of Independence: A Study in the History of Political Ideas,* New York: Alfred A. Knopf, Inc., 1962, pp. 185–192. Reprinted by permission.

minster. The mounting confrontation moved closer and closer to violence, developing a momentum of its own. Events such as the Boston Massacre in 1770 and the Boston Tea Party in 1773 produced the Coersive or Intolerable Acts of 1774, which in turn provoked the first and second Continental Congresses. The final stage, open warfare and independence, was begun at Lexington and Concord in 1775 and was confirmed by a declaration of independence in 1776.

Although not a part of the English constitution, the Unanimous Declaration of the Thirteen United States of America, as the title appears on the parchment copy, is most assuredly a product of it. It is in the tradition of Magna Carta, the Petition of Right, and the Bill of Rights, from an American point of view the fourth in a series of assertions of individual liberties. As in the first three, there is a statement of grievances against an English king and his government for violating the people's rights. George III, like James II in 1688, has "abdicated Government." And the British people, having not heard the cries of their brethren overseas, now become like "the rest of mankind, Enemies in War, in Peace Friends."

Besides the example of English practice and experience, one discerns the influence of John Locke's *Two Treatises of Government*. The rights claimed were not those of Englishmen alone: "they are endowed by their Creator with certain unalienable Rights . . . Life, Liberty and the pursuit of Happiness." As a result of the Declaration of Independence, English ideas of limited government, were made universal in their application, more apt for export than when they were, in Locke, simply a theory or a description of an English phenomenon. Through Locke and the success of the American Revolution, English constitutional experience acquired through many centuries was given to the world.

THE UNANIMOUS DECLARATION OF THE THIRTEEN UNITED STATES OF AMERICA

When in the Course of human events, it becomes necessary for one people to dissolve the political bands, which have connected them with another, and to assume among the powers of the earth, the separate and equal station to which the Laws of Nature and of Nature's God entitle them, a decent respect to the opinions of mankind requires that they should declare the causes which impel them to the separation.—We hold these truths to be self-evident, that all men are created equal, that they are endowed by their Creator with certain unalienable Rights, that among these are Life, Liberty and the pursuit of Happiness.—That to secure these rights, Governments are instituted among Men, deriving their just powers from the consent of the governed,—That whenever any Form of Government becomes destructive of these ends, it is the Right of the People to alter or to abolish it, and to institute new Government, laying its foundation on such principles and organizing its powers in such form, as to them shall seem most likely to effect their Safety and Happiness. Prudence, indeed, will dictate that Governments long established should not be changed for light and transient causes; and accordingly all experience hath shewn, that mankind are more disposed to suffer, while evils are sufferable, than to right themselves by abolishing the forms to which they are accustomed. But when a long train of abuses and usurpations, pursuing invariably the same Object evinces a design to reduce them under absolute Despotism, it is their right, it is their duty, to throw off such Government, and to provide new Guards for their future security.—Such has been the patient sufferance of these Colonies; and such is now the necessity which constrains them to alter their former Systems of Government. The history of the present King of Great Britain is a history of repeated injuries and usurpations, all having in direct object the establishment of an absolute Tyranny over these States. To prove this, let Facts be submitted to a candid world.—He has refused his Assent to Laws, the most wholesome and necessary for the public good.—He has forbidden his Governors to pass Laws of immediate and pressing importance, unless suspended in their operation till his Assent should be obtained; and when so suspended, he has utterly neglected to attend to them. . . . He has dissolved Representative Houses repeatedly, for opposing with manly firmness his invasions on the rights of the people.—He has refused for a long time, after such dissolutions, to cause others to be elected; whereby the Legislative powers, incapable of Annihilation, have returned to the People at large for their exercise; the State remaining in the meantime exposed to all the dangers of invasion from without, and convulsions within. . . . He has made Judges dependent on his Will alone, for the tenure of their offices, and the amount and payment of their salaries.—He has erected a multitude of New Offices, and sent hither swarms of Officers to harass our people, and eat out their substance.—He has kept among us, in times of peace, Standing Armies without the Consent of our legislatures.—He has affected to render the Military independent of and superior to the Civil power.—He has combined with others to subject us to a jurisdiction foreign to our constitution, and unacknowledged by our laws; giving his Assent to their Acts of pretended Legislation.—For quartering large bodies of armed troops among us:—For protecting them, by a mock Trial, from punishment for any Murders which they should commit on the Inhabitants of these States:—For cutting off our Trade with all parts of the world:—For imposing Taxes on us without our Consent:—For depriving us in many cases, of the benefits of Trial by Jury:—For transporting us beyond Seas to be tried for pretended offenses:—For abolishing the free System of English Laws in a neighboring Province, establishing therein an Arbitrary government, and enlarging its Boundaries so as to render it at once an example and fit instrument for introducing the same absolute rule into these Colonies:—For taking away our Charters, abolishing our most valuable Laws, and altering fundamentally the Forms of our Governments:—For suspending our own Legislatures, and declaring themselves invested with power to legislate for us in all cases whatsoever.—He has abdicated Government here, by declaring us out of his Protection and waging War against us.—He has plundered our seas, ravaged our Coasts, burnt our towns, and destroyed the lives of our people.—He is at this time transporting large Armies of foreign Mercenaries to compleat the works of death, desolation and tyranny, already begun with circumstances of Cruelty & perfidy scarcely paralleled in the most barbarous ages, and totally unworthy the Head of a civilized nation.—He has constrained our fellow Citizens taken Captive on the high Seas to bear Arms against their Country, to become the executioners of their friends and Brethren, or to fall themselves by their Hands.—He has excited domestic insurrections amongst us, and has endeavoured to bring on the inhabitants of our frontiers, the merciless Indian Savages, whose known rule of warfare, is an undistinguished destruction of all ages, sexes and conditions. In every stage of these Oppressions We have Petitioned for Redress in the most humble terms: Our repeated Petitions have been answered only by repeated injury. A Prince whose character is thus marked by every act which may define a Tyrant, is unfit to be the ruler of a free people. Nor have We been wanting in attentions to our Brittish brethren. We have warned them from time to time of attempts by their legislature to extend an unwarrantable jurisdiction over us. We have reminded them of the circumstances of our emigration and settlement here. We have appealed to their native justice and magnanimity, and we have conjured them by the ties of our common kindred to disavow these usurpations, which would inevitably interrupt our connections and correspondence. They too have been deaf to the voice of justice and of consanguinity. We must, therefore, acquiesce in the necessity, which denounces our Separation, and hold them, as we hold the rest of mankind, Enemies in War, in Peace Friends.—

We, therefore, the Representatives of the united States of America, in General Congress, Assembled, appealing to the Supreme Judge of the world for the rectitude of our intentions do, in the Name, and by Authority of the good People of these Colonies, solemnly publish and declare, That these United Colonies are, and of Right ought to be Free and Independent States; that they are Absolved from all Allegiance to the British Crown, and that all political connection between them and the State of

Great Britain, is and ought to be totally dissolved: and that as Free and Independent States, they have full Power to levy War, conclude Peace, contract Alliances, establish Commerce, and to do all other Acts and Things which Independent States may of right do.—And for the support of this Declaration, with a firm reliance on the protection of divine Providence, we mutually pledge to each other our Lives, our Fortunes and our sacred Honor.

77

Adam Smith, *The Wealth of Nations* (1776). An Attack on Mercantilism

Adam Smith (1723–1790), a Scot, a friend of David Hume, Samuel Johnson and Voltaire, and for a time a professor of moral philosophy at Glasgow, published in 1776 one of the world's most influential books. *An Inquiry into the Nature and Causes of the Wealth of Nations* was a refutation of the mercantilistic assertion that wealth consisted of bullion, gold and silver, and that it was the purpose of government to foster its accumulation by means of laws restricting imports and encouraging exports. Wealth, he argued, adapting an idea of the French physiocrats, was a country's means for production. Smith was in the spirit of the eighteenth century, looking for natural laws governing the conduct of things, in the tradition of Isaac Newton (1642–1727), who explained the workings of the material universe by the laws of gravity. Smith said that a nation's economy did not require government regulation, but that it was better regulated by the natural working of the

SOURCE. Adam Smith, *An Inquiry into the Nature and Causes of the Wealth of Nations,* ed. Edwin Cannan, New York: Random House, Inc., Modern Library, Inc., 1937, pp. 417–418, 421, 423–425.

marketplace. By "an invisible hand," the basic selfishness of man and his competitiveness with his fellows were converted into a self-regulating system which optimized the benefits available to man and produced a mounting prosperity. All restrictions on the free market, be they government regulations or private individuals' scheming together, served only as a brake on the growth of capital and, thus, on further production and prosperity.

Although Smith discerned the advantages of laissez-faire and of the division of labor, he did not envision the effects of the industrial revolution with its huge factories and corporations. Rather, he saw the bustling competition of countless small shops and manufactories, which characterized the Britain of his own day. That he coined the term "the mercantile system" to describe the restrictions he abhorred is indicative of his suspicion of merchants. In another place he wrote, "People of the same trade seldom meet together but the conversation ends in a conspiracy against the public, or in some diversion to raise prices." His concern was for the common man, the consumer. It is ironic that his fame came when merchants and manufacturers chose to ignore the slighting things he had written about them and championed his general idea that the market should operate freely, unhindered by regulations or restrictions. Thus *The Wealth of Nations* was appropriated by the defenders of untrammeled business and was cited to justify opposition to any government regulation.

I thought it necessary, though at the hazard of being tedious, to examine at full length this popular notion that wealth consists in money, or in gold and silver. Money in common language, as I have already observed, frequently signifies wealth; and this ambiguity of expression has rendered this popular notion so familiar to us, that even they, who are convinced of its absurdity, are very apt to forget their own principles, and in the course of their reasonings to take it for granted as a certain and undeniable truth. Some of the best English writers upon commerce set out with observing, that the wealth of a country consists, not in its gold and silver only, but in its lands, houses, and consumable goods of all different kinds. In the course of their reasonings, however, the lands, houses, and consumable goods seem to slip out of their memory, and the strain of their argument frequently supposes that all wealth consists in gold and silver, and that to multiply those metals is the great object of national industry and commerce.

The two principles being established, however, that wealth consisted in gold and silver, and that those metals could be brought into a country which had no mines only by the balance of trade, or by exporting to a greater value than it imported; it necessarily became the great object of political œconomy to diminish as much as possible the importation of foreign goods for home consumption, and to increase as much as possible the exportation of the produce of domestic industry. Its two great engines for enriching the country, therefore, were restraints upon importation, and encouragements to exportation. . . .

The general industry of the society never can exceed what the capital of the society can employ. As the number of workmen that can be kept in employment by any particular person must bear a certain proportion to his capital, so the number of those that can be continually employed by all the members of a great society, must bear a certain proportion to the whole capital of that society, and never can exceed that proportion. No regulation of commerce can increase the quantity of industry in any society beyond what its capital can maintain. It can only divert a part of it into a direction into which it might not otherwise have gone; and it is by no means certain that this artificial direction is likely to be more advantageous to the society than that into which it would have gone of its own accord.

Every individual is continually exerting himself to find out the most advantageous employment for whatever capital he can command. It is his own advantage, indeed, and not that of the society, which he has in view. But the study of his own advantage naturally, or rather necessarily leads him to prefer that employment which is most advantageous to the society. . . .

As every individual, therefore, endeavours as much as he can both to employ his capital in the support of domestic industry, and so to direct that industry that its produce may be of the greatest value; every individual necessarily labours to render the annual revenue of the society as great as he can. He generally, indeed, neither intends to promote the public interest, nor knows how much he is promoting it. By preferring the support of domestic to that of foreign industry, he intends only his own security; and by directing that industry in such a manner as its produce may be of the greatest value, he intends only his own gain, and he is in this, as in many other cases, led by an invisible hand to promote an end which was no part of his intention. Nor is it always the worse for the society that it was no part of it. By pursuing his own interest he frequently promotes that of the society more effectually than when he really intends to promote it. I have never known much good done by those who affected to trade for the public good. It is an affectation, indeed, not very common among merchants, and very few words need be employed in dissuading them from it.

What is the species of domestic industry which his capital can employ, and of which the produce is likely to be of the greatest value, every individual, it is evident, can, in his local situation, judge much better than any statesman or lawgiver can do for him. The statesman, who should attempt to direct private people in what manner they ought to employ their capitals, would not only load himself with a most unnecessary attention, but assume an authority which could safely be trusted, not only to no single person, but to no council or senate whatever, and which would nowhere be so dangerous as in the hands of a man who had folly and presumption enough to fancy himself fit to exercise it.

To give the monopoly of the home-market to the produce of domestic industry, in any particular art or manufacture, is in some measure to direct private people in what manner they ought to employ their capitals, and must, in almost all cases, be either a useless or a hurtful regulation. If the produce of domestic can be brought there as cheap as that of foreign industry, the regulation is evidently useless. If it cannot, it must generally be hurtful. It is the maxim of every prudent master of a family, never to attempt to make at home what it will cost him more to make than to buy. The taylor does not attempt to make his own shoes, but buys them of the shoemaker. The shoemaker does not attempt to make his own clothes, but employs a taylor. The farmer attempts to make neither the one nor the other, but employs those different artificers. All of them find it for their interest to employ their whole industry in a way in which they have some advantage over their neighbours, and to purchase with a part of its produce, or what is the same thing, with the price of a part of it, whatever else they have occasion for.

What is prudence in the conduct of every private family, can scarce be folly in that of a great kingdom. If a foreign country can supply us with a commodity cheaper than we ourselves can make it, better buy it of them with some part of the produce of our own industry, employed in a way in which we have some advantage. The general industry of the country, being always in proportion to the capital which employs it, will not thereby be diminished, no more than that of the above-mentioned artificers; but only left to find out the way in which it can be employed with the greatest advantage. It is certainly not employed to the greatest advantage, when it is thus directed towards an object which it can buy cheaper than it can make. The value of its annual produce is certainly more or less diminished, when it is thus turned away from producing commodities evidently of more value than the commodity which it is directed to produce. According to the supposition, that commodity could be purchased from foreign countries cheaper than it can be made at home. It could, therefore, have been purchased with a part only of the commodities, or, what is the same thing, with a part only of the price of the commodities, which the industry employed by an equal capital would have produced at home, had it been left to follow its natural course. The industry of the country, therefore, is thus turned away from a more, to a less advantageous employment, and the exchangeable value of its annual produce, instead of being increased, according to the intention of the lawgiver, must necessarily be diminished by every such regulation.

By means of such regulations, indeed, a particular manufacture may sometimes be acquired sooner that it could have been otherwise, and after a certain time may be made at home as cheap or cheaper than in the foreign country. But though the industry of the society may be thus carried with advantage into a particular channel sooner than it could have been otherwise, it will by no means follow that the sum total, either of its industry, or of its revenue, can ever be augmented by any such regulation. The industry of the society can augment only in proportion as its capital augments, and its capital can augment only in proportion to what can be gradually saved out of its revenue. But the immediate effect of every such regulation is to diminish its revenue, and what diminishes its revenue is certainly not very likely to augment its capital faster than it would have augmented of its own accord, had both capital and industry been left to find out their natural employments.

Though for want of such regulations the society should never acquire the proposed manufacture, it would not, upon that account, necessarily be the poorer in any one period of its duration. In every period of its duration its whole capital and industry might still have been employed, though upon different objects, in the manner that was most advantageous at the time. In every period its revenue might have been the greatest which its capital could afford, and both capital and revenue might have been augmented with the greatest possible rapidity.

78

Jeremy Bentham, *A Fragment on Government* (1776), and *An Introduction to the Principles of Morals and Legislation* (1780)

William Blackstone's *Commentaries on the Laws of England* (1765–1769) became justly famous as a description of the evolved perfection of the common law and the constitution of England. However, in many respects, what he had written was an idealization; he gloried in the fictions that hid the seamy realities. Jeremy Bentham (1748–1832), who as a young law student at Oxford had listened to the lectures that Blackstone later converted into his *Commentaries,* spent his long life protesting the contradictions between the law as it actually was and the idealization that Blackstone described.

Bentham countered Blackstone's justification of the law as tradition with his own utilitarian "measure of right and wrong." Law and governmental action should be aimed at promoting "the greatest happiness of the greatest number." In his first published work, *A Fragment on Government* (1776), he applied this principle of critcism specifically to a short passage from Blackstone. Four years later in the opening paragraphs of *An Introduction to the Principles of Morals and Legislation,* he wrote what is probably his clearest and most succinct description "Of the Principle of Utility." By the turn of the century he was attracting a school of followers. As "Utilitarians" or "Philosophical Radicals," they influenced reform and legislation across a wide spectrum of nineteenth-century life.

SOURCE. *The Works of Jeremy Bentham,* ed., John Bowring, 11 vols., 1838–1843, New York: Russell & Russell, 1962, I, 227, 230, 1–2. Reprinted by permission of Russell & Russell, Publishers.

It is not difficult to ridicule or poke holes in the hedonistic basis of utilitarianism. Is any pleasure as good as any other? Is poetry no better than "pushpin"—a petty form of gambling once popular in taverns? Nevertheless, Bentham and his followers, by asserting that each person could judge his own happiness, were expressing a principle that was at the heart of liberalism. Bentham's insistence that tradition need not be blindly revered but, instead, be judged by a principle as straightforward and understandable as utility provided what was probably the most effective argument for reform in the nineteenth century.

A FRAGMENT ON GOVERNMENT

Preface

The age we live in is a busy age; an age in which knowledge is rapidly advancing towards perfection. In the natural world, in particular, every thing teems with discovery and with improvement. The most distant and recondite regions of the earth traversed and explored—the all-vivifying and subtle element of the air so recently analyzed and made known to us, —are striking evidences, were all others wanting, of this pleasing truth.

Correspondent to *discovery* and *improvement* in the natural world, is *reformation* in the moral. . . . Perhaps among such observations as would be best calculated to serve as grounds for reformation, are some which, being observations of matters of fact hitherto either incompletely noticed, or not at all, would, when produced, appear capable of bearing the name of discoveries: with so little method and precision have the consequences of this fundamental axiom, *It is the greatest happiness of the greatest number that is the measure of right and wrong,* been as yet developed.

Be this as it may, if there be room for making, and if there be use in publishing, *discoveries* in the *natural* world, surely there is not much less room for making, nor much less use in proposing, *reformation* in the *moral.* If it be a matter of importance and of use to us to be made acquainted with *distant* countries, surely it is not a matter of much less importance, nor of much less use to us, to be made better and better acquainted with the chief means of living happily in our *own:* If it be of importance and of use to us to know the principles of the element we breathe, surely it is not of much less importance, nor of much less use, to comprehend the principles, and endeavour at the improvement of those *laws,* by which alone we breathe it in security. If to this endeavour we should fancy any author, especially any author of great name, to *be,* and as far as could in such case be expected, to *avow himself,* a determined and persevering enemy, what should we say of him? We should say that the interests of reformation, and through them the welfare of mankind, were inseparably connected with the downfall of his works: of a great part, at least, of the esteem and influence which these works might, under whatever title, have acquired.

Such an enemy it has been my misfortune (and not mine only) to see, or fancy at least I saw, in the Author of the celebrated COMMENTARIES *on the* LAWS *of* ENGLAND: an author whose works have had, beyond comparison, a more extensive circulation, have obtained a greater share of esteem, of applause, and consequently of influence (and that by a title on many grounds so indisputable), than any other writer who on that subject has ever yet appeared.

It is on this account that I conceived, some time since, the design of pointing out some of what appeared to me the capital blemishes of that work, particularly this grand and fundamental one, the antipathy to reformation; or rather, indeed, of laying open and exposing the universal inaccuracy and confusion which seemed to my apprehension to pervade the whole. . . .

It is wonderful how forward some have been to look upon it as a kind of presumption, and ingratitude, and rebellion, and cruelty, and I know not what besides, not to allege only, nor to own, but to suffer any one so much as to imagine, that an old-established law could in any respect be a fit object of condemnation. Whether it has been a kind of *personification* that has been the cause of this, as if the Law were a living creature, or whether it has been the mechanical veneration for antiquity, or what other delusion of the fancy, I shall not here inquire. For my part, I know not for what good reason it is that the merit of justifying a law when right, should have been thought greater than that of censuring it when wrong. Under a government of laws, what is the motto of a good citizen? *To obey punctually; to censure freely.*

Thus much is certain; that a system that is never to be censured, will never be improved: that if nothing is ever to be found fault with, nothing will ever be mended: and that a resolution to justify every thing at any rate, and to disapprove of nothing, is a resolution which, pursued in future, must stand as an effectual bar to all the *additional* happiness we can ever hope for; pursued hitherto, would have robbed us of that share of happiness which we enjoy already.

Nor is a disposition to find "every thing as it should be," less at variance with itself, than with reason and utility.

AN INTRODUCTION TO THE PRINCIPLES OF MORALS AND LEGISLATION

Chapter I.   Of the Principle of Utility

Nature has placed mankind under the governance of two sovereign masters, *pain* and *pleasure*. It is for them alone to point out what we ought to do, as well as to determine what we shall do. On the one hand the standard of right and wrong, on the other the chain of causes and effects, are fastened to their throne. They govern us in all we do, in all we say, in all we think: every effort we can make to throw off our subjection, will serve but to demonstrate and confirm it. In words a man may pretend to abjure their empire: but in reality he will remain subject to it all the while. The *principle of utility* recognizes this subjection, and assumes it for the foundation of that system, the object of which is to rear the fabric of felicity by the hands of reason and of law. Systems which attempt to question it, deal in sounds instead of sense, in caprice instead of reason, in darkness instead of light.

But enough of metaphor and declamation: it is not by such means that moral science is to be improved.

III.

By utility is meant that property in any object, whereby it tends to produce benefit, advantage, pleasure, good, or happiness (all this in the present case comes to the same thing), or (what comes again to the same thing) to prevent the happening of mischief, pain, evil, or unhappiness to the party whose interest is considered: if that party be the community in general, then the happiness of the community: if a particular individual, then the happiness of that individual.

IV.

The interest of the community is one of the most general expressions that can occur in the phraseology of morals: no wonder that the meaning of it is often lost. When it has a meaning, it is this. The community is a fictitious *body*, composed of the individual persons who are considered as constituting as it were its *members*. The interest of the community then is, what?—the sum of the interests of the several members who compose it.

V.

It is in vain to talk of the interest of the community, without understanding what is the interest of the individual. A thing is said to promote the interest, or to be *for* the interest, of an individual, when it tends to add to the sum total of his pleasures: or, what comes to the same thing, to diminish the sum total of his pains.

VI.

An action then may be said to be conformable to the principle of utility, or, for shortness sake, to utility (meaning with respect to the community at large), when the tendency it has to augment the happiness of the community is greater than any it has to diminish it.

79

James Ogden, *A Description of Manchester* (1783). The Industrial Revolution

James Ogden (1718–1802), although he witnessed a revolution, failed to appreciate the fact until late in life. He was born in Manchester, then a prosperous little textile town of perhaps 10,000 people. Like many of Manchester's young men, he was soon a part of the textile industry, which was still under the domestic system and devoid of large factories. Ogden later became a schoolmaster, spending much of his time writing volumes of "turgid" verse, including the never-to-be-remembered *British Lion Rous'd; or Acts of the British Worthies: a Poem in Nine Books* (8 vols., 1762). While Ogden was thus pleasantly engaged, Manchester was transformed by the Industrial Revolution. Canals to the nearby coal fields and to the port of Liverpool made the town after 1760 a natural center for large-scale industry.

SOURCE. James Ogden, *A Description of Manchester . . . By a Native of the Town,* Manchester, 1783, pp. 87–94.

The introduction of modern machinery into the textile industry inaugurated the factory system. By 1800 Manchester had changed; it was an industrial center with a population of almost 100,000.

Late in life, Ogden developed an interest in the economic changes occurring about him. His *Description of Manchester*, written in 1783, was later reprinted several times because of its historical value. In his discussion of the introduction of machinery, reprinted below, at least two things are worth noting. First, it is apparent that some people did not share his enthusiasm for the blessings of modern technology; many viewed the entire process of industrialization with skepticism if not distrust. Second, it is interesting that Ogden attributed much of Manchester's economic success to its lack of a corporate structure. It was fortunate in being "only a market town," without the traditional guild regulations which obstructed industrial growth and commerce, and without parliamentary representation, whose elections periodically distracted and divided the people. This attitude, widespread among the wealthy and educated, was in the nineteenth century a great obstacle to both social and political reform.

These were first used by the country people on a confined scale, twelve spindles being thought a great affair at first, and the aukward posture required to spin on them, was discouraging to grown up people, while they saw with a degree of surprize, children, from nine to twelve years of age, manage them with dexterity, which brought plenty into families, that were before overburthened with children, and delivered many a poor endeavouring weaver out of bondage to which they were exposed, by the insolence of spinners, and abatement of their work, for which evils there was no remedy till spinning-jennies were invented. . . .

The plenty of weft produced by this means gave uneasiness to the country people, and the weavers were afraid lest the manufacturers should demand finer weft woven at the former prices, which occasioned some risings, and the jennies were opposed, some being demolished before those who used them could be protected, or convince others of their general utility, till *Dorning Rasbotham,* Esq; a worthy magistrate who lived in that part of the country, towards *Bolton,* where they were used, convinced the weavers, in a sensible printed address, that it was their true interest to encourage jennies, urging the former insolence of spinners, and the happiness of such as had already relieved themselves, and procured employment for their children; and appealed to their own experience of the fly shuttle, against which the like clamour had been raised, and the inventor driven to *France,* where he found encouragement, while his shuttles are yet in such estimation here, as to be used generally even on narrow goods, to the benefit of trade in general, without any bad consequence in the experience of several years, but they are rather of particular benefit to the weavers.

This seasonable address produced a general acquiescence in the use of these engines, to a certain number of spindles, but they were soon multiplied to three or four times the quantity; nor did the invention of ingenious mechanics rest here, for the demand of twist for warps was greater as weft grew plenty, therefore engines were soon constructed for this purpose: one in particular was purchased at a price which was a considerable reward for the contriver's ingenuity, and exposed at the Exchange, where he spun on it, and all that were disposed to see the operation, were admitted gratis.

The improvements kept increasing till the capital engines for twist were perfected; and it is amazing to see what thousands of spindles may be put in motion by a water wheel, and managed mostly by children, without confusion, and with less waste of cotton than the former methods: but the carding and slubbing, preparatory to twisting, required a greater range of invention than the twisting engines, and there were sufficient motives to encourage the attempt; for while carding was performed by common cards, and slubbing by the hand, these operations took half the price of spinning.

The first attempts were in carding engines, which are very curious, and now brought to great perfection, though they are still improving; and an engine has now been contrived, for converting the carded wool to slubbing, by drawing it to about the thickness of candle-wick, preparatory to throwing it into twist.

We suppose, and even wish that the principle of this last engine may be applied to reduce combed sheeps wool to a slubbing, for the purpose of spinning it upon the more complex machines, which would be a great acquisition to some branches of trade here. It is already spun on the common flax wheel with a fly (which has been adopted by these engines) the length way of the combing, which is capable of being handled and divided at pleasure, and may be prepared as a slubbing for the spinning machines, by any contrivance in the drawing out, which has a respect to the length of staple and cohesion of parts, wherein combed wool differs from carded cotton.

When the larger machines were first set to work by water, they produced such excellent twist for warps, that they soon outrivalled the makers of warps on the larger jennies, some of whom had several at work, and had reaped a good harvest of profit by them; but as the larger machines were encouraged, they suffered abatement in proportion; and one of them concerned, making his complaint to others when they were intoxicated at the alehouse, a resolution was taken to destroy the water machines, and some were demolished before the owners could be protected, or the deluded country people who joined them could reflect, that if more warps were made, there would be a greater demand for weft from their jennies, and a better price for it. . . .

We had given in our manuscript a particular description of the principles and movements of these machines; but have suppressed it for the present, as it has been hinted that this publication might be translated into *French,* and communicated to our rivals in trade; which is giving a consequence we little expected to our description of *Manchester,* and history of its manufactures.

We are now hastening to a conclusion, and shall observe by the way, that perhaps nothing has more contributed to the improvements in trade here, than the free admission of workmen in every branch, whereby the trade has been kept open to strangers of every description, who contribute to its improvement by their ingenuity; for *Manchester* being only a market town, governed by Constables, is not subject to such regulations as are made in corporations, to favour freemen in exclusion of strangers: and, indeed, nothing could be more fatal to its trading interest, if it should be incorporated, and have representatives in Parliament. For such is the general course of popular contests, that in places where the immediate dependence of the inhabitants is not upon trade, the health and morals of the people are ruined upon those occasions. How much more fatal would the effects be in such a town as this, where, to the above evils, there would be added the interruption of trade, and perpetuation of ill-will between masters and workmen, who were independent; while those who had nothing to depend on but labour, would contract habits of idleness and drunkenness, or fly to other places, where they could be free from the tyrannical restrictions and partial usage which generally prevail in corporations.

80

Thomas Clarkson, Sermon (1787). The African Slave Trade

Originally destined for a career in the church, Thomas Clarkson (1760–1846) instead devoted his life to the greatest humanitarian movement of the late-eighteenth century—the crusade against the African slave trade. Joining with such established figures as Granville Sharp and William Wilberforce, he became a prominent member of the Clapham Sect. Within the movement, Clarkson had two primary functions. First, he was its chief investigator, spending a great deal of time in Bristol and Liverpool collecting data on the slave trade. He was particularly interested in, and appalled by, conditions on the slave vessels during the middle passage, the trip from Africa to the Western Hemisphere (see Plate A). The data he collected were used by Wilberforce in his parliamentary efforts to abolish the British slave trade, ultimately successful in 1807.

Clarkson was largely responsible for mobilizing public opinion against the slave trade and for gathering petitions for presentation to parliament. These petitions strengthened the position of reforming MPs like Wilberforce. On one occasion, in 1787, Clarkson preached a sermon in Manchester condemning the evils of the slave trade. In so doing, he was following the example of other social reformers. By preaching his message, a reformer was assured of a building, a ready audience and, in most instances, a favorable reaction that could be transformed into a parliamentary petition. The excerpts from Clarkson's sermon, reproduced below, are taken from his *History of the Abolition of the African Slave-Trade by the British Parliament* (1808), one of the most important sources of information on the actions

SOURCE. Thomas Clarkson, *The History of the Rise, Progress, and Accomplishment of the Abolition of the African Slave-Trade by the British Parliament,* 2 vols., London: Frank Cass, Reprint, 1968, I, 418, 420–425. Reprinted by permission of Valentine, Mitchell, London, 1968.

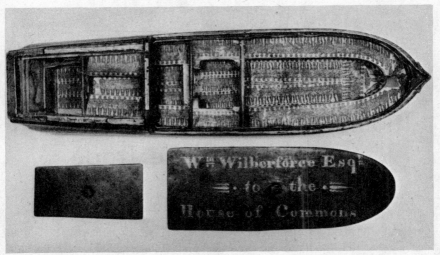

PLATE A
Model of Slave Ship (courtesy of Wilberforce House Museum, Hull).

of the Clapham Sect. Not content with their victory of 1807, Clarkson and his colleagues sought to insure that the antislave trade laws were enforced and, later, attacked the institution of slavery itself. In 1833, Clarkson, now an old man, saw parliament declare slavery illegal throughout the entire British empire.

Text. "Thou shalt not oppress a stranger, for ye know the heart of a stranger, seeing ye were strangers in the land of Egypt."

This being the case, and this law of Moses being afterwards established into a fundamental precept of Christianity, I must apply it to facts of the present day, and I am sorry that I must apply it to—ourselves.

And first, Are there no strangers, whom we oppress? I fear the wretched African will say, that he drinks the cup of sorrow, and that he drinks it at our hands. Torn from his native soil, and from his family and friends, he is immediately forced into a situation, of all others the most degrading, where he and his progeny are considered as cattle, as possessions, and as the possessions of a man to whom he never gave offence.

It is a melancholy fact, but it can be abundantly proved, that great numbers of the unfortunate strangers, who are carried from Africa to our colonies, are fraudulently and forcibly taken from their native soil. To descant but upon a single instance of the kind must be productive of pain to the ear of sensibility and freedom. Consider the sensations of the person, who is thus carried off by the ruffians, who have been lurking to intercept him. Separated from every thing which he esteems in life, without the possibility even of bidding his friends adieu, behold him overwhelmed in tears—wringing his hands in despair—looking backwards upon the spot where all his hopes and wishes lay,—while his family at home are waiting for him with anxiety and suspense—are waiting, perhaps, for sustenance—are agitated between hope and fear—till length of absence confirms the latter, and they are immediately plunged into inconceivable misery and distress.

If this instance, then, is sufficiently melancholy of itself, and is at all an act of oppression, how complicated will our guilt appear, who are the means of snatching away thousands annually in the same manner, and who force them and their families into the same unhappy situation, without either remorse or shame! . . .

If, then, we oppress the stranger, as I have shown, and if, by a knowledge of his heart, we find that he is a person of the same passions and feelings as ourselves, we are certainly breaking, by means of the prosecution of the Slave-trade, that fundamental principle of Christianity, which says, that we shall not do that unto another, which we wish should not be done unto ourselves, and, I fear, cutting ourselves off from all expectation of the Divine blessing. For how inconsistent is our conduct! We come into the temple of God; we fall prostrate before him; we pray to him, that he will have mercy upon us. But how shall he have mercy upon us, who have had no mercy upon others! We pray to him, again, that he will deliver us from evil. But how shall he deliver us from evil, who are daily invading the rights of the injured African, and heaping misery on his head! . . .

If, then, we wish to avert the heavy national judgment which is hanging over our heads (for must we not believe that our crimes towards the innocent Africans lie recorded against us in heaven) let us endeavour to assert their cause. Let us nobly withstand the torrent of the evil, however inveterately it may be fixed among the customs of the times; not, however, using our liberty as a cloak of maliciousness against those, who perhaps without due consideration, have the misfortune to be concerned in it, but upon proper motives, and in a proper spirit, as the servants of God; so that if the sun should be turned into darkness, and the moon into blood, and the very heaven should fall upon us, we may fall in the general convulsion without dismay, conscious that we have done our duty in endeavouring to succour the distressed, and that the stain of the blood of Africa is not upon us.

Edmund Burke, *Reflections on the Revolution in France* (1790)

Edmund Burke (1729–1797) wrote his *Reflections on the Revolution in France* in response to the popular support in England for the dramatic events then taking place in France. It was also a statement of the principles he had expressed and acted on consistently in his writing and during his political career. As the personal secretary of the Whig leader, the marquis of Rockingham, and as a Whig intellectual and a member of parliament himself, he had been an outspoken critic of the government of George III (1760–1820), especially for its policy toward the American colonies. Burke led the fight to reduce the influence of the king and his ministers in parliament, and he had spearheaded the movement to impeach and convict Warren Hastings for his highhanded treatment of natives during his governor-generalship of India. The apex of his career came in 1790 with the writing of his *Reflections*.

At the heart of Burke's political thinking was a profound distrust of abstract political theory and natural law based on reason. Like William Blackstone, he believed that a sound system of law and government must rest on a foundation of tradition, on institutions and practice that had evolved slowly and had been proved effective by generations of usage. The state "becomes a partnership not only between those who are living, but between those who are living, those who are dead, and those who are to be born." Unlike the Glorious Revolution of England and the American Revolution, which were movements to preserve and restore the constitutional usage of the past, the French Revolution was destroying tradition. Relying only on the false

SOURCE. Edmund Burke, *Reflections on the Revolution in France and Other Essays,* Introduction and Notes by A. J. Grieve, Everyman's Library Edition, Published by E. P. Dutton & Co., Inc., 1940, pp. 57–59, 242–243. Used with the permission of E. P. Dutton & Co., Inc. and J M Dent & Sons, Ltd. Publishers, London.

basis of abstract reason, the French would, he accurately predicted, only prove again how difficult or impossible it was to make legitimate and acceptible a revolutionary government.

When Burke wrote his *Reflections* in 1790, most Britons were still applauding the French for copying the good example of 1688. However, the popularity of Burke's book, which went through 11 editions the first year, and the radical and violent turn of events in France produced a rush toward conservatism. The political shift in parliament, led by Burke himself, and the parallel reaction in the country as a whole revived the Tory party and gave it unprecedented dominance for nearly 40 years. In the area of thought, Burke's ideas are still the beginning of any intelligent conservative political philosophy.

Government is not made in virtue of natural rights, which may and do exist in total independence of it; and exist in much greater clearness, and in a much greater degree of abstract perfection: but their abstract perfection is their practical defect. By having a right to everything they want everything. Government is a contrivance of human wisdom to provide for human *wants*. Men have a right that these wants should be provided for by this wisdom. Among these wants is to be reckoned the want, out of civil society, of a sufficient restraint upon their passions. Society requires not only that the passions of individuals should be subjected, but that even in the mass and body, as well as in the individuals, the inclinations of men should frequently be thwarted, their will controlled, and their passions brought into subjection. This can only be done *by a power out of themselves;* and not, in the exercise of its function, subject to that will and to those passions which it is its office to bridle and subdue. In this sense the restraints on men, as well as their liberties, are to be reckoned among their rights. But as the liberties and the restrictions vary with times and circumstances, and admit of infinite modifications, they cannot be settled upon any abstract rule; and nothing is so foolish as to discuss them upon that principle.

The moment you abate anything from the full rights of men, each to govern himself, and suffer any artificial, positive limitation upon those rights, from that moment the whole organization of government becomes a consideration of convenience. This it is which makes the constitution of a state, and the due distribution of its powers, a matter of the most delicate and complicated skill. It requires a deep knowledge of human nature and human necessities, and of the things which facilitate or obstruct the various ends, which are to be pursued by the mechanism of civil institutions. The state is to have recruits to its strength, and remedies to its distempers. What is the use of discussing a man's abstract right to food or medicine? The question is upon the method of procuring and administering them. In that deliberation I shall always advise to call in the aid of the farmer and the physician, rather than the professor of metaphysics. . . .

The science of government being therefore so practical in itself, and intended for such practical purposes, a matter which requires experience, and even more experience than any person can gain in his whole life, however sagacious and observing he may be, it is with infinite caution that any man ought to venture upon pulling down an edifice, which has answered in any tolerable degree for ages the common purposes of society, or on building it up again, without having models and patterns of approved utility before his eyes. . . .

To make a government requires no great prudence. Settle the seat of power; teach obedience: and the work is done. To give freedom is still more easy. It is not necessary to guide; it only requires to let go the rein. But to form a *free government*; that is, to temper together these opposite elements of liberty and restraint in one consistent work, requires much thought, deep reflection, a sagacious, powerful, and combining mind. This I do not find in those who take the lead in the National Assembly. Perhaps they are not so miserably deficient as they appear. I rather believe it. It would put them below the common level of human understanding. But when the leaders choose to make themselves bidders at an auction of popularity, their talents, in the construction of the state, will be of no service. They will become flatterers instead of legislators; the instruments, not the guides, of the people. If any of them should happen to propose a scheme of liberty, soberly limited, and defined with proper qualifications, he will be immediately outbid by his competitors, who will produce something more splendidly popular. Suspicions will be raised of his fidelity to his cause. Moderation will be stigmatized as the virtue of cowards; and compromise as the prudence of traitors; until, in hopes of preserving the credit which may enable him to temper, and moderate, on some occasions, the popular leader is obliged to become active in propagating doctrines, and establishing powers, that will afterwards defeat any sober purpose at which he ultimately might have aimed.

But am I so unreasonable as to see nothing at all that deserves commendation in the indefatigable labours of this Assembly? I do not deny that, among an infinite number of acts of violence and folly, some good may have been done. They who destroy everything certainly will remove some grievance. They who make everything new, have a chance that they may establish something beneficial. To give them credit for what they have done in virtue of the authority they have usurped, or which can excuse them in the crimes by which that authority has been acquired, it must appear, that the same things could not have been accomplished without producing such a revolution. Most assuredly they might; because almost every one of the regulations made by them, which is not very equivocal, was either in the cession of the king, voluntarily made at the meeting of the states, or in the concurrent instructions to the orders. Some usages have been abolished on just grounds; but they were such, that if they had stood as they were to all eternity, they would little detract from the happiness and prosperity of any state. The improvements of the National Assembly are superficial, their errors fundamental.

Whatever they are, I wish my countrymen rather to recommend to our neighbours the examples of the British constitution, than to take models from them for the improvement of our own. In the former they have got an invaluable treasure. They are not, I think, without some causes of apprehension and complaint; but these they do not owe to their constitution, but to their own conduct. I think our happy situation owing to our constitution; but owing to the whole of it, and not to any part singly; owing in a great measure to what we have left standing in our several reviews and reformations, as well as to what we have altered or superadded. Our people will find employment enough for a truly patriotic, free, and independent spirit, in guarding what they possess from violation. I would not exclude alteration neither; but even when I changed, it should be to preserve. I should be led to my remedy by a great grievance. In what I did, I should follow the example of our ancestors. I would make the reparation as nearly as possible in the style of the building.

82

Mary Wollstonecraft, *A Vindication of the Rights of Woman* (1792)

Mary Wollstonecraft (1759–1797) wrote what is perhaps still the most power-ful plea for the liberation of women. Her *Vindication of the Rights of Woman* (1792) was a product of the English debate on natural rights resulting from the French Revolution. It championed the liberal ideas of the Enlightenment against the conservative reaction. More specifically, it was a follow-up to her previous book, *A Vindication of the Rights of Men,* which she wrote hur-riedly in 1790 in reply to Edmund Burke. To Burke's assertion that the idea of natural rights was foolish and dangerous, she countered, "It is necessary emphatically to repeat that there are rights which men inherit at their birth, as rational creatures . . . not from their forefathers but from God." In her second book, she was simply extending to women in particular what she had formerly said of mankind in general. Only when women are taught and treated "as part of the human species" and not "as a kind of subordinate being" will they acquire the virtue of which they are capable and which is essential to make them the equals of men. Indeed, it is this same denial of human dignity that makes men unequal.

Mary Wollstonecraft was an emancipated woman, at least as much of one as the eighteenth century and her own inclinations would allow. After help-ing operate a private school and then working as a governess, from which position she was dismissed because the children loved her more than they did their mother, she became a writer. At first she wrote exclusively on women's and children's topics, but later she was accepted as capable of dealing even with contemporary intellectual topics. The success of her

---

SOURCE.   Mary Wollstonecraft, *A Vindication of the Rights of Woman with Strictures on Political and Moral Subjects,* ed., Charles W. Hagelman, Jr., pp. 31–33, 49–50, 52–53, 55, 283–284, 286–287. Norton Library Edition. Copyright © 1967 by W. W. Norton & Company, Inc., New York, N. Y.

Rights of Woman made her prominent in the literary circles of London and then of Paris, where she went in 1792 to view the Revolution. An affair with the American Gilbert Imlay gave Mary a daughter and, at its termination, led her to attempt to drown herself by jumping off the Putney bridge. In 1797 she married William Godwin, the English radical and freethinker, who had written denouncing the institution of marriage. This happy and successful union of two high-spirited and independent individuals ended when Mary died giving birth to their daughter.

A Vindication of the Rights of Woman went through two English editions in 1792 as well as two American and one Irish in that and the following year and has gone through numerous other editions since. Representing the rational spirit of the Enlightenment and championing the liberal idea of the free individual, it argues for the rights not only of women but of all personkind.

The conduct and manners of women, in fact, evidently prove that their minds are not in a healthy state; for, like the flowers which are planted in too rich a soil, strength and usefulness are sacrificed to beauty; and the flaunting leaves, after having pleased a fastidious eye, fade, disregarded on the stalk, long before the season when they ought to have arrived at maturity. One cause of this barren blooming I attribute to a false system of education, gathered from the books written on this subject by men who, considering females rather as women than human creatures, have been more anxious to make them alluring mistresses than affectionate wives and rational mothers; and the understanding of the sex has been so bubbled by this specious homage, that the civilized women of the present century, with a few exceptions, are only anxious to inspire love, when they ought to cherish a nobler ambition, and by their abilities and virtues exact respect. . . .

In the true style of Mahometanism, they are treated as a kind of subordinate beings, and not as a part of the human species, when improveable reason is allowed to be the dignified distinction which raises men above the brute creation, and puts a natural sceptre in a feeble hand. . . .

In the government of the physical world it is observable that the female in point of strength is, in general, inferior to the male. This is the law of nature; and it does not appear to be suspended or abrogated in favour of woman. A degree of physical superiority cannot, therefore, be denied —and it is a noble prerogative! But not content with this natural preeminence, men endeavour to sink us still lower, merely to render us alluring objects for a moment; and women, intoxicated by the adoration which men, under the influence of their senses, pay them, do not seek to obtain a durable interest in their hearts, or to become the friends of the fellow creatures who find amusement in their society.

I am aware of an obvious inference:—from every quarter have I heard exclamations against masculine women; but where are they to be found? If by this appellation men mean to inveigh against their ardour in hunting, shooting, and gaming, I shall most cordially join in the cry; but if it be against the imitation of manly virtues, or, more properly speaking, the attainment of those talents and virtues, the exercise of which ennobles the human character, and which raise females in the scale of animal being, when they are comprehensively termed mankind;—all those who view them with a philosophic eye must, I should think, wish with me, that they may every day grow more and more masculine. . . .

To account for, and excuse the tyranny of man, many ingenious arguments have been brought forward to prove, that the two sexes, in the acquirement of virtue, ought to aim at attaining a very different character; or, to speak explicitly, women are not allowed to have sufficient strength of mind to acquire what really deserves the name of virtue. Yet it should seem, allowing them to have souls, that there is but one way appointed by Providence to lead *mankind* to either virtue or happiness.

If then women are not a swarm of ephemeron triflers, why should they be kept in ignorance under the specious name of innocence? Men complain, and with reason, of the follies and caprices of our sex, when they do not keenly satirize our headstrong passions and grovelling vices. Behold, I should answer, the natural effect of ignorance! The mind will ever be unstable that has only prejudices to rest on, and the current will run with destructive fury when there are no barriers to break its force. Women are told from their infancy, and taught by the example of their mothers, that a little knowledge of human weakness, justly termed cunning, softness of temper, *outward* obedience, and a scrupulous attention to a puerile kind of propriety, will obtain for them the protection of man; and should they be beautiful, everything else is needless, for, at least, twenty years of their lives. . . .

Consequently, the most perfect education, in my opinion, is such an exercise of the understanding as is best calculated to strengthen the body and form the heart. Or, in other words, to enable the individual to attain such habits of virtue as will render it independent. In fact, it is a farce to call any being virtuous whose virtues do not result from the exercise of its own reason. This was Rousseau's opinion respecting men: I extend it to women, and confidently assert that they have been drawn out of their sphere by false refinement, and not by an endeavour to acquire masculine qualities. Still the regal homage which they receive is so intoxicating, that till the manners of the times are changed, and formed on more reasonable principles, it may be impossible to convince them that the illegitimate power, which they obtain, by degrading themselves, is a curse, and that they must return to nature and equality, if they wish to secure the placid satisfaction that unsophisticated affections impart. But for this epoch we must wait—wait, perhaps, till kings and nobles, enlightened by reason, and, preferring the real dignity of man to childish state, throw off their gaudy hereditary trappings: and if then women do not resign the arbitrary power of beauty—they will prove that they have *less* mind than man. . . .

As a proof that education gives this appearance of weakness to females, we may instance the example of military men, who are, like them, sent into the world before their minds have been stored with knowledge or fortified by principles. The consequences are similar; soldiers acquire a little superficial knowledge, snatched from the muddy current of conversation, and, from continually mixing with society, they gain, what is termed a knowledge of the world; and this acquaintance with manners and customs has frequently been confounded with a knowledge of the human heart. But can the crude fruit of casual observation, never brought to the test of judgment, formed by comparing speculation and experience, deserve such a distinction? Soldiers, as well as women, practice the minor virtues with punctilious politeness. Where is then the sexual difference, when the education has been the same? All the difference that I can discern, arises from the superior advantage of liberty, which enables the former to see more of life. . . .

Moralists have unanimously agreed, that unless virtue be nursed by liberty, it will never attain due strength—and what they say of man I extend to mankind, insisting that in all cases morals must be fixed on immutable principles; and that the being cannot be termed rational or virtuous who obeys any authority but that of reason.

To render women truly useful members of society, I argue that they should be led, by having their understandings cultivated on a large scale, to acquire a rational affection for their country, founded on knowledge, because it is obvious that we are little interested about what we do not understand. And to render this general knowledge of due importance, I have endeavoured to show that private duties are never properly fulfilled unless the understanding enlarges the heart; and that public virtue is only an aggregate of private. . . .

Asserting the rights which women in common with men ought to contend for, I have not attempted to extenuate their faults; but to prove them to be the natural consequence of their education and station in society. If so, it is reasonable to suppose that they will change their character, and correct their vices and follies, when they are allowed to be free in a physical, moral, and civil sense.

Let women share the rights and she will emulate the virtues of man; for she must grow more perfect when emancipated, or justify the authority that chains such a weak being to her duty. If the latter, it will be expedient to open a fresh trade with Russia for whips: a present which a father should always make to his son-in-law on his wedding day, that a husband may keep his whole family in order by the same means; and without any violation of justice reign, wielding this sceptre, sole master of his house, because he is the only being in it who has reason:—the divine, indefeasible earthly sovereignty breathed into man by the Master of the universe. Allowing this position, women have not any inherent rights to claim; and by the same rule their duties vanish, for rights and duties are inseparable.

Be just then, O ye men of understanding! and mark not more severely what women do amiss, than the vicious tricks of the horse or the ass for whom ye provide provender—and allow her the privileges of ignorance, to whom ye deny the rights of reason, or ye will be worse than Egyptian task-masters, expecting virtue where nature has not given understanding!

83

Thomas Robert Malthus, *An Essay on the Principle of Population* (1798)

There was a deep seam of optimism running through the eighteenth-century Enlightenment. By the use of reason, man was capable of discovering natural laws that governed not only the material universe but also the economic and political behavior of men. Such knowledge would enable men to transcend the shortcomings of the present and to produce in the future a

SOURCE. Thomas Robert Malthus, *Population: The First Essay*, Ann Arbor: University of Michigan Press, 1959, pp. 1, 4–6, 120–121.

utopian happy state. One of England's most radical and optimistic advocates of "progress" was William Godwin (1756–1836), the husband of Mary Wollstonecraft and the author of the weighty *Enquiry concerning Political Justice* (1793), which at a cost of three guineas was thought by the government to be sufficiently restricted not to merit censure.

Thomas Robert Malthus (1766–1834), a Church of England clergyman and later, at the East India Company college at Haileybury, the world's first professor of economics, was provoked by his father's enthusiasm for Godwin to write and then to publish his own counterarguments. Appearing as a pamphlet in 1798, Malthus's *Essay on the Principle of Population as it Affects the Future Improvement of Society,* crushed the optimists and has remained an anxiety to thinking men ever since. The passage below gives the gist of Malthus's argument, that the population will necessarily increase more rapidly than the food supply and will be kept in check by it. There will always be suffering and starving people. Politicians and others opposed to reform cited Malthus as proof that improvements in the condition of the poor were counterproductive. Any improvement could only be temporary, for it would be swamped by the increased population it encouraged. It is not surprising that Thomas Carlyle (1795–1881) on reading Malthus should have dubbed economics, perhaps unfairly, "the dismal science."

Malthus's own doubts regarding his conclusion can be detected in the lengthened edition of 1803. He removed some of the mathematical certainty that he had used to support his earlier conclusions and asserted that voluntary "moral restraint" might ease the pressure of population on the food supply. The expansion of arable land, especially in newly discovered and exploited continents, and better farming and manufacturing techniques bolstered and heartened the champions of progress. However, the growing world population, never far behind the expanding food supply, may yet demonstrate the awful applicability of Malthus's predictions.

It has been said that the great question is now at issue, whether man shall henceforth start forwards with accelerated velocity towards illimitable, and hitherto unconceived improvement, or be condemned to a perpetual oscillation between happiness and misery, and after every effort remain still at an immeasurable distance from the wished-for goal. . . .

In entering upon the argument I must premise that I put out of the question, at present, all mere conjectures, that is, all suppositions, the probable realization of which cannot be inferred upon any just philosophical grounds. . . .

I think I may fairly make two postulata.

First, That food is necessary to the existence of man.

Secondly, That the passion between the sexes is necessary and will remain nearly in its present state.

These two laws, ever since we have had any knowledge of mankind, appear to have been fixed laws of our nature, and, as we have not hitherto seen any alteration in them, we have no right to conclude that they will ever cease to be what they now are, without an immediate act of power in that Being who first arranged the system of the universe, and for the advantage of his creatures, still executes, according to fixed laws, all its various operations.

I do not know that any writer has supposed that on this earth man will ultimately be able to live without food. . . . Towards the extinction of the passion between the sexes, no progress whatever has hitherto been made. It appears to exist in as much force at present as it did two thousand or four thousand years ago. There are individual exceptions now as there always have been. But, as these exceptions do not appear to increase in number, it would surely be a very unphilosophical mode of arguing, to infer merely from the existence of an exception, that the exception would, in time, become the rule, and the rule the exception.

Assuming then, my postulata as granted, I say, that the power of population is indefinitely greater than the power in the earth to produce subsistence for man.

Population, when unchecked, increases in a geometrical ratio. Subsistence increases only in an arithmetical ratio. A slight acquaintance with numbers will shew the immensity of the first power in comparison of the second.

By that law of our nature which makes food necessary to the life of man, the effects of these two unequal powers must be kept equal.

This implies a strong and constantly operating check on population from the difficulty of subsistence. This difficulty must fall some where and must necessarily be severely felt by a large portion of mankind.

Through the animal and vegetable kingdoms, nature has scattered the seeds of life abroad with the most profuse and liberal hand. She has been comparatively sparing in the room and the nourishment necessary to rear them. The germs of existence contained in this spot of earth, with ample food, and ample room to expand in, would fill millions of worlds in the course of a few thousand years. Necessity, that imperious all pervading law of nature, restrains them within the prescribed bounds. The race of plants, and the race of animals shrink under this great restrictive law. And the race of man cannot, by any efforts of reason, escape from it. Among plants and animals its effects are waste of seed, sickness, and premature death. Among mankind, misery and vice. The former, misery, is an absolutely necessary consequence of it. Vice is a highly probable consequence, and we therefore see it abundantly prevail, but it ought not, perhaps, to be called an absolutely necessary consequence. The ordeal of virtue is to resist all temptation to evil.

This natural inequality of the two powers of population and of production in the earth and that great law of our nature which must constantly keep their effects equal form the great difficulty that to me appears insurmountable in the way to the perfectability of society. All other arguments are of slight and subordinate consideration in comparison of this. I see no way by which man can escape from the weight of this law which pervades all animated nature. No fancied equality, no agrarian regulations in their utmost extent, could remove the pressure of it even for a single century. And it appears, therefore, to be decisive against the possible existence of a society, all the members of which should live in ease, happiness, and comparative leisure; and feel no anxiety about providing the means of subsistence for themselves and families.

Consequently, if the premises are just, the argument is conclusive against the perfectibility of the mass of mankind. . . .

It is, undoubtedly a most disheartening reflection that the great obstacle in the way to any extraordinary improvement in society is of a nature that we can never hope to overcome. The perpetual tendency in the race of man to increase beyond the means of subsistence is one of the general laws of animated nature which we can have no reason to expect will change. Yet, discouraging as the contemplation of this difficulty must be to those whose exertions are laudably directed to the improvement of the human species, it is evident that no possible good can arise from any endeavours to slur it over or keep it in the back ground. On the contrary, the most baleful mischiefs may be expected from the unmanly conduct of not daring to face truth because it is unpleasing.

84

An Act for the Preservation
of the Health and Morals
# of Apprentices (1802)

The Industrial Revolution had by the 1790s transformed the economy, to say nothing of the landscape, of many parts of England. This was particularly true on the industrial frontier, the new factory towns in the midlands and the north of England. Slum housing, street crime, and child labor were only the most obvious of the many new hardships facing the people. For a number of reasons, however, the government was slow in attempting to alleviate the situation. Some problems, such as child labor, were simply not recognized as social evils, particularly by a government preoccupied with the war with France. Even more important, the laissez-faire principles of Adam Smith had become almost a dogma to many politicians, who were now convinced that any tampering with the "natural laws" of economics would only result in greater injury to the people and the nation. In view of these obstacles to reform, it is a testimony to the ability of Sir Robert Peel the elder (1750–1830), a wealthy cotton magnate, that he was able to persuade parliament to accept the reform legislation reproduced below.

Peel's Act for the Preservation of the Health and Morals of Apprentices has been variously interpreted by historians. Because it improved, if only slightly, working conditions and provided for "visitors" to ensure that its provisions were enforced, it has traditionally been viewed as a "factory act," establishing the government's right to regulate industry and providing a precedent for the factory acts of 1819, 1829, and 1833. There are, however, difficulties in accepting this view. As the following selection shows, the act dealt primarily with apprentice children, orphans sent to the factories by local officials anxious to cut welfare costs. As such children had not agreed to work in the factories, Peel could and did argue that this legislation was

SOURCE. *The Statutes At Large*, XLIII, 632–635 (42 George III. c. 73).

not an attack on laissez-faire. He viewed the 1802 act as an attempt to protect wards of the state. In other words, it was a poor law and not a factory act. Some historians would agree, arguing that the Factory Act of 1819, which dealt with "free" children, that is, those coerced by their parents, was more innovative and important. Still other historians emphasize the educational provisions in the act and see it as the first national education act. The fact that this legislation was and has remained controversial, subject to several interpretations, is probably the best indication of its importance.

AN ACT FOR THE PRESERVATION OF THE HEALTH AND MORALS OF APPRENTICES AND OTHERS, EMPLOYED IN COTTON AND OTHER MILLS, AND COTTON AND OTHER FACTORIES.

Whereas *it hath of late become a practice in cotton and woollen mills, and . . . factories, to employ a great number of male and female apprentices, and other persons, in the same building; in consequence of which certain regulations are become necessary to preserve the health and morals of such apprentices and other persons;* be it therefore enacted . . . That . . . all such mills and factories within *Great Britain* and *Ireland,* wherein three or more apprentices, or twenty or more other persons, shall at any time be employed, shall be subject to the several rules and regulations contained in this act. . . .

II. And be it enacted, That . . . the rooms and apartments in or belonging to any such mill or factory shall, twice at least in every year, be well and sufficiently washed with quick lime and water over every part of the walls and ceiling thereof; and that due care and attention shall be paid . . . to provide a sufficient number of windows and openings in such rooms . . . to insure a proper supply of fresh air. . . .

III. And be it further enacted, That every such master or mistress shall constantly supply every apprentice, during the term of his or her apprenticeship, with two whole and complete suits of cloathing, with suitable linen, stockings, hats, and shoes; one new complete suit being delivered to such apprentice once at least in every year.

IV. And be it further enacted, That no apprentice . . . shall be employed or compelled to work for more than twelve hours in any one day, (reckoning from six of the clock in the morning to nine of the clock at night), exclusive of the time that may be occupied by such apprentice in eating the necessary meals: provided always, that . . . no apprentice shall be employed . . . between the hours of nine . . . at night and six . . . in the morning.

VI. And be it further enacted, That every such apprentice shall be instructed, in some part of every working day, for the first four years at least of his or her apprenticeship . . . in the usual hours of work, in reading, writing, and arithmetick, or either of them, according to the age and abilities of such apprentice, by some discreet and proper person, to be provided and paid by the master or mistress of such apprentice, in some room or place in such mill or factory to be set apart for that purpose. . . .

IX. And be it further enacted, That the justices of the peace . . . yearly . . . appoint two persons, not interested in, or in any way connected with, any such mills or factories . . . one of whom shall be a justice of peace . . . and the other shall be a clergyman of the established church of *England* or *Scotland* and the said visitors, or either of them, shall have full power and authority . . . to enter into and inspect any such mill or factory, at any time of the day, or during the hours of employment, as they shall think fit; and such visitors shall report from time to time in writing, to the quarter sessions of the peace, the state and condition of such mills and factories, and of the apprentices therein, and whether the same are or are not conducted and regulated according to the directions of this act, and the laws of the realm.

85

The Times. The Battle of Trafalgar, 1805

The eighteenth century witnessed the birth and death of numerous newspapers, which today constitute for the historian a major source of evidence. Most of these newspapers were short-lived, because they were founded for a specific purpose and for a limited group of readers. For example, the most important early newspaper was probably *The Craftsman* (1726–1736),

SOURCE. *The Times*, November 7, 1805, p. 1. Reproduction from *The Times* by permission.

founded by Viscount Bolingbroke and William Pulteney to attack Sir Robert Walpole. One of these topical, partisan papers, however, did survive to become in the nineteenth century a national institution.

The founder of *The Times* was John Walter (1738–1812), a bankrupt coal merchant who became interested in printing. In 1784 Walter decided to found a newspaper, *The Daily Universal Register,* to cater to the business community and to promote his other printing enterprises. Soon, however, the title was changed to *The Times,* a reflection of Walter's decision to broaden the appeal of his paper. Although *The Times* in the 1790s had been a faithful supporter of Pitt's government, in the early nineteenth century it adopted a new, more critical approach to news coverage. Later, under its great editor Thomas Barnes (1831–1841), it became known popularly as "The Thunderer." To promote its independence from the government, *The Times* pioneered in the use of its own correspondents and acquired in the process a reputation for fresh, accurate news. By the early nineteenth century, *The Times* had become a well-established paper with a daily circulation of more than 5000.

Despite the use of its own correspondents, *The Times* in its early years still relied on governmental sources for much of its foreign news. The dispatch from Admiral Collingwood describing Horatio Nelson's naval victory and death off Cape Trafalgar on October 21, 1805, is typical of these official news releases. In this particular case, the government could afford to be honest with the public. The dispatch described the defeat of the combined navies of Spain and France. British naval supremacy was confirmed, and the English were given a new national hero.

ADMIRALTY-OFFICE, NOV. 6

Dispatches, of which the following are Copies, were received at the Admiralty this day, at one o'clock A.M. from Vice-Admiral Collingwood, Commander in Chief of his Majesty's ships and vessels off Cadiz:—

Euryalus, off Cape Trafalgar, Oct. 22, 1805

SIR,

The ever-to-be-lamented death of Vice-Admiral Lord Viscount Nelson, who, in the late conflict with the enemy, fell in the hour of victory, leaves to me the duty of informing my Lords Commissioners of the Admiralty, that on the 19th instant, it was communicated to the Commander in Chief, from the ships watching the motions of the enemy in Cadiz, that the Combined Fleet had put to sea; as they sailed with light winds westerly, his Lordship concluded their destination was the Mediterranean, and immediately made all sail for the Streights' entrance, with the British Squadron, consisting of twenty-seven ships, three of them sixty-fours, where his Lordship was informed, by Captain Blackwood (whose vigilance in watching, and giving notice of the enemy's movements, has been highly meritorious), that they had not yet passed the Streights.

On Monday the 21st instant, at day-light, when Cape Trafalgar bore E. by S. about seven leagues, the enemy was discovered six or seven miles to the Eastward, the wind about West, and very light; the Commander in Chief immediately made the signal for the fleet to bear up in two columns, as they are formed in order of sailing; a mode of attack his Lordship had previously directed, to avoid the inconvenience and delay in forming a line of battle in the usual manner. The enemy's line consisted of thirty-three ships (of which eighteen were French, and fifteen Spanish), commanded in Chief by Admiral Villeneuve: the Spaniards, under the direction of Gravina, wore, with their heads to the Northward, and formed their line of battle with great closeness and correctness. . . .

The Commander in Chief, in the *Victory,* led the weather column, and the *Royal Sovereign,* which bore my flag, the lee.

The action began at twelve o'clock, by the leading ships of the columns breaking through the enemy's line, the Commander in Chief about the tenth ship from the van, the Second in Command about the twelfth from the rear, leaving the van of the enemy unoccupied; the succeeding ships breaking through, in all parts, astern of their leaders, and engaging the enemy at the muzzles of their guns; the conflict was severe; the enemy's ships were fought with a gallantry highly honourable to their Officers; but the attack on them was irresistible, and it pleased the Almighty Disposer of all events to grant his Majesty's arms a complete and glorious victory. . . .

After such a Victory, it may appear unnecessary to enter into encomiums on the particular parts taken by the several Commanders; the conclusion says more on the subject than I have language to express; the spirit which animated all was the same: when all exert themselves zealously in their country's service, all deserve that their high merits should stand recorded; and never was high merit more conspicuous than in the battle I have described. . . .

A circumstance occurred during the action, which so strongly marks the invincible spirit of British seamen, when engaging the enemies of their country, that I cannot resist the pleasure I have in making it known to their Lordships; the *Temeraire* was boarded by accident, or design, by a French ship on one side, and a Spaniard on the other; the contest was vigorous, but, in the end, the Combined Ensigns were torn from the poop, and the British hoisted in their places.

Such a battle could not be fought without sustaining a great loss of men. I have not only to lament, in common with the British Navy, and the British Nation, in the Fall of the Commander in Chief, the loss of a

Hero, whose name will be immortal, and his memory ever dear to his country; but my heart is rent with the most poignant grief for the death of a friend, to whom, by many years intimacy, and a perfect knowledge of the virtues of his mind, which inspired ideas superior to the common race of men, I was bound by the strongest ties of affection; a grief to which even the glorious occasion in which he fell, does not bring the consolation which, perhaps, it ought: his Lordship received a musket ball in his left breast, about the middle of the action, and sent an Officer to me immediately with his last farewell; and soon after expired. . . .

Having thus detailed the proceedings of the fleet on this occasion, I beg to congratulate their Lordships on a victory which, I hope, will add a ray to the glory of his Majesty's crown, and be attended with public benefit to our country, I am, etc.

(Signed)
C. COLLINGWOOD

86

A Declaration by the Framework Knitters (1812). The Luddites

By a standard dictionary definition a Luddite is "one of a band of workmen who tried to prevent the use of labor-saving machinery by breaking it." The connotations attached to the term today make a Luddite an irrational opponent of progress, a man attempting to live in a world passing him by, a "featherbedder." This understanding is not entirely fair to the first Luddites, the framework knitters.

SOURCE. *English Historical Documents, Vol. XI, 1783–1832*, edited by A. Aspinall and E. Anthony Smith. 1959, Oxford University Press, Inc., p. 531. Reprinted by permission of Oxford University Press, Inc., and Eyre & Spottiswoode (Publishers) Ltd.

The framework knitters did not suddenly begin breaking machinery in 1811; they had a long and very English tradition of such activity. In fact, if there is a historical basis to the term Luddite, it derives from a Ned Lud, an unbalanced artisan who destroyed some knitting frames as early as 1779. Later he was transformed into a mythical General Lud or King Lud, who protected his subjects. Machine breaking was seldom the indiscriminate and mindless action of workers thrown out of work by machines. After all, the framework knitters used machines themselves.

As late as 1800 the framework knitters were a prosperous and well organized artisan class, possessing a charter from Charles II regulating their hosiery industry. The male leg adorned in fancy hose was still admired as an object of beauty, and thus business was good. However, because of changes in clothing styles in the early nineteenth century, their economic position was being eroded. Also, other knitters suffering from the general trade depression during the Napoleonic Wars began to use larger pantaloon frames to produce material for "cut up" goods, stockings with sewn seams rather than stockings produced from a single, continuous thread. Beginning in 1811, the framework knitters first complained that these inferior and cheaper goods were giving the trade a bad name and then began breaking the frames of their rivals. In their 1812 declaration they were not opposed to new machinery but to the new and unfair business practices of men using old machinery. Although they broke over 1000 frames, they remained selective in their destruction and, for that reason, they were initially supported by many employers. Only later, when other depressed classes adopted their techniques, did Luddism become a violent attack on machinery in general. The government then stepped in and suppressed the movement. And Ned Lud became, like Robin Hood, a hero to the oppressed in England's popular folk mythology.

BY THE FRAMEWORK KNITTERS

A Declaration

Whereas by the charter granted by our late sovereign Lord Charles II by the Grace of God King of Great Britain France and Ireland, the framework knitters are empowered to break and destroy all frames and engines that fabricate articles in a fraudulent and deceitful manner and to destroy all framework knitters' goods whatsoever that are so made and whereas a number of deceitful unprincipled and intriguing persons did attain an Act to be passed in the 28th year of our present sovereign Lord George III whereby it was enacted that persons entering by force into any house shop or place to break or destroy frames should be adjudged guilty of felony and as we are fully convinced that such Act was obtained in the most fraudulent interested and electioneering manner and that the honourable the Parliament of Great Britain was deceived as to the motives and intentions of the persons who obtained such Act we therefore the framework knitters do hereby declare the aforesaid Act to be null and void to all intents and purposes whatsoever as by the passing of this Act villainous and imposing persons are enabled to make fraudulent and deceitful manufactures to the discredit and utter ruin of our trade. And whereas we declare that the aforementioned Charter is as much in force as though no such Act had been passed. . . . And we do hereby declare to all hosiers lace manufacturers and proprietors of frames that we will break and destroy all manner of frames whatsover that make the following spurious articles and all frames whatsover that do not pay the regular prices heretofore agreed to [by] the masters and workmen—All print net frames making single press and frames not working by the rack and rent and not paying the price regulated in 1810: warp frames working single yarn or two coarse hole—not working by the rack, not paying the rent and prices regulated in 1809—whereas all plain silk frames not making work according to the gage—frames not marking the work according to quality, whereas all frames of whatsoever description the workmen of whom are not paid in the current coin of the realm will invariably be destroyed. . . .

Given under my hand the first day of January 1812.
God protect the Trade.

NED LUD'S OFFICE
Sherwood Forest

87

The Roman Catholic
Emancipation Act (1829)

English prejudices toward Roman Catholics had by the late eighteenth century begun to soften. By 1793 Roman Catholics enjoyed freedom of worship. Old laws limiting their political activity, however, still remained on the books. Specifically, the Corporation Act of 1661 prohibited non-Anglicans from being members of municipal governments. The Test Act of 1673 similarly restricted admission to offices of the royal government and required office holders to take an oath offensive to Roman Catholics. The Test Act of 1678 forbade Catholics to sit in either house of parliament. Protestant dissenters suffered less from this legislation, and in 1828 the applicability of these acts to them was completely removed.

An Irish crisis produced the Catholic Emancipation Act of 1829. Although in 1793 the Roman Catholic majority in Ireland obtained the right to vote in parliamentary elections and retained it by the Act of Union (1800), Catholics still could not hold public office. This disappointment, added to their dislike for the political union with Britain and their poor economic condition, led many Irish Catholics to rowdiness and disorder, which by the end of the 1820s was absorbing much of the attention of the British army. Daniel O'Connell (1775–1847), a Catholic barrister, and his Catholic Association, founded in 1823, worked for the election of members of parliament favorable to Catholic emancipation and to repeal of the union. In 1828, he contested a by-election, even though his Roman Catholicism would disqualify him from sitting in parliament. His winning demonstrated the possibility of scores of Roman Catholic victors at the next general election. If their victories were overturned by a Protestant parliament, Irish outrage was a certainty. The Tories, led by the duke of Wellington, therefore, passed the act that appears in part below. Besides giving Roman Catholics the political rights they had been denied for more than two and one-half centuries, it demonstrates that Catholics were still distrusted by the Protestant establishment. This is shown

SOURCE. *Statutes At Large,* LXV, pt. ii, 49–53, 57: (10 George IV, c. 7).

by the oath required of Catholic members of parliament and by the strictures against Jesuits, not to mention the act passed a short time later raising the property qualifications for voting in Ireland. In a different vein, this act can be considered as the beginning of nineteenth-century reform. It demonstrates the pragmatism of the Tories, passing legislation they did not believe in, because the situation demanded it. Also, by striking the first blow against the constitution, the Tories denied themselves the sanctity they later claimed as its chief defenders.

AN ACT FOR THE RELIEF OF HIS MAJESTY'S ROMAN CATHOLIC SUBJECTS (13th APRIL 1829)

Whereas by various Acts of Parliament certain Restraints and Disabilities are imposed on the Roman Catholic Subjects of His Majesty, to which other Subjects of His Majesty are not liable: And Whereas it is expedient that such Restraints and Disabilities shall be from henceforth discontinued: And Whereas by various Acts certain Oaths and certain Declarations, commonly called the Declaration against Transubstantiation, and the Declaration against Transubstantiation and the Invocation of Saints and the Sacrifice of the Mass, as practised in the Church of *Rome,* are or may be required to be taken, made, and subscribed by the Subjects of His Majesty, as Qualifications for sitting and voting in Parliament, and for the Enjoyment of certain Offices, Franchises, and Civil Rights": Be it enacted by the King's most Excellent Majesty, by and with the Advice and Consent of the Lords Spiritual and Temporal, and Commons, in this present Parliament assembled, and by the Authority of the same, That from and after the Commencement of this Act all such Parts of the said Acts as require the said Declarations, or either of them, to be made or subscribed by any of His Majesty's Subjects, as a Qualification for sitting and voting in Parliament, or for the Exercise or Enjoyment of any Office, Franchise, or Civil Right, be and the same are (save as hereinafter provided and excepted) hereby repealed.

II. And be it enacted, That from and after the Commencement of this Act it shall be lawful for any Person professing the Roman Catholic Religion, being a Peer, or who shall after the Commencement of this Act be returned as a Member of the House of Commons, to sit and vote in either House of Parliament respectively, being in all other respects duly qualified to sit and vote therein, upon taking and subscribing the following Oath, instead of the Oaths of Allegiance, Supremacy, and Abjuration:

I *A. B.* do sincerely promise and swear, That I will be faithful and bear true Allegiance to His Majesty King *George* the Fourth, and will defend him to the utmost of my Power against all Conspiracies and Attempts whatever, which shall be made against his Person, Crown, or Dignity; and I will do my utmost Endeavour to disclose and make known to His Majesty, His Heirs and Successors, all Treasons and traitorous Conspiracies which may be formed against Him or Them: And I do faithfully promise to maintain, support, and defend, to the utmost of my Power, the Succession of the Crown, which Succession, by an Act, intituled *An Act for the further Limitation of the Crown, and better securing the Rights and Liberties of the Subject,* is and stands limited to the Princess *Sophia,* Electress of *Hanover,* and the Heirs of her Body, being Protestants; hereby utterly renouncing and abjuring any Obedience or Allegiance unto any other Person claiming or pretending a Right to the Crown of this Realm: And I do further declare, That it is not an Article of my Faith, and that I do renounce, reject, and abjure the Opinion, that Princes excommunicated or deprived by the Pope, or any other Authority of the See of *Rome,* may be deposed or murdered by their Subjects, or by any Person whatsoever: And I do declare, That I do not believe that the Pope of *Rome,* or any other Foreign Prince, Prelate, Person, State, or Potentate, hath or ought to have any Temporal or Civil Jurisdiction, Power, Superiority, or Pre-eminence, directly or indirectly, within this Realm. I do swear, That I will defend to the utmost of my Power the Settlement of Property within this Realm, as established by the Laws: And I do hereby disclaim, disavow, and solemnly abjure any Intention to subvert the present Church Establishment, as settled by Law within this Realm: And I do solemnly swear, That I never will exercise any Privilege to which I am or may become entitled, to disturb or weaken the Protestant Religion or Protestant Government in the United Kingdom: And I do solemnly, in the presence of God, profess, testify, and declare, That I do make this Declaration, and every Part thereof, in the plain and ordinary Sense of the Words of this Oath, without any Evasion, Equivocation, or mental Reservation whatsoever.

So help me God. . . .

V. And be it further enacted, That it shall be lawful for Persons professing the Roman Catholic Religion to vote at Elections of Members to serve in Parliament for *England* and for *Ireland,* and also to vote at the Elections of Representative Peers of *Scotland* and of *Ireland,* and to be elected such Representative Peers, being in all other respects duly qualified, upon taking and subscribing the Oath hereinbefore appointed and set forth. . . .

X. And be it enacted, That it shall be lawful for any of His Majesty's

Subjects professing the Roman Catholic Religion to hold, exercise, and enjoy all Civil and Military Offices and Places of Trust or Profit under His Majesty, His Heirs or Successors, and to exercise any other Franchise or Civil Right, except as hereinafter excepted. . . .

XIV. And be it enacted, That it shall be lawful for any of His Majesty's Subjects professing the Roman Catholic Religion to be a Member of any Lay Body Corporate, and to hold any Civil Office or Place of Trust or Profit therein, and to do any Corporate Act, or vote in any Corporate Election or other Proceeding, upon taking and subscribing the Oath hereby appointed and set forth. . . .

XXIX. And be it further enacted, That if any Jesuit, or Member of any such Religious Order, Community, or Society as aforesaid, shall, after the Commencement of this Act, come into this Realm, he shall be deemed and taken to be guilty of a Misdemeanor, and being thereof lawfully convicted, shall be sentenced and ordered to be banished from the United Kingdom for the Term of his natural Life.

88

Lord John Russell, Speech in Commons (1831). The Great Reform Bill

In 1831, when Lord John Russell (1792–1878) delivered this speech, the House of Commons was a venerable institution, having served England well for centuries. Some of its features, however, had little relevance to present conditions, especially to the dramatic changes being produced by the Industrial Revolution. The county franchise had not been altered since it was established as the 40-shilling freeholder in 1430, and in the boroughs there

SOURCE. Hansard's Parliamentary Debates: Third Series, II, 1061, 1063–1064, 1066, 1068–1073, 1085, 1088–1089.

was a hodgepodge of different qualifications. No new boroughs had been created since 1677 and only one had been suppressed. Thus there were dilapidated boroughs like Old Sarum that had no residents at all. William Pitt the Elder (1708–1778), who once represented Old Sarum, in his speech on the Stamp Act referred to such phenomena as "the rotten part of the Constitution."

Although popular agitation for reform had existed as early as John Wilkes's Middlesex elections in 1768 and 1769, no ministry seriously proposed parliamentary reform until 1831 when Lord Grey (1765–1845) and the Whigs produced the bill proposed by Russell which appears below. When the bill, which was surprisingly radical, was defeated, Grey obtained a dissolution of parliament. The Whig cry of "the bill, the whole bill, and nothing but the bill" won the ensuing election, but the victorious Whigs' second reform bill was defeated by the Lords. The following year, a third bill was accepted by the Lords, but only after William IV (1830–1837) had pledged to create, if necessary, enough new peers to force its passage.

The final bill, much like the one Russell had introduced in 1831, did not make Britain a parliamentary democracy, nor did it intend to do so. It abolished only the worst of the rotten boroughs, distributing most of the seats thus redeemed among the counties and the new industrial towns. It extended the franchise and made it uniform in the counties and in the boroughs, doubling the number of eligible voters to nearly a million out of a total population of more than 16 million. Thus the middle-class well-to-do of the towns were added to the landed wealthy as the practical rulers of Britain. Although the Reform Act did not enfranchise the working class and, in fact, disfranchised some, it did momentarily quiet the popular unrest that many feared would lead to revolution on the European model of 1830. Though this bill was intended to be the final reform of parliament, it was in reality only the first of a series of reform bills that during the next century extended the suffrages to virtually all adult subjects.

Although the legal ban on publishing parliamentary debates was in practice ended in 1771, systematic recording and publishing did not begin until 1803 under the direction of William Cobbett (1762–1835). His printer, T. C. Hansard, however, assumed the primary responsibility for the project, which has continued to this day. Soon the debates were referred to simply as *Hansard*.

Lord *John Russell* then rose and spoke to the following effect:

The measure I have now to bring forward, is a measure, not of mine, but of the Government, in whose name I appear—the deliberate measure of a whole Cabinet, unanimous upon this subject, and resolved to place their measure before this House, in redemption of their pledge to their Sovereign, the Parliament, and to their country. . . .

Allow me to imagine, for a moment, a stranger from some distant country, who should arrive in England to examine our institutions. All the information he had collected would have told him that this country was singular for the degree which it had attained in wealth, in science, and in civilization. He would have learned, that in no country have the arts of life been carried further, no where the inventions of mechanical skill been rendered more conducive to the comfort and prosperity of mankind. He would have made himself acquainted with its fame in history, and above all, he would have been told, that the proudest boast of this celebrated country was its political freedom. If, in addition to this he had heard that once in six years this country, so wise, so renowned, so free, chose its Representatives to sit in the great Council, where all the ministerial affairs were discussed and determined; he would not be a little curious to see the process by which so important and solemn an operation was effected. What then would be his surprise, if he were taken by his guide, whom he had asked to conduct him to one of the places of election, to a green mound and told, that this green mound sent two Members to Parliament—or, to be taken to a stone wall, with three niches in it, and told that these three niches sent two Members to Parliament. . . . But his surprise would increase to astonishment if he were carried into the North of England, where he would see large flourishing towns, full of trade and activity, containing vast magazines of wealth and manufactures, and were told that these places had no Representatives in the Assembly which was said to represent the people. Suppose him, after all, for I will not disguise any part of the case, suppose him to ask for a specimen of popular election, and to be carried, for that purpose, to Liverpool; his surprise would be turned into disgust at the gross venality and corruption which he would find to pervade the electors. After seeing all this, would he not wonder that a nation which had made such progress in every kind of knowledge, and which valued itself for its freedom, should permit so absurd and defective a system of representation any longer to prevail? . . . The chief grievances of which the people complain are these;—First, the nomination of Members by individuals? Second, the Elections by close Corporations; third, the Expense of Elections. . . .

We propose that every borough which . . . had less than 2,000 inhabitants, shall altogether lose the right of sending Members to Parliament. The effect will be, utterly to disfranchise sixty boroughs. . . . We find that there are forty-seven boroughs, of only 4,000 inhabitants, and these we shall deprive of the right of sending more than one Member to Parliament . . . making in the whole 168 vacancies. . . . As I have already said, we do not mean to allow that the remaining boroughs should be in the hands of select Corporations—that is to say, in the possession of a small number of persons, to the exclusion of the great body of the inhabitants, who have property and interest in the place represented. . . . We therefore propose that the right of voting shall be given to householders paying rates for, or occupying a house of, the yearly value of 10*l.* and upwards. . . . I shall now proceed to the manner in which we propose to extend the franchise in counties. The Bill I wish to introduce will give all copyholders to the value of 10*l.* a year . . . and all leaseholders for not less than twenty-one years, . . . a right to vote for the return of Knights of the Shire. . . . The right will depend upon a lease for twenty-one years, where the annual rent is not less than fifty pounds. It will be recollected that, when speaking of the numbers disfranchised, I said, that 168 vacancies would be created. . . . We propose . . . to fill up a certain number of the vacancies, but not the whole of them. We intend that seven large towns shall send two Members each, and that twenty other towns shall send one Member each. . . . A great portion of the Metropolis and its neighbourhood, amounting in population to 800,000 or 900,000, is not represented, and we propose to give eight members to the unrepresented. . . .

Next we propose an addition to the Members for the larger counties . . . two additional Members to each of twenty-seven counties, where the inhabitants exceed 150,000. Everybody will expect that Yorkshire, divided into three Ridings—the East, West, and North—should have two Members for each Riding. . . . Besides this, it is proposed that the Isle of Wight shall return one Member. . . .

The names of electors are to be enrolled, by which means we hope that the disputes regarding qualification will be in a great measure avoided. We propose that all electors in counties, cities, towns, or boroughs, shall be registered, and for this purpose, machinery will be put in motion. . . .

I arrive at last at the objections which may be made to the plan we propose. I shall be told, in the first place, that we overturn the institutions of our ancestors. I maintain, that in departing from the letter, we preserve the spirit of those institutions. Our opponents say, our ancestors gave Old Sarum Representatives, therefore we should give Old Sarum Representatives.—We say, our ancestors gave Old Sarum Representatives, because it *was* a large town; therefore we give Representatives to Manchester, which *is* a large town. . . . I . . . think I am justified in saying, that we are to be believed when we come forward and state, that we consider some effectual measure of Reform to be necessary. I say, that we have a right to be believed when we assert that it is not for any sinister end of our own we bring forward the present measure, but because we are interested in the future welfare of this country, which welfare we conceive

to be best consulted by the adoption of a timely and an effective Reform
—because we think, that, by such a course alone we shall be enabled to
give permanency to that Constitution which has been so long the admiration of nations, on account of its popular, spirit, but which cannot
exist much longer, unless strengthened by an additional infusion of popular spirit, commensurate with the progress of knowledge and the increased intelligence of the age. To establish the Constitution on a firm
basis, you must show that you are determined not to be the representatives of a small class, or of a particular interest; but to form a body, who,
representing the people, springing from the people, and sympathising with
the people, can fairly call on the people to support the future burthens
of the country, and to struggle with the future difficulties which it may
have to encounter; confident that those who call upon them are ready to
join them heart and hand: and are only looking, like themselves, to the
glory and welfare of England. I conclude, Sir, by moving for leave to
bring in a bill for amending the state of the Representation in England
and Wales.

89

Ebenezer Elliott, *Corn Law Rhymes* (1831). The Free Trade Movement

The Corn Law of 1815 was the most consistently controversial statute in
early nineteenth-century England. This act, prohibiting the importation of
foreign corn, or grain, into England unless domestic wheat was selling for
at least 80s. a quarter (8 bushels), was an attempt by the landed interests to
maintain agricultural prices at the artificially high levels of the Napoleonic
Wars era. Other economic and social groups in England, however, regarded

SOURCE. Ebenezer Elliott, *Corn Law Rhymes,* 3rd ed., London: B. Steill, 1831, pp. 29–30, 31, 45, 60, 65.

the Corn Law as class legislation. Blaming the landlords for the high price of bread, the lower classes proceeded to riot in many English cities. Although the rioting eventually ceased, the resentment remained and festered into the 1830s. The middle classes argued that the protection of domestic grain necessarily resulted in higher wages and made English manufactured goods less competitive in world markets. In effect, the middle classes complained that industry was being forced to subsidize the inefficiency of the landlords, a policy that could result only in harm to England. Despite Robert Peel's attempted modifications of the 1820s, the Corn Law remained a major source of dispute. The Anti-Corn Law League, founded in 1838 under the leadership of Richard Cobden and John Bright, helped to persuade Peel in 1846 to repeal the corn duties. The victory of Cobden and Bright symbolized the economic triumph of free trade and the political ascendancy of the middle class. The destruction of the Corn Law, "the ark of the Tory Convenant," marked a major defeat for those who had previously regarded themselves as the rightful rulers of England.

Ebenezer Elliott (1781–1849) was one of the most vocal critics of the Corn Law. The son of an English Jacobin, "Devil Elliott," Ebenezer divided his time between poetry and business. He failed in both. Although some of his early poetry rose to the level of mediocrity, all of it was ignored. His iron business went bankrupt in the 1820s. Personally frustrated, Elliott began writing his famous "corn-law rhymes," directed against what he believed to be the source of his and England's economic woes. These rhymes, published in several editions and widely read, made him something of a popular hero. In the selections reproduced below, the intensity of his feelings is apparent. To the historian seeking to understand the passions aroused by the Corn Law, Elliott's rhymes are worth more than all of the cerebral speeches of Bright and Cobden entombed between the covers of *Hansard*.

What Is Bad Government?

WHAT is bad government, thou slave,
  Whom robbers represent?
What is bad government, thou knave,
  Who lov'st bad government?
It is the deadly *will*, that takes
  What labour ought to keep;
It is the deadly *power*, that makes
  Bread dear, and labour cheap.

The Four Dears

DEAR sugar, dear tea, and dear corn
  Conspired with dear representation,
To laugh worth and honour to scorn,
  And beggar the whole British nation.

Let us bribe the dear sharks, said dear tea;
  Bribe, bribe, said dear representation;
Then buy with their own the dear humbugg'd, and be
  The bulwarks of tory dictation.
Dear sugar and tea, said dear corn,
  Be true to dear representation;
And then the dear crown will be worn,
  But to dignify dearest taxation.

Dear sugar, dear corn, and dear tea,
  Stick to me, said dear representation;
Let us still pull together, and we
  Shall still rob the dear British nation.

How Different!

POOR weaver, with the hopeless brow,
  And bare woe-whiten'd head;
Thou art a pauper, all allow,
  All see thou begg'st thy bread;
And yet thou dost not plunder slaves,
  Then tell them they are free;
Nor hast thou join'd with tax-fed knaves,
  To corn-bill mine and me.

What borough dost thou represent?
  Whom bid'st thou toil and pay?
Why sitt'st not thou in pauperment,
  If baser beggars may?
Where are thy hounds, thy palaced w—e,
  To feed on mine and me?
Thy revered pimp, thy coach and four,
  Thy thieves in livery?

No house hast thou, no food, no fire;
  None bow to thee, alas!
A beggar! yet nor lord, nor squire,
  Say how comes this to pass?

While you proud pauper, dead to shame,
  Is fed by mine and me?
And yet behind the rascal's name
  The rascal writes M.P.!

Caged Rats

YE coop us up, and tax our bread,
  And wonder why we pine:
But ye are fat, and round, and red,
  And fill'd with tax-bought wine.
Thus, twelve rats starve while three rats thrive,
  (Like you on mine and me,)
When fifteen rats are caged alive,
  With food for nine and three.

Haste! havoc's torch begins to glow,
  The ending is begun;
Make haste; destruction thinks ye slow;
  Make haste to be undone!
Why are ye call'd 'my lord,' and 'squire,'
  While fed by mine and me,
And wringing food, and clothes, and fire
  From bread-tax'd misery?

Make haste, slow rogues! *prohibit* trade,
  Prohibit honest gain;
Turn all the good that God hath made
  To fear, and hate, and pain;
Till beggars all, assassins all,
  All cannibals we be,
And death shall have no funeral
  From shipless sea to sea.

The Jacobin's Prayer

AVENGE the plunder'd poor, oh Lord!
But not with fire, but not with sword,
Not as at Peterloo they died,
Beneath the hoofs of coward pride.
Avenge our rags, our chains, our sighs,
The famine in our children's eyes!
But not with sword—no, not with fire
Chastise Thou Britain's locustry!

Lord, let them feel thy heavier ire;
Whip them, oh Lord! with poverty!
Then, cold in soul as coffin'd dust,
Their hearts as tearless, dead, and dry,
Let them in outraged mercy trust,
And *find* that mercy they deny!

Yon cotton-prince, at Peterloo,
Found easy work, and glory, too,
Corn laws, quoth he, make labour cheap,
And famine from our trenches keep;
He sees but wealth in want and woe;
Men starve, he owns, and justly so;
But if they marry and get brats,
Must *he* provide their shirts and hats?
Lord, fill his ledger with bad debts!
Let him be learn'd in gazettes!

Sadler Committee, Testimony (1832). Child Labor in England

Despite Peel's apprentice act of 1802 and the later factory acts of 1819 and 1829, child labor remained a controversial social issue. This and similar problems of industrialization in the 1820s and 1830s produced demands that the government intervene and correct the worst abuses of laissez-faire capitalism. Logically, many of the early reformers were Tories, who represented not only the landed classes but an older, paternalistic concern for the welfare of England's poor. Richard Oastler and Michael Sadler in the early 1830s and Benjamin Disraeli's Young England movement later were representative of this sense of social responsibility.

Michael Sadler (1780–1835), a Tory MP associated with several reform movements in the 1820s, led the attack on the abuses of child labor. To publicize the problem, he persuaded parliament to appoint a select committee to hear testimony on the working conditions of children and, if necessary, to propose remedial legislation. Sadler's committee achieved the objective of its chairman, becoming, as one historian has described it, "the chief source of horror stories" about child labor, the impact of which can be judged from the excerpts below. The resulting Factories Regulations Act (1833) prohibited the employment in textile mills of children under the age of nine and limited the workday of children under the age of 13 and of youths under 18 to 9 and 12 hours, respectively. More important, the act provided for full-time factory inspectors to make certain that its provisions were enforced. The act represented a major attack on the economic principles of laissez-faire.

SOURCE. "Report of the Select Committee on the Factories Bill," *Industrial Revolution: Children's Employment,* II, 157–159, 163–164, in the Irish University Press 1000-volume series of *British Parliamentary Papers,* Shannon, 1968–1972.

The testimony before the Sadler Committee was published as a "parliamentary paper." These papers, beginning in about 1801 and totaling almost 7000 volumes for just the nineteenth century, are for the study of modern Britain the most important printed government records. These "Blue Books," so-called because of their original blue paper covers, consist of several different types of documents. Many, like the one below, are reports of select committees of parliament. Others are reports of Royal Commissions, composed of both members of parliament and outside specialists. There were also collections of official correspondence, frequently dealing with foreign or colonial policy, and statistical reports from government agencies. All were arranged chronologically according to parliamentary session, with no attempt at any topical organization.

No complete set of original parliamentary papers exists, although nearly complete sets are found in such obvious places as the British Museum. Most copies failed to survive the year of their publication, their folio size putting them in some demand as wrapping paper. Today, thanks to the marvels of photography, most major libraries possess microprint editions.

Veneris, 1º *die Junii*, 1832

MICHAEL THOMAS SADLER, ESQUIRE, IN THE CHAIR.

Joseph Hebergam, Called in and Examined

4143. Where do you reside?—At North Great Huddersfield, in Yorkshire.

4144. What age are you?—I was 17 on the 21st of April.

4145. Are your father and mother living?—No; I have been without a father six years on the 8th of August.

4146. Your mother survives?—Yes.

4147. Have you worked in factories?—Yes.

4148. At what age did you commence?—Seven years of age.

4149. At whose mill?—George Addison's, Bradley Mill, near Huddersfield.

4150. What was the employment?—Worsted-spinning.

4151. What were your hours of labour at that mill?—From 5 in the morning till 8 at night.

4152. What intervals had you for refreshment and rest?—Thirty minutes at noon.

4153. Had you no time for breakfast or refreshment in the afternoon?—No, not one minute; we had to eat our meals as we could; standing or otherwise.

4154. You had fourteen and a half hours of actual labour at 7 years of age?—Yes.

4155. What wages had you at that time?—Two shillings and sixpence a week.

4164. What means were taken to keep you at your work so long?—There were three overlookers; there was a head overlooker, and then there was one man kept to grease the machines, and then there was one kept on purpose to strap.

4165. Was the main business of one of the overlookers that of strapping the children up to this excessive labour?—Yes, the same as strapping an old restive horse that has fallen down and will not get up.

4166. Was that the constant practice?—Yes, day by day.

4167. Were there straps regularly provided for that purpose?—Yes, he is continually walking up and down with it in his hand.

4176. Where is your brother John working now?—He died three years ago.

4177. What age was he when he died?—Sixteen years and eight months.

4178. To what was his death attributed by your mother and the medical attendants?—It was attributed to this, that he died from working such long hours, and that it had been brought on by the factory. They have to stop the flies with their knees, because they go so swift they cannot stop them with their hands; he got a bruise on the shin by a spindle-board, and it went on to the degree that it burst; the surgeon cured that, then he was better; then he went to work again; but when he had worked about two months more his spine became affected, and he died.

4181. What effect had this labour upon your own health?—It had a great deal; I have had to drop it several times in the year.

4182. How long was it before the labour took effect on your health?—Half a year.

4183. And did it at length begin to affect your limbs?—When I had worked about half a year, a weakness fell into my knees and ankles; it continued, and it has got worse and worse.

4187. How far did you live from the mill?—A good mile.

4188. Was it very painful for you to move?—Yes, in the morning I could scarcely walk, and my brother and sister used out of kindness to take me under each arm, and run with me to the mill, and my legs dragged on the ground in consequence of the pain; I could not walk.

4189.　Were you sometimes too late?—Yes; and if we were five minutes too late, the overlooker would take a strap, and beat us till we were black and blue.

4190.　The overlooker nevertheless knew the occasion of your being a little too late?—Yes.

4191.　Did you state to him the reason?—Yes, he never minded that; and he used to watch us out of the windows.

4192.　Did the pain and weakness in your legs increase?—Yes.

4193.　Just show the Committee the situation in which your limbs are now?—

[The Witness accordingly stood up, and showed his limbs.]

4194.　Were you originally a straight and healthy boy?—Yes, I was straight and healthful as any one when I was 7 years and a quarter old.

4306.　How long have you been in the Leeds Infirmary?—A week last Saturday night; if I had been this week at Leeds I should have been a fortnight next Saturday.

4307.　Have any cases of accidents in mills or factories been brought into the Infirmary since you were there?—Yes, last Tuesday but one there was a boy brought in about 5 or 6 o'clock in the evening from a mill; he had got catched with the shaft, and he had both his thighs broke, and from his knee to his hip the flesh was ripped up the same as if it had been cut by a knife, his head was bruised, his eyes were nearly torn out, and his arms broken. His sister, who ran to pull him off, got both her arms broke and her head bruised, and she is bruised all over her body. The boy died last Thursday night but one, about 8 o'clock; I do not know whether the girl is dead, but she was not expected to live.

4310.　Something has been said about the fear of giving evidence regarding this factory question; do you know whether any threats have ever been used on that account?—Yes; Dr. Walker ordered me to wear irons from the ankle to the thigh; my mother was not able to get them, and he said he would write a note, and she might go to some gentlemen in the town, and give them that note, and see if they would not give her something towards them; and so she did, and I have got the bare irons made; and I was coming into the yard where I live; and there was a man who worked at the same place that I did, asked me to let him look at them; I told him I could not get money to line them with, and he said, "I will tell you where there is a gentleman who will give you the money;" he told me of Mr. Oastler, and he said, "I will go and see if he is at home, that you may not lose your trouble." Mrs. Oastler was at home, and said I was to be there at 8 o'clock in the morning, because he wanted to go off on a journey; I got there about half-past 8. Mr. Wood of Bradford gave me a sovereign, and Mr. Oastler gave me 3s. 6d., and so I had them made. He asked me questions what my lameness came on with, and I told him, and he happened to mention it at the County Meeting at York; my master saw it in the newspaper; I think it was in Mr. Baines's newspaper, of Leeds; he is an enemy to the Ten Hours' Bill, and he happened to see it in the paper, and he sent the foreman on to our house where I lived; he had not patience to read it, and he said to my mother, "I suppose it is owing to our place that your Joseph got the use of his limbs taken away?" and my mother said he was informed wrong, that he had it before he went to that factory; but he said, "If he has said anything about our factory, we shall certainly turn him off, and both his brothers." I have two little brothers working at the same place.

4311. Did the foreman say this to you?—To my mother and me; he said he did not know exactly how it was, but he would go back and see the paper himself, and if he found out that we said anything about the factory system, that we should be turned off.

4312. Have you been turned off?—I have not, but my master will not speak to me or look at me: I do not know whether he will let me start again or not.

4335. You stated that you found it your duty to go to those mills, in order to maintain your mother, who is a widow, and very poor?—Yes.

91

Thomas Babington Macaulay, Minute on Indian Education (1835)

In acquiring a world empire, Britain created a number of vexatious administrative problems, among the most serious and constant of which being the extent to which she should civilize, or "Anglicize," the native populations. Did economic and political imperialism require cultural assimilation? This question, first posed in connection with French Canada after 1763, remained in the African colonies a controversial issue well into the twentieth century.

The consolidation of British control in India in the early nineteenth century engendered a major debate between the "Orientalists" and the "Anglicists." The former defended the vitality and sophistication of Indian culture. The latter in the 1820s conducted a vigorous campaign against what they viewed as barbarism and superstition, attacking in particular the *suttee,* a Hindu religious practice of burning alive a man's widow on his funeral pyre. The decision of the East India Company in 1833 to admit Indians into their civil service precipitated a new round in this old conflict. Although both sides agreed that the education of Indians should be promoted, they differed on the form it should take. The "Orientalists" favored Arabic and Sanscrit learning. The "Anglicists" urged the introduction of western scholarship taught in English.

The most prominent of the westernizers was Thomas Babington Macaulay (1800–1859), a member of the Supreme Council of India. Already a distinguished essayist, and later to achieve renoun for his *History of England from the Accession of James the Second,* Macaulay had no doubt as to the superiority of English civilization. As he later stated, the history of England since 1688 was "eminently the history of physical, of moral, and of intel-

SOURCE. *Speeches by Lord Macaulay with his Minute on Indian Education,* ed. G. M. Young, London: Oxford University Press, 1935, pp. 348–350, 352–353, 357–359.

lectual improvement." It was England's duty therefore to uplift the Indians by providing them with western learning, an argument he made most dogmatically in his famous Minute on Indian Education (1835). Macaulay, it should be noted, was not a racist. Indians were not inferior as people; they simply had an inferior culture. As Greece had civilized Rome and Rome had civilized Britain, now England, a link in the chain of progress, must transfer that benefit to India.

Macaulay and others recognized that in so doing they might be contributing to the end of British political rule over India. Nevertheless, England would create a more enduring empire:

> The sceptre may pass from us. Victory may be inconstant to our arms. But there are triumphs which are followed by no reverse. There is an empire exempt from all natural cause of decay. Those triumphs are the pacific triumphs of reason over barbarism; that empire is the imperishable empire of our arts and our morals, our literature and our laws.

Regardless of the merits of the case, the decision of the government of India to adopt Macaulay's recommendations was of great importance. Although alienating many Indians and perhaps contributing to the Indian Mutiny of 1857, the westernization and modernization of India was begun.

We have a fund to be employed as Government shall direct for the intellectual improvement of the people of this country. The simple question is, what is the most useful way of employing it?

All parties seem to be agreed on one point, that the dialects commonly spoken among the natives of this part of India, contain neither literary nor scientific information, and are, moreover, so poor and rude that, until they are enriched from some other quarter, it will not be easy to translate any valuable work into them. It seems to be admitted on all sides, that the intellectual improvement of those classes of the people who have the means of pursuing higher studies can at present be effected only by means of some language not vernacular amongst them.

What then shall that language be? One-half of the Committee maintain that it should be the English. The other half strongly recommended the Arabic and Sanscrit. The whole question seems to me to be, which language is the best worth knowing?

I have no knowledge of either Sanscrit or Arabic.—But I have done what I could to form a correct estimate of their value. I have read translations of the most celebrated Arabic and Sanscrit works. I have conversed both here and at home with men distinguished by their proficiency in the Eastern tongues. I am quite ready to take the Oriental learning at the valuation of the Orientalists themselves. I have never found one among them who could deny that a single shelf of a good European library was worth the whole native literature of India and Arabia. The intrinsic superiority of the Western literature is, indeed, fully admitted by those members of the Committee who support the Oriental plan of education.

It will hardly be disputed, I suppose, that the department of literature in which the eastern writers stand highest is poetry. And I certainly never met with any Orientalist who ventured to maintain that the Arabic and Sanscrit poetry could be compared to that of the great European nations. But when we pass from works of imagination to works in which facts are recorded, and general principles investigated, the superiority of the Europeans becomes absolutely immeasurable. It is, I believe, no exaggeration to say, that all the historical information which has been collected from all the books written in the Sanscrit language is less valuable than what may be found in the most paltry abridgments used at preparatory schools in England. In every branch of physical or moral philosophy, the relative position of the two nations is nearly the same.

How, then, stands the case? We have to educate a people who cannot at present be educated by means of their mother-tongue. We must teach them some foreign language. The claims of our own language it is hardly necessary to recapitulate. It stands preeminent even among the languages of the west. It abounds with works of imagination not inferior to the noblest which Greece has bequeathed to us; with models of every species of eloquence; with historical compositions, which, considered merely as narratives, have seldom been surpassed, and which, considered as vehicles of ethical and political instruction, have never been equalled; with just and lively representations of human life and human nature; with the most profound speculations on metaphysics, morals, government, jurisprudence, and trade; with full and correct information respecting every experimental science which tends to preserve the health, to increase the comfort, or to expand the intellect of man. Whoever knows that language has ready access to all the vast intellectual wealth, which all the wisest nations of the earth have created and hoarded in the course of ninety generations. It may safely be said, that the literature now extant in that language is of far greater value than all the literature which three hundred years ago was extant in all the languages of the world together. Nor is this all. In India, English is the language spoken by the ruling class. It is spoken by the higher class of natives at the seats of Government. It is likely to become the language of commerce throughout the seas of the East. . . .

And what are the arguments against that course which seems to be alike recommended by theory and by experience? It is said that we ought to secure the co-operation of the native public, and that we can do this only by teaching Sanscrit and Arabic.

I can by no means admit that when a nation of high intellectual attainments undertakes to superintend the education of a nation comparatively ignorant, the learners are absolutely to prescribe the course which is to be taken by the teachers. It is not necessary, however, to say any thing on this subject. For it is proved by unanswerable evidence that we are not at present securing the co-operation of the natives. It would be bad enough to consult their intellectual taste at the expense of their intellectual health. But we are consulting neither,—we are withholding from them the learning for which they are craving, we are forcing on them the mock-learning which they nauseate. . . .

It is said that the Sanscrit and Arabic are the languages in which the sacred books of a hundred millions of people are written, and that they are, on that account, entitled to peculiar encouragement. Assuredly it is the duty of the British Government in India to be not only tolerant, but neutral on all religious questions. But to encourage the study of a literature admitted to be of small intrinsic value, only because that literature inculcates the most serious errors on the most important subjects, is a course hardly reconcileable with reason, with morality, or even with that very neutrality which ought, as we all agree, to be sacredly preserved. It is confessed that a language is barren of useful knowledge. We are to teach it because it is fruitful of monstrous superstitions. We are to teach false History, false Astronomy, false Medicine, because we find them in company with a false religion. We abstain, and I trust shall always abstain, from giving any public encouragement to those who are engaged in the work of converting natives to Christianity. And while we act thus, can we reasonably and decently bribe men out of the revenues of the state to waste their youth in learning how they are to purify themselves after touching an ass, or what text of the Vedas they are to repeat to expiate the crime of killing a goat?

It is taken for granted by the advocates of Oriental learning, that no native of this country can possibly attain more than a mere smattering of English. . . . They assume it as undeniable, that the question is between a profound knowledge of Hindoo and Arabian literature and science on the one side, and a superficial knowledge of the rudiments of English on the other. This is not merely an assumption, but an assumption contrary to all reason and experience. We know that foreigners of all nations do learn our language sufficiently to have access to all the most abstruse knowledge which it contains, sufficiently to relish even the more delicate graces of our most idiomatic writers. There are in this very town natives who are quite competent to discuss political or scientific questions with fluency and precision in the English language. I have heard the very question on which I am now writing discussed by native gentlemen with a liberality and an intelligence which would do credit to any member of the Committee of Public Instruction. Indeed it is unusual to find, even in the literary circles of the continent, any foreigner who can express himself in English with so much facility and correctness as we find in many Hindoos. Nobody, I suppose, will contend that English is so difficult to a Hindoo as Greek to an Englishman. Yet an intelligent English youth, in a much smaller number of years than our unfortunate pupils pass at the Sanscrit college, becomes able to read, to enjoy, and even to imitate, not unhappily, the compositions of the best Greek Authors. Less than half the time which enables an English youth to read Herodotus and Sophocles, ought to enable a Hindoo to read Hume and Milton.

To sum up what I have said, I think it clear that we are not fettered by the Act of Parliament of 1813; that we are not fettered by any pledge expressed or implied; that we are free to employ our funds as we choose; that we ought to employ them in teaching what is best worth knowing; that English is better worth knowing than Sanscrit or Arabic; that the natives are desirous to be taught English, and are not desirous to be taught Sanscrit or Arabic; that neither as the languages of law, nor as the languages of religion, have the Sanscrit and Arabic any peculiar claim to our engagement; that it is possible to make natives of this country thoroughly good English scholars, and that to this end our efforts ought to be directed.

In one point I fully agree with the gentlemen to whose general views I am opposed. I feel with them, that it is impossible for us, with our limited means, to attempt to educate the body of the people. We must at present do our best to form a class who may be interpreters between us and the millions whom we govern; a class of persons, Indian in blood and colour, but English in taste, in opinions, in morals, and in intellect. To that class we may leave it to refine the vernacular dialects of the country, to enrich those dialects with terms of science borrowed from the Western nomenclature, and to render them by degrees fit vehicles for conveying knowledge to the great mass of the population.

The National Petition (1839). The Chartist Program

In the late 1830s and 1840s, England witnessed a revival of lower-class political agitation. The "Hungry Forties" brought widespread unemployment, reduced wages, and poverty that in some cases became actual starvation. The suffering lower classes felt betrayed. The Reform Act of 1832, which had enfranchised the "moneymongers and shopocrats," appeared simply to have transferred power from an exploitive landed class to an oppressive middle class. This widely held view was confirmed by the Poor Act of 1834, which refused a person governmental assistance unless he entered a work-house, and by the Factory Act of 1833, which regulated the hours of work only of the young. Of these economic and political frustrations was born Chartism.

The Chartist movement, led initially by William Lovett (1800–1877), was on the surface a movement for political reform. The Chartist Petition of 1839 indicates, however, that the real objective was social and economic reform; political change was simply a means to an end. The petition of 1839 is also interesting in its moderate and deferential tone, indicating a willingness of Lovett and his followers to work within the system. Its rejection in the House of Commons by a vote of 235 to 46, however, undermined the moderates' position and contributed to the rise of "physical force" Chartists such as Feargus O'Connor, an Irish demagogue who radicalized but also weakened the movement in the 1840s. Finally, it should be noted that this petition mentions only five of the six political demands usually associated with Chartism, that for equal electoral districts being omitted.

The rejection of this petition foreshadowed the general failure of Chartism. The moderate middle class became more interested in the Anti-Corn Law

SOURCE. William Lovett, *The Life and Struggles of William Lovett*, London: Trübner & Co., 1876, pp. 469–473.

League. The moderate workingman turned increasingly to trade unionism. Only the radicals remained; and the failure of their monster petitions in 1842 and 1848 and the prosperity of the 1850s ended even this last phase. The failure of Chartism should not obscure its importance. It awakened people to the economic and political problems facing England; it developed in workingmen a class consciousness; and it forced politicians to realize that the political reform of 1832 might not in fact be final.

NATIONAL PETITION

Unto the Honourable the Commons of the United Kingdom of Great Britain and Ireland in Parliament assembled, the Petition of the undersigned, their suffering countrymen

HUMBLY SHEWETH,

That we, your petitioners, dwell in a land whose merchants are noted for enterprise, whose manufacturers are very skilful, and whose workmen are proverbial for their industry.

The land itself is goodly, the soil rich, and the temperature wholesome; it is abundantly furnished with the materials of commerce and trade; it has numerous and convenient harbours; in facility of internal communication it exceeds all others.

For three-and-twenty years we have enjoyed a profound peace.

Yet, with all these elements of national prosperity, and with every disposition and capacity to take advantage of them, we find ourselves overwhelmed with public and private suffering.

We are bowed down under a load of taxes; which, notwithstanding, fall greatly short of the wants of our rulers; our traders are trembling on the verge of bankruptcy; our workmen are starving; capital brings no profit, and labour no remuneration; the home of the artificer is desolate, and the warehouse of the pawnbroker is full; the workhouse is crowded, and the manufactory is deserted.

We have looked on every side, we have searched diligently in order to find out the causes of a distress so sore and so long continued.

We can discover none in nature, or in Providence.

Heaven has dealt graciously by the people; but the foolishness of our rulers has made the goodness of God of none effect.

The energies of a mighty kingdom have been wasted in building up the power of selfish and ignorant men, and its resources squandered for their aggrandisement.

The good of a party has been advanced to the sacrifice of the good of the nation; the few have governed for the interest of the few, while the interest of the many has been neglected, or insolently and tyrannously trampled upon.

It was the fond expectation of the people that a remedy for the greater part, if not for the whole, of their grievances, would be found in the Reform Act of 1832.

They were taught to regard that Act as a wise means to a worthy end; as the machinery of an improved legislation, when the will of the masses would be at length potential.

They have been bitterly and basely deceived.

The fruit which looked so fair to the eye has turned to dust and ashes when gathered.

The Reform Act has effected a transfer of power from one domineering faction to another, and left the people as helpless as before.

Our slavery has been exchanged for an apprenticeship to liberty, which has aggravated the painful feeling of our social degradation, by adding to it the sickening of still deferred hope.

We come before your Honourable House to tell you, with all humility, that this state of things must not be permitted to continue; that it cannot long continue without very seriously endangering the stability of the throne and the peace of the kingdom. . . .

We tell your Honourable House that the capital of the master must no longer be deprived of its due reward; that the laws which make food dear, and those which by making money scarce, makes labour cheap, must be abolished; that taxation must be made to fall on property, not on industry; that the good of the many, as it is the only legitimate end, so must it be the sole study of the Government.

As a preliminary essential to these and other requisite changes; as means by which alone the interests of the people can be effectually vindicated and secured, we demand that those interests be confided to the keeping of the people.

When the state calls for defenders, when it calls for money, no consideration of poverty or ignorance can be pleaded in refusal or delay of the call.

Required as we are, universally, to support and obey the laws, nature and reason entitle us to demand, that in the making of the laws, the universal voice shall be implicitly listened to.

We perform the duties of freemen; we must have the privileges of freemen.

WE DEMAND UNIVERSAL SUFFRAGE. . . .

WE DEMAND THE BALLOT. . . .

WE DEMAND ANNUAL PARLIAMENTS. . . .

We demand that in the future election of members of your Honourable House, the approbation of the constituency shall be the sole qualification; and that to every representative so chosen, shall be assigned, out of the public taxes, a fair and adequate remuneration for the time which he is called upon to devote to the public service. . . .

The management of this mighty kingdom has hitherto been a subject for contending factions to try their selfish experiments upon.

We have felt the consequences in our sorrowful experience—short glimmerings of uncertain enjoyment swallowed up by long and dark seasons of suffering.

If the self-government of the people should not remove their distresses, it will at least remove their repinings.

Universal suffrage will, and, it alone can, bring true and lasting peace to the nation; we firmly believe that it will also bring prosperity.

May it therefore please your honourable House to take this our petition into your most serious consideration; and to use your utmost endeavours, by all constitutional means, to have a law passed, granting to every male of lawful age, sane mind, and unconvicted of crime, the right of voting for members of Parliament; and directing all future elections of members of Parliament to be in the way of secret ballot; and ordaining that the duration of Parliaments so chosen shall in no case exceed one year; and abolishing all property qualifications in the members; and providing for their due remuneration while in attendance on their Parliamentary duties.

AND YOUR PETITIONERS, &c.

93

Lord Durham, *Report on the Affairs of British North America* (1839). Self-Government in the Colonies

Even after the loss of the 13 colonies, Britain retained settlements in North America. Besides those on the Atlantic coast—Nova Scotia, Newfoundland, Prince Edward Island, and New Brunswick—there was Quebec, initially French, but after the American Revolution enlarged by the influx of Loyalists. In 1791 Quebec was divided into two parts, Upper Canada, today called Ontario, populated by Loyalists and recent British immigrants, and Lower Canada, today called Quebec, populated primarily by the French. In 1837 almost simultaneous rebellions erupted in both colonies protesting the authority of the British governors and the power of the established local oligarchies. Although the revolts were easily suppressed, the British government recognized the danger and sent an important official to study the political problems facing the Canadas.

The man sent was John George Lambton, the earl of Durham (1792–1840), often called "Radical Jack" for his Benthamite leanings and for his outspoken liberalism. The son-in-law of prime minister Lord Grey, he had played an important role in the writing of the Great Reform Bill. He subscribed to Edward Gibbon Wakefield's ideas of "Systematic Colonization," which meant, among other things, a more rational alienation of crown lands in the colonies and greater colonial self-government. Thus Durham had the opportunity in Canada to practice both his liberalism and his advanced ideas on colonial government.

For five months in 1838, Durham ruled Canada as High Commissioner and

SOURCE. Arthur Berriedale Keith, ed., *Selected Speeches and Documents on British Colonial Policy, 1763–1917,* London: Oxford University Press, 1948, pp. 129–131, 134–135, 138–142. Reprinted by permission of Oxford University Press.

Governor-in-Chief. Resigning in a huff, he returned to England to write his report which, delivered in January 1839, advocated two things. First, the two Canadas should be united. The French, by being thrown in with the rapidly growing English population, would hopefully become Anglicized and thus would be more easily controlled. The political union was accomplished in 1840, but the French have never taken well to the idea of losing their "national" identity. Second, as the selection below shows, Durham advocated that Canada be given responsible government, that the governor, in internal affairs, accept the advice of members responsible to the legislative assembly; just as in England the monarch was supposedly controlled by a cabinet responsible to the House of Commons. This suggestion is especially interesting for its insight into English attitudes toward their own evolving governmental system. Although this recommendation was not endorsed by the British government, it was introduced in 1849 by Governor Lord Elgin. In this, Canada played her traditional role of colonial bellwether; almost immediately the principle' was extended to the other white settlement colonies, not only in North America but in Australasia and southern Africa as well.

Since the Revolution of 1688, the stability of the English constitution has been secured by that wise principle of our Government which has vested the direction of the national policy, and the distribution of patronage, in the leaders of the Parliamentary majority. However partial the monarch might be to particular ministers, or however he might have personally committed himself to their policy, he has invariably been constrained to abandon both, as soon as the opinion of the people has been irrevocably pronounced against them through the medium of the House of Commons. The practice of carrying on a representative government on a different principle, seems to be the rock on which the continental imitations of the British Constitution have invariably split; and the French Revolution of 1830 was the necessary result of an attempt to uphold a ministry with which no Parliament could be got to act in concert. It is difficult to understand how any English statesman could have imagined that representative and irresponsible government could be successfully combined. There seems, indeed, to be an idea, that the character of representative institutions ought to be thus modified in colonies; that it is an incident of colonial dependence that the officers of government should be nominated by the Crown, without any reference to the wishes of the community, whose interests are entrusted to their keeping. It has never been very clearly explained what are the imperial interests, which require this complete nullification of representative government. But if there be such a necessity, it is quite clear that a representative government in a colony must be a mockery, and a source of confusion. For those who support this system have never yet been able to devise, or to exhibit in the practical working of colonial government, any means for making so complete an abrogation of political influence palatable to the representative body. It is not difficult to apply the case to our own country. Let it be imagined that at a general election the opposition were to return 500 out of 658 members of the House of Commons, and that the whole policy of the ministry should be condemned, and every Bill introduced by it, rejected by this immense majority. Let it be supposed that the Crown should consider it a point of honour and duty to retain a ministry so condemned and so thwarted; that repeated dissolutions should in no way increase, but should even diminish, the ministerial minority, and that the only result which could be obtained by such a development of the force of the opposition were not the slightest change in the policy of the ministry, not the removal of a single minister, but simply the election of a Speaker of the politics of the majority; and, I think, it will not be difficult to imagine the fate of such a system of government. Yet such was the system, such literally was the course of events in Lower Canada, and such in character, though not quite in degree, was the spectacle exhibited in Upper Canada, and, at one time or another, in every one of the North American Colonies. . . .

The preceding pages have sufficiently pointed out the nature of those evils, to the extensive operation of which, I attribute the various practical grievances, and the present unsatisfactory condition of the North American Colonies. It is not by weakening, but strengthening the influence of the people on its Government; by confining within much narrower bounds than those hitherto allotted to it, and not by extending the interference of the imperial authorities in the details of colonial affairs, that I believe that harmony is to be restored, where dissension has so long prevailed; and a regularity and vigour hitherto unknown, introduced into the administration of these Provinces. It needs no change in the principles of government, no invention of a new constitutional theory, to supply the remedy which would, in my opinion, completely remove the existing political disorders. It needs but to follow out consistently the principles of the British constitution, and introduce into the Government of these great Colonies those wise provisions, by which alone the working of the representative system can in any country be rendered harmonious and efficient. We are not now to consider the policy of establishing representative government in the North American Colonies. That has been irrevocably done; and the experiment of depriving the people of their present constitutional power, is not to be thought of. To conduct their Government harmoniously, in accordance with its established principles, is now the business of its rulers; and I know not how it is possible to secure that harmony in any other way, than by administering the Government on those principles which have been found perfectly efficacious in Great Britain. . . .

I know that it has been urged that the principles, which are productive of harmony and good government in the mother country, are by no means applicable to a colonial dependency. It is said that it is necessary that the administration of a colony should be carried on by persons nominated without any reference to the wishes of its people; that they have to carry into effect the policy, not of that people, but of the authorities at home; and that a colony which should name all its own administrative functionaries, would, in fact, cease to be dependent. I admit that the system which I propose would, in fact, place the internal government of the colony in the hands of the colonists themselves; and that we should thus leave to them the execution of the laws, of which we have long entrusted the making solely to them. Perfectly aware of the value of our colonial possessions, and strongly impressed with the necessity of maintaining our connexion with them, I know not in what respect it can be desirable that we should interfere with their internal legislation in matters which do not affect their relations with the mother country. The matters, which so concern us, are very few. The constitution of the form of government,— the regulation of foreign relations, and of trade with the mother country, the other British Colonies, and foreign nations,—and the disposal of the public lands, are the only points on which the mother country requires a control. This control is now sufficiently secured by the authority of the Imperial Legislature; by the protection which the Colony derives from us against foreign enemies; by the beneficial terms which our laws secure to its trade; and by its share of the reciprocal benefits which would be conferred by a wise system of colonization. A perfect subordination, on the part of the Colony, on these points, is secured by the advantages which it finds in the continuance of its connexion with the Empire. It certainly is not strengthened, but greatly weakened, by a vexatious interference on the part of the Home Government, with the enactment of laws for regulating the internal concerns of the Colony, or in the selection of the persons entrusted with their execution. The colonists may not always know what laws are best for them, or which of their countrymen are the fittest for conducting their affairs; but, at least, they have a greater interest in coming to a right judgement on these points, and will take greater pains to do so, than those whose welfare is very remotely and slightly affected by the good or bad legislation of these portions of the Empire. If the colonists make bad laws, and select improper persons to conduct their affairs, they will generally be the only, always the greatest, sufferers; and, like the people of other countries, they must bear the ills which they bring on themselves, until they choose to apply the remedy. . . .

My own observation convinces me, that the predominant feeling of all the English population of the North American Colonies is that of devoted attachment to the mother country. . . . The attachment constantly exhibited by the people of these Provinces towards the British Crown and Empire has all the characteristics of a strong national feeling. They value the institutions of their country, not merely from a sense of the practical advantages which they confer, but from sentiments of national pride; and they uphold them the more, because they are accustomed to view them as marks of nationality, which distinguish them from their Republican neighbours. I do not mean to affirm that this is a feeling which no impolicy on the part of the mother country will be unable to impair; but I do most confidently regard it as one which may, if rightly appreciated, be made the link of an enduring and advantageous connexion. The British people of the North American Colonies are a people on whom we may safely rely, and to whom we must not grudge power. For it is not to the individuals who have been loudest in demanding the change, that I propose to concede the responsibility of the Colonial administration, but to the people themselves.

94

Lord Palmerston, Speech in Commons (1850). The Don Pacifico Affair

Britain reached the apex of her world power in the 50 years following the Congress of Vienna, a power based on industrial leadership, naval and imperial supremacy, and the relative political stability and self-confidence of her people. The man best symbolizing this preeminence was Henry John Temple, third Earl Palmerston (1784–1865). Palmerston, a man of great

SOURCE. *Hansard's Parliamentary Debates,* Third Series, CXII, 380–381, 383, 394–397, 443–444.

political ability, was the Tory secretary-at-war from 1809–1828, the Whig foreign secretary throughout the 1830s and from 1846 to 1851, and finally prime minister from 1855 to 1858 and again from 1859 to 1865. Unlike some patrician statesmen, he was loved by the public. Cartoonists often portrayed "Pam" with a straw in his mouth, symbolic of his devil-may-care attitude, which led him in 1840 at the age of 56 to attempt, unsuccessfully, to seduce one of the Queen's ladies-in-waiting.

Palmerston's foreign policy reflected his life-style; it was arrogant, unpredictable, and often controversial. Specifically, his use of gunboat diplomacy to protect Englishmen in foreign countries was the subject of much debate. To foreign governments and to his critics at home, Pam was the image of the "Ugly Englishman" of the nineteenth century, a meddlesome, overbearing bully. His admirers, however, saw him as John Bull, ever ready to defend a British subject in his just quarrel with a foreign government. As for his being a bully, Palmerston denied it, arguing that nations could not escape responsibility for their actions simply because they were small and poor: "The weaker a government is, the more inexcusable becomes its insolence or injustice."

Palmerston's greatest speech, reproduced below, was on the Don Pacifico affair, the reaction to which threatened his entire approach to diplomacy. Palmerston's aggressive attempts to collect from the Greek government damages for Don Pacifico, a Portuguese Jew born at Gibraltar, whose house in Athens had been burned by a mob in 1847, created grave diplomatic problems for England. When in 1850 France withdrew her ambassador from London in protest, the House of Lords voted censure on Palmerston for his handling of the dispute. Palmerston was forced to accept a reduced settlement for Pacifico and offer his resignation to a shaken prime minister, Lord John Russell. Russell, hoping to salvage British prestige as well as his foreign secretary, arranged for a vote of confidence in the House of Commons, thus giving Palmerston a chance to defend himself. Palmerston spoke on June 25, 1850, the second night of this dramatic four-day debate. Rising to speak at 9:45 in the evening, he concluded his moving, impromptu oration four and one-half hours later at 2:20 in the morning to prolonged cheers. The speech, particularly the last portion appealing to British patriotism to vindicate his actions, clinched his greatest parliamentary triumph. Winning a vote of 310 to 264, Palmerston not only saved his career, but added luster to a reputation that was fast becoming a legend.

When I say that this is an important question, I say it in the fullest expression of the term. It is a matter which concerns not merely the tenure of office by one individual, or even by a Government; it is a question that involves principles of national policy, and the deepest interests as well as the honour and dignity of England. . . .

Now, the resolution of the House of Lords involves the future as well as the past. It lays down for the future a principle of national policy, which I consider totally incompatible with the interests, with the rights, with the honour, and with the dignity of the country; and at variance with the practice, not only of this, but of all other civilised countries in the world. . . . The country is told that British subjects in foreign lands are entitled—for that is the meaning of the resolution—to nothing but the protection of the laws and the tribunals of the land in which they happen to reside. The country is told that British subjects abroad must not look to their own country for protection, but must trust to that indifferent justice which they may happen to receive at the hands of the Government and tribunals of the country in which they may be. . . .

I say, then, that our doctrine is, that, in the first instance, redress should be sought from the law courts of the country; but that in cases where redress cannot be so had—and those cases are many—to confine a British subject to that remedy only, would be to deprive him of the protection which he is entitled to receive.

Then the question arises, how does this rule apply to the demands we have made upon Greece? . . .

Then we come to the claim of M. Pacifico—a claim which has been the subject of much unworthy comment. . . . I don't care what M. Pacifico's character is. I do not, and cannot admit, that because a man may have acted amiss on some other occasion, and in some other matter, he is to be wronged with impunity by others.

The rights of a man depend on the merits of the particular case; and it is an abuse of argument to say, that you are not to give redress to a man, because in some former transaction he may have done something which is questionable. Punish him if you will—punish him if he is guilty, but don't pursue him as a Pariah through life.

What happened in this case? In the middle of the town of Athens, in a house . . . —a house as good as the generality of those which existed in Athens before the Sovereign ascended the throne—M. Pacifico, living in this house, within forty yards of the great street, within a few minutes' walk of a guardhouse, where soldiers were stationed, was attacked by a mob. Fearing injury, when the mob began to assemble, he sent an intimation to the British Minister, who immediately informed the authorities. Application was made to the Greek Government for protection. No protection was afforded. The mob, in which were soldiers and gens-d'armes, who, even if officers were not with them, ought, from a sense of duty, to have interfered and to have prevented plunder—that mob, headed by the sons of the Minister of War, not children of eight or ten years old, but older—that mob, for nearly two hours, employed themselves in gutting the house of an unoffending man, carrying away or destroying every single thing the house contained, and left it a perfect wreck.

Is not that a case in which a man is entitled to redress from somebody? I venture to think it is. . . .

The Greek Government having neglected to give the protection they were bound to extend, and having abstained from taking means to afford redress, this was a case in which we were justified in calling on the Greek Government for compensation for the losses, whatever they might be, which M. Pacifico had suffered. I think that claim was founded in justice. The amount we did not pretend to fix. If the Greek Government had admitted the principle of the claim, and had objected to the account sent in by M. Pacifico—if they had said, "This is too much, and we think a less sum sufficient," that would have been a question open to discussion. . . . But the Greek Government denied altogether the principle of the claim. . . .

M. Pacifico having, from year to year, been treated either with answers wholly unsatisfactory, or with a positive refusal, or with pertinacious silence, it came at last to this, either that his demand was to be abandoned altogether, or that, in pursuance of the notice we had given the Greek Government a year or two before, we were to proceed to use our own means of enforcing the claim. . . .

Well, then, was there anything so uncourteous in sending, to back our demands, a force which should make it manifest to all the world that resistance was out of the question? Why, it seems to me, on the contrary, that it was more consistent with the honour and dignity of the Government on whom we made those demands, that there should be placed before their eyes a force, which it would be vain to resist, and before which it would be no indignity to yield. . . .

I believe I have now gone through all the heads of the charges which have been brought against me in this debate. I think I have shown that the foreign policy of the Government, in all the transactions with respect to which its conduct has been impugned, has throughout been guided by those principles which . . . ought to regulate the conduct of the Government of England in the management of our foreign affairs. I believe that the principles on which we have acted are those which are held by the great mass of the people of this country. I am convinced these principles are calculated, so far as the influence of England may properly be exercised with respect to the destinies of other countries, to conduce to the maintenance of peace, to the advancement of civilization, to the welfare and happiness of mankind. . . .

While we have seen . . . the political earthquake rocking Europe from side to side—while we have seen thrones shaken, shattered, levelled; institutions overthrown and destroyed—while in almost every country of Europe the conflict of civil war has deluged the land with blood, from the Atlantic to the Black Sea, from the Baltic to the Mediterranean; this country has presented a spectacle honourable to the people of England, and worthy of the admiration of mankind.

We have shown that liberty is compatible with order; that individual freedom is reconcilable with obedience to the law. We have shown the example of a nation, in which every class of society accepts with cheerfulness the lot which Providence has assigned to it; while at the same time every individual of each class is constantly striving to raise himself in the social scale—not by injustice and wrong, not by violence and illegality—but by persevering good conduct, and by the steady and energetic exertion of the moral and intellectual faculties with which his Creator has endowed him. To govern such a people as this, is indeed an object worthy of the ambition of the noblest man who lives in the land; and therefore I find no fault with those who may think any opportunity a fair one, for endeavouring to place themselves in so distinguished and honourable a position. But I contend that we have not in our foreign policy done anything to forfeit the confidence of the country. We may not, perhaps, in this matter or in that, have acted precisely up to the opinions of one person or of another—and hard indeed it is, as we all know by our individual and private experience, to find any number of men agreeing entirely in any matter, on which they may not be equally possessed of the details of the facts, and circumstances, and reasons, and conditions which led to action. But, making allowance for those differences of opinion which may fairly and honourably arise among those who concur in general views, I maintain that the principles which can be traced through all our foreign transactions, as the guiding rule and directing spirit of our proceedings, are such as deserve approbation. I therefore fearlessly challenge the verdict which this House, as representing a political, a commercial, a constitutional country, is to give on the question now brought before it; whether the principles on which the foreign policy of Her Majesty's Government has been conducted, and the sense of duty which has led us to think ourselves bound to afford protection to our fellow subjects abroad, are proper and fitting guides for those who are charged with the Government of England; and whether, as the Roman, in days of old, held himself free from indignity, when he could say *Civis Romanus sum*; so also a British subject, in whatever land he may be, shall feel confident that the watchful eye and the strong arm of England, will protect him against injustice and wrong.

William Howard Russell, Dispatches to *The Times* (1854) The Charge of the Light Brigade

Britain's involvement in the Crimean War (1854–1856), to check Russian expansion against the Turks and potentially against India, proved in the end an embarrassment. It was viewed by many as unnecessary, the product of a series of unforgivable diplomatic blunders. Once begun the war revealed serious defects in the British war machine, especially in supply and medical facilities. Britain suffered 21,000 noncombat deaths in winning the Crimean War. The army was also poorly led, resulting in such glorious disasters as the charge of the Light Brigade described below. The commander-in-chief, Lord Raglan, had lost an arm at Waterloo (1815), and he had seen no combat since. The best that could be said for Lord Cardigan and Lord Lucan, who commanded the cavalry, was that they were gentlemen, both having purchased their commissions and never having been in battle. Cardigan, perhaps the most despised officer in the army, avoided the hardships of war by sleeping on his private yacht on the Black Sea.

The Crimean War was the first campaign fully covered by newspaper reporters, the most famous being William Howard Russell (1820–1907) of *The Times*. Russell's lively reports to *The Times* stirred in the English an admiration for the courage of the suffering British troops, the men of the Light Brigade and "the thin red line," as he described the infantry at Balaclava. His revelations of gross inefficiency in the army also produced outrage and contributed to the fall of the weak Melbourne government in 1855 and, later, to the reform of the civil service and the army. Russell subsequently covered the Indian Mutiny (1857), the American civil war

---

SOURCE. W. H. Russell, *The War: From the Landing at Gallipoli to the Death of Lord Raglan,* London: George Routledge & Co., 1855, pp. 230–232.

(1861–1865), Bismarck's wars (1866–1871), and the British invasion of Egypt (1882). His career, a reflection of a more literate public anxious for news and vicarious excitement, provided a model for such later war correspondents as H. M. Stanley, made famous by his expedition to Africa to find David Livingstone, and Winston Churchill.

And now occurred the melancholy catastrophe which fills us all with sorrow. It appears that the Quartermaster-General, Brigadier Airey, thinking that the Light Cavalry had not gone far enough in front when the enemy's horse had fled, gave an order in writing to Captain Nolan, 15th Hussars, to take to Lord Lucan, directing his Lordship "to advance" his cavalry nearer to the enemy. A braver soldier than Captain Nolan the army did not possess. . . .

Properly led, the British Hussar and Dragoon could in his mind break square, take batteries, ride over columns of infantry, and pierce any other cavalry in the world as if they were made of straw. He thought they had not had the opportunity of doing all that was in their power, and that they had missed even such chances as they had offered to them,—that, in fact, they were in some measure disgraced. A matchless horseman and a first-rate swordsman, he held in contempt, I am afraid, even grape and canister. He rode off with his orders to Lord Lucan. . . .

When Lord Lucan received the order from Captain Nolan, and had read it, he asked, we are told, "Where are we to advance to?" Captain Nolan pointed with his finger to the line of the Russians, and said, "There are the enemy, and there are the guns, sir, before them; it is your duty to take them," or words to that effect, according to the statements made since his death. Lord Lucan, with reluctance, gave the order to Lord Cardigan to advance upon the guns, conceiving that his orders compelled him to do so. The noble Earl, though he did not shrink, also saw the fearful odds against him. . . . It is a maxim of war, that "cavalry never act without a support," that "infantry should be close at hand when cavalry carry guns, as the effect is only instantaneous," and that it is necessary to have on the flank of a line of cavilry some squardons in column, the attack on the flank being most dangerous. The only support our light cavalry had was the reserve of heavy cavalry at a great distance behind them, the infantry and guns being far in the rear. There were no squadrons in column at all, and there was a plain to charge over, before the enemy's guns were reached, of a mile and a half in length.

At ten minutes past eleven, our Light Cavalry brigade advanced. The whole brigade scarcely made one effective regiment, according to the numbers of continental armies; and yet it was more than we could spare. As they rushed towards the front, the Russians opened on them from the guns in the redoubt on the right, with volleys of musketry and rifles. They swept proudly past, glittering in the morning sun in all the pride and splendour of war. We could scarcely believe the evidence of our senses! Surely that handful of men are not going to charge an army in position? Alas! it was but too true—their desperate valour knew no bounds, and far indeed was it removed from its so-called better part—discretion. They advanced in two lines, quickening their pace as they closed towards the enemy. A more fearful spectacle was never witnessed than by those who, without the power to aid, beheld their heroic countrymen rushing to the arms of death. At the distance of 1200 yards the whole line of the enemy belched forth, from thirty iron mouths, a flood of smoke and flame, through which hissed the deadly balls. Their flight was marked by instant gaps in our ranks, by dead men and horses, by steeds flying wounded or riderless across the plain. The first line is broken, it is joined by the second, they never halt or check their speed an instant; with diminished ranks, thinned by those thirty guns, which the Russians had laid with the most deadly accuracy, with a halo of flashing steel above their heads, and with a cheer which was many a noble fellow's death-cry, they flew into the smoke of the batteries, but ere they were lost from view the plain was strewn with their bodies and with the carcasses of horses. They were exposed to an oblique fire from the batteries on the hills on both sides, as well as to a direct fire of musketry. Through the clouds of smoke we could see their sabres flashing as they rode up to the guns and dashed between them, cutting down the gunners as they stood. We saw them riding through the guns, as I have said; to our delight we saw them returning, after breaking through a column of Russian infantry, and scattering them like chaff, when the flank of fire of the battery on the hill swept them down, scattered and broken as they were. Wounded men and dismounted troopers flying towards us told the sad tale—demi-gods could not have done what we had failed to do. At the very moment when they were about to retreat, an enormous mass of Lancers was hurled on their flank. Colonel Shewell, of the 8th Hussars, saw the danger, and rode his few men straight at them, cutting his way through with fearful loss. The other regiments turned and engaged in a desperate encounter. With courage too great almost for credence, they were breaking their way through the columns which enveloped them, when there took place an act of atrocity without parallel in the modern warfare of civilized nations. The Russian gunners, when the storm of cavalry passed, returned to their guns. They saw their own cavalry mingled with the troopers who had just ridden over them, and, to the eternal disgrace of the Russian name, the miscreants poured a murderous volley of grape and canister on the mass of struggling men and horses, mingling friend and foe in one common ruin. It was as much as our Heavy Cavalry brigade could do to cover the retreat of the miserable remnants of that band of heroes as they returned to the place they had so lately quitted in all the pride of life. At thirty-five minutes past eleven not a British soldier, except the dead and dying, was left in front of these bloody Muscovite guns.

96

Anthony Trollope, *The Three Clerks* (1858). The Unreformed Civil Service

Anthony Trollope (1815–1882) had two careers. He was a civil servant, a prominent postal official, and also a popular novelist. His novels, many of the most famous describing life in the imaginary provincial town of Barchester, dealt primarily with the middle class. He emphasized character development and atmosphere rather than action or plot and, partially for that reason, his novels were seen by many later critics as "Victorian," and hence respectable to the point of dullness. When Trollope died in 1882, *The Times* observed that, "It would be rash to prophesy that his work will long be read; most of it lacks some of the qualifications which that stern official who draws up the passports for the Land of Matters Unforgot insists upon." In the short run it was an accurate prediction. The poignancy of Charles Dickens's descriptions of the urban poor and the urbanity of William Makepeace Thackeray's portrayals of the aristocracy never lost their appeal, but Trollope to be again appreciated had to await the twentieth century's rediscovery of the charm and complexity of Victorian England.

SOURCE.   Anthony Trollope, *The Three Clerks,* introduction by W. Teignmouth Shore, London: Oxford University Press, 1907, pp. 10, 12–15. Reprinted by permission of Oxford University Press.

By studying the popular literature of any period, the historian can learn much about the attitudes and interests of the general public. In the case of Trollope, Dickens, and Thackeray, who often satirized or directly attacked the conditions they observed, the historian can gain insight into the problems facing Victorian England. In the selection from *The Three Clerks* (1858), Trollope ridicules in a gentle but effective manner the patronage system of recruitment for the civil service. A decade later, William Ewart Gladstone was to correct this problem by introducing open competition.

The London world, visitors as well as residents, are well acquainted also with Somerset House; and it is moreover tolerably well known that Somerset House is a nest of public offices, which are held to be of less fashionable repute than those situated in the neighbourhood of Downing Street, but are not so decidedly plebeian as the Custom House, Excise, and Post Office.

But there is one branch of the Civil Service located in Somerset House, which has little else to redeem it from the lowest depths of official vulgarity than the ambiguous respectability of its material position. This is the office of the Commissioners of Internal Navigation. The duties to be performed have reference to the preservation of canal banks, the tolls to be levied at locks, and disputes with the Admiralty as to points connected with tidal rivers. The rooms are dull and dark, and saturated with the fog which rises from the river, and their only ornament is here and there some dusty model of an improved barge. Bargees not unfrequently scuffle with hobnailed shoes through the passages, and go in and out, leaving behind them a smell of tobacco, to which the denizens of the place are not unaccustomed. . . .

Charles Tudor, the third of the three clerks alluded to in our title-page, is the son of a clergyman, who has a moderate living on the Welsh border, in Shropshire. Had he known to what sort of work he was sending his son, he might probably have hesitated before he accepted for him a situation in the Internal Navigation Office. He was, however, too happy in getting it to make inquiries as to its nature. We none of us like to look a gift-horse in the mouth. Old Mr. Tudor knew that a clerkship in the Civil Service meant, or should mean, a respectable maintenance for life, and having many young Tudors to maintain himself, he was only too glad to find one of them provided for.

Charley Tudor was some few years younger than his cousin Alaric when he came up to town, and Alaric had at that time some three or four years' experience of London life. The examination at the Internal Navigation was certainly not to be so much dreaded as that at the Weights and Measures; but still there was an examination; and Charley, who had not been the most diligent of schoolboys, approached it with great dread after a preparatory evening passed with the assistance of his cousin and Mr. Norman.

Exactly at ten in the morning he walked into the lobby of his future workshop, and found no one yet there but two aged seedy messengers. He was shown into a waiting-room, and there he remained for a couple of hours, during which every clerk in the establishment came to have a look at him. At last he was ushered into the Secretary's room.

"Ah!" said the Secretary, "your name is Tudor, isn't it?" Charley confessed to the fact. . . .

"And you wish to serve the Queen?" said the Secretary.

Charley, not quite knowing whether this was a joke or not, said that he did. . . .

"The Internal Navigation requires great steadiness, good natural abilities, considerable education, and—and—and no end of application. Come, Mr. Tudor, let us see what you can do." And so saying, Mr. Oldeschole, the Secretary, motioned him to sit down at an office table opposite to himself.

Charley did as he was bid, and took from the hands of his future master an old, much-worn quill pen, with which the great man had been signing minutes.

"Now," said the great man, "just copy the few first sentences of that leading article—either one will do," and he pushed over to him a huge newspaper.

To tell the truth, Charley did not know what a leading article was, and so he sat abashed, staring at the paper.

"Why don't you write?" asked the Secretary.

"Where shall I begin, sir!" stammered poor Charley, looking piteously into the examiner's face.

"God bless my soul! there; either of those leading articles," and leaning over the table, the Secretary pointed to a particular spot.

Hereupon Charley began his task in a large, ugly, round hand, neither that of a man nor of a boy, and set himself to copy the contents of the paper. "The name of Pacifico stinks in the nostril of the British public. It is well known to all the world how sincerely we admire the versitility of Lord Palmerston's genius; how cordially we simpathize with his patriotic energies. But the admiration which even a Palmerston inspires must have a bound, and our simpathy may be called on too far. When we find ourselves asked to pay——." By this time Charles had half covered the half-sheet of foolscap which had been put before him, and here at the word "pay" he unfortunately suffered a large blot of ink to fall on the paper.

"That won't do, Mr. Tudor, that won't do—come, let us look," and stretching over again, the Secretary took up the copy.

"Oh dear! oh dear! this is very bad; versatility with an 'i!'—sympathy with an 'i!' sympathize with an 'i!' Why, Mr. Tudor, you must be very fond of 'i's' down in Shropshire."

Charley looked sheepish, but of course said nothing.

"And I never saw a viler hand in my life. Oh dear, oh dear, I must send you back to Sir Gilbert. Look here, Snape, this will never do—never do for the Internal Navigation, will it?'

Snape, the attendant senior clerk said, as indeed he could not help saying, that the writing was very bad.

"I never saw worse in my life," said the Secretary. "And now, Mr. Tudor, what do you know of arithmetic?"

Charley said that he thought he knew arithmetic pretty well;—"at least some of it," he modestly added.

"Some of it!" said the Secretary, slightly laughing. "Well, I'll tell you what—this don't do at all;" and he took the unfortunate manuscript between his thumb and forefinger. "You had better go home and endeavour to write something a little better than this. Mind, if it is not very much better it won't do. And look here; take care that you do it yourself. If you bring me the writing of any one else, I shall be sure to detect you. I have not any more time now; as to arithmetic, we'll examine you in 'some of it' to-morrow." . . .

He worked thus for an hour before dinner, and then for three hours in the evening, and produced a very legible copy of half a chapter of the "Decline and Fall."

"I didn't think they examined at all at the Navigation," said Norman.

"Well, I believe it's quite a new thing," said Alaric Tudor. "The schoolmaster must be abroad with a vengeance, if he got as far as that."

And then they carefully examined Charley's work, crossed his t's, dotted his i's, saw that his spelling was right, and went to bed.

Again, punctually at ten o'clock, Charley presented himself at the Internal Navigation; and again saw the two seedy old messengers warming themselves at the lobby fire. On this occasion he was kept three hours in the waiting-room, and some of the younger clerks ventured to come and speak to him. At length Mr. Snape appeared, and desired the acolyte to follow him. Charley, supposing that he was again going to the awful Secretary, did so with palpitating heart. But he was led in another direction into a large room, carrying his manuscript neatly rolled in his hand. Here Mr. Snape introduced him to five other occupants of the chamber; he, Mr. Snape himself, having a separate desk there, being, in official parlance, the head of the room. Charley was told to take a seat at a desk, and did so, still thinking that the dread hour of his examination was soon to come. His examination, however, was begun and over. No one ever asked for his calligraphic manuscript, and as to his arithmetic, it may be presumed that his assurance that he knew "some of it," was deemed to be adequate evidence of sufficient capacity. And in this manner, Charley Tudor became one of the Infernal Navvies.

97

Samuel Smiles, *Self Help* (1859)

Samuel Smiles (1812–1904) is best remembered today as the author of *Self Help*, one of the most influencial and popular books of the Victorian period. *Self Help*, together with *Character* (1871), *Thrift* (1875), *Duty* (1880), and *Life and Labour* (1887), made Smiles the apostle of individual effort as the key to national progress, a position similar to that of Horatio Alger in the United States.

Smiles's popularity resulted from a number of factors. His message of self-reliance was congenial to the general laissez-faire atmosphere of the mid-nineteenth century. His forceful, pithy style was attractive to many readers. Finally, his examples of success, courage, and perseverance—such as the story of the conduct of the men aboard the sinking *Birkenhead*—were often drawn from English history and thus appealed to the national pride of his audience.

Smiles has certainly never lacked critics. As early as the 1880s socialists condemned him as an apologist for middle class values and an obstacle to meaningful reform. Fairness demands, however, a recognition of Smiles's

SOURCE.   Samuel Smiles, *Self Help with Illustrations of Conduct and Perseverance*, introduction by Asa Briggs, London: John Murray, 1958, pp. 35–36, 38, 57, 298–299, 360, 377–379. Reprinted by the permission of John Murray (Publishers) Ltd.

interest in and sympathy with the lower classes. As a young man he edited a radical newspaper and supported some of the ideas of Chartism. Although by the time he wrote *Self Help* he had grown doubtful of the ability of government to legislate solutions to social problems, he was never willing to equate personal success with wealth: wealth could easily be a bar to good character—the true index of success, well within the reach of every man.

Self Help with Illustrations of Conduct and Perseverance was originally published in 1859. It has since been reprinted numerous times and translated into several major languages.

"Heaven helps those who help themselves" is a well-tried maxim, embodying in a small compass the results of vast human experience. The spirit of self-help is the root of all genuine growth in the individual; and, exhibited in the lives of many, it constitutes the true source of national vigour and strength. Help from without is often enfeebling in its effects, but help from within invariably invigorates. Whatever is done *for* men or classes, to a certain extent takes away the stimulus and necessity of doing for themselves; and where men are subjected to over-guidance and over-government, the inevitable tendency is to render them comparatively helpless. . . .

The Government of a nation itself is usually found to be but the reflex of the individuals composing it. The Government that is ahead of the people will inevitably be dragged down to their level, as the Government that is behind them will in the long run be dragged up. In the order of nature, the collective character of a nation will as surely find its befitting results in its law and government, as water finds its own level. The noble people will be nobly ruled, and the ignorant and corrupt ignobly. Indeed, all experience serves to prove that the worth and strength of a State depend far less upon the form of its institutions than upon the character of its men. For the nation is only an aggregate of individual conditions, and civilization itself is but a question of the personal improvement of the men, women, and children of whom society is composed.

National progress is the sum of individual industry, energy, and uprightness, as national decay is of individual idleness, selfishness and vice. What we are accustomed to decry as great social evils, will, for the most part, be found to be but the outgrowth of man's own perverted life; and though we may endeavour to cut them down and extirpate them by means of Law, they will only spring up again with fresh luxuriance in some other form, unless the condition of personal life and character are radically improved. If this view be correct, then it follows that the highest patriotism and philanthropy consist, not so much in altering laws and modifying institutions, as in helping and stimulating men to elevate and improve themselves by their own free and independent individual action. . . .

The spirit of self-help, as exhibited in the energetic action of individuals, has in all times been a marked feature in the English character, and furnishes the true measure of our power as a nation. . . .

In fine, human character is moulded by a thousand subtle influences; by example and precept; by life and literature; by friends and neighbours; by the world we live in as well as by the spirits of our forefathers, whose legacy of good words and deeds we inherit. But great, unquestionably, though these influences are acknowledged to be, it is nevertheless equally clear that men must necessarily be the active agents of their own well-being and well-doing; and that, however much the wise and the good may owe to others, they themselves must in the very nature of things be their own best helpers. . . .

Worldly success, measured by the accumulation of money, is no doubt a very dazzling thing; and all men are naturally more or less the admirers of worldly success. But though men of persevering, sharp, dexterous, and unscrupulous habits, ever on the watch to push opportunities, may and do "get on" in the world, yet it is quite possible that they may not possess the slightest elevation of character, nor a particle of real goodness. He who recognizes no higher logic than that of the shilling, may become a very rich man, and yet remain all the while an exceedingly poor creature. For riches are no proof whatever of moral worth; and their glitter often serves only to draw attention to the worthlessness of their possessor, as the light of the glow-worm reveals the grub.

The manner in which many allow themselves to be sacrificed to their love of wealth reminds one of the cupidity of the monkey—that caricature of our species. In Algiers, the Kabyle peasant attaches a gourd, well fixed, to a tree, and places within it some rice. The gourd has an opening merely sufficient to admit the monkey's paw. The creature comes to the tree by night, inserts his paw, and grasps his booty. He tries to draw it back, but it is clenched, and he has not the wisdom to unclench it. So there he stands till morning, when he is caught, looking as foolish as may be, though with the prize in his grasp. The moral of this little story is capable of a very extensive application in life. . . .

Riches are oftener an impediment than a stimulus to action; and in many cases they are quite as much a misfortune as a blessing. The youth who inherits wealth is apt to have life made too easy for him, and he soon grows sated with it, because he has nothing left to desire. Having no special object to struggle for, he finds time hang heavy on his hands; he remains morally and spiritually asleep; and his position in society is often no higher than that of a polypus over which the tide floats. . . .

Character is human nature in its best form. It is moral order embodied in the individual. Men of character are not only the conscience of society, but in every well-governed State they are its best motive power; for it is moral qualities in the main which rule the world. . . .

Notwithstanding the wail which we occasionally hear for the chivalry that is gone, our own age has witnessed deeds of bravery and gentleness— of heroic self-denial and manly tenderness—which are unsurpassed in history. The events of the last few years have shown that our countrymen are as yet an undegenerate race. . . .

The wreck of the *Birkenhead* off the coast of Africa on February 27th, 1852, affords another memorable illustration of the chivalrous spirit of common men acting in this nineteenth century, of which any age might be proud. The vessel was steaming along the African coast with 472 men and 166 women and children on board. The men belonged to several regiments then serving at the Cape, and consisted principally of recruits who had been only a short time in the service. At two o'clock in the morning, while all were asleep below, the ship struck with violence upon a hidden rock, which penetrated her bottom; and it was at once felt that she must go down. The roll of the drums called the soldiers to arms on the upper deck, and the men mustered as if on parade. The word was passed to *save the women and children;* and the helpless creatures were brought from below, mostly undressed, and handed silently into the boats. When they had all left the ship's side, the commander of the vessel thoughtlessly called out, "All those that can swim, jump overboard and make for the boats." But Captain Wright, of the 91st Highlanders, said, "No! if you do that, *the boats with the women must be swamped";* and the brave men stood motionless. There was no boat remaining, and no hope of safety; but not a heart quailed; no one flinched from his duty in that trying moment. "There was not a murmur nor a cry amongst them," said Captain Wright, a survivor, "until the vessel made her final plunge." Down went the ship, and down went the heroic band, firing a *feu de joie* as they sank beneath the waves. Glory and honour to the gentle and the brave. The examples of such men can never die, but, like their memories, are immortal.

Charles Darwin, *On the Origin of Species* (1859). The Theory of Evolution

Charles Darwin (1809–1882), intending first to be a physician and then a clergyman, found his vocation when he was invited to become the naturalist aboard the exporer ship, H.M.S. *Beagle.* From 1830 to 1836, he collected and compared specimens found along the coast of South America and on the adjacent islands, particularly the Galápagus Islands. As he moved from north to south and from mainland to island or from one island to another the variations in his specimens argued increasingly for some form of biological evolution. The mechanism by which evolution operated remained, however, a mystery. It was not until 1838 that Thomas Malthus's *Essay on Population* gave him the idea of the "struggle for existence." "It at once struck me," he wrote, "that under these circumstances favourable variations would tend to be preserved and unfavourable ones to be destroyed. The result would be the formation of a new species. Here then I had at last got a theory by which to work." In 1859, after 20 years of observation and study, and after learning that another naturalist, Alfred Russel Wallace, had arrived at an identical conclusion, Darwin published *On the Origin of Species by Means of Natural Selection or the Preservation of Favoured Races in the Struggle for Life.*

His concluding paragraphs, reproduced below, summarize his theory that "Natural Selection" is a result of the "Struggle for Life," his confidence that things "will tend to progress toward perfection," and his belief that his

SOURCE. Charles Darwin, *On the Origin of Species: A Facsimile of the First Edition,* introduction by Ernst Mayr, New York: Atheneum, 1967, pp. 488–490. Reprinted by permission of Harvard University Press.

theory "accords better with what we know of the laws impressed on matter by the Creator." Just as Sir Isaac Newton (1642–1727) had taken the mystery out of the mechanical operation of the universe by formulating the universal laws of gravity, so Darwin explained how the world, in its present complexity, had evolved by natural means from simple beginnings.

Darwin's book was instantly famous and controversial, the first edition selling out the first day. T. H. Huxley (1825–1895), for his ardent support nicknamed "Darwin's Bulldog," on reading the *Origin of Species* said of himself, "How extremely stupid not to have thought of that." In spite of stubborn pockets of resistance, chiefly on religious grounds, some of which still exist, Darwin's theory of evolution by natural selection was an idea whose time had come. Not only did it gain acceptance in scientific circles but, because of its agreement with the ideas of laissez-faire and progress, it accorded well with popular beliefs in many fields. Indeed, rugged indivualism and competition between men and nations seemed by reference to the idea of the "survival of the fittest" to be inevitable and necessary and, with questionable justice to Darwin, came to be summarized by the term "Social Darwinism." It is indisputable that Darwin's *Origin of Species* has been one of the two or three most influencial books of the nineteenth and twentieth centuries.

Authors of the highest eminence seem to be fully satisfied with the view that each species has been independently created. To my mind it accords better with what we know of the laws impressed on matter by the Creator, that the production and extinction of the past and present inhabitants of the world should have been due to secondary causes, like those determining the birth and death of the individual. When I view all beings not as special creations, but as the lineal descendants of some few beings which lived long before the first bed of the Silurian system was deposited, they seem to me to become ennobled. Judging from the past, we may safely infer that not one living species will transmit its unaltered likeness to a distant futurity. And of the species now living very few will transmit progeny of any kind to a far distant futurity; for the manner in which all organic beings are grouped, shows that the greater number of species of each genus, and all the species of many genera, have left no descendants, but have become utterly extinct. We can so far take a prophetic glance into futurity as to foretel that it will be the common and widely-spread species, belonging to the larger and dominant groups, which will ultimately prevail and procreate new and dominant species. As all the living forms of life are the lineal descendants of those which lived long before the Silurian epoch, we may feel certain that the ordinary succession by generation has never once been broken, and that no cataclysm has desolated the whole world. Hence we may look with some confidence to a secure future of equally inappreciable length. And as natural selection works solely by and for the good of each being, all corporeal and mental endowments will tend to progress towards perfection.

It is interesting to contemplate an entangled bank, clothed with many plants of many kinds, with birds singing on the bushes, with various insects flitting about, and with worms crawling through the damp earth, and to reflect that these elaborately constructed forms, so different from each other, and dependent on each other in so complex a manner, have all been produced by laws acting around us. These laws, taken in the largest sense, being Growth with Reproduction; Inheritance which is almost implied by reproduction; Variability from the indirect and direct action of the external conditions of life, and from use and disuse; a Ratio of Increase so high as to lead to a Struggle for Life, and as a consequence to Natural Selection, entailing Divergence of Character and the Extinction of less-improved forms. Thus, from the war of nature, from famine and death, the most exalted object which we are capable of conceiving, namely, the production of the higher animals, directly follows. There is grandeur in this view of life, with its several powers, having been originally breathed into a few forms or into one; and that, whilst this planet has gone cycling on according to the fixed law of gravity, from so simple a beginning endless forms most beautiful and most wonderful have been, and are being, evolved.

99

John Henry Cardinal Newman, *Apologia Pro Vita Sua* (1864). The Oxford Movement

The Oxford Movement began in 1833 as a reaction to the liberal and Evangelical tendencies of England and the Anglican Church. In a series of *Tracts for the Times* (1834–1841), such men as John Henry Newman (1801–1890) and E. B. Pusey (1800–1882) emphasized the historic position of the church as a divine institution, not just a congregation of individual believers, and they urged a return to traditional beliefs and ceremonies. Low-church Evangelicals, to whom these ideas were perilously close to Roman Catholicism, had their worst fears realized in 1841 when Newman, the most attractive and talented of the Oxford group, argued in *Tract* XC that the Thirty-Nine Articles of the Church of England were compatible with Roman Catholicism. His misunderstood objective was to reassure men who were leaning toward Rome that they might safely remain Anglican. In the storm of public controversy that ensued, the *Tracts* were discontinued, and Newman left Oxford under a cloud of suspicion. In 1845, he officially joined, and became a priest in, the Roman Catholic Church.

In 1864, after two decades of personal frustration and practical exile, Newman was provoked to reply to an offhand remark impugning the honesty of the Roman Church and of himself personally. *Apologia Pro Vita Sua: Being a History of his Religious Opinions,* a few passages of which are reproduced below, recounts his attempts to understand his own faith and reveals how he was inevitably led to a break with the Anglican Church and

SOURCE.   John Henry Cardinal Newman, *Apologia Pro Vita Sua: Being a History of His Religious Opinions,* ed. Martin J. Svaglic, pp. 39–40, 54–55, 57, 113, 115, 181, 213. © 1967 Oxford University Press. By permission of The Clarendon Press.

to join that of Rome. The book was immediately recognized, by all but a few anti-Catholic diehards, as a literary masterpiece and a spiritual autobiography of the first magnitude. It brought a better and more sympathetic understanding not only of Newman but of Catholics in general. Catholics were finally readmitted to Oxford in 1871, and six years later Newman was appointed a fellow of Trinity College. Thus, after an absense of more than three decades, he was restored to his beloved university. In 1879 he became a cardinal in the Roman Catholic Church.

The Oxford Movement became, despite Newman's defection, a permanent tendency to restore to the Anglican Church the richness of its Catholic heritage and to emphasize it as well as the tradition of the Protestant Reformation. Newman's humanism, which was so alien to the narrow and beleaguered Catholicism of Pope Pius IX (1846–1878), was more acceptable to Leo XIII (1878–1903) and has been vindicated in the twentieth century by the papacy of John XXIII (1958–1963) and the second Vatican Council (1962–1965). Newman now appears as the outstanding English churchman of the nineteenth century—in importance the counterpart of John Wesley in the eighteenth—noteworthy for his individual talent and attractiveness and for his impact on both of the Christian communions to which he gave his allegiance.

Great events were happening at home and abroad, which brought out into form and passionate expression the various beliefs which had so gradually been winning their way into my mind. Shortly before, there had been a Revolution in France; the Bourbons had been dismissed: and I held that it was unchristian for nations to cast off their governors, and, much more, sovereigns who had the divine right of inheritance. Again, the great Reform Agitation was going on around me as I wrote. The Whigs had come into power; Lord Grey had told the Bishops to set their house in order, and some of the Prelates had been insulted and threatened in the streets of London. The vital question was, how were we to keep the Church from being liberalized? . . . I felt affection for my own Church, but not tenderness; I felt dismay at her prospects, anger and scorn at her do-nothing perplexity. I thought that if Liberalism once got a footing within her, it was sure of the victory in the event. I saw that Reformation principles were powerless to rescue her. As to leaving her, the thought never crossed my imagination; still I ever kept before me that there was something greater than the Established Church, and that that was the Church Catholic and

Apostolic, set up from the beginning, of which she was but the local presence and the organ. She was nothing, unless she was this. She must be dealt with strongly, or she would be lost. There was need for a second reformation. . . .

I have spoken of my firm confidence in my position; and now let me state more definitely what the position was which I took up, and the propositions about which I was so confident. These were three:—

1. First was the principle of dogma: my battle was with liberalism; by liberalism I mean the anti-dogmatic principle and its developments. This was the first point on which I was certain. . . . Under this first head I have the satisfaction of feeling that I have nothing to retract, and nothing to repent of. The main principle of the movement is as dear to me now, as it ever was. I have changed in many things: in this I have not. From the age of fifteen, dogma has been the fundamental principle of my religion: I know no other religion; I cannot enter into the idea of any other sort of religion; religion, as a mere sentiment, is to me a dream and a mockery. As well can there be filial love without the fact of a father, as devotion without the fact of a Supreme Being. What I held in 1816, I held in 1833, and I hold in 1864. Please God, I shall hold it to the end. . . .

2. Secondly, I was confident in the truth of a certain definite religious teaching, based upon this foundation of dogma; viz. that there was a visible Church, with sacraments and rites which are the channels of invisible grace. I thought that this was the doctrine of Scripture, of the early Church, and of the Anglican Church. Here again, I have not changed in opinion; I am as certain now on this point as I was in 1833, and have never ceased to be certain. . . .

3. But now, as to the third point on which I stood in 1833, and which I have utterly renounced and trampled upon since,—my then view of the Church of Rome;—I will speak about it as exactly as I can. When I was young, as I have said already, and after I was grown up, I thought the Pope to be Antichrist. . . . From my boyhood and in 1824 I considered, after Protestant authorities, that St. Gregory I. about A.D. 600 was the first Pope that was Antichrist, though, in spite of this, he was also a great and holy man; but in 1832–3 I thought the Church of Rome was bound up with the cause of Antichrist by the Council of Trent. When it was that in my deliberate judgment I gave up the notion altogether in any shape, that some special reproach was attached to her name, I cannot tell; but I had a shrinking from renouncing it, even when my reason so ordered me, from a sort of conscience or preju-dice, I think up to 1843. . . .

I had no longer a distinctive plea for Anglicanism. . . . I had, most painfully, to fall back upon my three original points of belief, which I have spoken so much of in a former passage,—the principle of dogma, the sacramental system, and anti-Romanism. Of these three, the first two were better secured in Rome than in the Anglican Church. The Apostolical Succession, the two prominent sacraments, and the primitive Creeds, belonged, indeed, to the latter; but there had been and was far less strictness on matters of dogma and ritual in the Anglican system than in the Roman: in consequence, my main argument for the Anglican claims lay in the positive and special charges, which I could bring against Rome. I had no positive Anglican theory. . . .

I underwent a great change of opinion. I saw that, from the nature of the case, the true Vicar of Christ must ever to the world seem like Antichrist, and be stigmatized as such, because a resemblance must ever exist between an original and a forgery; and thus the fact of such a calumny was almost one of the notes of the Church. . . .

I have nothing more to say on the subject of the change in my religious opinions. On the one hand I came gradually to see that the Anglican Church was formally in the wrong, on the other that the Church of Rome was formally in the right; then, that no valid reasons could be assigned for continuing in the Anglican, and again that no valid objections could be taken to joining the Roman. . . .

I took leave of my first College, Trinity, which was so dear to me, and which held on its foundation so many who had been kind to me both when I was a boy, and all through my Oxford life. Trinity had never been unkind to me. There used to be much snap-dragon growing on the walls opposite my freshman's rooms there, and I had for years taken it as the emblem of my own perpetual residence even unto death in my University.

On the morning of the 23rd I left the Observatory. I have never seen Oxford since, excepting its spires, as they are seen from the railway.

100

Walter Bagehot, *The English Constitution* (1867). England on the Eve of Democracy

Walter Bagehot (1826–1877) was a prosperous member of the middle class, a banker and businessman, and probably the foremost journalist of his day. In 1855, he became a joint editor of the *National Review* and, in 1860, the editor of *The Economist,* a postion he held until his death. His most famous works include *Lombard Street* (1873), a pioneering study of central banking, and *The English Constitution* (1867), which first appeared as a series of articles in *Fortnightly Review* in 1865 and 1866.

Bagehot's book is the classic description of the nineteenth-century English constitution. Like Jeremy Bentham, Bagehot detected the disparity between the fictions that people believed and the conditions of things as they really were, but unlike the Utilitarians he saw the value of both. The "dignified parts of government" gave it "its motive power." Primary among these parts were the monarchy, the House of Lords, and the old belief in a separation of powers between the executive and the legislature. The "efficient parts" enabled the government to "employ that power." Most important was the cabinet, the "connecting link" that joined the dignified and efficient parts together and gave the British government its remarkable strength. What Bagehot describes below is the system of responsible government that had evolved during the eighteenth century and had been amplified by the Great Reform Act in 1832. Essential to the working of this English constitution was the deferential character of the mass of the English people, their willingness to allow their betters, the landed aristocracy and the upper middle class, to rule on their behalf.

SOURCE. Walter Bagehot, *The English Constitution,* Garden City, N. Y.: Dolphin Books, Doubleday & Company, Inc., n.d., pp. 63–64, 68–73.

It is noteworthy that Bagehot wrote on the eve of the second reform bill, the Representation of the People Act of 1867, by which Benjamin Disraeli joyfully "dished the Whigs." By joining forces with the radicals he gave the British working class a share of the electorate and took the first large step, a "leap in the dark," toward Britain's becoming a democracy. Bagehot, a middle class liberal, not a democrat, wrote in his book's second edition in 1872 a long introduction explaining the new dangers of political leaders bidding against each other for popular support. He was certainly correct in seeing the passing of the British constitution as he knew it. With the rise of highly structured and disciplined political parties, made necessary by a democratic electorate, and with the resulting power now wielded by the prime minister, the House of Commons and the cabinet have since gone some distance in joining the monarch and the House of Lords as dignified rather than efficient parts of the government.

No one can approach to an understanding of the English institutions, or of others which, being the growth of many centuries, exercise a wide sway over mixed populations, unless he divide them into two classes. In such constitutions there are two parts (not indeed separable with microscopic accuracy, for the genius of great affairs abhors nicety of division): first, those which excite and preserve the reverence of the population—the *dignified* parts, if I may so call them; and next, the *efficient* parts—those by which it, in fact, works and rules. There are two great objects which every constitution must attain to be successful, which every old and celebrated one must have wonderfully achieved: every constitution must first *gain* authority, and then *use* authority; it must first win the loyalty and confidence of mankind, and then employ that homage in the work of government. . . .

The dignified parts of government are those which bring it force—which attract its motive power. The efficient parts only employ that power. . . .

The brief description of the characteristic merit of the English Constitution is, that its dignified parts are very complicated and somewhat imposing, very old and rather venerable; while its efficient part, at least when in great and critical action, is decidedly simple and rather modern. We have made, or rather stumbled on, a constitution which—though full of every species of incidental defect, though of the worst *workmanship* in all out-of-the-way matters of any constitution in the world—yet has two capital merits: it contains a simple efficient part which, on occasion, and when wanted, *can* work more simply and easily, and better, than any instrument of government that has yet been tried; and it contains likewise historical, complex, august, theatrical parts, which it has inherited from a long past—which *take* the multitude—which guide by an insensible but an omnipotent influence the associations of its subjects. Its essence is strong with the strength of modern simplicity; its exterior is august with the Gothic grandeur of a more imposing age. Its simple essence may, *mutatis mutandis,* be transplanted to many very various countries, but its august outside—what most men think it is—is narrowly confined to nations with an analogous history and similar political materials.

The efficient secret of the English Constitution may be described as the close union, the nearly complete fusion, of the executive and legislative powers. No doubt by the traditional theory, as it exists in all the books, the goodness of our constitution consists in the entire separation of the legislative and executive authorities, but in truth its merit consists in their singular approximation. The connecting link is *the cabinet.* By that new word we mean a committee of the legislative body selected to be the executive body. The legislature has many committees, but this is the greatest. It chooses for this, its main committee, the men in whom it has most confidence. It does not, it is true, choose them directly; but it is nearly omnipotent in choosing them indirectly. A century ago the Crown had a real choice of ministers, though it had no longer a choice in policy. During the long reign of Sir R. Walpole he was obliged not only to manage parliament, but to manage the palace. He was obliged to take care that some court intrigue did not expel him from his place. The nation then selected the English policy, but the Crown chose the English ministers. They were not only in name, as now, but in fact, the Queen's servants. Remnants, important remnants, of this great prerogative still remain. The discriminating favour of William IV made Lord Melbourne head of the Whig party when he was only one of several rivals. At the death of Lord Palmerston it is very likely that the Queen may have the opportunity of freely choosing between two, if not three statesmen. But, as a rule, the nominal prime minister is chosen by the legislature, and the real prime minister for most purposes—the leader of the House of Commons—almost without exception is so. There is nearly always some one man plainly selected by the voice of the predominant party in the predominant house of the legislature to head that party, and consequently to rule the nation. We have in England an elective first magistrate as truly as the Americans have an elective first magistrate. The Queen is only at the head of the dignified part of the constitution. The prime minister is at the head of the efficient part. The Crown is, according to the saying, the "fountain of honour"; but the Treasury is the spring of business. Nevertheless our first magistrate differs from the American. He is not elected directly by the people; he is elected by the representative of the people. He is an example of "double election." The legislature chosen, in name, to make laws, in fact finds its principal business in making and in keeping an executive. . . .

The cabinet, in a word, is a board of control chosen by the legislature, out of persons whom it trusts and knows, to rule the nation. The particular mode in which the English ministers are selected; the fiction that they are, in any political sense, the Queen's servants; the rule which limits the choice of the cabinet to the members of the legislature—are accidents unessential to its definition—historical incidents separable from its nature. Its characteristic is that it should be chosen by the legislature out of persons agreeable to and trusted by the legislature. Naturally these are principally its own members—but they need not be exclusively so. A cabinet which included persons not members of the legislative assembly might still perform all useful duties. Indeed the Peers, who constitute a large element in modern cabinets are members, nowadays, only of a subordinate assembly. The House of Lords still exercises several useful functions; but the ruling influence—the deciding faculty—has passed to what, using the language of old times, we still call the lower house—to an assembly which, though inferior as a dignified institution, is superior as an efficient institution. A principal advantage of the House of Lords in the present age indeed consists in its thus acting as a *reservoir* of cabinet ministers. Unless the composition of the House of Commons were improved, or unless the rules requiring cabinet ministers to be members of the legislature were relaxed, it would undoubtedly be difficult to find without the Lords, a sufficient supply of chief ministers. But the detail of the composition of a cabinet, and the precise method of its choice, are not to the purpose now. The first and cardinal consideration is the definition of a cabinet. We must not bewilder ourselves with the inseparable accidents until we know the necessary essence. A cabinet is a combining committee—a *hyphen* which joins, a *buckle* which fastens, the legislative part of the state to the executive part of the state. In its origin it belongs to the one, in its functions it belongs to the other. . . .

But a cabinet, though it is a committee of the legislative assembly, is a committee with a power which no assembly would—unless for historical accidents, and after happy experience—have been persuaded to entrust to any committee. It is a committee which can dissolve the assembly which appointed it; it is a committee with a suspensive veto—a committee with a power of appeal. Though appointed by one parliament, it can appeal if it chooses to the next. Theoretically, indeed, the power to dissolve parliament is entrusted to the sovereign only; and there are vestiges of doubt whether in *all* cases a sovereign is bound to dissolve parliament when the cabinet asks him to do so. But neglecting such small and dubious exceptions, the cabinet which was chosen by one House of Commons has an appeal to the next House of Commons. The chief committee of the legislature has the power of dissolving a predominant part of that legisture—that which at a crisis is the supreme legislature. The English system, therefore, is not an absorption of the executive power by the legislative power; it is a fusion of the two. Either the cabinet legislates and acts, or else it can dissolve. It is a creature, but it has the power of destroying its creators. It is an executive which can annihilate the legislature, as well as an executive which is the nominee of the legislature. It *was* made, but it *can* unmake; it was derivative in its origin, but it is destructive in its action.

101

Queen Victoria, Letters to Gladstone (1870-1886). The Nineteenth-Century Monarchy

Two dominant figures of the late nineteenth century were Victoria (1819–1901), Queen of England from 1837 to 1901, and William Ewart Gladstone (1809–1898), four times Liberal prime minister: 1868–1874, 1880–1885, 1886, 1892–1894. Although their official positions brought them into personal contact for half a century, their association was seldom cordial. Following the death of Prince Albert in 1861, Victoria was a lonely woman needing affec-

SOURCE.   Philip Guedalla, *The Queen and Mr. Gladstone*, 2 vols., London: Hodder & Stoughton, Ltd., 1933, I, 218, 227–228; II, 90, 161, 220, 273–274, 286, 405.

tion and understanding; the aloof, unbending Gladstone could provide neither. Instead of flattering the queen and seeming to seek her advice as Disraeli did, Gladstone lectured her on all manner of things, including her duties as monarch. The difficulty was also in part political. As Gladstone aged he became, at least to the queen, increasingly radical, attacking the House of Lords, advocating home rule for Ireland, and proposing social and political reforms. Victoria in 1880 was so upset with "the Peoples' William" that she considered abdicating rather than accepting as her prime minister "that *half-mad fire-brand.*"

Gladstone and Victoria also differed on the function of monarchy in Britain. As Walter Bagehot observed in 1867, the English constitution was divided into two parts—the "dignified," headed by the queen, and the "efficient," headed by her prime minister. Victoria had no intention of being a "dignified" rubber stamp, particularly for Gladstone. Albert had taught her the virtues of hard work; she spent long hours each day familiarizing herself with the details of government policy, expecting to be consulted on the major decisions taken by "her" ministers. Gladstone had a radically different view of her duties. Following one of many royal complaints involving political appointments, Gladstone exploded: "I think this intolerable. It is by courtesy only that these appointments are made known to H. M." To Gladstone, monarchy was a revered and valuable part of the constitution, but its usefulness was symbolic. He frequently urged Victoria to become more visible to the public, performing such public functions as opening parliament. Victoria viewed this advice as insulting to a woman of her age and importance. The conflict continued past Gladstone's death in 1898; when Victoria's son, the future Edward VII (1901–1910), agreed to be a pallbearer, Victoria felt compelled to express her displeasure.

Victoria's letters to Gladstone are on permanent loan to the British Museum. The originals of Gladstone's letters to the queen are in the Royal Archives at Windsor Castle.

OSBORNE. *Jan.* 30. 1870.

The Queen has waited till *within* 10 *days* of the Opening of Parliament to give her final decision as to her doing so in person or not. She hardly thinks that Mr. Gladstone *can expect* any decision but what she must give:—viz: that it is *totally out of the question* that the Queen c^{LD} *undertake* it.—

After such repeated severe suffering w^h has weakened & shaken her v^y much & w^h obliges her to take the v^y g^{test} care when she goes out like *sitting backwards* when she drives & covering her face & hands with end-less wraps—besides avoiding excitement & fatigue,—it w^{ld} be *madness* to expose herself to the fatigue of a journey up in this severe weather & to the g^t agitation & excitement of going to open Parl^t & above *all* to the *totally unavoidable* exposure to Cold Drafts & heat.

Till these attacks showed themselves since the 2nd of Jany the Queen had *seriously* intended to try & make the effort of doing so;—tho' this g^t tendency to neuralgia w^h has hung about her for the last year & $\frac{1}{2}$ —but almost incessantly ever since Aug:—made her apprehensive that she might be unable to undertake it.

OSBORNE. *May* 6. 1870.

. . . The circumstances respecting the Bill to give women the same po-sition as men with respect to Parliamentary franchise gives her an oppor-tunity to observe that she had for some time past wished to call Mr. Glad-stone's attention to the mad & utterly demoralizing movement of the present day to place women in the same position as to professions—as *men*;—& amongst others, in the *Medical Line*. . . .

The Queen is a woman herself—& knows what an anomaly her *own* position is:—but that can be reconciled with reason & propriety tho' it is a terribly difficult & trying one. But to tear away all the barriers w^h sur-round a woman, & to propose that they sh^{ld} study with *men*—things w^h c^{ld} not be named before them—certainly not *in a mixed* audience—w^{ld} be to introduce a total disregard of what must be considered as belonging to the rules & principles of morality.

The Queen feels so strongly upon this dangerous & unchristian & un-natural *cry* & movement of "woman's rights,"—in w^h she knows Mr. Glad-stone *agrees*; (as he sent her that excellent Pamphlet by a Lady) that she is most anxious that Mr. Gladstone & others sh^{ld} take some steps to check this alarming danger & to make whatever use they can of her name.

She sends the letters w^h speak for themselves.

Let woman be what God intended; a helpmate for a man—but with totally different duties & vocations.

WINDSOR CASTLE. *April* 27. 1880.

The Queen acknowledges Mr. Gladstone's 2 letters just rec^d. She does not wish to object—if she can, to any persons who he submits to her as Members of the Government but she regrets to *see* the names of such very advanced Radicals as Mr. Chamberlain & Sir C. Dilke. It will alarm moderate Liberals as well as Conservatives & she cannot think will add to the harmony of the Cabinet. Before agreeing to either the Queen w^{ld} wish to feel *sure* that Mr. Chamberlain has never spoken disrespectfully of the Throne or expressed openly Republican principles.—The Queen must also ask, before she consents to Sir C. Dilke's appt to the office of Under Sec^y for Foreign Affairs that he sh^{ld} give a written explanation, or make one in Parlt. on the subject of his very offensive Speeches on the Civil List & Royal family. . . .

BALMORAL CASTLE. *May* 25. 1881.

The Queen has to thank Mr. Gladstone for a very kind letter on the occasion of her now somewhat ancient birthday.

The aff^{te} loyalty of her subjects is vy gratifying to her.—Her constant object, which only increases with years—is the welfare, prosperity, honour & glory of her dear Country.—

But the work & anxiety weigh heavily on her unsustained by the strong arm & loving advice of Him who now 19$\frac{1}{2}$ years ago was taken to a higher & better World!

WINDSOR CASTLE. *Dec*. 12. 1882.

. . . She asked Ld. Hartington to speak to Mr. Gladstone on the subject of the proposed changes in the Gov^t & the addition of Ld Derby & Sir C. Dilke.

The Queen must again refer to the Speeches of Sir C. Dilke w^h though spoken ten years ago, contain statements w^h have never been withdrawn. Mr. Gladstone in then replying lamented his Republican tendencies— & Sir C. Dilke *avowed* his Anti Monachical principles.—

Does he still maintain these views? If so, he *cannot* be a *Minister* in the Govt of a *Monarchy*.

Has he changed his principles? If so, there *can* be *no difficulty* in *avowing* it *publicly*.

BALMORAL CASTLE. *June* 5. 1884.

. . . She cannot alter her *decided* opinion that to put *any* limit to our occupation of Egypt—as vy *fatal* mistake. But to lessen the 5 years *even* —when the state of Egypt is such that one cannot at all foresee any speedy improvement (in wh. case other Powers w^{ld} *inevitably* step in)— w^{ld} be most *shortsighted* & truckling to insolent France, & have the vy worst effect & results.—*One year*—if a g^t object is to be obtained (it might be yielded) but *not more* & the Queen will *not* give *her consent* to it.

How *often & often* on many questions within the last few years have her warnings been disregarded & alas! (when too late) justified!— Let this not happen again now!

WINDSOR CASTLE. *July* 15. 1884.

The Queen thanks Mr. Gladstone for his letter rec^d this mor^g.

She is sorry that she *cannot* agree with him in his opinion of the House of Lords w^h has rendered such important services to the Nation & w^h at this moment is believed to represent the true feeling of the Country. The House of Lords is in no way opposed to the *people.*

The existence of an independent body of men acting solely for the good of the Country & free from the terror w^h forces so many Commoners to vote against their consciences, is an element of strength in the state & a guarantee for its welfare & freedom.—

To protect the Moderate Men from being swamped by extreme partizans as the Peers now desire to do, is an object in which in itself, Mr. Gladstone himself concurs, & the Queen cannot therefore, understand why this legitimate act of theirs is to expose them to the storm which noisy agitators for *their own* ends are preparing to raise against the House of Lords.

Many most useful measures for the benefit of the *people at large,* w^h had taken a long time to pass in the House of Commons, passed the House of Lords at once!

The Queen fears that the passions once roused by an imaginary grievance will not be easily quelled but will threaten the existence of the Monarchy & the stability of the Empire itself!

Those who do not do *all* in their power to prevent such wild & senseless passion from being raised incur a frightful responsibility! . . .

BUCKINGHAM PALACE. *May* 6. 1886.

The Queen is anxious before leaving for Windsor to repeat to Mr. Gladstone what she tried to express but w^h she thinks perhaps she did not do vy clearly—viz: that her silence on the momentous Irish measures which *he* thinks it *his duty* to bring forward—does not imply her *approval* of or *acquiescence in* them.—Like so many of Mr. Gladstone's best friends—& faithful followers—& so many of the best & wisest statesmen, the Queen can *only* see danger to the Empire in the course he is pursuing.

The Queen writes this with pain as she always *wished to be able* to *give* her Prime Minister her *full support,* but it is *impossible* for her to do so, when the Union of the Empire is in danger of disintegration & serious disturbance.

In conclusion she wishes to add that she fully believes that *Mr. Glad-stone* is actuated solely with the belief that he is doing what is best not only for Ireland but for the whole Empire.

102

Punch (1868-1879). The Modern Political Cartoon

Punch, or The London Charivari, born on July 17, 1841, filled the journalistic void between the solid, respectable publications such as *The Times* and the *Edinburgh Review* and the transient, nearly pornographic radical papers so popular in the 1830s. *Punch* sought and found a middle ground, by being critical but also humorous, reforming but never bitter or crude, sophisticated but still attractive to a broad spectrum of the English population. Its title was derived from Punchinello, the humpbacked figure in the Punch and Judy puppet shows, who ostensibly had become the editor of the new weekly. The subtitle, "Charivari," meaning a babel of noise, specifically referred to a popular Parisian magazine that served as a model for *Punch*. In its early years, *Punch* was viewed as a radical, reforming journal. Beginning about 1850, however, it began to shed its partisan biases, becoming by the 1870s a respectable, but still irreverent, middle – class publication. The secret of its success was probably the ability to change and to reflect the dominant attitudes of successive generations, a process that has made *Punch* a national institution.

Perhaps the most famous feature of *Punch* is the cartoon, adopted very early by the editors as a most effective weapon against people and institutions' taking themselves too seriously. Thus was continued an English tradition developed by Hogarth (1697–1764) and George Cruikshank (1792–

SOURCE.   *Punch,* LIV (1868), 51; LXIII (1872), 5; LXXVII (1879), 271; LXXIV (1878), 19; LXXV (1878), 55.

1878). Through its cartoons, *Punch* made familiar such figures as Mrs. Britannia and her daughter, Johnny Bull, Columbia, Dr. Punch and, of course, the British Lion (see document 117). In the cartoons from the Disraeli-Gladstone era, reproduced below, it is apparent that neither political party, nor England itself, was spared the satire that is the stock in trade of the cartoonist. The *Alabama* claims dispute, taken seriously by both Britain and the United States, is ridiculed (Plate A). In the 1870s, both the Conservative program of Disraeli (Plate B) and Gladstone's Liberal platform (Plate C) were regarded with more than a little skepticism. In a more serious vein, Disraeli's eastern policy of 1878 is viewed with considerable apprehension (Plate D). The last cartoon (Plate E) is a plague-on-both-your-houses criticism of the partisanship of Disraeli and Gladstone in the late 1870s. By studying the cartoons of an obviously popular journal, the historian can learn a great deal about how events were viewed by the public. This may be more important than a knowledge of the event itself.

" HOITY-TOITY ! ! ! "

Mrs. Britannia. " HOITY-TOITY ! WHAT'S ALL THIS FUSS ABOUT ! "
Johnny Bull. " IT'S COUSIN COLUMBIA, MA, AND SHE SAYS I BROKE HER SHIPS, AND I DIDN'T—
AND I WANT TO BE FRIENDS—AND SHE'S A CROSS THING—AND WANTS TO HAVE IT ALL HER OWN
WAY ! "

PLATE A
(Punch, February 1, 1868.)

THE CONSERVATIVE PROGRAMME.

"DEPUTATION BELOW, SIR.—WANT TO KNOW THE CONSERVATIVE PROGRAMME."
Rt. Hon. Ben. Diz. "EH!—OH!—AH!—YES!—QUITE SO! TELL THEM, MY GOOD ABERCORN, WITH MY
COMPLIMENTS, THAT WE PROPOSE TO RELY ON THE SUBLIME INSTINCTS OF AN ANCIENT PEOPLE!!"
[See Speech at Crystal Palace.

PLATE B
(Punch, July 6, 1872.)

THE COLOSSUS OF WORDS.

PLATE C
(Punch, December 13, 1879.)

ON THE DIZZY BRINK.

Lord B. "JUST A LEETLE NEARER THE EDGE?"
Britannia. "NOT AN INCH FURTHER. I'M A GOOD DEAL NEARER THAN IS PLEASANT ALREADY!"

PLATE D
(Punch, January 19, 1878.)

A BAD EXAMPLE.

Dr. Punch. "WHAT'S ALL THIS? YOU, THE TWO HEAD BOYS OF THE SCHOOL, THROWING MUD!
YOU OUGHT TO BE ASHAMED OF YOURSELVES!"

PLATE E
(Punch, August 10, 1878.)

103

Benjamin Disraeli, Crystal Palace Speech (1872). The New Imperialism

Benjamin Disraeli, earl of Beaconsfield (1804–1881), prime minister in 1868 and again from 1874 to 1880, is often considered the founder of the modern Conservative party. His entire career was indicative of the political changes produced by the social and political tensions in Victorian England. Born a Jew, Disraeli was distrusted early in life because of his "dandyism," his social and literary indiscretions, and his brilliant but undisciplined oratory. When Sir Robert Peel's free trade policies split the Conservative party in 1846, Disraeli was catapulted to political prominence as the spokesman of the otherwise leaderless country squires. Even then he was an outsider, more tolerated than trusted. It was not until 1868 that he became prime minister or, as he stated, he had "climbed to the top of the greasy pole." Within a year he and the Conservatives were swept from power by the urban classes, recently enfranchised by the Reform Act of 1867. Despite his disappointment and his advanced age, Disraeli formulated "conservative" policies that enabled his party to survive in an increasingly democratic era. The most enduring of these were the preservation of traditional British institutions, the improvement of the working and living conditions of the lower classes, and the maintenance and strengthening of the empire.

Disraeli developed these policies in his famous Crystal Palace Speech of June 24, 1872, stressing his belief in and concern for the British Empire. Traditionally, this speech has been viewed as one of several indications in the 1870s of renewed British interest in imperial expansion and consolidation, a reaction to the supposedly "separatist" policies of Gladstone's Liberal government and to the growing might of other European nations. Disraeli is

SOURCE. W. F. Monypenny and George Earl Buckle, *The Life of Benjamin Disraeli, Earl of Beaconsfield,* 6 vols., New York: The Macmillan Company, 1920, V, 194–196.

seen as a new prophet of imperialism, instilling in the British public attitudes that would contribute to the "partition" of Africa in the 1880s and 1890s and to the programs of imperial federation and preference associated with Joseph Chamberlain at the turn of the century. To many historians, however, this view of the Crystal Palace Speech is an oversimplification. Disraeli never developed these ideas in any detail. When he became prime minister again in 1874, he remained indifferent to the practical problems facing the empire. In fact, it can be argued that because of the growth of colonial nationalism Disraeli's theories were incapable of implementation. Disraeli, who had earlier referred to the colonies as a "millstone" around Britain's neck, nevertheless saw the political utility of associating the concept of imperialism with the Conservative party.

If you look to the history of this country since the advent of Liberalism —forty years ago—you will find that there has been no effort so continuous, so subtle, supported by so much energy, and carried on with so much ability and acumen, as the attempts of Liberalism to effect the disintegration of the Empire of England. And, gentlemen, of all its efforts, this is the one which has been the nearest to success. Statesmen of the highest character, writers of the most distinguished ability, the most organised and efficient means, have been employed in this endeavor. It has been proved to all of us that we have lost money by our Colonies. It has been shown with precise, with mathematical demonstration, that there never was a jewel in the Crown of England that was so truly costly as the possession of India. How often has it been suggested that we should at once emancipate ourselves from this incubus! Well, that result was nearly accomplished. When those subtle views were adopted by the country under the plausible plea of granting self-government to the Colonies, I confess that I myself thought that the tie was broken. Not that I for one object to self-government; I cannot conceive how our distant Colonies can have their affairs administered except by self-government.

But self-government, in my opinion, when it was conceded, ought to have been conceded as part of a great policy of Imperial consolidation. It ought to have been accompanied by an Imperial tariff, by securities for the people of England for the enjoyment of the unappropriated lands which belonged to the Sovereign as their trustee, and by a military code which should have precisely defined the means and the responsibilities by which the Colonies should be defended, and by which, if necessary, this country should call for aid from the Colonies themselves. It ought, further, to have been accompanied by the institution of some representative council in the metropolis, which would have brought the Colonies into constant and continuous relations with the Home Government. All this, however, was omitted because those who advised that policy—and I believe their convictions were sincere—looked upon the Colonies of England, looked even upon our connection with India, as a burden upon this country; viewing everything in a financial aspect, and totally passing by those moral and political considerations which make nations great, and by the influence of which alone men are distingushed from animals.

Well, what has been the result of this attempt during the reign of Liberalism for the disintegration of the Empire? It has entirely failed. But how has it failed? Through the sympathy of the Colonies for the Mother Country. They have decided that the Empire shall not be destroyed; and in my opinion no Minister in this country will do his duty who neglects any opportunity of reconstructing as much as possible our Colonial Empire, and of responding to those distant sympathies which may become the source of incalculable strength and happiness to this land.

The issue is not a mean one. It is whether you will be content to be a comfortable England, modelled and moulded upon Continental principles and meeting in due course an inevitable fate, or whether you will be a great country, an Imperial country, a country where your sons, when they rise, rise to paramount positions, and obtain not merely the esteem of their countrymen, but command the respect of the world.

104

William Ewart Gladstone, Speech in Commons (1886). Irish Home Rule

The Act of Union of 1800, binding Ireland and Great Britain together as a political unit, was from the beginning unacceptable to many Irish. Daniel O'Connell (1775–1847), even after he had achieved Catholic emancipation in 1829, continued to work for repeal of the Act of Union. Such political agitation, interrupted in the 1840s by the horrors of the potato famine, was by the 1860s again becoming a fact of Irish life. The first in England to recognize the legitimacy of Ireland's complaint was William Ewart Gladstone (1809–1898). On learning that his Liberal party had won the election of 1868 and that he would become prime minister, he asserted, "My mission is to pacify Ireland."

In 1869 he disestablished the Church of Ireland. His land acts of 1870 and 1881 attempted, with limited success, to deal with the problem of English absentee landlords and oppressed Irish tenants. By 1886, when he became prime minister for a third time, protest in Ireland had become so violent and Irish obstruction in the House of Commons so annoying that he concluded the only solution was to give Ireland its own parliament for local affairs. Below are excerpts from Gladstone's speech of April 8, in which he introduced his Home Rule Bill. In it, he applies to Ireland the Liberal party's traditional policy toward foreign countries: they should be allowed to conduct their own affairs.

Gladstone's bill failed in the House of Commons because of opposition from the Conservatives and also from the Liberal Unionists, the 93 Liberals who supported the union of Britain and Ireland. Typical of the opposition was Lord Randolph Churchill, a Conservative who decided to play "the Orange card," and who insisted with some foresight that "Ulster will fight," and

SOURCE. *Hansard's Parliamentary Debates*, Third Series, CCCIV, 1080–1085.

then added his own opinion that "Ulster will be right." Seven years later, in 1893, Gladstone attempted a second Home Rule Bill, which this time was defeated in the House of Lords. A third bill was introduced in 1912, after the power of the Lords to defeat it had been destroyed by the Parliament Act of 1911. When its implementation was delayed by World War I, if not by Protestant Ulster's readiness to resist, the Catholic South also prepared to fight. The Easter Rebellion of 1916 in Dublin and the division of Ireland in 1921 set the stage for the trouble that has come since.

Gladstone's Irish policy, by which he risked his own political career and the tenure of his political party, is often cited as the courageous stance of a statesman acting on principle rather than on political expediency. Or was it, on the other hand, the pursuit of an unrealistic objective, doomed from the beginning to failure and not worth the political turmoil it caused?

I do not deny the general good intentions of Parliament on a variety of great and conspicuous occasions, and its desire to pass good laws for Ireland. But let me say that, in order to work out the purposes of government, there is something more in this world occasionally required than even the passing of good laws. It is sometimes requisite not only that good laws should be passed, but also that they should be passed by the proper persons. The passing of many good laws is not enough in cases where the strong permanent instincts of the people, their distinctive marks of character, the situation and history of the country require not only that these laws should be good, but that they should proceed from a congenial and native source, and besides being good laws should be their own laws. . . .

The principle that I am laying down I am not laying down exceptionally for Ireland. It is the very principle upon which, within my recollection, to the immense advantage of the country, we have not only altered, but revolutionized our method of governing the Colonies. I had the honour to hold Office in the Colonial Department—perhaps I ought to be ashamed to confess it—51 years ago. At that time the Colonies were governed from Downing Street. It is true that some of them had Legislative Assemblies; but with these we were always in conflict. We were always fed with information by what was termed the British Party in those Colonies. A clique of gentlemen constituted themselves the British Party; and the non-British Party, which was sometimes called the "Disloyal Party," was composed of the enormous majority of the population. We had continual shocks, continual debates, and continual conflicts. All that has changed. England tried to pass good laws for the Colonies at that period; but the Colonies said—"We do not want your good laws; we want our own." We admitted the reasonableness of that principle, and it is now coming home to us from across the seas. We have to consider whether it is applicable to the case of Ireland. Do not let us disguise this from ourselves. We stand face to face with what is termed Irish nationality. Irish nationality vents itself in the demand for local autonomy, or separate and complete self-government in Irish, not in Imperial affairs. Is this an evil in itself? Is it a thing that we should view with horror or apprehension? Is it a thing which we ought to reject or accept only with a wry face, or ought we to wait until some painful and sad necessity is incumbent upon the country, like the necessity of 1780 or the necessity of 1793? Sir, I hold that it is not. . . .

I hold that there is such a thing as local patriotism, which, in itself, is not bad, but good. The Welshman is full of local patriotism—the Scotchman is full of local patriotism; the Scotch nationality is as strong as it ever was, and should the occasion arise—which I believe it never can—it will be as ready to assert itself as in the days of Bannockburn. I do not believe that that local patriotism is an evil. I believe it is stronger in Ireland even than in Scotland. Englishmen are eminently English; Scotchmen are profoundly Scotch; and, if I read Irish history aright, misfortune and calamity have wedded her sons to her soil. The Irishman is more profoundly Irish; but it does not follow that, because his local patriotism is keen, he is incapable of Imperial patriotism. . . . I say that the Irishman is as capable of loyalty as another man—I say that if his loyalty has been checked in its development, why is it? Because the laws by which he is governed do not present themselves to him, as they do to us in England and Scotland, with a native and congenial aspect; and I think I can refer to two illustrations which go strongly to support the doctrine I have advanced. Take the case of the Irish soldier and of the Irish Constabulary. Have you a braver or a more loyal man in your Army than the Irishman, who has shared every danger with his Scotch and English comrades, and who has never been behind them, when confronted by peril, for the sake of the honour and safety of his Empire? Compare this case with that of an ordinary Irishman in Ireland. The Irish soldier has voluntarily placed himself under military law, which is to him a self-chosen law, and he is exempted from that difficulty which works upon the population in Ireland—namely, that they are governed by a law which they do not feel has sprung from the soil. . . .

However this may be, we are sensible that we have taken an important decision—our choice has been made. It has not been made without thought; it has been made in the full knowledge that trial and difficulty may confront us on our path. We have no right to say that Ireland, through her constitutionally-chosen Representatives, will accept the plan

I offer. Whether it will be so I do not know—I have no title to assume it; but if Ireland does not cheerfully accept it, it is impossible for us to attempt to force upon her what is intended to be a boon; nor can we possibly press England and Scotland to accord to Ireland what she does not heartily welcome and embrace. There are difficulties; but I rely upon the patriotism and sagacity of this House; I rely on the effects of free and full discussion; and I rely more than all upon the just and generous sentiments of the two British nations. Looking forward, I ask the House to assist us in the work which we have undertaken, and to believe that no trivial motive can have driven us to it—to assist us in this work which, we believe, will restore Parliament to its dignity and legislation to its free and unimpeded course. I ask you to stay that waste of public treasure which is involved in the present system of government and legislation in Ireland, and which is not a waste only, but which demoralizes while it exhausts. I ask you to show to Europe and to America that we, too, can face political problems which America 20 years ago faced, and which many countries in Europe have been called upon to face, and have not feared to deal with. I ask that in our own case we should practise, with firm and fearless hand, what we have so often preached—the doctrine which we have so often inculcated upon others—namely, that the concession of local self-government is not the way to sap or impair, but the way to strengthen and consolidate unity. I ask that we should learn to rely less upon merely written stipulations, and more upon those better stipulations which are written on the heart and mind of man. I ask that we should apply to Ireland that happy experience which we have gained in England and in Scotland, where the course of generations has now taught us, not as a dream or a theory, but as practice and as life, that the best and surest foundation we can find to build upon is the foundation afforded by the affections, the convictions, and the will of the nation; and it is thus, by the decree of the Almighty, that we may be enabled to secure at once the social peace, the fame, the power, and the permanence of the Empire.

105

Sidney Webb, "The Historic Basis of Socialism," *Fabian Essays* (1889)

The outstanding political fact of the late nineteenth century was the new democratic electorate created by the reform acts of 1867 and 1884. The traditional political parties—the Liberals (formerly Whigs) and the Conservatives (formerly Tories)—attempted to marshal the new voters but, in fact, offered little of tangible benefit to them. Walter Bagehot's prediction that politicians would seek to outbid one another for popular support was not immediately realized. The Liberals, at first championing laissez-faire individualism and then becoming absorbed in Ireland, had little time or inclination to cater to the needs of the new working-class electorate. The Conservatives, although occasionally advocating paternalistic Tory Democracy, were more interested in maintaining the *status quo* at home and in defending the British Empire.

This political neglect and the anxiety caused by the economic depression of the 1870s and 1880s led some people to search for more radical solutions. Socialism, espoused in a Utopian form by Robert Owen (1771–1858) in the 1820s and 1830s, had recently been made scientific and more resolute by Karl Marx (1818–1883), who after 1849 lived in London and wrote, from his desk in the British Museum, his revolutionary masterpiece, *Das Kapital*. Such socialistic ideas, however, seemed to many people either too utopian and impractical or, as in the case of Marx, too violent and un-English.

The Fabian Society, organized in 1884, was one of several socialist groups formed about the same time. It was unique however it its respectability, disavowing violent revolutionary means and attracting to its membership notable intellectuals like the historian Sidney Webb (1859–1947) and the playwright

SOURCE. George Bernard Shaw et al., *Fabian Essays,* sixth edition, introduction by Asa Briggs, London: George Allen & Unwin, Ltd., 1962, pp. 64, 66–67, 90–93. Reprinted by permission of George Allen & Unwin, Ltd.

George Bernard Shaw (1856–1950). It took its name from the Roman general Quintus Fabius Maximus, who had bested Hannibal by refusing a direct confrontation, confident that by being patient and prepared the victory would ultimately be his. Thus the characteristic activity of the Fabians was teaching, speaking to any group that would listen, preaching that socialistic cooperation was destined peacefully and constitutionally to replace capitalistic competitiveness: the "economic side of the democratic ideal is, in fact, Socialism." The following selection, originally a speech by Sidney Webb, is filled with typically Fabian ideas. It and seven other essays by other Fabians were edited by Shaw and published in 1889. These *Fabian Essays*, a publishing success from the very beginning, did much to establish the authority of the Society and to publicize its ideals. In 1900 the Fabians joined with other socialist groups and labor unions to form the Labour Representation Committee, which in 1906 became the Labour party.

Socialism is by this time a wave surging throughout all Europe; and for want of a grasp of the series of apparently unconnected events by which and with which it has been for two generations rapidly coming upon us—for want, in short, of knowledge of its intellectual history, we in England today see our political leaders in a general attitude of astonishment at the changing face of current politics; both great parties drifting vaguely before a nameless undercurrent which they fail utterly to recognize or understand. With some dim impression that Socialism is one of the Utopian dreams they remember to have heard comfortably disposed of in their academic youth as the impossible ideal of Humanity-intoxicated Frenchmen, they go their ways through the nineteenth century as a countryman blunders through Cheapside. . . .

In the present Socialist movement . . . two streams are united: advocates of social reconstruction have learnt the lesson of Democracy, and know that it is through the slow and gradual turning of the popular mind to new principles that social reorganization bit by bit comes. All students of society who are abreast of their time, Socialists as well as Individualists, realize that important organic changes can only be (1) democratic, and thus acceptable to a majority of the people, and prepared for in the minds of all; (2) gradual, and thus causing no dislocation, however rapid may be the rate of progress; (3) not regarded as immoral by the mass of the people, and thus not subjectively demoralizing to them; and (4) in this country at any rate, constitutional and peaceful. Socialists may therefore be quite at one with Radicals in their political methods. Radicals, on the other hand, are perforce realizing that mere political levelling is insufficient to save a State from anarchy and despair. Both sections have been driven to recognize that the root of the difficulty is economic; and there is every day a wider consensus that the inevitable outcome of Democracy is the control by the people themselves, not only of their own political organization, but, through that, also of the main instruments of wealth production; the gradual substitution of organized co-operation for the anarchy of the competitive struggle; and the consequent recovery, in the only possible way, of what John Stuart Mill calls "the enormous share which the possessors of the instruments of industry are able to take from the produce." The economic side of the democratic ideal is, in fact, Socialism itself. . . .

We must abandon the self-conceit of imagining that we are independent units, and bend our jealous minds, absorbed in their own cultivation, to this subjection to the higher end, the Common Weal. Accordingly, conscious "direct adaptation" steadily supplants the unconscious and wasteful "indirect adaptation" of the earlier form of the struggle for existence; and with every advance in sociological knowledge Man is seen to assume more and more, not only the mastery of "things," but also a conscious control over social destiny itself.

This new scientific conception of the Social Organism has put completely out of countenance the cherished principles of the Political Economist and the Philosophic Radical. . . .

The result of this development of Sociology is to compel a revision of the relative importance of liberty and equality as principles to be kept in view in social administration. In Bentham's celebrated "ends" to be aimed at in a civil code, liberty stands predominant over equality, on the ground that full equality can be maintained only by the loss of security for the fruits of labour. That exposition remains as true as ever; but the question for decision remains, how much liberty? Economic analysis has destroyed the value of the old criterion of respect for the equal liberty of others. Bentham, whose economics were weak, paid no attention to the perpetual tribute on the fruits of others' labour which full private property in land inevitably creates. In his view liberty and security to property meant that every worker should be free to obtain the full result of his own labour; and there appeared no inconsistency between them. The political economist now knows that with free competition and private property in land and capital, no individual can possibly obtain the full result of his own labour. The student of industrial development, moreover, finds it steadily more and more impossible to trace what is precisely the result of each separate man's toil. Complete rights of liberty and property necessarily involve, for example, the spoliation of the Irish cottier tenant for the benefit of Lord Clanricarde. What then becomes of the Benthamic principle of the greatest happiness of the greatest number? When the Benthamite comes to understand the Law of Rent, which of the two will he abandon? For he cannot escape the lesson of the century, taught alike by the economists, the statesmen, and the "practical men," that complete individual liberty, with unrestrained private ownership of the instruments of wealth production, is irreconcilable with the common weal. The free struggle for existence among ourselves menaces our survival as a healthy and permanent social organism. Evolution, Professor Huxley declares, is the substitution of consciously regulated co-ordination among the units of each organism, for blind anarchic competition. Thirty years ago Herbert Spencer demonstrated the incompatibility of full private property in land with the modern democratic State; and almost every economist now preaches the same doctrine. The Radical is rapidly arriving, from practical experience, at similar conclusions; and the steady increase of the Government regulation of private enterprise, the growth of municipal administration, and the rapid shifting of the burden of taxation directly to rent and interest, mark in treble lines the statesman's unconscious abandonment of the old Individualism, and our irresistible glide into collectivist Socialism.

It was inevitable that the Democracy should learn this lesson. With the masses painfully conscious of the failure of Individualism to create a decent social life for four-fifths of the people, it might have been foreseen that Individualism could not survive their advent to political power. If private property in land and capital necessarily keeps the many workers permanently poor (through no fault of their own) in order to make the few idlers rich (from no merit of their own), private property in land and capital will inevitably go the way of the feudalism which it superseded. The economic analysis confirms the rough generalization of the suffering people. The history of industrial evolution points to the same result; and for two generations the world's chief ethical teachers have been urging the same lesson. No wonder the heavens of Individualism are rolling up before our eyes like a scroll and even the Bishops believe and tremble. . . .

Every increase in the political power of the proletariat will most surely be used by them for their economic and social protection. In England, at any rate, the history of the century serves at once as their guide and their justification.

Charles Booth, *Life and Labour* *of the People of London* (1889)

Charles Booth's 17-volume *Life and Labour* is one of the most important and interesting sources on London life in the late nineteenth century. It was more than simply an academic exercise, however; the information contained in it was used to support many of the social reforms introduced into England at the turn of the century. Booth (1840–1916) was an unlikely candidate for such a momentous and pioneering sociological undertaking. Born to comfort, he devoted his early life to his successful shipping business. It was not until he had become middle aged and wealthy that he committed himself to the great survey, a decision that is still something of a mystery. Most likely his natural curiosity was reinforced by a desire to prove that the socialists were exaggerating the extent of urban poverty. He concluded that they were not.

Booth's study is composed of a number of different parts. Much of it is simply a detailed description of various London neighborhoods (as in this selection on Parker Street), of the industries of London, and of the habits and morals of the different social classes. He also attempted to offer solutions to the problems he observed. Like Smiles, he remained a defender of capitalism and considered "self-reliance" the key to progress in most areas. As a result, Beatrice Potter, one of his early associates, deserted him and embraced the Fabian Socialism of her future husband, Sidney Webb. Booth, perhaps simply aware of the social implications of democracy, was more willing than Smiles to grant government a limited role in solving obvious

SOURCE. *Charles Booth's London,* eds. Albert Fried and Richard M. Elman, New York: Pantheon Books, 1968, pp. 70–71, 74–75, 190–191, 197, 199, 202, 334–335. Reprinted by the permisson of Random House, Inc., and Hutchinson Publishing Group Ltd.

social problems. For example, he was an early and strong advocate of old age pensions, introduced into England in 1908.

Life and Labour came out piecemeal between 1889 and 1903. When completed it consisted of four volumes on poverty, five volumes on London industry, seven volumes on religious influences, and a *Final Volume* containing his conclusions.

This street differs in some respects from Shelton Street, and, bad as Shelton Street is, Parker Street touches a little lower level. In Shelton Street the rooms were not taken by the night, but by the week. In Parker Street it was not unusual to let by the night, so that any man and woman who had met could find accommodation. . . .

No. 2, Parker Street has two entrances, the one being numbered at 159, Drury Lane. One of the parlour floors is used for the sale of coal and coke, and the room over for living in. . . . In one of those rooms there was at one time a Mrs. Carter, a woman with a fiery temper, almost fit to commit murder, and her husband has been in prison for ill-using her. She was, however, a clean, hard-working woman. These people were at times very poor. On the second floor to the right there were a man and woman (English) who had lived unmarried for fourteen years. There were no children; the room clean, with a few comforts. In the other room lived another pair in the same fashion; the woman very unhappy, brutally treated by the man, whom she says she would leave if she knew how else to get a living. Such cases are not uncommon. The man was a drunkard. On the third floor lived an old woman and her son, Irish, who declined to be visited by a Protestant missionary. . . .

No. 24 is let in furnished apartments. It was in the occupation of a Mr. Holden, a quiet man who died about a year ago, and his widow carries on the business. The characters occupying the rooms are very low indeed; one of them, a girl of eighteen, mentioned that she had been confirmed by a Bishop but had been a b—— sight worse since. About two or three years ago a woman was found dead in the parlour of this house; she appeared to have been strangled. . . .

No. 1 on the north side, at the corner of Drury Lane, does not really belong to Parker Street at all. The shop entrance is in Drury Lane, the house only enters from Parker Street, and with its inhabitants, who in position and appearance are much above the dwellers in Parker Street, we need not concern ourselves. Nos. 3 to 5 are warehouses. No. 7 has been pulled down. . . . The whole house for eleven years past was noted for poverty, dirt, and drink, and deaths were at one time so frequent in it that it got a bad name for "ill-luck." . . .

Drinking habits and the disorderliness resulting from them could not but be continually mentioned in the course of the long walks taken in all parts of London day after day with the picked police officers who were permitted to assist us during the revision of our maps; and we had the advantage of discussing these and other cognate subjects with their divisional superiors. . . .

Whether the people drink less or not, the police are practically agreed in saying that they are much less rowdy than formerly: "Totally different people to what they were thirty-three years ago," said one who joined the force then; an improvement which he claims has extended also to publicans and the police themselves, of whom the latter are now an almost entirely sober body of men, while the former are much more respectable and steady, and for the most part careful as to the conduct of their houses. "The modern publican is of a totally different type to the man of twenty years ago, with his white hat and black band, and his bull-dog: the decayed prize-fighter type. The publican now is usually well educated; respectable, and a keen man of business, who can keep his own accounts in proper order, and fully realizes that it is to his interest that the law should be strictly observed in his house." As to drink, this last witness reiterated the opinion that there had been a great decrease, if not of drinking, certainly of drunkenness, and was one of the few who asserted that the alleged increase among women was not a fact, the true way of putting it being that drink had decreased among men, but not, or at all events not in the same degree, among women. As to drunkenness he said, "Go and look at Hampstead Heath on Bank Holiday and compare it with what it was twenty years ago, or walk in the streets on Saturday night." . . .

Upon the connection of poverty, or at any rate the poverty that seeks charitable relief, with drink, the statements are uncompromising. A Wesleyan minister, referring to claims on their relief fund, stated that in almost every application the necessity was traced ultimately to drink on the part of man or wife "or both." A Congregationalist says that "he came to London believing that the influence of drink was much exaggerated, but has been convinced that it is at the root of all the poverty and distress with which they come into contact; with every case of distress that is relieved they always find afterwards that drink has been the cause of leakage." A Church of England vicar speaks of it as "the great trouble; the main cause of all the poverty. In almost every application for relief there is a history of drink." He began with a determination not to help when either parent was a drunkard, but has found this impossible. Apart from drunkenness he emphasized the fearful extravagance in drink. A lay church worker, while agreeing that though there might be no actual decrease in drinking, "there were fewer outward signs of drunkenness in the streets," said that "in almost every case that came under his notice for assistance there was a history of drink, not necessarily in the life of the actual applicant, but at least somewhere in the background." And a relieving officer of an adjoining Union confirms this, saying that "though there is less rowdiness, the general habits of drinking have not decreased," and that in his experience "in all applications for relief, except from widows, cripples, and the aged, the ultimate, if not immediate cause of poverty is drink." . . .

From the religious point of view it is remarked that teetotalism is apt to become a cult of its own, of a rather narrow kind, and it is added that "those who yield to the seductions of temperance are sometimes too much bitten by the idea of saving." But carping such as this leaves untouched the great main fact to which we have endless testimony, that "Christian people are nearly all temperate and thrifty," and the better in every way for being so. . . .

Improvement must be sought, first of all, in the deepening of the sentiment of Individual Responsibility. This sentiment rests no doubt upon right feeling, but is subject to stimulation by the opinion of others, and may finally be enforced by law. Of these three, public opinion seems to me to be the most lax. The expectation of evil, the attributing of bad motives, and the ready acceptance of a low standard constitute the first difficulty we have to meet. Cynicism is accounted so clever that men pretend to be worse than they are rather than be thought fools. Clear views of right and wrong in matters of daily action, however firmly they may be rooted in the hearts of men, seldom find utterance; and when this polite rule is broken some surprise is always felt. . . .

It would seem inevitable that the sense of duty must be weakened by the loss of the habit of judging and of the experience of being judged, as well as by laxity, but nevertheless I venture to assert that it is maintained at a far higher level than is generally thought or claimed. Thus legal enactment, if carefully aimed and measured, becomes doubly and trebly valuable, serving first to check the evil-doer, and secondly to awaken the individual conscience, while it also, by impressing an undeniable seal of condemnation, crystallizes the looseness of public opinion as to any particular offence. Legislation can never go far beyond the sanction of existing public opinion, but may yet lead the way, and in many cases has done so.

107

Rudyard Kipling, "Recessional" (1897)

Rudyard Kipling (1865–1936) is usually regarded as the high priest of British imperialism. Born in India, he became a journalist, writing a number of popular short stories about India and the army. In 1889 he settled in England, where he continued to develop the imperial theme, producing such widely read works as *Barrack-Room Ballads* (1892), the *Jungle Books* (1894–95), and *Captains Courageous* (1897). To most readers these works reflected the imperial spirit that pervaded Britain in the late nineteenth century.

Kipling was, however, always suspicious of Britain's jingo imperialism. For one thing, British power had been purchased at a great price.

> If blood be the price of admiralty,
> Lord God, we ha' paid in full!

More important, he believed in an older, humanitarian imperialism. Power implied duty and responsibility; Britain must rule for the benefit of the "lesser breeds without the Law," a belief developed most forcefully in his "White Man's Burden" (1899). Loving India as he did and respecting the "Fuzzy-Wuzzy," who "bruk a British square," Kipling regretted the arrogance bred of power and the contempt bred of familiarity. His concern was the same as that of Queen Victoria when she wrote, "Coloured races should be treated with every kindness and affection, as brother, not—as, alas, Englishmen too often do."

It was in this somber mood that Kipling approached the Diamond Jubilee of 1897 commemorating Victoria's 60 years on the throne. The resulting

---

SOURCE. Rudyard Kipling, *The Five Nations,* London: Methuen and Co., 1903, pp. 214–215. Reprinted by permission of Mrs. George Bambridge, Methuen & Co. Ltd., the Macmillan Co. of Canada, and Doubleday & Co., Inc.

pageantry was to many British an opportunity for self-congratulation, and even of boastfulness. Kipling's "Recessional," perhaps his greatest poem, struck a melancholy note during the joyous proceedings, warning of the danger of becoming "drunk with sight of power," and drawing a comparison between Britain's empire and those of Nineveh and Tyre. Only he, the imperialist, could have written such lines and not have lost public respect. His warning was apt; two years later the Boer War began. This messy and morally dubious conflict produced in Britain a reaction not only against the aggressive imperialism of Joseph Chamberlain and Alfred Milner but also against the literature of Kipling himself. When he received the Nobel Prize for literature in 1907, his literary career was largely over.

RECESSIONAL
(1897)

GOD of our fathers, known of old,
   Lord of our far-flung battle-line,
Beneath whose awful Hand we hold
   Dominion over palm and pine—
Lord God of Hosts, be with us yet,
Lest we forget—lest we forget!

The tumult and the shouting dies;
   The captains and the kings depart:
Still stands Thine ancient sacrifice,
   An humble and a contrite heart.
Lord God of Hosts, be with us yet,
Lest we forget—lest we forget!

Far-called, our navies melt away;
   On dune and headland sinks the fire:
Lo, all our pomp of yesterday
   Is one with Nineveh and Tyre!
Judge of the Nations, spare us yet,
Lest we forget—lest we forget!

If, drunk with sight of power, we loose
   Wild tongues that have not Thee in awe,
Such boastings as the Gentiles use,
   Or lesser breeds without the Law—
Lord God of Hosts, be with us yet,
Lest we forget—lest we forget!

For heathen heart that puts her trust
  In reeking tube and iron shard,
All valiant dust that builds on dust,
  And guarding, calls not Thee to guard,
For frantic boast and foolish word—
Thy Mercy on Thy People, Lord!

Amen.

108

Eyre Crowe, Memorandum (1907). England and Germany

Britain's world position was seriously eroded in the late nineteenth century because of the creation of a strong German Empire (1871), the industrialization of Europe and the United States, the growth of nationalism in many of the colonies, and the division of Europe in the 1880s and 1890s into two strong alliance systems. Despite these developments, British statesmen remained reluctant to make formal diplomatic commitments, preferring instead the freedom of Britain's traditional policy of "splendid isolation." By the turn of the century, however, this policy appeared increasingly unrealistic. The Boer War revealed that England had few, if any, friends in Europe, and England's relative wealth was no longer sufficient to support an independent foreign policy. England's emergence from diplomatic isolation was signaled by the Anglo-Japanese Treaty of 1902 and, more importantly, by the *Entente Cordiale* with France in 1904, a "friendly under-

SOURCE. G. P. Gooch and Harold Temperley, eds., *British Documents on the Origins of the War, 1898–1914*, Vol. III: *The Testing of the Entente, 1904–6*, London: His Majesty's Stationery Office, 1928, pp. 402–403, 414–416, 419–420. Reprinted by permission of the Controller of Her Britannic Majesty's Stationery Office.

standing" backed up by a series of colonial agreements. This *entente,* although perhaps not so intended, was seen by many as anti-German, especially when England supported France against Germany in the Moroccan Crisis of 1905 to 1906.

Eyre Crowe (1864–1925), who entered the Foreign Office in 1885, observed this change in foreign policy at close quarters. In early 1907 he wrote a long memorandum, part of which is reproduced below, justifying Britain's support of France. He sought to portray this action as simply a reflection of Britain's traditional foreign policy, the use of sea power to maintain freedom of commerce and the balance of power. If Britain appeared to be anti-German, it was only because Germany currently represented the greatest threat to this balance of power. It is also apparent that Crowe was no supporter of "appeasement"; peace could best be maintained by resisting German demands, which he compared to blackmail. This memorandum provoked considerable controversy within the Foreign Office, some of his colleagues arguing that he was overly suspicious of German intentions. Nevertheless, Sir Edward Grey (1862–1933), the foreign secretary, regarded his memo as "most valuable." As Germany's challenge to British naval supremacy intensified, Crowe's views became increasingly prevalent within the Foreign Office, contributing ultimately to Britain's support of France in 1914.

Crowe's secret memorandum, distributed only to select members of the cabinet, was deposited in the Public Record Office in London with the rest of the voluminous Foreign Office papers. Being secret, it was never printed as part of a "parliamentary paper." It was made public only in 1928, when the British government authorized the publication of a large collection of official documents designed to explain and to justify Britain's pre-World War I diplomacy.

The general character of England's foreign policy is determined by the immutable conditions of her geographical situation on the ocean flank of Europe as an island State with vast oversea colonies and dependencies, whose existence and survival as an independent community are inseparably bound up with the possession of preponderant sea power. . . . Sea power is more potent than land power, because it is as pervading as the element in which it moves and has its being. Its formidable character makes itself felt the more directly that a maritime State is, in the literal sense of the word, the neighbour of every country accessible by sea. It would, therefore, be but natural that the power of a State supreme at sea should inspire universal jealousy and fear, and be ever exposed to the danger of being overthrown by a general combination of the world. Against such a combination no single nation could in the long run stand, least of all a small island kingdom not possessed of the military strength of a people trained to arms, and dependent for its food supply on oversea commerce. The danger can in practice only be averted—and history shows that it has been so averted—on condition that the national policy of the insular and naval State is so directed as to harmonize with the general desires and ideals common to all mankind, and more particularly that it is closely identified with the primary and vital interests of a majority, or as many as possible, of the other nations. Now, the first interest of all countries is the preservation of national independence. It follows that England, more than any other non-insular Power, has a direct and positive interest in the maintenance of the independence of nations, and therefore must be the natural enemy of any country threatening the independence of others, and the natural protector of the weaker communities.

Second only to the ideal of independence, nations have always cherished the right of free intercourse and trade in the world's markets, and in proportion as England champions the principle of the largest measure of general freedom of commerce, she undoubtedly strengthens her hold on the interested friendship of other nations, at least to the extent of making them feel less apprehensive of naval supremacy in the hands of a free trade England than they would in the face of a predominant protectionist Power. This is an aspect of the free trade question which is apt to be overlooked. It has been well said that every country, if it had the option, would, of course, prefer itself to hold the power of supremacy at sea, but that, this choice being excluded, it would rather see England hold that power than any other State.

History shows that the danger threatening the independence of this or that nation has generally arisen, at least in part, out of the momentary predominance of a neighbouring State at once militarily powerful, economically efficient, and ambitious to extend its frontiers or spread its influence, the danger being directly proportionate to the degree of its power and efficiency, and to the spontaneity or "inevitableness" of its ambitions. The only check on the abuse of political predominance derived from such a position has always consisted in the opposition of an equally formidable rival, or of a combination of several countries forming leagues of defence. The equilibrium established by such a grouping of forces is technically known as the balance of power, and it has become almost an historical truism to identify England's secular policy with the maintenance of this balance by throwing her weight now in this scale and now in that, but ever on the side opposed to the political dictatorship of the strongest single State or group at a given time.

If this view of British policy is correct, the opposition into which England must inevitably be driven to any country aspiring to such a dictatorship assumes almost the form of a law of nature. . . .

By applying this general law to a particular case, the attempt might be made to ascertain whether, at a given time, some powerful and ambitious State is or is not in a position of natural and necessary enmity towards England; and the present position of Germany might, perhaps, be so tested. Any such investigation must take the shape of an inquiry as to whether Germany is, in fact, aiming at a political hegemony with the object of promoting purely German schemes of expansion, and establishing a Germany primacy in the world of international politics at the cost and to the detriment of other nations. . . .

The immediate object of the present inquiry was to ascertain whether there is any real and natural ground for opposition between England and Germany. It has been shown that such opposition has, in fact, existed in an ample measure for a long period, but that it has been caused by an entirely one-sided aggressiveness, and that on the part of England the most conciliatory disposition has been coupled with never-failing readiness to purchase the resumption of friendly relations by concession after concession.

It might be deduced that the antogonism is too deeply rooted in the relative position of the two countries to allow of its being bridged over by the kind of temporary expedients to which England has so long and so patiently resorted. On this view of the case it would have to be assumed that Germany is deliberately following a policy which is essentially opposed to vital British interests, and that an armed conflict cannot in the long run be averted, except by England either sacrificing those interests, with the result that she would lose her position as an independent Great Power, or making herself too strong to give Germany the chance of succeeding in a war. This is the opinion of those who see in the whole trend of Germany's policy conclusive evidence that she is consciously aiming at the establishment of a German hegemony, at first in Europe, and eventually in the world. . . .

It might be suggested that the great German design is in reality no more than the expression of a vague, confused, and unpractical statesmanship, not fully realizing its own drift. A charitable critic might add, by way of explanation, that the well-known qualities of mind and temperament distinguishing for good or for evil the present Ruler of Germany may not improbably be largely responsible for the erratic, domineering, and often frankly aggressive spirit which is recognizable at present in every branch of German public life, not merely in the region of foreign policy; and that this spirit has called forth those manifestations of discontent and alarm both at home and abroad with which the world is becoming familiar: that, in fact, Germany does not really know what she is driving at, and that all her excursions and alarums, all her underhand intrigues do not contribute to the steady working out of a well conceived and relentlessly followed system of policy, because they do not really form part of any such system. This is an hypothesis not flattering to the German Government, and it must be admitted that much might be urged against its validity. But it remains true that on this hypothesis also most of the facts of the present situation could be explained. . . .

If, merely by way of analogy and illustration, a comparison not intended to be either literally exact or disrespectful be permitted, the action of Germany towards this country since 1890 might be likened not inappropriately to that of a professional blackmailer, whose extortions are wrung from his victims by the threat of some vague and dreadful consequences in case of a refusal. To give way to the blackmailer's menaces enriches him, but it has long been proved by uniform experience that, although this may secure for the victim temporary peace, it is certain to lead to renewed molestation and higher demands after ever-shortening periods of amicable forbearance. The blackmailer's trade is generally ruined by the first resolute stand made against his exactions and the determination rather to face all risks of a possibly disagreeable situation than to continue in the path of endless concessions. But, failing such determination, it is more than probable that the relations between the two parties will grow steadily worse. . . .

Although Germany has not been exposed to such a rebuff as France encountered in 1898, the events connected with the Algeciras Conference appear to have had on the German Government the effect of an unexpected revelation, clearly showing indications of a new spirit in which England proposes to regulate her own conduct towards France on the one hand and to Germany on the other. That the result was a very serious disappointment to Germany has been made abundantly manifest by the turmoil which the signature of the Algeciras Act has created in the country, the official, semi-official, and unofficial classes vying with each other in giving expression to their astonished discontent. The time which has since elapsed has, no doubt, been short. But during that time it may be observed that our relations with Germany, if not exactly cordial, have at least been practically free from all symptoms of direct friction, and there is an impression that Germany will think twice before she now gives rise to any fresh disagreement. In this attitude she will be encouraged if she meets on England's part with unvarying courtesy and consideration in all matters of common concern, but also with a prompt and firm refusal to enter into any one-sided bargains or arrangements, and the most unbending determination to uphold British rights and interests in every part of the globe. There will be no surer or quicker way to win the respect of the German Government and of the German nation.

109

David Lloyd George, Campaign Speech (1910). Attack on the House of Lords

The Liberal party of William Ewart Gladstone, standing for laissez-faire individualism and economy in government, had by 1910 been transformed. A large part of the middle class, frightened by Gladstone's Irish policy, had transferred its allegiance to the Conservatives. Increasingly the Liberal party was led by men either from, or appealing to the interests of, the lower classes. This new posture was best personified by David Lloyd George (1863–1945), who spoke with the fire and moral fervor of his Welsh noncomformist background, abhorring aristocratic privilege and demanding social and economic justice for the poor. Achieving national prominence because of his outspoken opposition to the Boer War (1899–1902), in 1905 he became a member of the new Liberal government, first as president of the Board of Trade and then in 1908 as chancellor of the exchequer.

Lloyd George consistently championed social welfare legislation, but his greatest domestic achievement was his Budget of 1909 and the resulting reform of the House of Lords. The budget was controversial not only because of its size, necessary to pay for the new welfare programs and the naval race with Germany, but because it increased the amounts levied on the wealthy by such means as a graduated income tax and death duties on

SOURCE. *The Times,* November 22, 1910, p. 8. Reproduced from *The Times* by permission.

land. When the Conservative-dominated House of Lords, which had already rejected several Liberal bills, now, on doubtful constitutional grounds, rejected the budget also, the lines of battle were drawn. The election of January 1910 was a referendum on the specific issue of the budget, and the Liberals were returned to power. The Lords bowed to the obvious wishes of the electorate and passed the budget, but it then threw out the subsequent Parliament Bill that would have reduced its ability to reject legislation to a suspensive veto, effective for 30 days in the case of money bills and for two years in the case of other legislation. In December 1910, there was another election, this one on the issue of the Parliament Bill. The Liberals were again successful, and the Lords in 1911 accepted the Parliament Act, although the king, as in 1832, had to threaten to create additional peers.

In defending the budget and the Parliament Bill to the working-class voters of London, at Limehouse on July 30, 1909, and then at Mile-end-road on November 21, 1910, Lloyd George was in his element. From *The Times* report of the latter speech, one can see his unabashed radicalism and the popular reaction to his fiery and emotional oratory. From his success in inaugurating the budget and the reform of the House of Lords, Lloyd George gained in stature with the Liberal party and, of course, with the electorate. This victory, however, was to be the last for the Liberal party. Being dependent on the support of Labour and the Irish, it was now burdened with political debts that could not easily be paid. Its last, best excuse for not being able to enact all it had promised—rejection in the House of Lords—had, by its own hand, been destroyed. The unhappy sequel to the events of 1909 to 1911 has been described as "The Strange Death of Liberal England."

MR. LLOYD GEORGE AT MILE-END

Attack on the Peers

Mr. Lloyd George last night addressed a meeting of 5,000 men at the Paragon Music Hall, Mile-end-road. His speech was intended to mark the opening of the Liberal election campaign in the Tower Hamlets, and the interest which had been aroused by the announcement of his visit was shown by the great crowd outside the hall who clamoured in vain to be admitted to its already over-burdened balconies and boxes.

The Chancellor of the Exchequer, as he recalled at the beginning of his speech, had opened his first campaign against the Lords in the neighbouring district of Limehouse. That was 18 months ago, but it seemed to be fresh in the minds of his audience, who greeted his references to his former speech with a cheer of encouragement and invitation to further exploits in the same field. The great majority of his hearers had clearly come to hear another Limehouse speech, and Mr. Lloyd George did not disappoint them. They were restless and unenthusiastic while he was detailing the merits of his Budget, . . . but they became keenly attentive and fiercely demonstrative when he began a violent attack upon the aristocracy. . . . A few of his supporters on the platform winced at the tone of these remarks, . . . but it was greatly to the liking of the "East-enders," as the chairman, Mr. B. S. Straus, called the audience, and Mr. Lloyd George was enthusiastically cheered when, at the end of an hour and a half, he sat down.

The meeting was several times interrupted by the intervention and immediate ejection, mercilessly carried out, of a number of male supporters of woman suffrage. The only other disturber of the meeting was a Socialist with a message to deliver.

Mr. Lloyd George's Speech

Mr. Lloyd George said: . . . I came here to talk to you tonight about the grave issue which has arisen out of a series of events which culminated in the rejection of that Budget. . . . The government needed money for the defence of the country. . . . We also needed money for the purpose of great schemes of social reform long promised, long promised by both parties—much too long deferred. (Cheers.) That was our need. No one denied it. How did we meet it? We met it by taxing great incomes, great fortunes, and the luxuries of all classes. That was our proposal. We sent it to the House of Lords. What did they demand? That great wealth should be spared, that we should pass luxuries by untaxed and untolled, and the money squandered on luxuries also, and that we should impose the burden on the bread and meat of the people. (Cries of "Shame.") What was our answer? We said not an ounce would be taken out of the necessaries of life of the people. (Cheers.) Then the Lords said, "Out with your Budget then." (More cries of "Shame.") And we have come here to ask you to help us to put them out. (Cheers.)

Success of the Budget

The Budget . . . has been in operation six months. Some resolutions have been in operation 18 months. Out of the money from the Budget we voted 20 millions last year and this, out of the new taxes, to raise the old people above need. Twenty millions! What more have we done? They talk as if we had done nothing for the Navy. Why, out of the money raised by that very abused Budget we have spent ten millions more upon building ships and upon the equipment of the Navy, and we have found every penny of it. But that is not all. We are going to bring in an additional 200,000 poor old people who are now branded with the stain of pauperism. We are going to make them State pensioners—like the dukes. . . .

The Imaginary Trip to Australia

Let [the Lords] take a trip to Australia to persuade the Australians to set up a House of Lords on our plan. Well now, let us go there with them. Now we go to Australia, . . . and before we landed we would ask, "Have you a Second Chamber here?" and they would say, "Yes." Then we would say, "We will stay the night." (Laughter.) "Would you mind telling us how it is composed and of what class of people?" "Oh," they would say, "just the class of people you see all around you. It is elected by all the people, male and female, who are of age." "But," our Tariff Reform friends would say, "surely you give more votes to the owners of property than to a mere man who works for his living?" And they would say, "No; here we want to be governed by souls not sods." (Cheers.) Then our Tory friends would say, "Is life safe here?" "Absolutely," they would be told. "Is property secure?" "Quite." "Can a man safely bring his capital to this country?" and the Australian would say, "From all I hear it would be much safer here than it would be in many quarters in the City of London." "Well, then," we would say to them, "Mind you, we are a mission to convert the heathen to the principles of an hereditary Chamber." (Laughter.) . . . "Ah! what shall Australia do to be saved? Give us an aristocracy." "How are we to get one?" they would say. "Nothing easier in the world. I will tell you how we got ours. I will give you our oldest and most ancient stock, and consequently our best, because aristocracy is like cheese—the older it is (Voice,—"The more it stinks.") (Laughter) the higher it becomes.

Family Origins

Now I will tell you how we got our first and best quality. A few shiploads of French filibusters came over from the coast of Normandy. They killed all the owners of property they could lay their hands on. (Laughter.) Having done so, they levied for their own uses death duties of 100 per cent. upon the rest. (Laughter.) Unfortunately their descendants ever since have been cutting each other's throats and there are very few of them left. Consequently they are very rare and very costly, and I need hardly assure you that such a common and vulgar doctrine as the survival of the fittest does not apply to them." (Laughter.) Now that is how we started. And we would say to the Australians:—"Have you anything like that?" And they would say:—"Well, stop a minute. We had a few years ago bushrangers (cheers) ; but we must inform you that they only stole cattle." "Oh," we say, "cattle won't do; it must be land, and that on a large scale." "Well," says the Australian, "it really doesn't matter. We hanged the last of them a short time ago before they had an opportunity of founding a family. Have you anything else?" (Laughter.) "Well, let's give you our second quality. Our second quality arose in this way. We had a great religious Reformation in this country and we had a certain number of people who took advantage of it to appropriate to their own uses land and buildings which had been consecrated to feed the needy and to attend the sick. (Shame.) . . . And they are the people whose descendants hurl at us the epithets of robbers, thieves, spoliators, because we dare put a tax of a halfpenny upon the land they purloined. . . . I would . . . say, "Have you anything to match that?" and they would say, "We have never been quite as bad as that in our worst days in this country." "Well then," I would say, "I am afraid we cannot help you. We have given you our two best qualities. We might go on and spread out a few more of those goods—the peerages created to enoble the indiscretions of kings. (Laughter.) We could go on, but it is hopeless. Don't you think you could found an aristocracy out of something of that sort?" They would say, "Here, rather than be governed by men like that we would have a Senate of Kangaroos." (Loud laughter and cheers.) . . .

"A Ludicrous Assembly"

It is no use going to the Colonies: there is no country in the world that would look at our Second Chamber. It is a ludicrous Assembly. Had it not been for the fact that for centuries the British-race has somehow got accustomed to them, their sense of humour would not tolerate them for half an hour. They may have been useful hundreds of years ago, but it must have been before my time, and it is no use trying to tinker at reform. They are past it. (Laughter.) Their system is just like the sort of thing I saw in London when they first introduced the electric trams—it is just like running an old horse tram and the electric cars on the same track. It ends in blocking the traffic. It is true the Tory Party now are doing their very best to put life into the old horse. (Laughter.) They are fitting up electric wires to his tail just to make him go for a time. . . . Well, on humanitarian principles I am opposed to cruelty to animals (Laughter), and I would turn the poor old thing to grass and convert his old tram into a cucumber frame.

Emmeline Pankhurst, *My Own Story* (1914). The Suffragette Movement

Women in nineteenth-century Britain made steady, if unspectacular, progress toward achieving equality of status with men. Divorce was obtainable at law after 1857. Oxford and Cambridge began to admit women in the 1870s, and employment opportunities for women began to improve about the same time. In 1893 parliament gave a married woman the same property rights as if she had remained single, freeing her from total economic dependence on her husband. Politically, women meeting the necessary property qualifications could vote in some local elections and, by the 1890s, even hold office. At the end of the century, however, women could still not vote in national elections, a restriction that was increasingly viewed as an anomaly in "democratic" Britain. The Women's Social and Political Union (WSPU), founded in 1903, undertook to win this fundamental right. Led by Mrs. Emmeline Pankhurst (1858–1928), the widow of a radical labor leader, and her two daughters, Sylvia and Christabel, the WSPU attempted at first peacefully to pursuade the Liberals to sponsor the necessary legislation. When this failed, the Pankhursts turned to "guerilla warfare," as described below in the selection from Mrs. Pankhurst's autobiography.

It is interesting to note that the Pankhursts, like most English revolutionaries, attempted to portray themselves as acting within established tradition. The Americans had rebelled to save their freedom; the men in England had used force to obtain their political rights. As Emmeline Pankhurst stressed, "The argument of broken glass is the most valuable argument in modern politics." Not everyone accepted this logic, however, and the violence of the WSPU by polarizing the issue perhaps delayed women's

SOURCE. Emmeline Pankhurst, *My Own Story*, New York: Kraus Reprint Co., 1971, pp. 116, 280–283, 306–307.

suffrage. Actually, some suffragettes appear to have lost sight of their objective—the right to vote. The "rapture of battle" became more important than victory, resulting by 1913 in a split between the moderate Sylvia and her mother and sister, who were turning to arson and bombing. World War I ended the movement; the militant suffragettes could now hate the "Huns." Following the war in 1918, parliament enfranchised women over thirty, that is, those who were mature and responsible and in numbers, insufficient to be able to outvote the men.

Published autobiographies are of great value to the historian. However, because they naturally attempt to justify the author's actions, they must be used with care.

Now we had reached a point where we had to choose between two alternatives. We had exhausted argument. Therefore either we had to give up our agitation altogether, as the suffragists of the eighties virtually had done, or else we must act, and go on acting, until the selfishness and the obstinacy of the Government was broken down, or the Government themselves destroyed. Until forced to do so, the Government, we perceived, would never give women the vote.

We realised the truth of John Bright's words, spoken while the reform bill of 1867 was being agitated. Parliament, John Bright then declared, had never been hearty for any reform. The Reform Act of 1832 had been wrested by force from the Government of that day, and now before another, he said, could be carried, the agitators would have to fill the streets with people from Charing Cross to Westminster Abbey. . . .

We had tried every other measure, as I am sure that I have demonstrated to my readers, and our years of work and suffering and sacrifice had taught us that the Government would not yield to right and justice, what the majority of members of the House of Commons admitted was right and justice, but that the Government would, as other governments invariably do, yield to expediency. Now our task was to show the Government that it was expedient to yield to the women's just demands. In order to do that we had to make England and every department of English life insecure and unsafe. We had to make English law a failure and the courts farce comedy theatres; we had to discredit the Government and Parliament in the eyes of the world; we had to spoil English sports, hurt business, destroy valuable property, demoralise the world of society, shame the churches, upset the whole orderly conduct of life—

That is, we had to do as much of this guerilla warfare as the people of

England would tolerate. When they came to the point of saying to the Government: "Stop this, in the only way it can be stopped, by giving the women of England representation," then we should extinguish our torch.

Americans, of all people, ought to see the logic of our reasoning. There is one piece of American oratory, beloved of schoolboys, which has often been quoted from militant platforms. In a speech now included among the classics of the English language your great statesman, Patrick Henry, summed up the causes that led to the American Revolution. He said: "We have petitioned, we have remonstrated, we have supplicated, we have prostrated ourselves at the foot of the throne, and it has all been in vain. We must fight—I repeat it, sir, we must fight."

Patrick Henry, remember was advocating killing people, as well as destroying private property, as the proper means of securing the political freedom of men. The Suffragettes have not done that, and they never will. In fact the moving spirit of militancy is deep and abiding reverence for human life. In the latter course of our agitation I have been called upon to discuss our policies with many eminent men, politicians, literary men, barristers, scientists, clergymen. One of the last named, a high dignitary of the Church of England, told me that while he was a convinced suffragist, he found it impossible to justify our doing wrong that right might follow. I said to him: "We are not doing wrong—we are doing right in our use of revolutionary methods against private property. It is our work to restore thereby true values, to emphasise the value of human rights against property rights. You are well aware, sir, that property has assumed a value in the eyes of men, and in the eyes of the law, that it ought never to claim. It is placed above all human values. The lives and health and happiness, and even the virtue of women and children—that is to say, the race itself—are being ruthlessly sacrificed to the god of property every day of the world."

To this my reverend friend agreed, and I said: "If we women are wrong in destroying private property in order that human values may be restored, then I say, in all reverence, that it was wrong for the Founder of Christianity to destroy private property, as He did when He lashed the money changers out of the Temple and when He drove the Gaderene swine into the sea."

It was absolutely in this spirit that our women went forth to war. In the first month of guerilla warfare an enormous amount of property was damaged and destroyed. On January 31st a number of putting greens were burned with acids; on February 7th and 8th telegraph and telephone wires were cut in several places and for some hours all communication between London and Glasgow were suspended; a few days later windows in various of London's smartest clubs were broken, and the orchid houses at Kew were wrecked and many valuable blooms destroyed by cold. The jewel room at the Tower of London was invaded and a showcase broken. The residence of H. R. H. Prince Christian and Lambeth Palace, seat of the Archbishop of Canterbury, were visited and had windows broken. The refreshment house in Regents Park was burned to the ground on February 12th and on February 18th a country house which was being built at Walton-on-the-Hill for Mr. Lloyd-George was partially destroyed, a bomb having been exploded in the early morning before the arrival of the workmen. A hat pin and a hair pin picked up near the house—coupled with the fact that care had been taken not to endanger any lives—led the police to believe that the deed had been done by women enemies of Mr. Lloyd-George. Four days later I was arrested and brought up in Epsom police court, where I was charged with having "counselled and procured" the persons who did the damage. Admitted to bail for the night, I appeared next morning in court, where the case was fully reviewed. Speeches of mine were read, one speech, made at a meeting held on January 22nd, in which I called for volunteers to act with me in a particular engagement; and another, made the day after the explosion, in which I publicly accepted responsibility for all militant acts done in the past, and even for what had been done at Walton. At the conclusion of the hearing I was committed for trial at the May Assizes at Guildford. Bail would be allowed, it was stated, if I would agree to give the usual undertaking to refrain from all militancy or incitement to militancy. . . .

That struggle is not a pleasant one to recall. Every possible means of breaking down my resolution was resorted to. The daintiest and most tempting food was placed in my cell. All sorts of arguments were brought to bear against me—the futility of resisting the Cat and Mouse Act, the wickedness of risking suicide—I shall not attempt to record all the arguments. They fell against a blank wall of consciousness, for my thoughts were all very far away from Holloway and all its torments. I knew, what afterwards I learned as a fact, that my imprisonment was followed by the greatest revolutionary outbreak that had been witnessed in England since 1832. From one end of the island to the other the beacons of the women's revolution blazed night and day. Many country houses—all unoccupied —were fired, the grand stand of Ayr race course was burned to the ground, a bomb was exploded in Oxted Station, London, blowing out walls and windows, some empty railroad carriages were blown up, the glass of thirteen famous paintings in the Manchester Art Gallery were smashed with hammers—these are simply random specimens of the general outbreak of secret guerilla warfare waged by women to whose liberties every other approach had been barricaded by the Liberal Government of free England. The only answer of the Government was the closing of the British Museum, the National Gallery, Windsor Castle, and other tourist resorts. As for the result on the people of England, that was exactly what we had anticipated. The public were thrown into a state of emotion of insecurity and frightened expectancy. Not yet did they show themselves ready to demand of the Government that the outrages be stopped in the only way they could be stopped—by giving votes to women. I knew that it would be so. Lying in my lonely cell in Holloway, racked with pain, oppressed with increasing weakness, depressed with the heavy responsibility of unknown happenings, I was sadly aware that we were but approaching a far goal. The end, though certain, was still distant. Patience, and still more patience, faith and still more faith, well, we had called upon these souls' help before and it was certain that they would not fail us at this greatest crisis of all.

111

Wilfred Owen, Poems (1917-1918). The Western Front

World War I was a traumatic experience. The initial enthusiasm evaporated quickly among the machine guns, heavy artillery, and mustard gas—the harsh realities of trench warfare. Exhilaration turned to a sullen acceptance of a conflict that produced not the expected victory, but a military stalemate and, of course, lengthy casualty lists. This despair produced the poetry of men like Robert Graves, Siegfried Sassoon, and Wilfred Owen. Earlier wars had inspired poets too, but most of them had been noncombatants concerned with glorifying the deeds of their nations' warriors. The best poetry of World War I was written, however, by men who fought and, in some cases, died in the trenches. It reflects a questioning of the morality and utility of war, an attitude that survived the war and became the pacifist movement of the 1920s and 1930s.

Wilfred Owen (1893–1918) owed both his fame and his death to World War I. In 1915 he volunteered as a private in the Artists' Rifles. He fought in France for three years, being seriously wounded in 1917 but recovering and becoming a company commander. He was killed in action on November 4, 1918, one week before the armistice. Because his best poetry was written between August 1917 and September 1918, his literary fame was post-humous. His poetry reflects the cynicism, anger, and frustration of the men who were sent to fight on the Western Front. Poetry like Owen's adds another dimension to the study of World War I and the attitudes of the people who survived it, supplementing the traditional evidence of more conventional documents.

THE PARABLE OF THE OLD MAN AND THE YOUNG

So Abram rose, and clave the wood, and went,
And took the fire with him, and a knife.
And as they sojourned both of them together,
Isaac the first-born spake and said, My Father,
Behold the preparations, fire and iron,
But where the lamb for this burnt-offering?
Then Abram bound the youth with belts and straps,
And builded parapets and trenches there,
And stretched forth the knife to slay his son.
When lo! an angel called him out of heaven,
Saying, Lay not thy hand upon the lad,
Neither do anything to him. Behold,
A ram, caught in a thicket by its horns;
Offer the Ram of Pride instead of him.
But the old man would not so, but slew his son,
And half the seed of Europe, one by one.

SPRING OFFENSIVE

Halted against the shade of a last hill,
They fed, and lying easy, were at ease
And, finding comfortable chests and knees,
Carelessly slept. But many there stood still
To face the stark, blank sky beyond the ridge,
Knowing their feet had come to the end of the world.

Marvelling they stood, and watched the long grass swirled
By the May breeze, murmurous with wasp and midge,
For though the summer oozed into their veins
Like an injected drug for their bodies' pains,
Sharp on their souls hung the imminent line of grass,
Fearfully flashed the sky's mysterious glass.

• • •

So, soon they topped the hill, and raced together
Over an open stretch of herb and heather
Exposed. And instantly the whole sky burned
With fury against them; earth set sudden cups
In thousands for their blood; and the green slope
Chasmed and steepened sheer to infinite space.

Of them who running on that last high place
Leapt to swift unseen bullets, or went up
On the hot blast and fury of hell's upsurge,
Or plunged and fell away past this world's verge,
Some say God caught them even before they fell.

But what say such as from existence' brink
Ventured but drave too swift to sink,
The few who rushed in the body to enter hell,
And there out-fiending all its fiends and flames
With superhuman inhumanities,
Long-famous glories, immemorial shames—
And crawling slowly back, have by degrees
Regained cool peaceful air in wonder—
Why speak not they of comrades that went under?

PLATE A
Battle of Passchendaele (from the Imperial War Museum; courtesy of
Camera Press, Ltd., London).

SOLDIER'S DREAM

> I dreamed kind Jesus fouled the big-gun gears;
> And caused a permanent stoppage in all bolts;
> And buckled with a smile Mausers and Colts;
> And rusted every bayonet with His tears.
> And there were no more bombs, of ours or Theirs,
> Not even an old flint-lock, nor even a pikel.
> But God was vexed, and gave all power to Michael;
> And when I woke he'd seen to our repairs.

The Balfour Report (1926).
From Empire to Commonwealth

John Stuart Mill in the nineteenth century defined Great Britain as "the Power which, of all in existence, best understands liberty." If this premise is accepted, the evolution of Britain's nineteenth-century empire into the twentieth-century Commonwealth of Nations becomes a natural, almost inevitable, process. Following the introduction of responsible government in the 1840s and 1850s, the colonies of white settlement in British North America, Australasia, and southern Africa asserted increasing control over their own affairs, including commerce and, to a more limited extent, foreign policy. The participation of these colonies, or dominions as they were called after 1907, in World War I and in the postwar deliberations at Versailles gave them a new standing in the international community. The dominions' new, practical independence was registered by their membership in the League of Nations.

There remained in the 1920s, however, constitutional difficulties connected with "dominion status." Most important, the Colonial Laws Validity Act (1865) declared void any colonial statute conflicting with a British law extended to the colony. Furthermore, the British parliament still had the theoretical power to pass legislation affecting the dominions. The Imperial Conference of 1926, therefore, appointed the Inter-Imperial Relations Committee to clarify the status of the dominions and named Lord Balfour (1848–1930), the former British prime minister, as its chairman. His report, issued as a parliamentary paper, is reproduced in part below.

The Balfour Report, although widely recognized as an important statement of principle, was typically British in its ambiguity and flexibility. It firmly

SOURCE. "Report of the Inter-Imperial Relations Committee," Cmd. 2768, pp. 14–15, 20, 22, 25–26, *Parliamentary Papers*, 1926, XI. Reprinted by permission of the Controller of Her Britannic Majesty's Stationery Office.

stated that Britain and the dominions were "freely associated" "autonomous communities." It also stated the obvious, that in the areas of defense and foreign policy "the major share of responsibility" would continue to rest with Britain. But, if the dominions were autonomous, what held the British Commonwealth together? Was it simply a semi-mystical "unity in diversity" as Stanley Baldwin, the prime minister, described it? It is apparent that this "piece of Scottish, Balfourian metaphysics" did not actually give the dominions the legal independence sought by some of them. To do that, the British parliament in the Statute of Westminster (1931) repealed the Colonial Laws Validity Act, forbade Britain to legislate for a dominion without its consent, and granted the dominions the authority to pass legislation with extraterritorial effect. A dominion could now, if it chose, legislate itself out of the British Commonwealth, as Ireland immediately began to do. On the other hand, the Balfour Report and the Statute of Westminster made it possible for the colonies in Asia and Africa to aspire to independence and yet remain within the Commonwealth, instead of following the American example.

II. STATUS OF GREAT BRITAIN AND THE DOMINIONS

The Committee are of opinion that nothing would be gained by attempting to lay down a Constitution for the British Empire. Its widely scattered parts have very different characteristics, very different histories, and are at very different stages of evolution; while, considered as a whole, it defies classification and bears no real resemblance to any other political organisation which now exists or has ever yet been tried.

There is, however, one most important element in it which, from a strictly constitutional point of view, has now, as regards all vital matters, reached its full development—we refer to the group of self-governing communities composed of Great Britain and the Dominions. Their position and mutual relation may be readily defined. *They are autonomous Communities within the British Empire, equal in status, in no way subordinate one to another in any aspect of their domestic or external affairs, though united by a common allegiance to the Crown, and freely associated as members of the British Commonwealth of Nations.*

A foreigner endeavouring to understand the true character of the British Empire by the aid of this formula alone would be tempted to think that it was devised rather to make mutual interference impossible than to make mutual co-operation easy.

Such a criticism, however, completely ignores the historic situation. The rapid evolution of the Oversea Dominions during the last fifty years has involved many complicated adjustments of old political machinery to changing conditions. The tendency towards equality of status was both right and inevitable. Geographical and other conditions made this impossible of attainment by the way of federation. The only alternative was by the way of autonomy: and along this road it has been steadily sought. Every self-governing member of the Empire is now the master of its destiny. In fact, if not always in form, it is subject to no compulsion whatever.

But no account, however accurate, of the negative relations in which Great Britain and the Dominions stand to each other can do more than express a portion of the truth. The British Empire is not founded upon negations. It depends essentially, if not formally, on positive ideals. Free institutions are its life-blood. Free co-operation is its instrument. Peace, security, and progress are among its objects. Aspects of all these great themes have been discussed at the present Conference: excellent results have been thereby obtained. And, though every Dominion is now, and must always remain, the sole judge of the nature and extent of its co-operation, no common cause will, in our opinion, be thereby imperilled.

Equality of status, so far as Britain and the Dominions are concerned, is thus the root principle governing our Inter-Imperial Relations. But the principles of equality and similarity, appropriate to *status,* do not universally extend to function. Here we require something more than immutable dogmas. For example, to deal with questions of diplomacy and questions of defence, we require also flexible machinery—machinery which can, from time to time, be adapted to the changing circumstances of the world. . . .

V. *RELATIONS WITH FOREIGN COUNTRIES*

It was agreed in 1923 that any of the Governments of the Empire contemplating the negotiation of a treaty should give due consideration to its possible effect upon other Governments and should take steps to inform Governments likely to be interested of its intention. . . .

When a Government has received information of the intention of any other Government to conduct negotiations, it is incumbent upon it to indicate its attitude with reasonable promptitude. So long as the initiating Government receives no adverse comments and so long as its policy involves no active obligations on the part of the other Governments, it may proceed on the assumption that its policy is generally acceptable. It must, however, before taking any steps which might involve the other Governments in any active obligations, obtain their definite assent.

Where by the nature of the treaty it is desirable that it should be ratified on behalf of all the Governments of the Empire, the initiating Government may assume that a Government which has had full opportunity of indicating its attitude and has made no adverse comments will concur in the ratification of the treaty. In the case of a Government that prefers not to concur in the ratification of a treaty unless it has been signed by a plenipotentiary authorised to act on its behalf, it will advise the appointment of a plenipotentiary so to act. . . .

It was frankly recognized that in this sphere, as in the sphere of defence, the major share of responsibility rests now, and must for some time continue to rest, with His Majesty's Government in Great Britain. Nevertheless, practically all the Dominions are engaged to some extent, and some to a considerable extent, in the conduct of foreign relations, particularly those with foreign countries on their borders. A particular instance of this is the growing work in connection with the relations between Canada and the United States of America which has led to the necessity for the appointment of a Minister Plenipotentiary to represent the Canadian Government in Washington. We felt that the governing consideration underlying all discussions of this problem must be that neither Great Britain nor the Dominions could be committed to the acceptance of active obligations except with the definite assent of their own Governments.

113

The British Gazette (1926).
The General Strike

Following two years of economic prosperity immediately after the Armistice in 1918, Britain encountered economic difficulties. These were characterized primarily by a permanent condition of unemployment, about 10 percent of the work force being without jobs throughout the entire decade of the 1920s. Hardest hit were the coal miners, whose industry had been artificially expanded by the needs of World War I and then bolstered for a time by government subsidies. A reduction in wages provoked the miners on April 26, 1926, to strike. This action was supported by the Trade Union Congress (TUC), which called a general, sympathetic strike on May 3.

The General Strike lasted only nine days. Although people sympathized with the plight of the miners, they viewed the strike as a threat to constitutional authority and supported prime minister Stanley Baldwin's refusal to bow to the demands of the TUC. Abandoned by their fellow labor unionists, the miners continued to strike for six months until they were forced to accept lower wages, longer hours, and increased unemployment. The collapse of the General Strike brought a realization that working men had more to gain from a strong labor party than by direct action.

One surprising characteristic of the General Strike was the goodwill shown between the combatants; football matches between strikers and police were hardly the prelude to revolution. In many areas, the inconveniences and hardships produced by the strike provoked a spirit of civic cooperation and gaiety. In fact, one of Baldwin's major concerns was restraining hot heads such as Winston Churchill (1874–1965), the chancellor of the ex-

SOURCE. *The British Gazette,* No. 1 (May 5, 1926), p. 1; No. 2 (May 6, 1926), p. 3. Reprinted by permission of the Controller of Her Britannic Majesty's Stationery Office.

chequer, who wanted to call out the troops and suppress "the enemy." Fortunately, Churchill was fully occupied by his work as editor of *The British Gazette,* a government newspaper created to replace the private papers, most of which had been closed by the strike. Baldwin later boasted that this appointment was the "cleverest" thing that he had ever done; otherwise Churchill "would have wanted to shoot someone."

The British Gazette is an interesting piece of historical evidence, especially in view of the absence of other press accounts of the General Strike. However, because of Churchill's anti-labor bias, it must be used with more than the usual caution. It is obvious from both the article and the editorial reproduced below that *The British Gazette* made no pretense at objectivity and was more inflammatory in tone and style than the strike itself. It is important, nevertheless, as a reflection of Churchill's combative personality, a fighting spirit that seemed inappropriate in 1926 but that, in 1940, was to become an invaluable national asset.

FIRST DAY OF GREAT STRIKE.
NOT SO COMPLETE AS HOPED BY ITS PROMOTERS.
PREMIER'S AUDIENCE OF THE KING.
MINERS AND THE GENERAL COUNCIL MEET AT HOUSE OF COMMONS.

The great strike began yesterday. There are already signs, however, that it is by no means so complete as its promoters hoped. There were far more trains running than was the case on the first day of the railway strike in 1919.

The King received the Prime Minister in audience at Buckingham Palace yesterday morning.

Reports from all parts of the country indicate that satisfactory arrangements have been set up for recruiting. Volunteers came forward in large numbers in London and all the important provincial centres. . . .

Never-Ending Queue

The wooden huts in the courtyard of the Foreign Office were besieged yesterday by an eager crowd anxious to do their bit. In the never-ending queue were representatives of every walk of life fairly evenly divided between men and women.

Inside the huts the officials and their volunteer helpers had a hard time of it, with never a minute to look up from their work or to cease their relentless fire of questions. "What can you do? What are you willing to do?" The answer to the first part of the question was usually something to do with motors, and the answer to the second question was invariably "anything."

This overwhelming flood of willing volunteers provided an interesting study in types. Here was the obvious City man, the lady from Mayfair, the "charlady," and an extraordinary number of young girls. The younger men, who by the queue held a majority ranged from the bareheaded motor-bicycle type to the newsboy and the van boy.

A casual inquiry as to what one of the latter was willing to do met with a unanimous cry from everybody in the vicinity, "Anything." "That," remarked the patient policeman at the door, "is the right spirit, and the sort of spirit we have had here in large quantities for the last two days."

Outside in Downing-street, the Police managed to keep the roadway fairly clear, but in Whitehall half a dozen mounted men had their work cut out to keep the curious on the move. Everywhere, however, good temper prevailed. . . .

Londoners' Trek to Work

On foot, squeezed into cars, standing in vans, riding pillion, pedaling on cycles, swarming Citywards by every road and route, London came yesterday morning doggedly and cheerially to work.

Whoever has struggled along the choked highway to Epsom Downs on Derby Day may form a mental picture of the first day's strike pilgrimmage to the East of Temple Bar. The congestion was as bad, and the temper of the people was as good.

No newspaper came to many houses to tell whether the conflict had in the eleventh hour been averted, but to read the news one had only to look out of the window. The streets with their press of private vehicles, with their streams of walkers settled to a long and steady stride, and, with never a sign of red omnibus or clanging tram, told emphatically as print that the great general strike had begun.

Every thoroughfare was a one-way street—to London. The luxurious 1920 limousines and the drab and coughing relics of prewar motoring crept along side by side in the crowded fraternity of the road. At every crossing the police beckoned on the unending line, and their task was made easy, because every man and woman at the wheel drove with consideration and a new courtesy.

In the inevitable blocks and jams, conversation rose above the throbbing of the engines. "How long will it last?" "They say that the Government—" And there Englishmen are gathered together. "Was that Mr. Ford's first sample?" demanded a lorry driver stuck level with a sorry machine whose radiator oozed little rivulets. "Never mind," retorted the anxious owner, "it moves, and"—indicating three laughing girls in the back seat—"I've a better cargo than you."

[May 5, 1926]

THE NATIONAL ISSUE.
Constitution To Be Vindicated.
ASSAULT ON RIGHTS OF THE NATION.
Union Leaders' Personal Responsibility.

Everyone must realize that, so far as the General Strike is concerned, there can be no question of compromise of any kind. Either the country will break the General Strike, or the General Strike will break the country.

Not only is the prosperity of the country gravely injured; not only is immense and increasing loss and suffering inflicted upon the whole mass of the people; but the foundations of the lawful Constitution of Great Britain are assailed.

His Majesty's Government will not flinch from the issue, and will use all the resources at their disposal and whatever measures may be necessary to secure in a decisive manner the authority of Parliamentary government.

The Prime Minister's message to *The British Gazette* expresses a decision from which there can be no withdrawal. All loyal citizens, without respect to party or class, should forthwith range themselves behind his Majesty's Government and Parliament in the task of defending in an exemplary fashion the deliberate and organized assault upon the rights and freedom of the nation. The stronger the rally of loyal and faithful men to the cause of Parliamentary government, the sooner will the victory be achieved and the shorter the period of waste and suffering.

Extremists' Pressure

No doubt it is true that the majority of the Trades Union leaders did not intend, when they launched the General Strike, to raise the constitutional issue. They drifted weakly forward under the pressure of more extreme men. Perhaps they thought that the Government would collapse and Parliament bow down before the threat of so much injury to the Commonwealth. But whatever they may have wished or thought, a national issue has been raised of supreme magnitude.

Moreover, the responsibility of these Trades Union leaders is grievous. It is also a personal responsibility. They made no attempt to consult by ballot those whom they claim to represent. They broke in many directions contracts and engagements to which their good name was pledged, and they yielded themselves to a course of action reckless, violent, and, but for the strength and good sense of the British nation, immeasurable in its possibilities.

It would be the manly course on their part, and one which they have a perfect right to take, to reconsider their action now that they can see into what deep and deepening waters it is daily carrying them. It is not yet too late.

But whatever they may do, the authority of Parliamentary government over any sectional combination must be vindicated. Every man and every woman must consider where duty lies, and, if duties seem to conflict, where the greater duty lies. The first of all duties, a duty greater than all others put together, is owed to the nation as a whole and to that system of democratic and representative Parliamentary government which has for so many generation been the mainstay of British progress and of British freedom.

[May 6, 1926]

114

Lord Birkenhead, Speech in Lords (1928). Equal Voting Rights for Women

The House of Lords remained, despite the Parliament Act of 1911, an important part of the constitution. Although it could no longer kill legislation outright, it could and did continue to make suggestions and to correct the

SOURCE. *The Parliamentary Debates* (House of Lords), Fifth Series, LXXI, 251–254.

oversights of the busy House of Commons. Ironically, the Lords had always been the less formal of the two houses in its proceedings and rules of debate. Its membership, continually augmented by the ennobling of successful men from many walks of life, invariably contained a number of capable and diligent statesmen.

Such a man was F. E. Smith (1872–1930), a successful barrister, a member of parliament and the cabinet, and certainly one of the most intelligent men in Britain. In 1919 he had been made lord chancellor and elevated to the peerage as baron, later earl of, Birkenhead. In the Lords his dramatic sarcasm and sense of humor were more appropriate and better appreciated than in the serious and workaday House of Commons. In the speech below, which Birkenhead delivered on May 22, 1928, one can see the history of women's emancipation from the viewpoint of a witty but pragmatic male chauvinist. With the passage of this act, the Representation of the People (Equal Franchise) Act of 1928, women attained the same voter qualifications as men.

It is worth while going into the history of this matter. . . . It was in the year 1918, after the War, that the disaster took place. Had it not been for the War in my judgment we should have continued successfully to resist this measure for an indefinite period of time. But what happened? In that year, in which nearly everybody went mad, when the phrases of President Wilson and his predictions were translated into logical and mathematical conclusions, and we talked of self-determination when we made the Peace Treaty—it was in that year that a discussion arose as to the extension of the franchise. . . .

Let me describe to your Lordships how gradually, yet how inevitably, we descended the slippery slope. First of all, it was not proposed that women should be included. Then a member of the House of Commons, and an important one, said that whoever was included or was not included, it was quite impossible to exclude from the franchise the brave men who had supported our cause in the field. Although it is not a political or a philosophic certainty that a man who has supported your cause in the field is necessarily equally qualified to support your cause at the polls, that argument in the spirit of the moment was accepted with facile enthusiasm, and accordingly the soldiers were admitted, subject to the qualification of age and without reference to any other very rigorous examination. Then another member of the House arose and said: "If you are extending the franchise to our brave soldiers in recognition of their valour on the field how about our brave munition workers, many to whom would greatly have desired to serve in the field, but who were not allowed to do so because of the immensely greater services which they were rendering to the nation by their work in relation to munitions?" That argument, too, was difficult to resist when once you had yielded to the first. Then an insidious and subtle member of the House said: "How about our brave women munition workers?" and, having once on principle yielded to the first argument, it was absolutely impossible to resist the second. . . .

In those circumstances—preserving, as I made it plain to the House of Commons of that day in not opposing that Bill that I did preserve, all my old objections and prejudices—was I to say: "I will leave this Government because I am in a small minority in the House of Commons?" I have spent nearly the whole of my political life in giving wise advice to my fellow countrymen, which they have almost invariably disregarded, and if I had resigned every time that my wise and advantageous advice was rejected I should seldom, indeed, during that critical period have been in office. I, therefore, reasonably took the view, making a frank explanation to the House of Commons of the position in which I found myself, that it was my duty as Attorney-General to carry out the wishes of the Government; but I expressly made my advocacy of that Bill conditional upon my complete freedom to explain the circumstances in which I found myself at the moment as its paradoxical champion. I claim the same freedom to-night.

Let me for a moment discuss the real issue which is before this House. Nearly all the arguments that have been addressed to your Lordships have been arguments that would have been valuable, timely and relevant in the year 1919. I have not heard one argument in the course of debate which has the slightest value in the period which we have reached. . . . Suppose your Lordships took the grave and most unwise responsibility of rejecting this Bill to-night, what would happen at the next General Election? The Leader of the Labour Party, the Leader of the Liberal Party and the Leader of the Conservative Party would all go to the country and say: "We profoundly resent the attitude of the House of Lords and we all of us pledge ourselves to re-introduce this Bill at once the moment the Election has taken place." I picture Lord Banbury taking the field and informing the country that if he is returned to power it is his purpose to refuse to carry this Bill into law. These things are not done by members of this House without organisation, or Parties, or followings. When you are to attempt a prognosis of that which the country will do you must address yourselves to it in the spirit of practical politicians. Once you know that the Leaders of all the Parties and the organisations of all the Parties are deeply pledged to this change it is folly to make a recommendation to your Lordships which, if adopted, would cover this House with ridicule. We know that such a course could never be taken by an Assembly which, upon so many grave and critical occasions, has given evidence of prudence and sanity.

We have to-day to meet a new situation. I have made it plain that I did and do contemplate the results with anxiety, but let us realise that when once both Houses have affirmed as a matter of principle in the Preamble to the 1919 Act, as the noble and learned Lord upon the Woolsack reminded us, that men and women were to be equal, there was indeed a kind of hypocrisy an insincerity in relation to which we had little defence, when we put it off year after year and said that women of twenty-one are not as mature and not as sophisticated as men of twenty-one. Everyone of us in our hearts knows that a woman of twenty-one is far more mature and far more sophisticated than a man of twenty-one. The moment, therefore, you had settled the principle that women were to have votes at all it became a lost cause to argue that there should be differentiation between people of the same ages. . . . My recommendation to your Lordships is to go into the Lobby in favour of this Bill, if without enthusiasm yet in a spirit of resolute resignation.

115

John Maynard Keynes, "Can Lloyd George Do It?" (1929)

The general election of May 1929 focused on the problem of unemployment. The Conservatives, led by Prime Minister Stanley Baldwin (1867–1949), emphasized that 90 percent of the work force had jobs, and they adopted as their slogans "Trust Baldwin" and "Safety First." As evidence that economic

SOURCE. *The Collected Writings of John Maynard Keynes*, Vol. IX: *Essays in Persuasion*, London: Macmillan for the Royal Economic Society, 1972, pp. 92–93, 121–122, 124–125. Reprinted by permission of Professor E. A. G. Robinson and Lord Kahn, Executor of the Estate of Lord Keynes.

progress was being made, Baldwin cited the expanded broccoli exports to Europe. Although Labour naturally believed in socialism and wanted to end "the capitalist dictatorship," its leader, Ramsay MacDonald (1866–1937), was primarily concerned with appearing moderate and responsible; thus he proposed few specific reforms. Actually, the most radical and innovative program was that of the Liberal party, now reunited under the leadership of David Lloyd George (1863–1945). The Liberals' campaign manifesto, "We Can Conquer Unemployment," incorporated many of the ideas of John Maynard Keynes (1883–1946), one of the leading economists in Britain.

Keynes, a Treasury official from 1915 to 1919, became famous because of his *Economic Consequences of the Peace* (1919), a violent attack on the Treaty of Versailles, which he felt would retard the revival of German and, hence, European prosperity. In 1925 he protested Britain's return to the gold standard by criticizing the chancellor of the exchequer in a pamphlet, "The Economic Consequences of Mr. Churchill." He proposed, unsuccessfully, to promote economic growth by means of programs financed and directed by the government. His ideas struck a responsive chord in the fertile mind of Lloyd George, and Keynes became a part of the Liberal brain trust. Together with H. D. Henderson, a similarly-minded colleague, Keynes wrote in 1929 a pamphlet in support of the Liberals, "Can Lloyd George Do It?"

As is shown in the excerpts from this pamphlet below, Keynes advocated bold governmental experimentation in the field of economic planning and an end to blind, do-nothing reliance on the natural laws of laissez-faire economics. He strongly supported Lloyd George's plan for government-sponsored programs of public works, financed at least in part by deficit spending. This, he argued, was less costly than unemployment insurance and the unproductiveness of unemployed labor. His ideas were, as he himself stated, regarded by most people as "extreme and reckless utterances" and, in the 1929 election, the Liberals received only 59 seats in the House of Commons compared to 288 for Labour and 260 for the Conservatives. Although the Liberals and Lloyd George were dead, Keynes's ideas were not. Following the Wall Street Crash of late 1929, Keynes's economic theories, most forcefully and completely articulated in his *General Theory of Employment, Interest and Money* (1936), gradually gained acceptance. Keynesian economics received its most complete test in the New Deal programs of President Franklin Roosevelt in the United States and in the wartime government of Winston Churchill.

Except for a brief recovery in 1924 before the return to the gold standard, one-tenth or more of the working population of this country have been unemployed for eight years—a fact unprecedented in our history. The number of insured persons counted by the Ministry of Labour as out of work has never been less than one million since the initiation of their statistics in 1923. Today (April 1929) 1,140,000 work-people are unemployed.

This level of unemployment is costing us out of the Unemployment Fund a cash disbursement of about £50 million a year. This does not include poor relief. Since 1921 we have paid out to the unemployed in cash a sum of about £500 million—and have got literally nothing for it. This sum would have built a million houses; it is nearly double the whole of the accumulated savings of the Post Office Savings Bank; it would build a third of all the roads in the country; it far exceeds the total value of all the mines, of every description, which we possess; it would be enough to revolutionise the industrial equipment of the country; or to proceed from what is heavy to what is lighter, it would provide every third family in the country with a motor-car or would furnish a fund enough to allow the whole population to attend cinemas for nothing to the end of time.

But this is not nearly all the waste. There is the far greater loss to the unemployed themselves, represented by the difference between the dole and a full working wage, and by the loss of strength and morale. There is the loss in profits to employers and in taxation to the Chancellor of the Exchequer. There is the incalculable loss of retarding for a decade the economic progress of the whole country. . . .

It is important to know and appreciate these figures because they put the possible cost of Mr Lloyd George's schemes into its true perspective. He calculates that a development programme of £100 million a year will bring back 500,000 men into employment. *This expenditure is not large in proportion to the waste and loss accruing year by year* through unemployment, as can be seen by comparing it with the figures quoted above. It only represents 5 per cent of the loss already accumulated on account of unemployment since 1921. It is equal to about 2½ per cent of the national income. If the experiment were to be continued at the rate of £100 million per annum for three years, and if the whole of it were to be entirely wasted, the annual interest payable on it hereafter would increase the budget by less than 2 per cent. In short, it is a *very modest programme*. The idea that it represents a desperate risk to cure a moderate evil is the reverse of the truth. It is a negligible risk to cure a monstrous anomaly.

Nothing has been included in the programme which cannot be justified as worth doing for its own sake. Yet even if half of it were to be wasted, *we should still be better off*. Was there ever a stronger case for a little boldness, for taking a risk if there be one? . . . Our whole economic policy during recent years has been dominated by the preoccupation of the Treasury with their departmental problem of debt conversion. The less the government borrows, the better, they argue, are the chances of converting the national debt into loans carrying a lower rate of interest. In the interests of conversion, therefore, they have exerted themselves to curtail, as far as they can, all public borrowing, all capital expenditure by the State, no matter how productive and desirable in itself. We doubt if the general public has any idea how powerful, persistent, and far-reaching this influence has been.

To all well-laid schemes of progress and enterprise, they have (whenever they could) barred the door with, No! Now it is quite true that curtailing capital expenditures exerts some tendency towards lower interest rates for government loans. But it is no less true that it makes for increased unemployment and that it leaves the country with a pre-war outfit. . . . It is not an accident that the Conservative government have landed us in the mess where we find ourselves. It is the natural outcome of their philosophy:

> You must not press on with telephones or electricity, because this will raise the rate of interest.
>
> You must not hasten with roads or housing, because this will use up opportunities for employment which we may need in later years.
>
> You must not try to employ everyone, because this will cause inflation.
>
> You must not invest, because how can you know that it will pay?
>
> You must not do anything, because this will only mean that you can't do something else.
>
> Safety first! The policy of maintaining a million unemployed has now been pursued for eight years without disaster. Why risk a change?
>
> We will not promise more than we can perform. We, therefore, promise nothing.

This is what we are being fed with.

They are slogans of depression and decay—the timidities and obstructions and stupidities of a sinking administrative vitality.

Negation, restriction, inactivity—these are the government's watchwords. Under their leadership we have been forced to button up our waistcoats and compress our lungs. Fears and doubts and hypochondriac precautions are keeping us muffled up indoors. But we are not tottering to our graves. We are healthy children. We need the breath of life. There is nothing to be afraid of. On the contrary. The future holds in store for us far more wealth and economic freedom and possibilities of personal life than the past has ever offered.

There is no reason why we should not feel ourselves free to be bold, to be open, to experiment, to take action, to try the possibilities of things. And over against us, standing in the path, there is nothing but a few old gentlemen tightly buttoned-up in their frock coats, who only need to be treated with a little friendly disrespect and bowled over like ninepins.

Quite likely they will enjoy it themselves, when once they have got over the shock.

116

The Times (1933). The Body-line Bowling Controversy

The British have always been a sporting people, one historian arguing that organized games "rank among England's leading contributions to world culture." Archery, bowls, hunting, shooting, prizefighting, croquet, and polo (from India) were all popular sports in the nineteenth century. The revival of horseracing (St. Leger, the Derby, and Ascot) and steeplechasing (the Grand National at Aintree) was assisted by the reforms of Lord George Bentinck and the introduction of handicapping. Golf, originally a "peculiarity of Scotsmen," was introduced into England in the 1860s and grew rapidly. Lawn tennis, patented in 1874, was regulated after 1877 by the Wimbledon All England Croquet and Lawn Tennis Club. Most significant in the long run was the development of "football," regularized by the Football Association (1863) and the Rugby Union (1871). "Association" football, or soccer, has swept the world, becoming without question the premier sport of modern time. The first international match was between England and Scotland in 1872. And then there was cricket.

Cricket, an old game, was already recognized as the national sport by the early nineteenth century. It was viewed as peculiarly English, because it developed qualities such as courage and grace, individualism and teamwork,

SOURCE. *The Times,* January 19, 1933, pp. 3, 12; January 20, 1933, p. 9; January 24, 1933, p. 10; March 1, 1933, p. 15. Reproduced from *The Times* by permission.

THE "LEAGUE THEORY."

Mr. Punch. "COME ALONG, LET'S REFER THIS LITTLE SQUABBLE TO GENEVA."

PLATE A
(© *Punch* 1933).

sportsmanship and, of course, honesty. The popularity of cricket as a spectator sport was signaled by the opening of Lord's Cricket Ground in 1827 and the emergence of such cricketers as Alfred Mynn (1807–1861) and W. G. Grace (1848–1915), who became national heroes. Cricket was also a good export, especially to the colonies. In 1859 the All England XI journeyed to Canada and the United States. The first eleven to visit England was a team of Australian Aborigines in 1868. This led to the first Test Match between England and Australia in 1871. These matches were seen as more than important sporting events: they were a bond uniting the empire.

Because cricket was a gentlemanly sport, which taught fair play and respect for rules, there was dismay in both England and Australia at the bitterness and controversy produced in the 1932 to 1933 Test Matches. Douglas Jardine, the coach of the English team sponsored by the Marylebone Cricket Club (MCC), attempted to neutralize the strong Australian batsmen by instructing his premier bowler, Harold Larwood, to bowl on the leg side or, as the Australians claimed, at the batsman rather than the wicket. When in the second match two of Australia's best batsmen were carried from the field, the situation became explosive. The Australians regarded this body-line bowling or leg-theory bowling as unsportsmanlike, as "not cricket." The resulting controversy can be judged from the selections below taken from the sports pages of *The Times*. The problem was so serious that the Dominions Secretary called the MCC officials to Downing Street for a conference (see Plate A). Although the crisis was short-lived, the following year the British government took the precaution of insisting that Larwood be dropped from the English team.

THE THIRD TEST MATCH.
ENGLAND'S WINNING POSITION.
AUSTRALIA PROTEST AT LEG-THEORY.

England seems almost certain to beat Australia in the Third Test Match for, after scoring 412 in their second innings and leaving the Australians 532 to make in order to win, they succeeded in dismissing four of their best batsmen in the second innings for 120 before stumps were pulled up to-day. At the close of play Ponsford, Fingleton, McCabe, and Bradman were all out, and Woodfull and Richardson may be regarded as Australia's last hope, though Oldfield, if he is able to go in, which seems unlikely, is capable of a good performance. The wicket was still in excellent order when Australia went in a second time. On the form of this match the English team have proved themselves superior all round. . . .

The only bright feature of the match from the Australian point of view was Bradman's bright innings to-day. In a little over an hour he showed his best form. He hit the bowling hard at a critical period, and he made it look playable, which other Australians have hitherto failed to do. The crowd applauded heartily while Jardine kept his bowlers to the off theory, but when he reverted to leg theory against Bradman, who seemed to be getting the better of the bowling, they howled and hooted loudly. . . .

When Australia went in Larwood began bowling to an off-field. His first few opening overs were very fast and he completely beat Fingleton with his pace. Ponsford went in at the fall of the first wicket. He began well, but was out to a good stroke. Larwood had, so far taken two for one run. Larwood continued bowling to an orthodox field for a few overs, but, after Bradman had begun to score freely off him, he reverted to the leg theory. Woodfull and Bradman continued to make runs off Larwood

and Bradman hit eight 4's and a 6 before he was caught and bowled by
Verity.

The Australian Board of Control have cabled a protest against "body-
line bowling" to the M.C.C., which is printed on p. 12.

[*The Times,* January 19, 1933]

"LEG-THEORY" BOWLING.
AUSTRALIAN PROTEST.

The Australian Cricket Board of Control has sent the following telegram to the M.C.C.:

> Body-line bowling has assumed such proportions as to menace the
> best interests of the game, making the protection of his body by a
> batsman his main consideration. It is causing intensely bitter feel-
> ing between the players as well as injury to them. In our opinion it
> is unsportsmanlike. Unless it is stopped at once it is likely to upset
> the friendly relations existing between Australia and England. . . .

The M.C.C. received the telegram sent by the Australian Cricket Board
of Control on the subject of leg-theory bowling shortly before noon yesterday. It is not yet known when the matter will be discussed.

[*The Times,* January 19, 1933]

LEG BOWLING.
OTHER DAYS AND OTHER GROUNDS.
"IS IT A BETTER GAME?"

To the Editor of *The Times*

Sir,

The discussion in your paper on "leg bowling" revives old memories
and old desires. Pitches like billiard tables and spectators numbered in
thousands make people forget what cricket used to be. Fifty years ago
this new danger was a common incident of every match played outside the
few places where groundsmen guarded the turf. Fast bowlers—*quorum
parvissima pars fui*—were regarded as essential and were often, as I was,
most erratic. I have often seen a ball pitch once and then bounce straight
into the backstop's hands.

Nor were these bowling eccentricities confined to local grounds. I remember on one occasion the first ball of a match slung with immense violence straight at the big black beard of W. G. Grace. Did he object? Certainly not: he simply hit it out of the ground and waited for the next.

In the country there were some pitches renowned for their fiery qualities. On one of these I recall a game in which Ranjitsinhji took part. Two benches from the village school provided the grand stand and on these were seated the squire, the local doctor—whose patients were long-suffering and few—the publican, and some countrymen.

Ranjitsinhji was clean bowled by the village postman, who wore his official costume, and all the four innings were finished in the day. As for leg balls and head balls and body balls, they formed the feature of the match, which no one seemed more thoroughly to enjoy than Ranjitsinhji himself.

The world has been made smooth for the game and its lords, but is it a better game?

Yours faithfully,
BUCKMASTER

1, Porchester Terrace, W. 2.

[The Times, January 20, 1933]

M.C.C. REPLY TO AUSTRALIA.
"FULLEST CONFIDENCE" IN JARDINE.

The Committee of the M.C.C. met at Lord's yesterday to consider the message which they had received from the Australian Board of Control, . . . and replied:

We, the Marylebone Cricket Club, deplore your cable. We deprecate your opinion that there has been unsportsmanlike play. We have the fullest confidence in our captain, team, and managers, and we are convinced that they would do nothing to infringe either the laws of cricket or the spirit of the game. We have no evidence that our confidence has been misplaced. Much as we regret the accidents to Woodfull and Oldfield, we understand that in neither case was the bowler to blame. If the Australian Board of Control wish to propose a new law or rule it shall receive our careful consideration in due course. We hope the situation is not now as serious as your cable would seem to indicate, but if it is such as to jeopardize the good relations between English and Australian cricketers, and you consider it desirable to cancel the remainder of the programme, we would consent, but with great reluctance.

(Signed) FINDLAY, Secretary.

[*The Times*, January 24, 1933]

FIFTY-ONE FIFTY-ONE

In four out of five of this season's Test Matches between England and Australia the English Captain has lost the toss; in four of the five he and his side have easily won the game. That, in brief, is the whole story of the struggle between the two countries which ended yesterday on the Sydney ground. It is the outcome of the indomitable will-power with which Jardine has played his part and managed his team, and of the loyal and willing teamspirit with which, to a man, they responded. In the whole series of these matches, of which the Mother Country and the Dominion have so far each won fifty-one, no English captain, however great and distinguished, has been more in evidence as a controlling factor of the play. He had under his command what is admittedly on this year's form the better of the two sides—and he had Larwood. But if Woodfull and Bradman and the other Australian batsmen found themselves up against an unfamiliar type of bowling, the practice as well as the theory of which was not on the whole to their liking, it is no less true that Larwood and his captain in particular have had to face a style of criticism which they must have found at least as distasteful and nerveracking.

Happily that is all over now. Several of the Dominion batsmen have shown that they can deal successfully with the bowling to which objections were raised—a natural evolution of the bowler's art to cope with the modern predominance of the batsman, and largely due, as many think, to the batsman's own fault—and time and reflection may perhaps lead its critics to question whether the maintenance of their protest is worth while. For the moment England has the better team, every member of which from first to last has good reason to be proud of his share in England's victory. But by the law of averages Australia's turn will come again. The two countries are now level in the number of matches won, and for the good of the game and the enjoyment of the players on both sides nothing must ever be allowed to interfere with the friendly feelings and close rivalry that have bound them together so long.

[*The Times*, March 1, 1933]

117

Edward VIII, Radio Speech (1936). The Abdication Crisis

The monarchy's decline in power was not accompanied by a drop in public interest in the royal family. This interest was heightened in late 1936, when monarchy became controversial for the first time since the republican criticism of Victoria in the 1860s. The issue was the right of the king, Edward VIII (January 20–December 11, 1936), to order his personal life as he saw fit. Specifically, Edward, a bachelor of 41, wanted to marry Mrs. Wallis Simpson, an American divorcee who had remarried. The news of the king's association with Mrs. Simpson was kept out of the English papers, largely because of the voluntary restraint of the editors. In October 1936 Mrs. Simpson was granted her divorce, making her marriage to Edward possible. Prime Minister Stanley Baldwin, concerned about the effect of such a marriage on the institution of monarchy, gave the king a simple choice: give up Mrs. Simpson or the throne. In early December the news broke in the press, creating a public sensation. The attempts to work out a compromise failed, and on December 11, 1936, Edward abdicated and with his bride went into dignified exile.

Edward's abdication speech is interesting in two ways. First, it illustrates how Edward's personal crisis had been transformed into a constitutional issue. Edward's remark that earlier he had not been free to speak indicates that he, a good constitutional monarch, had accepted Baldwin's argument that the monarch's private and public lives could not be separated. In both areas the king must act on the advice of his ministers, and Baldwin had forbidden him while he remained king to make an appeal for public support. Second, Edward's use of the BBC for his announcement reflects the obvious

SOURCE. Edward, Duke of Windsor, *A King's Story: The Memoirs of the Duke of Windsor,* New York: G. P. Putnam's Sons, 1947, pp. 411–412.

growth in the importance of the electronic news media, a development also of significance to the historian.

At long last I am able to say a few words of my own.

I have never wanted to withhold anything, but until now it has not been constitutionally possible for me to speak.

A few hours ago I discharged my last duty as King and Emperor, and now that I have been succeeded by my brother, the Duke of York, my first words must be to declare my allegiance to him. This I do with all my heart.

You all know the reasons which have impelled me to renounce the Throne, but I want you to understand that in making up my mind I did not forget the Country or the Empire, which, as Prince of Wales and lately as King, I have for 25 years tried to serve.

But you must believe me when I tell you that I have found it impossible to carry the heavy burden of responsibility and to discharge my duties as King, as I wish to do, without the help and support of the woman I love, and I want you to know that the decision I have made has been mine, and mine alone. This was a thing I had to judge for myself. The other person most nearly concerned has tried, up to the last, to persuade me to take a different course. I have made this, the most serious decision of my life, only upon the single thought of what would in the end be best for all.

This decision has been made less difficult to me by the sure knowledge that my brother, with his long training in the public affairs of this Country and with his fine qualities, will be able to take my place forthwith without interruption or injury to the life and progress of the Empire, and he has one matchless blessing, enjoyed by so many of you, and not bestowed on me, a happy home with his wife and children.

During these hard days I have been comforted by my Mother and by my Family.

The Ministers of the Crown, and in particular Mr. Baldwin, the Prime Minister, have always treated me with full consideration. There has never been any constitutional difference between me and them and between me and Parliament. Bred in the constitutional tradition by my Father, I should never have allowed any such issue to arise.

Ever since I was Prince of Wales, and later on when I occupied the Throne, I have been treated with the greatest kindness by all classes wherever I have lived or journeyed throughout the Empire. For that I am very grateful.

I now quit altogether public affairs, and I lay down my burden. It may be some time before I return to my native land, but I shall always follow the fortunes of the British race and Empire with profound interest, and if, at any time in the future, I can be found of service to His Majesty in a private station, I shall not fail.

And now we all have a new King.

I wish Him, and you, His people, happiness and prosperity with all my heart.

God bless you all.

God Save The King.

118

Neville Chamberlain, Speech in Commons (1938). The Munich Crisis

The British foreign policy of appeasement in the 1930s is today usually condemned as a policy of weakness and the sacrifice of moral principles in the face of danger. That appeasement is ineffectual is also taken as self-evident: aggressors whose initial demands are met simply increase their demands. The great appeaser was, of course, Neville Chamberlain (1869–1940), the prime minister from 1937 to 1940. Chamberlain came to power a highly regarded administrator who, in the 1920s, had done creative work in dealing with domestic problems such as housing. It was perhaps unfortunate that he became prime minister just when public and parliamentary concern was shifting away from the depression and toward Hitler's Germany.

Chamberlain, perhaps because of his administrative background, took

SOURCE. Parliamentary Debates (House of Commons), Fifth Series, Vol. 339, pp. 41–42, 45, 47–49; Vol. 351, p. 292.

pride in his rational approach to world problems. He believed that most international disputes resulted from misunderstandings that could be settled by reasonable compromise. Indeed, this seemed the lesson to be learned from World War I. Like many in England, he listened sympathetically to the demands made by Hitler, believing that they often represented legitimate German grievances. He therefore believed in active appeasement, the settlement of difficulties before they became crises threatening the peace of Europe. The great test of appeasement was the dispute between Czechoslovakia and Germany over the Sudetenland, an area of Czechoslovakia inhabited largely by Germans and desired by Hitler. In September 1938 Chamberlain made three trips to Germany, first agreeing to and then at Munich helping to arrange the details of the partition of Czechoslovakia.

In the Commons on October 3, 1938, Chamberlain defended his foreign policy, which he had already described as insuring "peace for our time." It is clear that he was not ashamed of his actions. They represented a step toward "the pacification of Europe," the laying of the "foundations of peace." Other members, however, including Winston Churchill, condemned the Munich agreement, arguing that it was a stain on British honor and would, in fact, promote war rather than avert it. Following the dismemberment of the remainder of Czechoslovakia in March 1939, most of it being absorbed by Germany, and the general acknowledgment of the failure of appeasement, Britain's policy hardened. When Britain came to the defense of Poland in September 1939, the war was accepted by almost everyone as necessary and morally correct. Chamberlain acknowledged that everything he had worked for had "crashed into ruins."

The Prime Minister (Mr. Chamberlain): . . . When the House met last Wednesday, we were all under the shadow of a great and imminent menace. War, in a form more stark and terrible than ever before, seemed to be staring us in the face. Before I sat down, a message had come which gave us new hope that peace might yet be saved, and to-day, only a few days after, we all meet in joy and thankfulness that the prayers of millions have been answered, and a cloud of anxiety has been lifted from our hearts. Upon the Members of the Cabinet the strain of the responsibility of these last few weeks has been almost overwhelming. Some of us, I have no doubt, will carry the mark of it for the rest of our days. . . .

Before I come to describe the Agreement which was signed at Munich in the small hours of Friday morning last, I would like to remind the House of two things which I think it is very essential not to forget when those terms are being considered. The first is this: We did not go there to decide whether the predominantly German areas in the Sudetenland should be passed over to the German Reich. That had been decided already. Czechoslovakia had accepted the Anglo-French proposals. What we had to consider was the method, the conditions and the time of the transfer of the territory. The second point to remember is that time was one of the essential factors. All the elements were present on the spot for the outbreak of a conflict which might have precipitated the catastrophe. We had populations inflamed to a high degree; we had extremists on both sides ready to work up and provoke incidents; we had considerable quantities of arms which were by no means confined to regularly organised forces. Therefore, it was essential that we should quickly reach a conclusion, so that this painful and difficult operation of transfer might be carried out at the earliest possible moment and concluded as soon as was consistent with orderly procedure, in order that we might avoid the possibility of something that might have rendered all our attempts at peaceful solution useless. . . .

Before giving a verdict upon this arrangement, we should do well to avoid describing it as a personal or a national triumph for anyone. The real triumph is that it has shown that representatives of four great Powers can find it possible to agree on a way of carrying out a difficult and delicate operation by discussion instead of by force of arms, and thereby they have averted a catastrophe which would have ended civilisation as we have known it. The relief that our escape from this great peril of war has, I think, everywhere been mingled in this country with a profound feeling of sympathy—[HON. MEMBERS: "Shame."] I have nothing to be ashamed of. Let those who have, hang their heads. We must feel profound sympathy for a small and gallant nation in the hour of their national grief and loss. . . .

In my view the strongest force of all, one which grew and took fresh shapes and forms every day was the force not of any one individual, but was that unmistakable sense of unanimity among the peoples of the world that war somehow must be averted. The peoples of the British Empire were at one with those of Germany, of France and of Italy, and their anxiety, their intense desire for peace, pervaded the whole atmosphere of the conference, and I believe that that, and not threats, made possible the concessions that were made. I know the House will want to hear what I am sure it does not doubt, that throughout these discussions the Dominions, the Governments of the Dominions, have been kept in the closest touch with the march of events by telegraph and by personal contact, and I would like to say how greatly I was encouraged on each of the journeys I made to Germany by the knowledge that I went with the good wishes of the Governments of the Dominions. They shared all our anxieties and all our hopes. They rejoiced with us that peace was preserved, and with us they look forward to further efforts to consolidate what has been done.

Ever since I assumed my present office my main purpose has been to work for the pacification of Europe, for the removal of those suspicions and those animosities which have so long poisoned the air. The path which leads to appeasement is long and bristles with obstacles. The question of Czechoslovakia is the latest and perhaps the most dangerous. Now that we have got past it, I feel that it may be possible to make further progress along the road to sanity. . . .

In our relations with other countries everything depends upon there being sincerity and good will on both sides. I believe that there is sincerity and good will on both sides in this declaration. That is why to me its significance goes far beyond its actual words. If there is one lesson which we should learn from the events of these last weeks it is this, that lasting peace is not to be obtained by sitting still and waiting for it to come. It requires active, positive efforts to achieve it. No doubt I shall have plenty of critics who will say that I am guilty of facile optimism, and that I should disbelieve every word that is uttered by rulers of other great States in Europe. I am too much of a realist to believe that we are going to achieve our paradise in a day. We have only laid the foundations of peace. The superstructure is not even begun.

[October 3, 1938]

The Prime Minister (Mr. Chamberlain): This is a sad day for all of us, and to none is it sadder than to me. Everything that I have worked for, everything that I have hoped for, everything that I have believed in during my public life, has crashed into ruins. There is only one thing left for me to do; that is, to devote what strength and powers I have to forwarding the victory of the cause for which we have to sacrifice so much. I cannot tell what part I may be allowed to play myself; I trust I may live to see the day when Hitlerism has been destroyed and a liberated Europe has been re-established.

[September 3, 1939]

119

Winston Churchill, Speeches in Commons (1940). The Battle of Britain

Seldom have a man and his mission come together so dramatically or so happily for both as did Winston Churchill (1874–1965) and the salvation of Britain in May 1940. Churchill, then 65 years old, had already had a life-time full of excitement, controversy, and frustration. As an intrepid young army officer and newspaper correspondent, he had been with the Malakand Field Force in India and with Lord Kitchener in the Sudan, a participant in the cavalry charge at Omdurman; captured by the Boers in South Africa, he had effected one of the most daring and lucky escapes in history. In parliament he had pushed welfare legislation, urged the Dardanelles campaign, and defended the British Empire. He was acknowledged to be talented and hardworking but, equally, he was thought to be erratic, overly daring, and pugnacious. During the 1930s he was out of power and out of favor. He warned of the danger of Germany's rearming. When Chamberlain returned from Munich talking of peace with honour, he countered that Britain had "sustained a total and unmitigated defeat." But no one listened. If he had died before 1940, he would have been likened to his father, Lord Randolph, a brilliant failure.

Britain in 1940 was still suffering from the shock of World War I and from two decades of timid and unimaginative leadership. At first unwilling to prevent Germany from becoming powerful, she then seemed unable to stop the march of German aggression. Austria, Czechoslovakia, and Poland had been digested. Denmark and Norway were recent conquests. And on

SOURCE. *The Parliamentary Debates* (House of Commons), Fifth Series, Vol. 360, p. 1502; Vol. 361, pp. 795–796; Vol. 362, pp. 60–61; Vol. 364, pp. 1170–1171.

May 10, Holland, Belgium, and France were invaded. Under severe attack in parliament, Neville Chamberlain resigned as prime minister, and Churchill was asked to form a national coalition government. In the dangerous months that followed, Churchill's speeches expressed Britain's resolve: "We shall never surrender." On May 13, he had just assumed power and was making his first address to parliament as prime minister. On June 4, Britain's army had just been safely exacuated from the sands of Dunkirk, but the serious consequences of its expulsion, even the fall of France, were apparent. By June 18, France had fallen and Churchill was careful to point out the present danger to "the whole world, including the United States." On August 20, when the Battle of Britain was raging, he expanded the theme of British and American common interests. Churchill's attitude toward the United States was in part pragmatic, but also an acknowledgment of his own dual ancestry and of his sense of the community of all "English Speaking Peoples."

Britain's survival was, in the end, surely contributed to by the United States. Yet, Britain's holding out alone for a full year against the onslaught of Hitler's war machine was due to the British people themselves, to the British Empire, and also to Winston Churchill. It was his own as well as Britain's "finest hour." Of his role, he later said that the lion's heart had been that of the British people; he had merely been allowed to give the lion's roar.

May 13, 1940

I would say to the House, as I said to those who have joined this Government: "I have nothing to offer but blood, toil, tears and sweat."

We have before us an ordeal of the most grievous kind. We have before us many, many long months of struggle and of suffering. You ask, what is our policy? I will say: It is to wage war, by sea, land and air, with all our might and with all the strength that God can give us; to wage war against a monstrous tyranny, never surpassed in the dark, lamentable catalogue of human crime. That is our policy. You ask, what is our aim? I can answer in one word: It is victory, victory at all costs, victory in spite of all terror, victory, however long and hard the road may be; for without victory, there is no survival. Let that be realised; no survival for the British Empire, no survival for all that the British Empire has stood for, no survival for the urge and impulse of the ages, that mankind will move forward towards its goal. But I take up my task with buoyancy and hope. I feel sure that our cause will not be suffered to fail among men. At this time I feel entitled to claim the aid of all, and I say, "Come then, let us go forward together with our united strength."

June 4, 1940

I have, myself, full confidence that if all do their duty, if nothing is neglected, and if the best arrangements are made, as they are being made, we shall prove ourselves once again able to defend our island home, to ride out the storm of war, and to outlive the menace of tyranny, if necessary for years, if necessary alone. At any rate, that is what we are going to try to do. That is the resolve of His Majesty's Government—every man of them. That is the will of Parliament and the nation. The British Empire and the French Republic, linked together in their cause and in their need, will defend to the death their native soil, aiding each other like good comrades to the utmost of their strength. Even though large tracts of Europe and many old and famous States have fallen or may fall into the grip of the Gestapo and all the odious apparatus of Nazi rule, we shall not flag or fail. We shall go on to the end. We shall fight in France, we shall fight on the seas and oceans, we shall fight with growing confidence and growing strength in the air, we shall defend our island, whatever the cost may be. We shall fight on the beaches, we shall fight on the landing grounds, we shall fight in the fields and in the streets, we shall fight in the hills; we shall never surrender, and even if, which I do not for a moment believe, this island or a large part of it were subjugated and starving, then our Empire beyond the seas, armed and guarded by the British Fleet, would carry on the struggle, until, in God's good time, the new world, with all its power and might, steps forth to the rescue and the liberation of the old.

June 18, 1940

What General Weygand called the "Battle of France" is over. I expect that the battle of Britain is about to begin. Upon this battle depends the survival of Christian civilisation. Upon it depends our own British life and the long continuity of our institutions and our Empire. The whole fury and might of the enemy must very soon be turned on us. Hitler knows that he will have to break us in this island or lose the war. If we can stand up to him all Europe may be free, and the life of the world may move forward into broad, sunlit uplands; but if we fail then the whole world, including the United States, and all that we have known and cared for, will sink into the abyss of a new dark age made more sinister, and perhaps more prolonged, by the lights of a perverted science.

Let us therefore brace ourselves to our duty and so bear ourselves that if the British Commonwealth and Empire lasts for a thousand years men will still say, "This was their finest hour."

August 20, 1940

We have to think not only for ourselves but for the lasting security of the cause and principles for which we are fighting and of the long future of the British Commonwealth of Nations. Some months ago we came to the conclusion that the interests of the United States and of the British Empire both required that the United States should have facilities for the naval and air defence of the Western hemisphere against the attack of a Nazi power which might have acquired temporary but lengthy control of a large part of Western Europe and its formidable resources. We had therefore decided spontaneously, and without being asked or offered any inducement, to inform the Government of the United States that we would be glad to place such defence facilities at their disposal by leasing suitable sites in our Transatlantic possessions for their greater security against the unmeasured dangers of the future. The principle of association of interests for common purposes between Great Britain and the United States had developed even before the war. Various agreements had been reached about certain small islands in the Pacific Ocean which had become important as air fueling points. In all this line of thought we found ourselves in very close harmony with the Government of Canada.

Presently we learned that anxiety was also felt in the United States about the air and naval defence of their Atlantic seaboard, and President Roosevelt has recently made it clear that he would like to discuss with us, and with the Dominion of Canada and with Newfoundland, the development of American naval and air facilities in Newfoundland and in the West Indies. There is, of course, no question of any transference of sovereignty—that has never been suggested—or of any action being taken, without the consent or against the wishes of the various Colonies concerned, but for our part, His Majesty's Government are entirely willing to accord defence facilities to the United States on a 99 years' leasehold basis, and we feel sure that our interests no less than theirs, and the interests of the Colonies themselves and of Canada and Newfoundland will be served thereby. These are important steps. Undoubtedly this process means that these two great organisations of the English-speaking democracies, the British Empire and the United States, will have to be somewhat mixed up together in some of their affairs for mutual and general advantage. For my own part, looking out upon the future, I do not view the process with any misgivings. I could not stop it if I wished; no one can stop it. Like the Mississippi, it just keeps rolling along. Let it roll. Let it roll on full flood, inexorable, irresistible, benignant, to broader lands and better days.

120

The Atlantic Charter (1941). Churchill and the United States

World War II united the two principal parts of the English-speaking community in a crusade against Nazism. This new cooperation was reinforced by the nine wartime meetings between Winston Churchill and Franklin Roosevelt, the first on August 9 to 12, 1941, aboard H.M.S. *Prince of Wales* in Placentia Bay, Newfoundland. Britain's position was then precarious—the Battle of Britain had been a costly victory; her new ally, Russia, was in precipitous retreat before the German *Wehrmacht;* Egypt was threatened by Rommel's Afrika Korps; and, finally, the Battle of the Atlantic against German U-boats was not going well. Churchill had hoped that this meeting would result in further American military and economic support. Instead, it produced the Atlantic Charter.

The Atlantic Charter, issued jointly on August 14, 1941, is in some ways a perplexing document. It was not the purpose of the meeting, largely a discussion of Lend Lease and war strategy. Nor was it an official document, one historian describing it as "technically . . . nothing more than a press release." Only later was it generally accepted as the war objectives of the Grand Alliance formed after Pearl Harbor. Also, despite its general principles

SOURCE. *The Times,* August 15, 1941, p. 4. Reproduced from *The Times* by permission.

and flowery rhetoric, harking back to Wilson's "Fourteen Points" and, more recently, to Roosevelt's "Four Freedoms," the Atlantic Charter represented a compromise, which revealed some important differences between the two powers. Article 4 sought to reconcile the British Empire's system of economic preference with the American demand for "access, on equal terms" to world markets. Article 5, on social security, was insisted on by Churchill, after his communication by telegraph with the British cabinet, headed in his absence by Clement Attlee (1883–1967), the leader of the Labour party. Article 7 was included because of American insistence. Finally, Article 8, vaguely hinting at an Anglo-America peacekeeping force following the war, was a subtle attempt by Churchill to insure continuing American participation in world affairs.

The Atlantic Charter did, however, represent a symbolic victory for Churchill. America was now committed in principle to the "final destruction of Nazi tyranny." A more substantial assurance came on December 8, 1941, when after Pearl Harbor the United States declared war not only on Japan but also on Germany. Of the latter event Churchill later wrote: "We had won the war. England would live. . . . Once again in our long island history we should emerge, however mauled or mutilated, safe and victorious. We should not be wiped out. Our history would not come to an end. . . . Being saturated and satiated with emotion and sensation, I went to bed and slept the sleep of the saved and thankful."

MR. CHURCHILL MEETS THE PRESIDENT.
THREE DAYS OF CONFERENCE AT SEA.
JOINT DECLARATION OF PEACE AIMS.
"FREEDOM FROM FEAR AND WANT."
NEW SURVEY OF MUNITIONS SUPPLY.

After three days of secret conference at sea Mr. Churchill and Mr. Roosevelt have drawn up a joint declaration of principles upon which a better world should be based "after the final destruction of Nazi tyranny."

The Eight Points of the Joint declaration proclaim that all states, victor or vanquished, should have equal access to the trade and raw materials of the world; that the peace to be established should let all men live "in freedom from fear and want;" and that, until there is a permanent system of security, the aggressor nations should be disarmed.

The whole problem of the supply of munitions of war was also further examined, and Lord Beaverbrook, who was with Mr. Churchill, has arrived in Washington to continue the discussions.

Mr. Attlee's Broadcast

AGREED STATEMENT ON THE MEETING

The announcement of Mr. Churchill's meeting with Mr. Roosevelt and of their joint declaration of peace aims was made by Mr. Attlee, Lord Privy Seal and Deputy Prime Minister, in a special broadcast from Downing Street yesterday afternoon. He said:

"I have come to tell you about an important meeting between the President of the United States and the Prime Minister which has taken place and of a Declaration of Principles which has been agreed between them. Here is the statement which they have agreed to issue:

'The President of the United States and the Prime Minister, Mr. Churchill, representing his Majesty's Government in the United Kingdom, have met at sea.

'They have been accompanied by officials of their two Governments, including high-ranking officers of their military, naval, and air services.

'The whole problem of the supply of munitions of war, as provided by the Lease-Lend Act, for the armed forces of the United States and for those countries actively engaged in resisting aggression has been further examined.

'Lord Beaverbrook, Minister of Supply of the British Government, has joined in these conferences. He is going to proceed to Washington to discuss further details with appropriate officials of the United States Government. These conferences will also cover the supply problem of the Soviet Union.

'The President and the Prime Minister have had several conferences. They have considered the dangers to world civilization arising from the policy of military domination by conquest upon which the Hitlerite Government of Germany and other Governments associated therewith have embarked, and have made clear the steps which their countries are respectively taking for their safety in facing these dangers.'

EIGHT POINTS

"They have agreed upon the following joint declaration:

'The President of the United States and the Prime Minister, Mr. Churchill, representing his Majesty's Government in the United Kingdom, being met together, deem it right to make known certain common principles in the national policies of their respective countries on which they base their hopes for a better future for the world.

'*First,* their countries seek no aggrandisement, territorial or other.

'*Second,* they desire to see no territorial changes that do not accord with the freely expressed wishes of the peoples concerned.

'*Third,* they respect the right of all peoples to choose the form of Government under which they will live; and they wish to see sovereign rights and self-government restored to those who have been forcibly deprived of them.

'*Fourth,* they will endeavour, with due respect for their existing obligations, to further enjoyment by all States, great or small, victor or vanquished, of access, on equal terms, to the trade and to the raw materials of the world which are needed for their economic prosperity.

'*Fifth,* they desire to bring about the fullest collaboration between all nations in the economic field, with the object of securing for all improved labour standards, economic advancement, and social security.

'*Sixth,* after the final destruction of Nazi tyranny, they hope to see established a peace which will afford to all nations the means of dwelling in safety within their own boundaries, and which will afford assurance that all the men in all the lands may live out their lives in freedom from fear and want.

'*Seventh,* such a peace should enable all men to traverse the high seas and oceans without hindrance.

'*Eighth,* they believe all of the nations of the world, for realistic as well as spiritual reasons, must come to the abandonment of the use of force. Since no future peace can be maintained if land, sea, or air armaments continue to be employed by nations which threaten, or may threaten, aggression outside of their frontiers, they believe, pending the establishment of a wider and permanent system of general security, that the disarmament of such nations is essential. They will likewise aid and encourage all other practicable measures which will lighten for peace-loving peoples the crushing burden of armament.' "

121

The Beveridge Report (1942).
Program for the Welfare State

Even while the outcome of the Battle of Britain was in the balance, people in Britain were thinking ahead to postwar reconstruction. There was a general determination to avoid the failure following World War I to make good the pledge that Britain should be a land "fit for heroes to live in." The community of danger and sacrifice and the extent of government planning and intervention in people's lives necessitated by Britain's all-out war effort made more acceptable the idea that government planning should extend beyond the restoration of peace. Thus a number of government commissions were appointed to investigate problems that might be anticipated. The most important of these was that chaired by Sir William Beveridge (1879–1963) dealing with "Social Insurance and Allied Services." The Beveridge Report, presented to parliament and published in December 1942, contained goals far more tangible and meaningful to the average Briton than were the global generalities of the Atlantic Charter.

The Report asserted that Britain's aim should be "the abolition of want," and that this should be part of a "comprehensive policy of social progress," for the elimination as well of "Disease, Ignorance, Squalor and Idleness." Required were a comprehensive and compulsory scheme of insurance to replace the present array of specialized programs and a system of "children's allowances" to adjust earning power to family needs. The proposal was not that the state should assume complete responsibility for all needs but that there be a cooperative venture of individuals and government working together. All subjects would be equal in the insurance premiums they paid and in the benefits they received.

The report met with immediate acclaim in Britain and abroad, everywhere

SOURCE. *Social Insurance and Allied Services: Report by Sir William Beveridge* (Cmd. 6404), London: His Majesty's Stationery Office, 1942, pp. 5–9.

that is except in the British government. The crisis year of 1942 was just ending, and the tide was turning in favor of the allies. It was not surprising that Churchill was absorbed more with the conduct of the war than with the problems of peace and reconstruction. Although a short time later he spoke in favor of an insurance scheme that would provide security for all "from the cradle to the grave," his attitude toward the Report remained cool and uncommitted. Disillusionment with Churchill's leadership consequently increased. While he was concentrating on the defeat of the Axis powers, the people at home were increasingly concerned with what peace would bring for them personally. The Labour party was quick to endorse the Report and awaited the postwar election. When the election came in 1945, the voters remembered the troubles after World War I and the failure of Churchill to accept the challenge of the Beveridge Report. Instead of honoring the hero for his triumphs in war, they looked to the Labour party, whose election slogan invited, "Let us face the future."

1.   The Inter-departmental Committee on Social Insurance and Allied Services were appointed in June, 1941, by the Minister without Portfolio, then responsible for the consideration of reconstruction problems. The terms of reference required the Committee "to undertake, with special reference to the inter-relation of the schemes, a survey of the existing national schemes of social insurance and allied services, including workmen's compensation and to make recommendations." The first duty of the Committee was to survey, the second to recommend. . . .

2.   The schemes of social insurance and allied services which the Inter-departmental Committee have been called on to survey have grown piece-meal. Apart from the Poor Law, which dates from the time of Elizabeth, the schemes surveyed are the product of the last 45 years beginning with the Workmen's Compensation Act, 1897. . . . Together with this growth of social insurance and impinging on it at many points have gone developments of medical treatment, particularly in hospitals and other institutions; developments of services devoted to the welfare of children, in school and before it; and a vast growth of voluntary provision for death and other contingencies, made by persons of the insured classes through Industrial Life Offices, Friendly Societies and Trade Unions.

3.   In all this change and development, each problem has been dealt with separately, with little or no reference to allied problems. The first task of the Committee has been to attempt for the first time a comprehensive survey of the whole field of social insurance and allied services, to show just what provision is now made and how it is made for many

different forms of need. . . . The picture presented is impressive in two ways. First, it shows that provision for most of the many varieties of need through interruption of earnings and other causes that may arise in modern industrial communities has already been made in Britain on a scale not surpassed and hardly rivalled in any other country of the world. In one respect only of the first importance, namely limitation of medical service, both in the range of treatment which is provided as of right and in respect of the classes of persons for whom it is provided, does Britain's achievement fall seriously short of what has been accomplished elsewhere; it falls short also in its provision for cash benefit for maternity and funerals and through the defects of its system for workmen's compensation. In all other fields British provision for security, in. adequacy of amount and in comprehensiveness, will stand comparison with that of any other country; few countries will stand comparison with Britain. Second, social insurance and the allied services, as they exist today, are conducted by a complex of disconnected administrative organs, proceeding on different principles, doing invaluable service but at a cost in money and trouble and anomalous treatment of identical problems for which there is no justification. In a system of social security better on the whole than can be found in almost any other country there are serious deficiencies which call for remedy.

6. In proceeding from this first comprehensive survey of social insurance to the next task—of making recommendations—three guiding principles may be laid down at the outset.

7. The first principle is that any proposals for the future, while they should use to the full the experience gathered in the past, should not be restricted by consideration of sectional interests established in the obtaining of that experience. Now, when the war is abolishing landmarks of every kind, is the opportunity for using experience in a clear field. A revolutionary moment in the world's history is a time for revolutions, not for patching.

8. The second principle is that organisation of social insurance should be treated as one part only of a comprehensive policy of social progress. Social insurance fully developed may provide income security; it is an attack upon Want. But Want is one only of five giants on the road of reconstruction and in some ways the easiest to attack. The others are Disease, Ignorance, Squalor and Idleness.

9. The third principle is that social security must be achieved by cooperation, between the State and the individual. The State should offer security for service and contribution. The State in organising security should not stifle incentive, opportunity, responsibility; in establishing a national minimum, it should leave room and encouragement for voluntary action by each individual to provide more than that minimum for himself and his family.

10.   The Plan for Social Security set out in this Report is built upon these principles. It uses experience but is not tied by experience. It is put forward as a limited contribution to a wider social policy, though as something that could be achieved now without waiting for the whole of that policy. It is, first and foremost, a plan of insurance—of giving in return for contributions benefits up to subsistence level, as of right and without means test, so that individuals may build freely upon it.

11.   The work of the Inter-departmental Committee began with a review of existing schemes of social insurance and allied services. The Plan for Social Security, with which that work ends, starts from a diagnosis of want. . . . [This is] the main conclusion to be drawn from these surveys: abolition of want requires a double re-distribution of income, through social insurance and by family needs.

12.   Abolition of want requires, first, improvement of State insurance, that is to say provision against interruption and loss of earning power. . . . To prevent interruption or destruction of earning power from leading to want, it is necessary to improve the present schemes of social insurance in three directions: by extension of scope to cover persons now excluded, by extension of purposes to cover risks now excluded, and by raising the rates of benefit.

13.   Abolition of want requires, second, adjustment of incomes, in periods of earning as well as in interruption of earning, to family needs, that is to say in one form or another it requires allowances for children. . . .

14.   By a double re-distribution of income through social insurance and children's allowances, want, as defined in the social surveys, could have been abolished in Britain before the present war. . . . The income available to the British people was ample for such a purpose. The Plan for Social Security set out in . . . this Report takes abolition of want after this war as its aim. It includes as its main method compulsory social insurance, with national assistance and voluntary insurance as subsidiary methods. It assumes allowances for dependent children, as part of its background. The plan assumes also establishment of comprehensive health and rehabilitation services and maintenance of employment, that is to say avoidance of mass unemployment, as necessary conditions of success in social insurance.

17.   The main feature of the Plan for Social Security is a scheme of social insurance against interruption and destruction of earning power and for special expenditure arising at birth, marriage or death. The scheme embodies six fundamental principles: flat rate of subsistence benefit; flat rate of contribution; unification of administrative responsibility; adequacy of benefit; comprehensiveness; and classification. . . . Based on them and in combination with national assistance and voluntary insurance as subsidiary methods, the aim of the Plan for Social Security is to make want under any circumstances unnecessary.

122

Letters to *The Times* (1946).
The National Health Service

Following its decisive victory in the general election of 1945, the Labour party, led by Clement Attlee (1883–1967), set out to redeem its pledge to build a "Socialist Commonwealth." Several basic industries, totaling about 20 percent of the British economy, were nationalized and placed under the control of public corporations. These included the Bank of England, coal, electricity and gas, inland transport, railroads, and iron and steel. Of more interest to the general public was Labour's implementation of the Beveridge Report. The twin pillars of the new welfare state were the National Insurance Act (1946) and the National Health Service Act (1948). The former, supported in principle by all three parties, consolidated earlier legislation dealing with benefits for illness, unemployment, and disability, embracing "not certain occupations and income groups, but the entire population." New assistance was also provided for the aged, widowed, orphaned, and pregnant. More controversial was the National Health Service Act.

The need for a national health service, providing free, voluntary medical and dental treatment for all, even including visitors to Britain, was never a matter of real debate. The British Medical Association (BMA) had accepted the principle in the 1930s. The Conservatives also conceded the need for, as one member stated, "a national, comprehensive, 100 per cent health service." The debate centered primarily on control of the new medical system. Aneurin Bevan, the fiery Minister of Health, insisted that it be run by a government agency responsible to parliament. The BMA, as shown below, argued that a government-controlled bureaucracy would make medicine a salaried profession and destroy initiative. The intimate, voluntary, doctor-patient relationship so essential to good medical treatment would thus be weakened. The government prevailed. The National Health Service,

SOURCE. *The Times*, April 2, 1946, p. 5; April 17, 1946, p. 5; April 20, 1946, p. 5; April 23, 1946, p. 5.

which went into effect on July 5, 1948, however, preserved freedom of choice for both doctors and patients. Within a year 95 percent of the British public was enrolled in the plan; the doctors soon joined them.

Something of the nature of the controversy surrounding nationalized medicine can be seen in the letters to *The Times* reprinted below. Although perhaps not the most accurate means of determining public opinion, letters of this kind give the historian insight into what issues were of public concern.

To the Editor of the Times

April 2, 1946

Sir,

The monstrosity of the present system of private practice in medicine is that it gives the doctors a vested interest in disease which they are defending desperately. We, the victims, support them because we want doctors of our own friendly choice and not strangers planted on us by the State.

The solution is simple. In Sweden, the most civilised country in western Europe, the private doctor is paid an agreed fee for keeping the family well throughout the year. He gains nothing and has more to do when there is illness in the family. He loses nothing and has less work when all is well.

My Swedish acquaintances have found no difficulty in inducing English doctors to make this arrangement. Why not make it obligatory, and abolish payment by the job ruthlessly?

Faithfully,
G. Bernard Shaw,
Ayot St. Lawrence, Welwyn,
Hertfordshire.

To the Editor of the Times

April 17, 1946

Sir,

It is stated in the leading article in *The Times* of April 11 that the statement of the council of the B. M. A. contains no issues which justify "talk of a fight for medical freedom." While it is true that the selections made from the council's report may justify this comment, the parts to which no reference is made contain ample evidence of the council's views on the fundamental issues of public and professional freedom. . . .

For the medical profession to be converted into a technical branch of government would be disastrous both to medicine and the public. The doctor's primary loyalty and responsibility should be to his patient. He should be free to act, to speak, and to write unhampered by interference from above. The doctor should be the patient's doctor and not the Government's doctor. A whole-time salaried service is inconsistent with free choice of doctor. It would tend to impose a uniformity in a form of work in which initiative and originality are essential. It would tend to bureaucratize a human service. It would destroy a proper incentive, the relationship between remuneration and the amount and value of work done or responsibility accepted. It might tend to replace competition for patients by competition to avoid them.

The Government's proposals in their present form mean that the general practitioner in the future, no longer owning the goodwill of his practice, will be allowed to practice in the public service in the area of his choice only with the permission of a committee appointed by the Minister. He will, as the Minister has informed the negotiating committee of the profession, be remunerated under a system which provides that a substantial part of his income will be salary. In the council's view these proposals do lead to the general practitioner becoming the full-time salaried servant of the State. . . .

Is it too much to ask that there should be accorded to a profession, which is not without pride in its past achievements and in its contribution to the public good, the same amount of discussion and, indeed, negotiation which Governments of all complexions have accorded, and rightly so, to the trade unions of this country on legislative proposals affecting them? This Bill contains proposals which all will welcome. But the recognition of this truth should not be allowed to obscure the fact that, unless the Bill is modified in certain important features, there is a very real danger that some essential freedoms would be lost to the profession and so to the public.

Yours faithfully,
CHARLES HILL, Secretary,
British Medical Association
Havistock Square, W.C.1

To the Editor of the Times

April 20, 1946

SIR,

In his letter published on April 17 Dr. Charles Hill wholly fails to substantiate his disagreement with your view that there are no issues in the statement of the B.M.A. which justify "talk of a fight for medical freedom."

Dr. Hill writes: "The doctor's primary loyalty and responsibility should be to his patient. . . . The doctor should be the patient's doctor and not the Government's doctor." We agree, but consider the implied antithesis fallacious. The antithesis of the doctor dominated by the Government is the doctor dominated by the necessity of earning a living in a commercial market into which he has probably sunk most of his capital. This Bill does not emperil the relationship between doctor and patient. It reconciles the economic needs of the doctor with the medical needs of the patient—and this must be for the benefit of all. The patient is free to choose his own doctor under the service, and their relationship is the same as before except that the doctor's remuneration comes from public funds.

Dr. Hill further states that a doctor will be able to practise in the area of his choice "only with the permission of a committee appointed by the Minister." He does not mention that it will be mainly professional in character and that it will not be able to withhold permission on any ground other than that "there are already enough doctors practising in the public service in the area in question." Without this provision, the Minister could not ensure the proper distribution of doctors in accordance with the needs of the community. In the past the miners, who needed doctors most, had the fewest and lowest-paid doctors of all. We are glad that the Minister provides for the health of Merthyr Tydfil as well as that of Maidenhead.

Doctors will be free to practise outside the service wherever they like. Doctors practising under the service can take private patients outside it provided that such patients are not on their lists as public patients or on the lists of their partners in a health centre. It is a misuse of language for Dr. Hill to allege that the scheme may "lead to the general practitioner becoming the full-time salaried servant of the State."

Dr. Hill complains that the medical profession were not fully consulted by the Minister. They were given the fullest opportunity to express their views to him and are now assured of the fullest Parliamentary discussion of the Bill in principle and detail.

We do not deny that there are risks inherent in every far-reaching venture of social reform. It is the business of all of us, including doctors and members of Parliament, to minimize them by vigilance and wise administration. Dr. Hill has not produced one valid argument to show that any part of the scheme is inconsistent with a sound professional ethic. In these circumstances we are entitled to ask whether the B.M.A. is to join us in the battle for public health or to discredit itself by continuing to cry "Wolf."

We are, Sir, your obedient servants,

RAYMOND BLACKBURN,
JOHN FREEMAN,
WILLIAM WELLS
House of Commons, April 18

To the Editor of the Times

April 23, 1946

SIR,

In your leading article "Doctors and the Bill" which the secretary of the B.M.A. stigmatizes as partial, you refer to the emergency fund. As a long-standing member of the B.M.A., belonging to no other political body, may I mention that this £100,000, together with a further £100,000 from the National Insurance Defence Trust, comes in part from subsriptions of many members who are completely out of sympathy with the policy of the leaders of the B.M.A.? The latter are in the main elderly men firmly entrenched in secure positions who resent any innovation likely to disturb them. They make great play through the secretary of the B.M.A. with freedom of choice. What chance has a young doctor lacking capital to settle in a practice of his own choosing? Similarly, where large blocks of patients are bought and sold, what price freedom of choice for the patient?

Yours faithfully,
WILFRED KILROE
116, Kenley Road,
Merton Park, S.W. 19

123

Sir Anthony Eden, Speech on BBC (1956). The Suez Crisis

Britain's role in defeating Hitler's Germany confirmed in most people's minds her standing as a world power. The euphoria of victory and the long tradition of her great-power status made it difficult for the British to recognize, let alone to accept, her decline after 1945, a decline occasioned by economic difficulties, American military dominance, and colonial nationalism. The event that ended Britain's lingering illusions of world power was the Suez Crisis of 1956.

As elsewere after 1945, the Middle East demonstrated the erosion of British power. Although Britain gave up her mandates over Transjordan in 1946 and Palestine in 1948, her ownership and military control of the Suez Canal seemed to guarantee her dominance in the area. Nevertheless, in 1954 British troops were forced to withdraw from the canal zone in the face of demands by Colonel Gamal Abdel Nasser, the new Egyptian strongman and the symbol of Arab nationalism. Following the cancellation of American and British financial support for Egypt's proposed Aswan Dam, Nasser seized control of the canal and nationalized it. Following unsatisfactory negotiations, Sir Anthony Eden, British prime minister from 1955 to 1957, authorized a British, French, and Israeli attack on Egypt. On the evening of November 3, 1956, the day British troops landed in Egypt, Eden appealed for public support on BBC radio and television. Reprinted below is part of his speech as it appeared in *The Listener,* a weekly publication summarizing the major broadcasts carried on BBC.

Eden's speech is interesting in its unreality. He attempted to justify Britain's assertion of power independent of the United Nations, the Commonwealth and, more importantly, the United States. Nasser, whom Eden

SOURCE. *The Listener,* LVI, 735–736 (November 8, 1956). By permission of Lord Avon.

characterized elsewhere as a "megalomaniacal dictator," was seen as a new Hitler. Eden, a critic of appeasement in the 1930s, argued that Nasser must learn the lesson that Hitler should have been taught earlier. The situation in 1956 was different, however, and most nations looked on Britain as the aggressor. The United States joined Russia in the UN to denounce Britain, and most of the Commonwealth nations disagreed with British policy. One Canadian remarked that hearing of Britain's invasion was "like finding a beloved uncle arrested for rape." Nehru of India could not think of "a grosser case of naked aggression." British public opinion was divided, and Eden was eventually forced from office. The lesson of Suez was clear: Britain's policy in the Middle East had failed because she lacked the independent power needed to carry it out. Her influence in the Middle East evaporated, and in the world at large she was now recognized as a former great power.

I know that you would wish me, as Prime Minister, to talk to you tonight on the problem which is in everybody's mind; and to tell you what has happened, what the Government has done, and why it has done it. . . .

As a Government we have had to wrestle with the problem of what action we should take. So have our French friends. The burden of that decision was tremendous but inescapable. In the depths of our conviction we decided that here was the beginning of a forest fire, of immense danger to peace. We decided that we must act, and act quicky.

What should we do? We put the matter to the Security Council. Should we have left it to them? Should we have been content to wait to see whether they would act? How long would this have taken? And where would the forest fire have spread in the meantime? Would words have been enough? What we did was to take police action at once: action to end the fighting and to separate the armies. We acted swiftly and reported to the Security Council, and I believe that before long it will become apparent to everybody that we acted rightly and wisely.

Our friends inside the Commonwealth, and outside, could not in the very nature of things be consulted in time. You just cannot have immediate action and extensive consultation as well. But our friends are coming—as Australia and New Zealand have already done and I believe that Canada and the United States will soon come—to see that we acted with courage and speed, to deal with a situation which just could not wait.

There are two things I would ask you never to forget. We cannot allow

—we could not allow—a conflict in the Middle East to spread; our survival as a nation depends on oil and nearly three-quarters of our oil comes from that part of the world. . . .

The other reflection is this. It is a personal one. All my life I have been a man of peace, working for peace, striving for peace, negotiating for peace. I have been a League of Nations man and a United Nations man, and I am still the same man, with the same convictions, the same devotion to peace. I could not be other, even if I wished, but I am utterly convinced that the action we have taken is right.

Over the years I have seen, as many of you have, the mood of peace at any price: many of you will remember that mood in our own country and how we paid for it. Between the wars we saw things happening which we felt were adding to the danger of a great world war. Should we have acted swiftly to deal with them—even though it meant the use of force? Or should we have hoped for the best, and gone on hoping and talking—as in fact we did?

There are times for courage, times for action—and this is one of them —in the interests of peace. I do hope we have learned our lesson. Our passionate love of peace, our intense loathing of war, have often held us back from using force even at times when we knew in our heads, if not in our hearts, that its use was in the interest of peace. And I believe with all my heart and head—for both are needed—that this is a time for action, effective and swift. Yes, even by the use of some force in order to prevent the forest fire from spreading—to prevent the horror and devastation of a larger war.

The Government knew, and they regretted it, that this action would shock and hurt some people: the bombing of military targets, and military targets only; it is better to destroy machines on the ground than let them destroy people from the air. We had to think of our troops and of the inhabitants of the towns and villages. After all, it was our duty to act and act swiftly, for only by such action could we secure peace. . . .

So finally, my friends, what are we seeking to do? First and foremost, to stop the fighting, to separate the armies, and to make sure that there is no more fighting. We have stepped in because the United Nations could not do so in time. If the United Nations will take over the police action we shall welcome it. Indeed, we proposed that course to them. And police action means not only to end the fighting now but also to bring a lasting peace to an area which for ten years has lived, or tried to live, under the constant threat of war.

Edward Heath, Speech in Commons (1971). From Commonwealth to Common Market

Following World War II, Great Britain was closely associated with three areas or power blocs, the United States, the Empire-Commonwealth, and Western Europe. During the 1950s and early 1960s, however, Britain's relations with each changed to her disadvantage. The dependent empire evaporated, beginning with Indian independence in 1947. Although most former colonies in Asia and Africa remained in the Commonwealth, this expanded and now multiracial organization was not a force on which Britain could rely. Britain's "special relationship" with the United States was strained by the latter's denunciation of the 1956 Suez operation and then later by the Americans' taking Britain's support for granted during the Cuban Crisis. Britain increasingly appeared a junior partner. Finally, by the Treaty of Rome (1957), France, West Germany, Italy and the Benelux nations formed the European Economic Community (EEC), a "Common Market" which Britain chose not to join. In 1962 Dean Acheson, who had been the American secretary of state from 1949 to 1953, characterized the situation: "Great Britain has lost an empire and has not yet found a role."

In an attempt to find a role, Harold Macmillan, the Conservative prime minister from 1957 to 1963, announced in 1961 that Britain was applying belatedly for membership in the Common Market. This decision naturally alarmed the other Commonwealth nations, which feared the loss of their economic privileges in the British market. It also upset many people in Britain. Some feared higher food prices. Others were simply repelled by the idea of the British becoming Europeans and, as one member of parlia-

---

SOURCE. *Parliamentary Debates* (House of Commons), Fifth Series, Vol. 823, pp. 2076, 2202–2205, 2211–2212.

ment argued, turning their backs on "a thousand years of history." Charles de Gaulle solved Britain's problem by vetoing this application in 1963. In Britain, however, the debate continued, and by 1966 both the Labour party of Harold Wilson and the Conservative party, now led by Edward Heath, supported entry into Europe in principle. Serious negotiations were resumed in July 1970 by Heath, who had just become prime minister; with De Gaulle out of the way, they proved successful. In October 1971 the approval of the British parliament was sought. This historic debate was concluded on October 28 by a brief speech by Heath, reprinted in part below.

Interestingly, Heath did not stress the economic rationale for membership in the EEC. Although he believed that England's industry must have access to the larger European market, Heath viewed the decision as a political one. The Commonwealth had not become "a reality." The United States was preoccupied with "its relationships with other super Powers." Britain, a European nation, must seek its future as a part of the "United Europe." Parliament, despite strong Labour objections, supported Heath and, following further detailed deliberations, Britain entered the Common Market on January 1, 1973. Many believed that a new, European era in Britain's history was beginning.

Order read for resuming adjourned debate on Question [21st October]: That this House approves Her Majesty's Government's decision of principle to join the European Communities on the basis of the arrangements which have been negotiated.—[*Sir Alec Douglas-Home.*]

Question again proposed. . . . 9.31 p.m.

The Prime Minister (Mr. Edward Heath): I do not think that any Prime Minister has stood at this Box in time of peace and asked the House to take a positive decision of such importance as I am asking it to take tonight. I am well aware of the responsibility which rests on my shoulders for so doing. After 10 years of negotiation, after many years of discussion in this House and after 10 years of debate, the moment of decision for Parliament has come. The other House has already taken its vote and expressed its view—[HON. MEMBERS: "Backwoodsmen!"]; 451 frontwoodsmen have voted in favour of the Motion and, for the rest, 58. . . .

Earlier, the world was watching New York. They were waiting to see whether China was going to become a member of the Security Council and of the General Assembly. Tonight, the world is similarly watching Westminster, waiting to see whether we are going to decide that Western

Europe should now move along the path to real unity—or whether the British Parliament, now given the choice, not for the first time but probably for the last time for many years to come, will reject the chance of creating a united Europe.

There can be absolutely no doubt of the world interest in this matter —of those physically watching and those waiting for the outcome. Nor can there be any doubt of the reasons why. It is natural that we in this House, in this long debate, have been largely concerned with the impact on our own country, but our decision tonight will vitally affect the balance of forces in the modern world for many years to come. . . .

The right hon. Gentleman [Mr. Callaghan] described the pursuit of a united Europe as an ideal which he respected. It inspired the founders of the European Communities after the war. At that time we in Britain held back, conscious of our ties with the Commonwealth and of our relationship with the United States, both of which had been so strongly reinforced in war. We did not then see how we could fit that into the framework of European unity.

The Commonwealth has, since then, developed into an association of independent countries with now only a few island dependencies remaining. It is a unique association which we value, but the idea that it would become an effective economic or political, let alone military, *bloc* has never materialised. It has never become a reality. [*Interruption.*]

Our relationship with the United States is close, friendly and natural, but it is not unique. It is not fundamentally different from that of many other countries of Western Europe, except, again, for our natural ties of language and common law, tradition and history. The United States is now inevitably and increasingly concerned with its relationships with the other super Powers. This applies also in the economic field, because in the situation which I have described the United States is bound to find itself involved more and more with the large economic powers, Japan and the European Community.

This is a time of profound change. It is a time in which United States policy towards Soviet Russia and Soviet China, and in the trade and monetary field, is changing. It is a time when we must see how these problems can best be handled by Britain. . . .

When it comes to dealing with the major economic Powers in creating what has now to be a changed, if not a new, trading and financial policy, the strength of this country alone, or of any individual member of the Community, were it to act alone, is not enough to ensure a sensible or satisfactory outcome to the current monetary and trading discussions which, I believe, are bound to go on for some time.

We as a country are dangerously vulnerable to protectionist pressure if such a satisfactory outcome of a new financial and trading system is not achieved. But in Europe we can share and reinforce the strength and experience of the Community. We can work with partners whose interests are the same as ours. . . .

Surely we must consider the consequences of staying out. We cannot delude ourselves that an early chance would be given us to take the decision again. We should be denying ourselves and succeeding generations the opportunities which are available to us in so many spheres; opportunities which we ourselves in this country have to seize. We should be leaving so many aspects of matters affecting our daily lives to be settled outside our own influence. That surely cannot be acceptable to us. We should be denying to Europe, also—let us look outside these shores for a moment —its full potential, its opportunities of developing economically and politically, maintaining its security, and securing for all its people a higher standard of prosperity.

All the consequences of that for many millions of people in Europe must be recognised tonight in the decision the House is taking. In addition, many projects for the future of Europe have been long delayed. There has been great uncertainty, and tonight all that can be removed —[Hon. Members: "No."] . . .

Throughout my political career, if I may add one personal remark, it is well known that I have had the vision of a Britain in a united Europe; a Britain which would be united economically to Europe and which would be able to influence decisions affecting our own future, and which would enjoy a better standard of life and a fuller life. I have worked for a Europe which will play an increasing part in meeting the needs of those parts of the world which still lie in the shadow of want. . . .

I want Britain as a member of a Europe which is united politically, and which will enjoy lasting peace and the greater security which would ensue.

Nor do I believe that the vision of Europe . . . is an unworthy vision, or an ignoble vision or an unworthy cause for which to have worked— [*Interruption.*] I have always made it absolutely plain to the British people that consent to this course would be given by Parliament—[Hon. Members: "Resign."] Parliament is the Parliament of all the people.

When we came to the end of the negotions in 1963, after the veto had been imposed, the negotiator on behalf of India said:

When you left India some people wept. And when you leave Europe tonight some will weep. And there is no other people in the world of whom these things could be said.

That was a tribute from the Indian to the British. But tonight when this House endorses this Motion many millions of people right across the world will rejoice that we have taken our rightful place in a truly United Europe.

Question put:—

The House divided: Ayes 356, Noes 244.

125

Bernadette Devlin, Interview in *Playboy* (1972). Northern Ireland

England's Irish question or, as some would say, Ireland's English question appears to the world at large as the tragic outgrowth of unfulfilled national-ism and religious bigotry. This troublesome issue, bequeathed to the twen-tieth century by the failure of Gladstone's plans of Home Rule, was further aggravated by Lloyd George's partition of Ireland in 1921. Southern Ireland, the Irish Free State, was granted responsible government within the British Commonwealth and in 1949 became the Republic of Eire, free from all British control. Northern Ireland or Ulster chose, however, to remain united with Britain. Its "Home Rule" parliament, dominated by the Protestant Unionist party, continued systematically to discriminate against the Roman Catholic minority.

In 1967 the Catholic minority in Ulster launched a moderate civil rights movement. The initial concessions granted were too extreme for the Orange-men, or ultra-Protestants, led by Ian Paisley, and insufficient to satisfy the Roman Catholics. Attitudes hardened, violent demonstrations began, and in 1969 British troops were sent to maintain order. Gradually, the civil rights movement merged with that of the Irish Republican Army, to unite all of

Ireland under the government of Eire in Dublin. One of the leading spokespersons for unification is Bernadette Devlin.

Bernadette Devlin, a Roman Catholic, was, in 1969 at the age of 21, elected one of the 12 Northern Irish members of the House of Commons. There she quickly established herself as a fiery and intrepid debater. After serious disturbances in Londonderry, she spent time in prison for inciting to riot. In an effort to publicize Irish grievances, Devlin has granted countless television and press interviews, like that in *Playboy* in 1972, part of which is reprinted below. Although she vigorously condemns British policy toward Ireland, it is interesting that she does not see Ireland's present difficulties solely as the result of British political and religious oppression. Besides being an Irish nationalist, she is also a socialist, seeing "independent socialism" and the destruction of capitalism as essential if Ireland and other small nations are to be completely free.

Ms. Devlin's interview in *Playboy* and her earlier lecture tour of American cities with large Irish-American populations are in the established tradition of Irish appeals to the United States for support, a practice dating back to the Fenians of the 1860s. The argumentative nature of this interview requires that it be used with great care. Its usefulness is, as with most interviews, as an expression of the interviewee's attitudes and not as a source of reliable evidence concerning the actual historical events.

Playboy: . . . What was it like growing up as a Catholic in Protestant Northern Ireland?

Devlin: Well, it was an education in more ways than one. I was born in Cookstown, in County Tyrone, a small farming community that's sort of a microcosm of Ulster. It was originally a plantation, settled by the Scots Presbyterians the British imported in the 17th Century to take over the land from us restless natives. To this day, the town is divided almost evenly between the descendants of the original Protestant settlers and the Catholics they subjugated; both groups are still segregated in the geographical areas of the town where their ancestors lived 300 years ago. And attitudes haven't changed much, either; the Protestants still have a sense of settler superiority and expect the Catholics to stay in their place and not get uppity, pretty much the way your own American colonists once viewed the Indians, or the way many white Southerners still feel about blacks. And, like the Indians and the blacks, we were poor, virtually disenfranchised and very angry. We still are. . . .

To understand the present struggle in Ireland, you must see it from the perspective of 800 years of invasion, oppression, exploitation and genocide. Irish history is written in Irish blood.

Playboy: Since that history seems to have a direct bearing on what's happening today, let's talk about it. When did the English first become involved in Ireland?

Devlin: It all began, ironically enough in light of what's happened since, when Pope Adrian IV, an Englishman, granted Ireland as an "inheritance" to the Norman king of England, Henry II, in 1154. Until then, there was no united Ireland as such, only a loose confederation of independent kingdoms, which united against Henry's invading armies and eventually drove them off. Over the next several hundred years, the English mounted sporadic, unsuccessful campaigns to conquer the island. Then, with the rise of the Tudors, a bloodier page was opened. Before this, the conflict between Ireland and England had had no religious overtones; both were Catholic powers fighting the kind of territorial war that was common in those days. But Henry VIII's break with Rome introduced the bitter note of religious antagonism, because the earls of Ireland remained loyal to the Pope. Their resistance was finally broken in 1601, under Elizabeth I. Protestantism became the official religion of all Ireland, and harsh penalties were imposed on any Irishman who refused to convert.

The vast landholdings of the Irish earls, comprising the richest farmland in Ireland, were seized and granted to English and Scots farmers, Protestants, of course. The original Irish inhabitants were driven into the woods and mountains by British troops. The seaport of Derry was renamed Londonderry, to be settled by London emigrants. For a while, Parliament debated whether the Irish would be transported to the New World as slaves or allowed to stay and work as serfs for the English. Although large numbers were transported, it was decided to keep the majority in Ireland as an agricultural labor force.

In 1638, the embittered Irish revolted against the British and the Protestant landlords, and fighting spread across the country; an Irish *Tet* offensive, you might call it. The situation grew so grave that Oliver Cromwell, the Puritan fanatic who had just beheaded his own king for alleged Catholic leanings, invaded Ireland and put city after city to the torch; in the town of Drogheda alone, he massacred more than 4000 people. After he had "pacified" Ireland, Cromwell accelerated the expropriation of Irish land and the importation of Protestant settlers. By 1660, the British had seized 12,000,000 out of 15,000,000 arable acres in Ireland.

After Cromwell's death, the Irish saw a vain glimmer of hope in the Stuart restoration. King James II was a secret Catholic and favorably disposed to the Irish. But then James was deposed and exiled by William of Orange, a staunch Dutch Protestant. James landed in Ireland to organize a war to regain his throne, and Irish Catholics rallied behind him; but after a bloody campaign, he was decisively defeated by the armies of King William at the Battle of the Boyne—July 1, 1690. That battle snuffed out the Irish Catholics' last real hope of freedom. From then on, Protestant hegemony over Ireland was total. The Orangemen still celebrate the Battle of the Boyne each year with huge parades. One of these, in 1969, triggered the rioting that led to the present crisis. Members of the Orange Order, a fascist group that effectively controlled Ulster until recently, used to recite an old toast on the anniversary of the Battle of the Boyne:

> To the glorious, pious and immortal memory of King William III, who saved us from Rogues and Roguery, Slaves and Slavery, Popes and Popery; and whoever denies this toast may he be slammed, crammed and jammed into the muzzle of the great gun of Athlone, and the gun fired into the Pope's belly, and the Pope into the Devil's belly, and the Devil into Hell, and the door locked and the key kept in an Orangeman's pocket.

In Northern Ireland, the Battle of the Boyne is still being fought. . . .

Playboy: As a professed believer in self-determination for all peoples, don't you grant the Northern Protestants the right to remain with Britain, if that's the desire of the majority?

Devlin: The partition of Ireland was no more acceptable to farseeing Irishmen that the secession of your own Southern states was to Abraham Lincoln. If you'd taken a plebiscite within the Confederacy in 1861, you would have found that a majority of Southerners preferred to split off from the United States. Lincoln put the good of the entire country ahead of regional sectarianism, and this led to your Civil War. In Ireland, too, we had civil war—between the government of the new Irish Free State and the militant Republicans.

Playboy: A civil war won by the Irish leaders who accepted partition.

Devlin: Oh, they won, all right. And in the process, the hopes of the Irish people for social progress and human dignity were brutally crushed. The rulers of the Free State, who had the support of the Church and the Irish middle class—and, tacitly and ironically, of the British and the Unionists in the North—wanted no social revolution, only a nice tidy little bourgeois capitalist country, rigidly Roman Catholic and linked to Britain by preferential trade agreements. They ruthlessly suppressed the I.R.A. rebels, hundreds of whom were shot by their old comrades in arms. By the mid-Twenties, our revolution had been sold down the river and the Irish people, North and South, faced *two* enemies: the British and the Dublin government.

Playboy: Many people would contend that the leaders who eventually accepted partition were not traitors but realists. Wasn't partition preferable to another 10 or 15 years of armed struggle?

Devlin: Most historians believe the British would have caved in completely if the Irish negotiating team had just held on a little longer. The British public had suffered terribly in the first war; they were fed up with the mess in Ireland. Lloyd George knew his own political survival depended upon negotiating immediate British withdrawal. He would have been ready to surrender Ulster if the Irish had presented a united front. But, tragically, we played right into his hands, and the result was the loss of half our country, the continued exploitation of our people in the North and, ultimately, the institutionalization of a reactionary and corrupt capitalist regime in the South, which was just as rotten as the Protestant caste system in the North. James Connolly, who if he'd lived might have tipped the scales against partition, summed it up better than I can when he said 75 years ago:

> If you remove the English army tomorrow and hoist the green flag over Dublin Castle, unless you set about the organization of the Socialist Republic, your efforts would be in vain. England would still rule you. She would rule you through her capitalists, through her landlords, through her financiers, through the whole army of commercial and individualist institutions she has planted in this country and watered with the tears of our mothers and the blood of our martyrs.

Sure, we did get our own flag after partition, and that's about all we got. We didn't even get half a loaf; we lost the whole bakery. . . .

Playboy: Can you see no grounds for reconciliation with England? Or will your bitterness, violence and misery be handed down to the next generation?

Devlin: There's a solution to any human problem. In this case, I can actually see two solutions, short term and long term. For the short term, hostilities could cease tomorrow if the British would unconditionally release all internees and other political prisoners, declare an amnesty for all those currently charged with crimes against the state and withdraw all troops to their barracks with a specified date for total withdrawal from Northern Ireland.

Stormont and the whole Unionist state apparatus would have to be permanently dismantled, not just temporarily suspended as it is now, under Westminster's direct rule. All parties in Ireland, Protestant and Catholic, conservative and revolutionary, could then get together to determine conditions for the peaceful reunification of their country and the protection of minority rights. That would be a short-term solution for the immedite suffering and bloodshed. It's far from perfect and it might not work at all, given our hardened sectarian attitudes. . . .

The ultimate long-range solution for Ireland, which I realize won't come about overnight, is independent socialism. Until we have a society in which we solve our own economic and social problems and control our own destiny, the present problems of exploitation and injustice will remain. That's why I'm a committed socialist and why more and more of our people are turning toward socialism as the only viable alternative. We can't have true freedom without social justice; and in Ireland, we can't have either without socialism. It won't come today, tomorrow or the day after. But it will come. It *has* to come.